PROPERTY LAW IN A GLOBALIZING WORLD

Property Law in a Globalizing World identifies the paramount challenges that contemporary processes of globalization pose for the study and practice of property law. It offers a straightforward analysis of legal scenarios implicating cross-border property rights, covering a broad range of resources, from land, goods, and intangible financial assets to intellectual property, data, and digital assets. This is the first scholarly book offering a detailed study of legal strategies that can decrease the gap between the domestic tenets of property law and the cross-border nature of markets, interpersonal networks, and technology. It shows how strategies of soft law, conflict of laws, approximation, and supranationalism rely to various degrees on cross-border property norms and institutions, and studies the proprietary features of security interests and priorities to assets in insolvency in a global setting. It also shows how digital technology such as blockchain can revolutionize the system of cross-border property rights.

AMNON LEHAVI is Dean and Atara Kaufman Professor of Real Estate, Harry Radzyner Law School, and Academic Director, Gazit-Globe Real Estate Institute, Interdisciplinary Center (IDC) Herzliya, Israel. Lehavi is a leading authority on property, real estate, land use controls, international economic law, and law and globalization. He is the author of *The Construction of Property: Norms, Institutions, Challenges* (2013) and editor of *100 Years of Zoning and the Future of Cities* (2018) and *Private Communities and Urban Governance: Theoretical and Comparative Perspectives* (2016). Lehavi serves as a Co-President of the Law Schools Global League (2018–2020).

GLOBAL LAW SERIES

The series provides unique perspectives on the way globalization is radically altering the study, discipline, and practice of law. Featuring innovative books in this growing field, the series explores those bodies of law that are becoming global in their application, and the newly emerging interdependency and interaction of different legal systems. It covers all major branches of the law and includes work on legal theory, history, and the methodology of legal practice and jurisprudence under conditions of globalization. Offering a major platform on global law, these books provide essential reading for students and scholars of comparative, international, and transnational law.

Books in the Series

Intimations of Global Law
Neil Walker

Legalized Families in the Era of Bordered Globalization
Daphna Hacker

Transnational Sustainability Laws
Phillip Paiement

The Sociology of Law and the Global Transformation of Democracy
Chris Thornhill

Authority and the Globalisation of Inclusion and Exclusion
Hans Lindahl

PROPERTY LAW IN A GLOBALIZING WORLD

AMNON LEHAVI
Harry Radzyner Law School
Interdisciplinary Center (IDC) Herzliya

CAMBRIDGE
UNIVERSITY PRESS

CAMBRIDGE
UNIVERSITY PRESS

University Printing House, Cambridge CB2 8BS, United Kingdom

One Liberty Plaza, 20th Floor, New York, NY 10006, USA

477 Williamstown Road, Port Melbourne, VIC 3207, Australia

314–321, 3rd Floor, Plot 3, Splendor Forum, Jasola District Centre, New Delhi – 110025, India

79 Anson Road, #06–04/06, Singapore 079906

Cambridge University Press is part of the University of Cambridge.

It furthers the University's mission by disseminating knowledge in the pursuit of education, learning, and research at the highest international levels of excellence.

www.cambridge.org
Information on this title: www.cambridge.org/9781108425124
DOI: 10.1017/9781108595391

First published 2019

Printed and bound in Great Britain by Clays Ltd, Elcograf S.p.A.

A catalogue record for this publication is available from the British Library.

Library of Congress Cataloging-in-Publication Data
Names: Lehavi, Amnon, author.
Title: Property law in a globalizing world / Amnon Lehavi, Harry Radzyner Law School.
Description: Cambridge, United Kingdom ; New York, NY : Cambridge University Press, 2018. | Series: Global law series | Includes index.
Identifiers: LCCN 2018026582 | ISBN 9781108425124 (hardback : alk. paper) | ISBN 9781108441193 (pbk. : alk. paper)
Subjects: LCSH: Property (International law) | Real property. | Intellectual property (International law)
Classification: LCC K720 .L47 2018 | DDC 346.04/8–dc23
LC record available at https://lccn.loc.gov/2018026582

ISBN 978-1-108-42512-4 Hardback

CONTENTS

Introduction

This book identifies the various challenges that contemporary processes of globalization pose for the study and practice of property law. Along the lines of the Global Law Series, this book offers a clear and straightforward analysis of prominent legal scenarios implicating cross-border property interests and ties these quandaries to the underlying normative and institutional features of property law. The analysis throughout the book is premised on what I depict as a pragmatic and context-based view of globalization. This view underscores the quantitative and qualitative impact of the increasing movement of capital, goods, services, and persons across national borders, but at the same time, it avoids attempts to entirely undermine the role of nation-states or of domestic legal ordering. As a positive matter, we are not likely to have any time soon a single world court, legislature, or executive body with general and universal jurisdiction that would overwhelmingly preempt national legal institutions. Accordingly, the book typifies the current development of cross-border activities and processes, generally referred to as *globalization*, as inherently manifesting a fragmented and incomplete phenomenon. This means that we do not currently observe, nor should we anticipate to witness, a complete unification of the geopolitical, economic, or legal landscape. Globalization is not about turning the world into a single indivisible space, which is devoid of any local, national, or regional meaning. Consequently, processes of globalization are not expected to follow a single route in responding to pressures placed on legal systems by markets, interpersonal networks, and technology. Moreover, in contrast to much of the conventional wisdom in the literature about globalization, the book argues that some extra-legal forces, such as culture, political ideologies, and other social systems that generate values and beliefs, do not necessarily push human activity to bringing down borders or to otherwise doing away with nationally based legal systems.[1]

[1] Thus, for example, the potential political backlash against globalization has been a hot-button issue in public discourse, especially following the results of the November 2016 US

In this context, the book emphasizes the unique features of property being both a public law and a private law discipline and explains how the institutional and structural features of property law exhibit particular modes of tension between cross-border activities and current legal systems. Such tension is due particularly to the *in rem* or third-party applicability feature of property, by which property law is based on establishing a single set of rights, priorities, and powers in regard to assets. Such ranking of proprietary interests should also govern relations among distant parties that have no privity of contract or another preset legal basis for governing conflicting claims.

The *in rem* feature of property law also places practical limits on the ability of parties to engage in private ordering to circumvent potential problems of uncertainty due to differences among legal systems. Direct parties to an international commercial transaction can privately decide on the forum that would resolve contractual disputes and on the applicable law that would govern such matters, with little, if any, constraints on this exercise of party autonomy. However, such private ordering could prove of only limited value when the legal interests of third parties must also be considered. Thus, for example, if a US manufacturer sells goods to a Dutch buyer, and the buyer fails to pay and also defaults on other debts, then the insolvency proceedings would most likely take place in the debtor's "centre of main interests,"[2] which could very well be the Netherlands. This means that the legal standing of the US manufacturer as creditor vis-à-vis other creditors of the Dutch buyer would be resolved by the Dutch bankruptcy court. Moreover, the law that the court would apply in deciding how to rank and enforce the various debtors' claims – typically, the law of the state in which the insolvency proceedings were

presidential elections. *See* J. Eilperin, "Obama in Athens: 'The Current Path of Globalization Needs a Course Correction,'" *The Washington Post*, November 16, 2016; P. Baker and A. Swanson, "Trump Authorizes Tariffs, Defying Allies at Home and Abroad," *The New York Times*, March 8, 2018.

2 This standard is based on the provisions of the Council Regulation (EC) No 1346/2000 of 29 May 2000 on Insolvency Proceedings, OJ (L 160/5), June 30, 2000 (2000 EC Insolvency Regulation). It establishes in Article 3(1) that "[t]he courts of the Member States within the territory of which the centre of debtor's main interests is situated shall have jurisdiction to open insolvency proceedings." A recast of the 2000 EC Insolvency Regulation was promulgated in Regulation (EU) 2015/848 of the European Parliament and the Council of 20 May 2015 on Insolvency Proceedings, OJ (L 141/19), June 5, 2015 (2015 EU Insolvency Regulation). The 2015 regulation reiterates the "centre of main interests" principle in its Article 3(1) with regard to "main insolvency proceedings."

opened – could preempt any seller–buyer specific contractual arrangements about granting the creditor priority to the debtor's assets.[3]

Therefore, any such proceedings must also consider the validity and enforceability of legal mechanisms, designed by the parties and intended to have a third-party effect. Thus, if the US seller wishes to protect itself vis-à-vis third parties by including a reservation of title clause, by which it maintains ownership of the goods until payment is made in full, regardless of whether possession in the goods has already been surrendered to the buyer, then the authorized court should account for potential differences among the relevant legal systems in recognizing and enforcing such a legal interest. Would such a right be considered a security interest, and if so, might it have required the seller to publish or register the interest, and then – in which national registry?[4]

Such a cross-border property scenario could vividly illustrate the particular challenges that property law faces in an age of increasing cross-border legal actions. On the one hand, the third-party applicability feature of property law, and the subsequent need to inform third parties of the existence of such legal interests, has traditionally led national legal systems to embrace some sort of a *numerus clausus* (closed list) principle in property law. This has typically meant that new types of legal interests that would bind third parties should be designed top-down by the legislative or judicial branches and cannot be created solely by private parties through contract. Each legal system establishes its own list of recognized property interests, which may include, alongside ownership, rights in assets owned by others (*iura in re aliena*), such as life interests, usufructs, types of leases, and security interests (mortgage, lien, etc.). Anglo-American law generally goes further than civil law in recognizing

[3] 2015 EU Insolvency Regulation, Art. 7(1). This in mind, Article 8 reads: "The opening of insolvency proceedings shall not affect the rights *in rem* of creditors or third parties in respect of tangible or intangible, moveable or immoveable assets, both specific assets and collections of indefinite assets as a whole which change from time to time, belonging to the debtor which are situated within the territory of another Member State at the time of the opening of proceedings." This provision would be, however, irrelevant to the case at hand, because the United States is not an EU Member State. Moreover, even within the EU, the creditor has to show that the asset is "situated" in another Member State and that the creditor's interest is covered as one of the *in rem* rights listed in Article 8's subsections.

[4] Within an internal EU context, Article 10 of the 2015 EU Insolvency Regulation validates a reservation of title provision agreed to by the parties, where the asset is "situated" in another Member State. This, however, would not apply to the scenario of a US seller and/or when the asset is situated outside one of the EU's Member States.

the third-party effects of trusts and other types of interests, including temporary and future ones, which typically originate in the law of equity.

At the same time, however, the very need to design property law, at least to some extent, in a centralized manner, highlights the current tension between the property-related aspects of the cross-border movement of capital, goods, services, and persons, and the fragmented nature of cross-border or supranational institutions and norms designated to address such scenarios. Property law, while considered one of the most "domestic" fields of law, also requires a particularly dramatic move toward interstate ordering. This is so because property law cannot rely on private ordering to ease the friction between cross-border markets, interpersonal networks, and technology, and the *in rem* ordering of rights to assets. Accordingly, a cross-border ranking of property interests requires, to varying degrees, effective cross-border institutions – legislative, administrative, and adjudicative. Property law must therefore go a long way from old-style localism to cross-border ordering, even if it is otherwise normatively committed to preserving national lawmaking power.

The abundance of cross-border property scenarios, involving distant parties that have no privity of contract or another preset legal mechanism for resolving potential disputes, calls for a systematic evaluation of the future of property law in the age of globalization. I suggest that just as processes of globalization do not take a single route, so the appropriate legal strategy for addressing the various cross-border scenarios need not take a single form. Accordingly, the book examines four legal strategies that can be employed to decrease the gap between property law and the cross-border nature of markets, interpersonal networks, and technology. These strategies are soft law, conflict of laws, approximation, and supranationalism. The book develops methodological principles for evaluating these globalization strategies, by offering a quantitative versus qualitative analysis, emphasizing the need for an interdisciplinary approach, highlighting the role of institutions, and examining the functional/normative tradeoff in choosing a globalization strategy.

The book is structured as follows. Chapter 1, "Why Property Law Needs Globalization Strategies," starts by illustrating the prevalence of cross-border property disputes that stem from current processes of globalization, and the challenge that such scenarios pose for legal governance because of disparities across national legal systems and the limited scope of cross-border norms. This chapter then identifies the structural features of property law, and in particular the need to create a set of norms for the *in rem* ranking of rights, powers, and priorities in regard to assets. It shows how such structural features translate to the creation of a closed list (*numerus clausus*) of property rights for each legal system, with national systems diverging from one another in the rigidity of the list, the types of rights included, and the specific content given to each such right. Showing that such disparities result not only from historical reasons, but also from economic, political, and cultural ones, Chapter 1 presents the four globalization strategies (soft law, conflict of laws, approximation, and supranationalism) that could be utilized to mitigate the gaps between the domestic basis of property law and the current economic, social, and technological processes of globalization, and defines the methodological principles that can guide the choice of strategies.

Chapter 2, "Local to Global: An Institutional Analysis," identifies the key role that institutions play, in various ways, in implementing the various globalization strategies. The nature of property rights requires a dominant role for legislative institutions and administrative agencies, alongside courts or tribunals with effective enforcement power. In a global context, this feature of property law requires a cross-border legal ordering by an array of domestic and supranational institutions. Whereas soft law instruments do not require binding supranational institutions, the need for such institutions proves critical for more ambitious strategies for globalization, such as attempts to provide supranational constitutional protection of the right to property or to establish a binding legal infrastructure for a global market in capital, goods, and services. The chapter looks, for example, at the European Union's institutions and how the structure of exclusive, shared, and supporting competences within it may apply to property law. It then looks at the broader landscape of supranational conventions and other legislative instruments and how their property provisions are enforced by supranational judiciaries, such as the European Court of Human Rights or the Inter-American Court of Human Rights. It identifies the key role that arbitration tribunals are playing in the enforcement of bilateral investment treaties and investment chapters in free-trade agreements. Chapter 2 also highlights, in the context of the various strategies for globalizing property law, the role of other international organizations, such as the World Trade Organization (WTO), United Nations Conference on Trade and Development (UNCTAD), United Nations Commission on International Trade Law (UNCITRAL), International Institute for the Unification of Private Law (UNIDROIT), and the Hague Conference on Private International Law (HCCH).

Chapters 3–5 analyze different types of assets or objects of property, while examining the key differences and similarities in regard to these assets across national legal systems, the current state of cross-border norms and institutions, and the future potential of globalization strategies.

Chapter 3, "Land," identifies the changing landscape of real-estate markets and the need to accommodate land systems to numerous types of cross-border activities. These actions include mass-scale transactions in arable and other extractable lands, mostly in developing countries in sub-Saharan Africa and some parts of Latin America and Southeast Asia, referred to critically as *land grabs*. There are, however, many other types of foreign interests in real estate, including investments by sovereign wealth funds and private investors coming from emerging economies, as well as thousands of bilateral investment treaties (BITs) which implicate the power of host governments to take, regulate, or distribute land while protecting cross-border investments. Chapter 3 also studies the complex relations between customary land tenure, national lawmaking, and human rights conventions, and how bodies such as the Inter-American Court of Human Rights become involved in such matters. Examining the various globalization strategies, the chapter explains why the *lex rei sitae* rule (law of the place where the asset is located) is likely to continue to dominate the conflict of laws strategy for land, and how the supranationalism strategy invokes complex normative and institutional questions about the private/public interface in land law.

Chapter 4, "Tangible Goods, Monetary Claims, and Investment Securities," studies the cross-border proprietary aspects of various types of movable assets. It looks at tangible assets (chattels), intangible financial assets (such as monetary claims), and investment securities (such as shares or bonds). Identifying the enormous scope of cross-border movement of such assets in today's economy, the chapter shows the limited role that the *lex rei sitae* rule can play in governing proprietary disputes. This is especially so because of the growing role of bulks of chattels such as inventories or portfolios of monetary claims in contemporary trade and finance, meaning that it is normatively and practically difficult to identify a single locus for the assets. The chapter focuses on conflicting transactions and *bona fide* purchases of stolen/embezzled movable assets, and analyzes distinct cross-border norms that developed in the context of artwork and cultural artifacts.

Chapter 5, "Intellectual Property, Data, and Digital Assets," analyzes the apparent tension between the borderless nature of technology, innovation, and digitization, and the fragmentation of legal norms in regard to intellectual property, data, and digital assets. In some cases, the move toward a globalization strategy evolves over time, when the political, economic, or technological circumstances so permit, such as in the case of the 1994 signing of the Trade-Related Aspects of Intellectual Property Rights (TRIPS) Agreement as part of the establishment of the World Trade Organization (WTO). That said, national differences, even for new resources such as digital assets, may reflect core normative choices and ideological bents, such as those applying to the tension between strong monopoly rights for pharmaceutical innovators and affordable access to life-saving medicines, or the conflict between the benefits of data processing and protection of privacy. The chapter identifies the unique role that the blockchain technology may play in establishing a new decentralized, yet verifiable and transparent, system for cross-border *in rem* rights in such assets.

Chapter 6, "Security Interests and Proprietary Priorities in Insolvency," highlights the changing role of financial institutions and other providers of credit in a globalizing economy; the growth of economic instruments, such as portfolio financing, syndication of loans, or securitization of mortgages; and the challenges that these developments pose for the ranking of creditors and distribution of assets upon cross-border insolvency in view of the local basis of property law. The chapter examines the different types of assets that serve as collaterals, analyzes the disparities among national legal systems about the status of quasi-security interests, such as reservation of title or transfer of ownership for security purposes, and underscores the normative considerations that drive national systems to establish a particular ordering of creditors upon insolvency. The chapter then identifies the various globalization strategies employed to govern cross-border settings, which involve security interests and proprietary priorities in insolvency, from soft law and conflict of laws instruments promoted by bodies such as UNCITRAL, Organization of American States (OAS), or the European Union, up to more ambitious strategies, such as the one embedded in the creation of a single registry for international security interests in aircrafts under the UNIDROIT Cape Town Convention on International Interests in Mobile Equipment. In the context of cross-border insolvencies, Chapter 6 shows that the future of cross-border norms may lie not only in promoting conflicts of laws principles such as the debtor's "centre of main interests" (COMI), but also in innovative bottom-up schemes that foster information exchange and interjurisdictional coordination among stakeholders, such as in the case of the *Lehman Brothers Protocol*, or among national bankruptcy courts, such as in the *Nortel* cross-border bankruptcy trial.

***

It is my hope that the book will appeal to a broad audience coming from a cross-section of disciplines, such as law, economics, business, political science, and cultural studies, and that it will generate interest not only among scholars and students, but also among practitioners, public officials, and NGO members in various countries.

Chapters 1–3 are based in part on my earlier writing: "Unbundling Harmonization: Public versus Private Law Strategies to Globalize Property," *Chicago Journal of International Law* (2015); "Land Law in the Age of Globalization and Land Grabbing," *in* M. Graziadei & L. Smith (eds.), *Comparative Property Law: Global Perspectives* (Edward Elgar Publ., 2017); and "Globalizing Property Law: An Institutional Analysis," *Vanderbilt Journal of Transnational Law* (2017).

I wish to thank the general editors of the Global Law Series, and in particular Morag Goodwin and Randall Lesaffer for promoting this project, and the editorial team of Cambridge University Press for its great help throughout the process. Thanks to Ariel Amir for her research assistance. Finally, I thank my wife Sharon and daughter Lia – this book is dedicated to you with much love.

1

Why Property Law Needs Globalization Strategies

1.1 What Property Law Conflicts Increasingly Look Like

The following themes illustrate, at the outset, the growing prevalence of legal scenarios that have implications for cross-border property rights and interests:

(a) Bankruptcy of a multinational corporation that holds a substantial portfolio of intangible assets, such as rights to monetary claims or investment securities, and conversely, debts, vis-à-vis numerous parties located throughout the world. Creditors across borders, who have no privity between them, compete for a limited pool of assets. The inherent task of an insolvency proceeding, i.e., collecting all the assets and ranking claims in regard to them, becomes particularly challenging in view of the current fragmentation of judicial forums and applicable laws, and the absence of an explicit body of international bankruptcy law.

(b) Perils of mortgage-based (or any other asset-based) securitization, as clearly demonstrated in the aftermath of the 2007 subprime crisis. Insolvency of a single mortgage is traditionally governed by the *lex rei sitae* rule (law of the place where the asset is located), and jurisdiction is correspondingly granted to the national court in whose territory the land is situated. In contrast, once mortgages are massively bundled into investment securities – which could be then traded in various stock exchange markets across the world, with derivative instruments further pushed away from the underlying assets – any attempt to restructure the debt, or simply to liquidate the assets, would come across various problems of procedural and substantive cross-border legal fragmentation.

(c) Foreign investment that is covered by a bilateral investment treaty (BIT) between the host country and the investor's country of origin. Under BITs, investment typically covers practically all types of assets, from land to intellectual property and up to monetary claims. This is also the case with provisions on protection of investment in trade-based treaties, such as Chapter 11 of the North American Free Trade Agreement (NAFTA).[1] The gist of BITs lies in the additional layer of legal protection, beyond the host country's laws that would otherwise govern property disputes in regard to the asset. BITs' commitments to standards of protection, such as "fair and equitable treatment" or abstention from uncompensated expropriations, have resulted in the past few years in an unprecedented wave of litigation before independent arbitration tribunals, with extensive damages awarded at times against host countries. The investor's claim for extraterritorial protection under the *lex specialis* resulting from a certain BIT may exceed the public law aspect of property. Thus, when a foreign investor in land argues that the BIT protection of its property interests should also weigh against applying local laws of adverse possession or validating local users' customary rights, if such doctrines undercut the investor's property rights, then the BIT's cross-border norms may also implicate the private law facet of proprietary conflicts.

(d) Protection of property rights in regional human rights conventions, including the European Convention for the Protection of Human Rights and Fundamental Freedoms,[2] American Convention on Human Rights,[3] and African Charter on Human and Peoples' Rights.[4] With respective supranational tribunals, such as the European Court of Human Rights, entrusted with interpreting and enforcing the conventions' property clauses, the legal landscape of property law has been dramatically affected. In some cases, regional/supranational conventions and other instruments are geared specifically toward the cross-border protection of proprietary interests. The leading example is the European Union (EU), whose treaties are principally

[1] North American Free Trade Agreement, Ch. 11, December 17, 1992, 32 ILM 605 (1993). In late 2018, the United States, Canada, and Mexico agreed on a new trade deal that will replace NAFTA. See A. Rappeport, "A Last-Minute Deal With Canada Salvages a Trade Agreement," *The New York Times*, October 1, 2018.

[2] European Convention for the Protection of Human Rights and Fundamental Freedoms, November 4, 1950, 213 UNTS 221. The right to property was included in Article 1 of the Protocol (Protocol No. 1), signed in Paris on March 20, 1952. For the consolidated and amended version of the Convention and Protocol No. 1, see Council of Europe, Treaty Office, at www.coe.int/en/web/conventions/full-list/-/conventions/webContent/en_GB/7435985.

[3] American Convention on Human Rights, November 22, 1969, OASTS No. 36, 1144 UNTS 143.

[4] African Charter on Human and Peoples' Rights, June 27, 1981, 21 ILM 58.

committed to protecting the free movement of capital, goods, services, and persons within the internal market. The legal ties between such free movement across borders and the protection of property rights became more manifest with the 2009 entry into force of the EU Charter of Fundamental Rights.[5]

(e) Proliferation of good-faith buyer scenarios, in which goods, from artwork to digital assets, cross national borders and end up in the hands of consumers/buyers who pay consideration, despite flaws in the chain of title that may be revealed only in retrospect. Cases of theft or other types of unlawful dispossession from the original owner, followed by the flipping of the asset across various countries until it ends up in the hands of a good-faith buyer who pays consideration to the last intermediary in the process, have been a paradigm of such property conflicts. But many other such types of disputes among cross-border parties may take place. These conflicts may also contain an intellectual property requirement, such as when garments or electronic devices that infringe on a certain trademark, copyright, or patent are sold to retailers or end-consumers in the global markets. The parties to the conflict may be dispersed across various countries, having no privity of contract among them or another type of arrangement about the forum for dispute resolution or the applicable law.

(f) Rise in international marriages or registered spousal partnerships, resulting also from the increasing cross-border movement of persons, such as within the European Union or because of visa-waiver programs signed between the United States and various countries. This may lead to cross-border property conflicts upon dissolution of marriage or death. Such disputes may often implicate not only former spouses, or heirs, in case of death, but also various third parties. Thus, a former spouse requiring, upon dissolution of marriage, an equitable distribution of assets registered in the name of the other spouse (from land and chattels to career assets and social-security benefits) may become involved in a conflict also with the spouse's creditors or other parties who assert property rights in the same assets. As Chapter 2 shows, the growing international component of such property disputes has led eighteen of the twenty-eight Member States of the European Union to move forward in 2016 with a joint framework for uniform conflict of laws rules across these

[5] Charter of Fundamental Rights of the European Union, Art. 17 ("right to property"), adopted on December 13, 2007, OJ (C 326/02), October 26, 2012.

countries. Consequently, in June 2016, the EU Council adopted regulations for implementing "enhanced cooperation in the area of jurisdiction, applicable law and enforcement of decisions" in property matters concerning both married couples[6] and registered partners.[7]

(g) Finally, new domains and technologies – from digital communications and 3D printing up to biotechnology and genome research – require, more than ever, a property ordering of the "global commons." From outer space to cyberspace, physical and intangible assets become more valuable and capable of practical use. This calls for coordination at the international level, and for the development of legal mechanisms that establish the proprietary aspects of such assets and the distribution of rights in them across borders. A prominent example is the mechanism of tradable emission allowances devised by the 1997 Kyoto Protocol to the UN Framework Convention on Climate Change,[8] followed by the 2015 Paris Agreement that entered into force in November 2016.[9] Conceptualizing emissions of carbon dioxide and other greenhouse gases as an object of property entitlements, and creating a mechanism for trading in them, the Kyoto framework represents one of the most ambitious attempts at introducing a property regime for global commons. Similar cap-and-trade mechanisms exist on the regional level within the European Union,[10] and in other areas around the world.[11]

[6] Council Regulation (EU) 2016/1103 of 24 June 2016 Implementing Enhanced Cooperation in the Area of Jurisdiction, Applicable Law and the Recognition and Enforcement of Decisions in Matters of Matrimonial Property Regimes, OJ (L 183/1), July 8, 2016.

[7] Council Regulation (EU) 2016/1104 of 24 June 2016 Implementing Enhanced Cooperation in the Area of Jurisdiction, Applicable Law and the Recognition and Enforcement of Decisions in Matters of the Property Consequences of Registered Partnerships, OJ (L 183/30), July 8, 2016.

[8] Kyoto Protocol to the United Nations Framework Convention on Climate Change, December 11, 1997, 2303 UNTS 162.

[9] See, generally, United Nations Framework Convention on Climate Change, "The Paris Agreement," available at http://unfccc.int/paris_agreement/items/9485.php (accessed on March 1, 2018). For the full text of the Paris Agreement under the United Nations Framework Convention on Climate Change, signed on December 12, 2015, see http://unfccc.int/files/essential_background/convention/application/pdf/english_paris_agreement.pdf (accessed on March 1, 2018).

[10] The EU Emissions Trading System, set up in 2005, accounts for over three-fourths of international carbon trading. It currently includes 31 countries: The 28 EU Member States, Iceland, Norway, and Liechtenstein. European Commission, "The EU Emissions Trading System," available at http://ec.europa.eu/clima/policies/ets/index_en.htm (accessed on March 1, 2018).

[11] M. Roh, "Carbon as Commodity: Is Cap-and-Trade's Market Approach Flawed?" *ENERPO Journal*, 4 Q2 (2015), available at https://enerpojournal.com/2016/10/19/carbon-as-commodity-is-cap-and-trades-market-approach-flawed/ (accessed on March 1, 2018).

As this nonexhaustive list of scenarios shows, current economic, social, and technological processes of globalization increasingly challenge property law and may require the establishment of cross-border norms and institutions that would allow for an effective ordering of entitlements to assets.

To realize why the move toward various types of globalization strategies is far from being trivial, the following sections demonstrate why property law has been conventionally considered an inherently domestic field of law. Section 1.2 highlights the key structural features of property law. Section 1.3 illustrates how these structural features translate into the creation of a more-or-less closed list of property rights in each legal system, while demonstrating how national systems diverge from one another in the rigidity of the list, the types of property rights recognized, and the specific content given to each such right in a certain national legal system. Section 1.4 shows why such national differences are not merely the result of professional style or historical path-dependence, but are also embedded in social, political, economic, and cultural considerations. This analysis sets the stage for the presentation of four globalization strategies in Section 1.5, and the articulation of methodological principles for choosing among such strategies in Section 1.6.

1.2 The Structure of Property Law

This section identifies three structural features of property law: (1) third-party applicability, (2) contraints on private ordering, and (3) an intricate public/private interface. These structural features are inherent, while differently applied, across national legal systems. As this book shows, preserving these features may prove a considerable challenge in moving from local to global governance of property rights and interests.

1.2.1 Third-Party Applicability

I use the term *third-party applicability* interchangeably with the more familiar Latin term *in rem.*[12] This concept refers to the ways in which

[12] I do not address here the voluminous debate on whether the longstanding distinction between *in rem* and *in personam* rights holds true. This debate was invigorated much due to two seminal articles by American jurist Wesley Newcomb Hohfeld in the early twentieth century. See W. N. Hohfeld, "Some Fundamental Legal Conceptions as Applied in Judicial Reasoning," *Yale Law Journal*, 23 (1913), pp. 16–59; W. N. Hohfeld, "Fundamental Legal Conceptions as Applied in Judicial Reasoning," *Yale Law Journal*, 26 (1917), pp. 710–770. I address this issue in detail in A. Lehavi, *The Construction of Property:*

legal interests typically enumerated as property rights – such as ownership, security interests, or servitudes (as detailed in Section 1.3) – possess a qualitative trait of general applicability toward a broad class of persons in establishing the set of legal rights, powers, and priorities in regard to assets. Although property relations may be combined with contract- or tort-based relations, property rights in the broader sense do not merely break down into bilateral legal relations among specifically defined parties. This is particularly so because of the way in which legal rights, powers, and priorities regarding both specific assets and categories of resources (e.g., land, chattels, intangible financial assets, or digital assets) simultaneously implicate numerous parties with diverging legal interests. The third-party applicability of property rights is manifested most clearly, in civil law terminology – but with similar application in common law systems – in the *droit de suite* (right to appropriate the asset or to pursue any interest pertaining to it, such as when a secured creditor repossesses the collateralized asset or appropriates its value in case of insolvency of the owner/debtor), and the *droit de préférence* (preferential status of a proprietary right over other third-party interests).[13]

Unlike pure contractual relations, parties affected by proprietary legal rights, powers, and priorities may not be in privity or have prior explicit legal relations and are often strangers that find themselves *ex post facto* entangled in a clash over competing claims to the same asset. Consider, for example, the legal setting in which a tract of land is owned by one person, leased by another, mortgaged in favor of a third party, burdened by a right-of-way easement in favor of a neighboring landowner, and subject to a tax lien or future expropriation in favor of the government. Property rights reveal their true complexity when actors diverge in the particular set of legal interests they hold in regard to the asset and are not interconnected by a contractual arrangement.

Moreover, property law reveals its complex nature in scenarios involving a good-faith buyer of voidable or void title (demonstrated above in a cross-border context in Section 1.1), conflicting transactions, and other types of legal triangles where parties who are not in contractual privity

Norms, Institutions, Challenges (Cambridge, UK: Cambridge University Press, 2013), pp. 1–2, 26–28.

13 J. Dalhuisen, *Dalhuisen on Transnational, Comparative, Commercial, Financial and Trade Law, Vol. II: Contract and Movable Property Law* (Oxford: Hart, 2016), pp. 302–304.

assert simultaneous claims to the asset, and property law is required to prioritize the claims.[14]

Bankruptcy and other scenarios of default or insolvency also exemplify the distinctiveness of property rights. In such settings, proprietary rights (typically, security interests) have categorical priority over mere contractual or obligatory rights, with a further internal ranking occurring within each of these categories of rights, as shown in Chapter 6 in both domestic and cross-border settings.

Beyond the fact that parties to property conflicts may not be known to one another in advance, they often turn out to be more heterogeneous in their epistemological, cultural, and social attributes than are typical contractual counterparts. One could think about the potential tensions between owners of patented or copyrighted materials (such as pharmaceutical or software companies, respectively) and different groups of potential users, from competitors to end-users; or of the ways in which corporations involve not only various groups of shareholders (e.g., controlling shareholders, institutional investors, and minority shareholders), but also creditors, suppliers, employees, or personal creditors of shareholders – all competing over the corporation's assets.[15]

Accordingly, for a legal system to function well in creating, allocating, and enforcing *in rem* rights, it must establish a broad-based understanding among otherwise-diverse audiences about how proprietary rights are structured and prioritized in cases of conflict. While this challenge may prove significant even within a certain domestic legal system, it becomes manifestly more complex in the cross-border context, in which heterogeneity is inherently the pervasive reality.

1.2.2 Constraints on Private Ordering

Party autonomy and contractual freedom are key concepts in contract law.[16] Subject to only few limits, such as the unconscionability doctrine,[17]

[14] M. Mautner, "'The Eternal Triangles of the Law': Toward a Theory of Priorities in Conflicts Involving Remote Parties," *Michigan Law Review*, 90 (1991), pp. 95–154.

[15] Lehavi, *The Construction of Property*, pp. 179–213.

[16] H. Dagan and M. Heller, *The Choice Theory of Contracts* (Cambridge, UK: Cambridge University Press, 2017), pp. 19–47, 67–78.

[17] Ibid., pp. 86–87.

parties to a contract are at liberty to design the contract and the substantive and procedural rights under it as they deem fit, and they may further opt out of contract law's default rules on enforcement and dispute resolution. In the cross-border context, party autonomy plays a key role in the ability of parties to an international transaction to include specific provisions about jurisdiction, applicable law, procedure, and so forth. Professional parties, such as merchants and financial institutions, articulate their elaborate and sophisticated rules for implementation, enforcement, and dispute resolution, opting often for independent arbitration/mediation, as part of such private ordering.[18]

Property is different. To the extent that property law sets up certain requirements for a party to prevail over other parties with whom he or she has no contractual privity, the ability to engage in private ordering is practically limited because it would not be binding on noncontractual parties. This limit on private ordering has implications both at the initial stage of creating, transferring, or otherwise crafting the proprietary rights pertaining to a certain asset, and at the later stage of enforcing such rights or otherwise engaging in dispute resolution. As for the initial stage, the need to design property rights, unlike contractual rights, as ones that apply broadly and are "good against the world" is the key reason why practically every legal system embraces the principle of a closed list (*numerus clausus)* of recognized property rights, although legal systems may diverge in the rigidity of the list, the specific menu of rights, and the content of each such right.[19] The key idea is, however, that the power to create the list of property rights and change/adapt it over time is granted to the state institutions: legislative, administrative, and judicial normmakers. A privately ordered permutation on such rules can be enforced between contractual parties, but not beyond.[20]

At the stage of enforcement or dispute resolution, the limits on private ordering become particularly manifested in the cross-border setting. Contractual parties are generally free to choose the forum for dispute resolution, applicable law, and procedural and evidentiary rules, with

[18] For the prevalence of such provisions and their nexus to the prospects of creating a self-standing *lex mercatoria*, see G. Cuniberti, "Three Theories of Lex Mercatoria," *Columbia Journal of Transnational Law*, 52 (2014), pp. 369–434.

[19] N. M. Davidson, "Standardization and Pluralism in Property Law," *Vanderbilt Law Review*, 61 (2008), pp. 1597–1663.

[20] T. W. Merrill and H. E. Smith, "Optimal Standardization in the Law of Property: The Numerus Clausus Principle," *Yale Law Journal*, 110 (2000), pp. 1–70; B. Akkermans, *The Principle of Numerus Clausus in European Property Law* (Antwerp: Intersentia, 2008).

such principle of party autonomy also enshrined in international or regional instruments.[21]

In contrast, the ability for such type of private ordering is limited in the case of *in rem* rights,[22] with jurisdiction and applicable law being determined by the conflict of laws' rules established by international/ regional legal instruments or otherwise by domestic legal institutions. Traditionally, the most prominent rule has been the *lex rei sitae*, governing both jurisdiction and applicable law, although as the next chapters show, the rules may diverge across different types of assets. In contrast, party autonomy has been validated only rarely by either national courts or international instruments in cross-border contexts.[23] Accordingly, while professional international actors, such as merchants and financial institutions, increasingly develop industry-specific practices for the resolution of cross-border disputes between them, with an eye toward the creation of a new *lex mercatoria*,[24] such types of private ordering are still limited in that these do not bind third parties who do not follow such practices, such as in the case of a multiparty, cross-border insolvency.[25]

1.2.3 The Public/Private Interface

A third distinctive structural facet of property law concerns the complex interface between public law and private law aspects. The general challenge faced by legal systems in designing property law is how to delineate the borders of permissible government interference (or adversely, positive intervention) with property, while simultaneously defining the scope

[21] See, e.g., Regulation (EU) 1215/2012 of the European Parliament and of the Council of 12 December 2012 on Jurisdiction and the Recognition and Enforcement of Judgments in Civil and Commercial Matters, Art. 25, OJ (L 351/1), December 12, 2012 (allowing parties to grant jurisdiction to one of the courts of an EU Member State).

[22] Ibid., Art. 24(1) (in "proceedings which have as their object *in rem* rights in immovable property or tenancies in immovable property, the courts of the Member State in which the property is situated" shall have "exclusive jurisdiction").

[23] One such instance is a 1997 decision by the Dutch Supreme Court, by which when parties agree on the law that governs the assignment of claims, it also applies to the proprietary aspects of the assignment. *Brandsma qq/Hansa Chemie AG*, HR May 16, 1997, NJ 1998, 585 (Neth.) (in Dutch). For a detailed review of the case, see T. H. D. Struycken, "The Proprietary Aspects of International Assignment of Debts and the Rome Convention, Article 12," *Lloyd's Maritime and Commercial Law Quarterly*, 3 (1998), pp. 345–360. See also Chapter 6, Section 6.3.2.

[24] Dalhuisen, Vol. II, pp. 332–337.

[25] See Chapter 6, Section 6.4.

and nature of property rights of a person vis-à-vis the entire spectrum of private third parties.

Although the task of drawing the lines between public/constitutional legal norms and those controlling private conduct is familiar in many other fields of law, property does seem to introduce a special challenge. That the very same term, *property*, is used in both the private law field that orders legal relations among persons with regard to assets and the public/constitutional realm is not merely a matter of historical accident or conceptual confusion. While the standard, mostly liberal arguments in favor of some differentiation between government conduct and private conduct may apply to property, any attempt to hermetically separate the two realms of property law would be both impractical and normatively awkward. The result is one of constant tension between public and private. Whereas different legal systems may reach different results in attempting to draw the lines between public and private, the normative debate is not free of constraints and is implicated by how the structure of property rights encompasses both realms.[26] As the following chapters show, this complex interface may manifest itself in numerus cross-border settings, such as resolving whether regional/international human rights conventions that protect the right to property also have a bearing on the allocation and enforcement of property rights among private parties. From a broader normative or even political perspective, the potential application of property law norms to both realms may implicate the willingness of states and other local actors to bind themselves by cross-border norms and jurisdiction of respective institutions.

1.3 The Closed (but Country-Specific) List of Property Rights

As noted in Section 1.2, each national legal system establishes its own menu of property rights. Such property law templates may diverge from one another in the rigidity of the list of rights as a closed system (both at a certain point in time and over the course of time); the sources of law that are authorized to set or amend the list (i.e., whether courts can establish new property rights); the substantive and remedial content of each right; the types of assets that are objects of property; and the internal consistency or divergence of the rights' content across different assets.

[26] For a more detailed discussion of this point, see Lehavi, *The Construction of Property*, pp. 43–45.

To illustrate just the latter point – internal consistency or divergence – consider, for example, how the right of ownership (discussed in more detail under the next heading in this section) may prove to be very different, both conceptually and practically, for different types of assets within the same legal system. Thus, for example, while ownership of land or chattels is essentially perpetual (meaning typically that the right exists indefinitely until the owner transfers ownership of the asset to someone else through sale, gift, or inheritance or the right to the asset is lawfully expropriated by the government), ownership of most types of intellectual property is time-limited: a patent is normally protected for 20 years; a copyright exists for a period that runs typically for the life of the author plus 50–70 years. Moreover, some legal systems (e.g., Germany) struggle with defining a right of ownership in an intangible asset, such as a monetary claim, such that a party can only be "entitled" to the asset.[27] Moreover, while ownership of one's body is recognized in some aspects across legal systems – such as the growing recognition of the *right of publicity*, which protects the images and voices of persons from commercial exploitation without their consent[28] – other elements defy the typical incidents of ownership, such that the sale of (certain) organs is flatly prohibited.[29]

While the focus of most property jurisprudence and scholarship – and this book is no exception – is on private property, every legal system establishes its own approach to common property (i.e., an asset owned and/or held collectively by a group of persons), public property (i.e., an asset owned and/or held by a public entity), and hybrid property regimes.[30] These forms of property ownership are essential across all societies and economies, even those driven by a strong market orientation (in the case of common property, consider joint tenancy by spouses, corporations, or common property/amenities in a condominium). Accordingly, each legal system is tasked with defining legal similarities and differences for different subjects of ownership (person, group, state)

[27] S. van Erp, "Ownership of Data and the Numerus Clausus of Legal Objects," Maastricht European Private Law Institute Working Paper No. 2017/6 (October 2017), p. 17, available at https://ssrn.com/abstract=3046402 (accessed on March 1, 2018).

[28] Merrill and Smith, "Optimal Standardization," p. 20.

[29] See, generally, M. J. Radin, "From Baby-Selling to Boilerplates: Reflections on the Limits of the Infrastructures of the Market," *Osgoode Hall Law Journal*, 54 (2017), pp. 339–376; M. J. Radin, *Contested Commodities: The Trouble with Trade in Sex, Children, Body Parts, and Other Things* (Cambridge, MA: Harvard University Press, 2011).

[30] See Lehavi, *The Construction of Property*, pp. 97–150.

regarding a certain object of property. Thus, for example, while in some countries state land enjoys sovereign immunity against claims of adverse possession, in other countries publicly owned land is treated similarly to privately owned land in this respect.[31] Moreover, while the protection of the right to property in state constitutions, or in statutory law, is typically geared toward private property (while not practically denying such protection to other subjects), some states may promote a different agenda. Thus, Article 4 of the 2007 Property Rights Law of the People's Republic of China provides that the "property rights of the State, collective, individual and other obligees shall be protected by laws and shall not be infringed by any institute or individuals,"[32] thus emphasizing the particular importance of state ownership and its protection.

The following paragraphs briefly highlight the key property rights that are recognized, in one version or another, across many or all legal systems. A more elaborate discussion of such rights, in the context of specific types of assets, will be offered in the subsequent chapters of this book.

1.3.1 Ownership

In civil law systems, the right of ownership (*dominium*) is the starting point for property law. It is considered the most extensive property right, and it typically grants the owner the powers to use, enjoy, and alienate the asset, while excluding others or preventing them from interfering with the object of ownership.[33] Thus, under Article 903 of the German Civil Code:

[31] Compare W. Q. Impert, Comment, "Whose Land Is It Anyway: It's Time to Reconsider Sovereign Immunity from Adverse Possession," *UCLA Law Review*, 49 (2001), pp. 447–470 (analyzing sovereign immunity for federal and state government in the United States) with P. O'Connor, "The Private Taking of Land: Adverse Possession, Encroachment by Buildings and Improvement Under a Mistake," *UWAL Review*, 33 (2006), pp. 31–62 at 35 (noting the different approach that is taking hold in England against exemption of public land from limitation periods).

[32] Property Rights Law of the People's Republic of China, promulgated by the National People's Congress, March 16, 2007, effective October 1, 2007, 2007 Standing Committee National People's Congress Gazette 291. An unofficial English version is available at www.lehmanlaw.com/resource-centre/laws-and-regulations/general/property-rights-law-of-the-peoples-republic-of-china.html (accessed on March 1, 2018).

[33] S. van Erp and B. Akkermans, *Cases, Materials and Text on Property Law* (Oxford: Hart Publishing, 2012), pp. 213–215.

> The owner of an asset, when this does not contradict with the law or rights of third parties, can do with the object as he deems fit and exclude others from interfering.[34]

As this definition shows, ownership also has a residual character, in the sense that all other rights and powers, even if not specifically enumerated in the underlying statute, belong to the owner, unless such elements are otherwise prohibited by law or belong to other parties.

In contrast, the concept of ownership is much more subtle and complex in common law systems. This is particularly so because of the way in which the system of rights in land developed historically in England. The system that grew out of feudalism in medieval England was one of estates in land, or tenures, under which the tenant was entitled to possess the land and use it in return for certain services to his lord, with the King located on top of the feudal ladder.[35] The types of estates differed in the time of the tenure and any other conditions attached to them. The estate could be absolute or defeasible, i.e., subject to extinction under certain scenarios. The fee simple was in principle indefinite, with the life estate restricted to the life of the tenant, and shorter tenures fixed for a limited period of time. Over the course of time, the fee simple absolute became an inheritable and alienable right, so that in contemporary Anglo-American legal systems, the fee simple is practically equivalent to civil law ownership in land.[36]

For other types of assets, common law has essentially recognized title as an equivalent of ownership and has proven more flexible, as compared with at least some civil law systems, in recognizing title or ownership in intangibles. More generally, in contemporary Anglo-American jurisprudence, ownership occupies a central role, understood as comprising various incidents:

> [T]he right to possess, the right to use, the right to manage, the right to the income of the thing, the right to the capital, the right to security, the rights or incidents of transmissibility and absence of term, the duty to prevent harm, liability to execution, and the incident of residuarity.[37]

[34] "Der Eigentümer einer Sache kann, soweit nicht das Gesetz oder Rechte Dritter entgegenstehen, mit der Sache nach Belieben verfahren und andere von jeder Einwirkung ausschließen." German Civil Code (Bürgerliches Gesetzbuch), Art. 903, available at www.gesetze-im-internet.de/bgb/__903.html (in German) (accessed on March 1, 2018).

[35] J. Dukeminier et al., *Property*, 9th ed. (New York: Wolters Kluwer, 2018), pp. 249–253.

[36] Ibid., pp. 255–261.

[37] T. Honoré, *Making Law Bind: Essays Legal and Philosophical* (Oxford: Clarendon Press, 1989), p. 165.

As noted above, these incidents of ownership or title may operate differently or only partially for some types of assets – for example, ownership of patents or copyrights is time-limited.

1.3.2 Possessory Rights

The concept of possession has developed differently in civil law systems as compared with common law ones. In civil law, possession is typically an incident of an underlying right, most prominently ownership, allowing its holder to possess the asset. Possession is ownership's "appearance or shadow," and not a self-standing right.[38]

Accordingly, in civil law, the lease (or rent) allows a person to hold and use an asset for a set period of time, against consideration paid to the owner, although the prevalent legal view in civil law systems is that the lease is a personal right, and not a proprietary one.[39] A person may also lawfully possess an asset by virtue of a loan (time-limited right to hold and use for no consideration), usufruct, possessory security interest such as a pledge, or lien, which are discussed separately. In the case of holdership, a person merely holds an asset for someone else.[40]

In common law, possession plays a much more dominant role as a source, and not only as an incident of rights. The origin of this approach lies in the system of estates in land, with the fee simple, life estate, and other types of fees focusing on the physical (*seisin*) notion of possession. Modern types of leases in land, although not part of the system of estates, also came to be largely recognized in common law systems as having proprietary attributes.[41]

The force of possession in common law was traditionally manifested in the case of bailment in chattels, which refers to a category of cases in which ownership is separated from possession, through a voluntary act by the owner, with the purpose that the person in possession would temporarily use it or enjoy its profits (such as in a loan or hire), hold the

[38] Dalhuisen, Vol. II, pp. 348–349.

[39] van Erp and Akkermans, *Cases on Property Law*, pp. 298–299.

[40] Typically, the holdership is done in service of the owner. Dalhuisen, Vol. II, pp. 348–351.

[41] van Erp and Akkermans, *Cases on Property Law*, p. 309; T. W. Merrill and H. E. Smith, "The Property/Contract Interface," *Columbia Law Review*, 101 (2001), pp. 773–852 at 820–823 (pointing to American law's recognition of only four types of leases – the term of years, the periodic tenancy, the tenancy at will, and the tenancy at sufferance – as a manifestation of the *numerus clausus* principle, while not determining if the lease should be classified as property).

asset passively as a pawn or deposit, or perform a certain service or work on the asset for the owner (e.g., valet parking or dry cleaning). Historically, the owner/bailor would only have a contractual retrieval right and would have to rely on a tort action against the bailee, with the bailee having the option to pay damages instead of returning the asset. The bailee would also have a legal standing to act against third parties. With time, however, the common law came to recognize the right of immediate repossession, or a property right in *replevin*, in favor of the owner/bailor versus the bailee.[42] More broadly, in current Anglo-American law, the owner/bailor is considered as retaining the *in rem* rights associated with ownership (with only practical limits on uses that require actual possession), and there is a lingering dispute as to whether the bailee holds some type of a proprietary right by virtue of his or her possession.[43]

1.3.3 Usufruct (and Other Personal Servitudes)

Personal servitudes are prevalent mostly in civil law countries. Such rights grant a specific person or group of persons a right to enjoy land or a movable asset owned by another. The most prominent type of right is the usufruct, originating in Roman law, which grants its holder the right to use and enjoy an asset owned by someone else, as well the right to take the fruits that the asset produces. Consequently, during the period in which the right of usufruct is in force, the owner cannot exercise his or her rights to use and enjoy the asset and can only transfer ownership to another person. The new owner would be subjected, however, to the right of usufruct, such that the usufruct has the status of a property right, rather than a mere contractual status.[44] Some civil law systems also recognize other types of personal servitudes, based on Roman law distinctions, such as rights of use or habitation (with the right of habitation applying only to immovable assets).[45]

Common law systems do not generally follow the same lines. One such partial equivalent can be found in the historic right of *profits à prendre*, i.e., right to take off a land things that are otherwise considered part of the land, such as timber, minerals, or wild animals (game).[46] In contemporary common law systems, however, rights to remove oil, gas, or

[42] Dalhuisen, Vol. II, pp. 318–321.
[43] Merrill and Smith, "The Property/Contract Interface," pp. 811–813.
[44] van Erp and Akkermans, *Cases on Property Law*, p. 253.
[45] Ibid., pp. 262–267.
[46] Dukeminier et al., *Property*, pp. 763–765.

minerals operate under a distinct branch of doctrine, with nonmineral profits generally being governed by the same rules of easements,[47] analyzed in the following paragraphs as real servitudes.

1.3.4 *Real Servitudes*

Unlike personal servitudes, real servitudes burden one parcel of land for the benefit of another parcel, with such burdens and benefits sometimes having also a reciprocal nature.[48] This means that the effect of a real servitude extends beyond the original parties to the legal arrangement creating the servitude, such that the servitude also applies to any transferees or other third parties. The real servitude may grant right-holders in the dominant land the right to access, use, or take another action in the burdened (servient) land, or to limit the right-holders in the burdened land from doing something they could have otherwise done as owners/possessors. In civil law systems, real servitudes are based on Roman law principles. Accordingly, in such legal systems, right-holders in burdened lands are usually subject only to negative duties, and not to affirmative/positive ones, i.e. they cannot be compelled to do something. This distinction is based on the Roman maxim *servitus in faciendo consistere nequit* ("a servitude cannot continue by obliging" [action]).[49]

The development of real servitudes has been more complex in Anglo-American systems, with current distinctions among different types of servitudes often reflecting historical trajectories rather than functional considerations, and thus often creating confusion. The primary modern forms of servitudes – easements, real covenants, and covenants enforceable in equity (also known as equitable servitudes) – developed mostly in the nineteenth century. Generally, an *affirmative easement* focuses on the ability of a person to enter or perform an act on the servient land. An *easement appurtenant* gives this right to whomever owns the dominant land, and an *easement in gross* gives the right to a certain person regardless of ownership (and is thus closer to a personal servitude).[50]

47 Ibid., p. 764, n. 5.
48 A reciprocal system of burdens and benefits exists, for example, in common interest developments, such as in planned-unit developments or condominiums in the United States and in other legal systems. See A. Lehavi, "Concepts of Power: Majority Control and Accountability in Private Legal Organizations," *Virginia Law and Business Review*, 8 (2014), pp. 1–58 at 19–22.
49 van Erp and Akkermans, *Cases on Property Law*, pp. 243–246.
50 Dukeminier et al., *Property*, pp. 765–766.

While an affirmative easement is usually created by agreement, in some cases it may be created by implication or prescription, usually based on long-term use.[51] A *negative easement* entitles the owner of the dominant land to stop the owner of the servient land from doing something on the servient land.

Real covenants in the Anglo-American legal system grew out of the reluctance of courts to recognize new types of negative easements beyond those known historically, thus causing landowners to turn in the early nineteenth century to the law of contracts. A real covenant can be a negative promise (a promise not to do an act) or an affirmative promise (a promise to do an act) and is enforceable against any assignee who has notice of it. English and American law diverge in the sense that American courts have been more willing to recognize affirmative covenants.

An equitable servitude, enforceable by injunction or specific performance, is a covenant relating to the use of land and enforceable in equity against successor owners or possessors regardless of its enforceability in law. Accordingly, the traditional difference in Anglo-American law between real covenants and equitable servitudes relates to the remedy sought in case of a breach: damages in the case of a real covenant and injunction or performance in the case of an equitable servitude.[52]

1.3.5 Security Interests

The key role of a security interest is to give a creditor a preferred legal status to secure a debt, one which is applicable not only vis-à-vis the debtor, but also against other creditors and third parties who claim an interest in regard to the debtor's assets – thus making the security interest a proprietary right. Security interests are discussed in detail in Chapter 6.

Security interests can be roughly divided into possessory and nonpossessory securities, such that under the former type, the secured creditor possesses or otherwise controls the asset until payment is made, whereas under the latter model the debtor continues to possess and use the asset but is subject to surrendering the asset upon default. In today's economy, most security interests are nonpossessory. The mortgage or hypothec (as it is known in civil law terminology) applies to land, whereas other types of charges or pledges apply to different types of assets, tangible or intangible ones. The term *lien* is in some legal systems a synonym for a

[51] Ibid., p. 765.
[52] Ibid., pp. 838–853.

consensual charge or pledge, but it also has a distinct meaning in the sense that a right of possessory lien can emerge from a tax liability; or when a contractor, mechanic, or another person, who performs work on an asset but is not paid, is allowed by law to hold on to the asset until payment is made (this is known as *artificer's lien* or *mechanic's lien*). Finally, as Chapter 6 shows in detail, legal systems have different approaches to designing various quasi-security interests, such as reservation of title in the case of a credit sale, or transfer of ownership of an asset, or bulk of assets, to secure a debt.

1.3.6 Trust

In common law systems, the term *trust* refers to a situation in which a person holds rights in an asset on behalf of another person, or in limited circumstances, for a certain purpose. The person creating the trust is called the settlor, the person holding the rights is the trustee, and the person for whom such rights are held is the beneficiary.[53] While the trustee typically holds the formal legal title to the asset, his or her property rights are subjected to the terms of the trust, such that the nature of the trustee's ownership or title is very different than in nontrust settings.

A trust beneficiary has a personal right that the trustee would comply with the duties set out in the terms of trust, but the beneficiary's interest can also be seen as a kind of property right. This is so both in the sense that the beneficiary may assign to third parties his or her rights – such as a right to receive payments when the asset generates income[54] – and in that unauthorized transfers of the asset by the trustee to another person, who is not a *bona fide* purchaser, could be invalidated. Moreover, the beneficiary can also trace his or her equitable interests by virtue of the trust through substitution of one kind of property rights to another, such as when an authorized sale is made to a *bona fide* purchaser and the beneficiary interest is transferred to the proceeds from the sale.[55]

The concept of trust is more ambiguous in civil law systems. Civil law systems are familiar with a potential split in the substantive core of ownership, such as in the case of a usufruct that practically undercuts the owner's rights.[56] Such systems are also familiar with the idea of

[53] van Erp and Akkermans, *Cases on Property Law*, pp. 554–557.
[54] J. Penner, *The Law of Trusts*, 9th ed. (Oxford: Oxford University Press, 2014), pp. 27–28.
[55] Ibid., p. 312.
[56] Dalhuisen, Vol. II, pp. 490–491.

certain funds being set aside for certain purposes, not truly belonging to the person holding them. That said, civil law does not have an integrated system of equitable rights that can override legal ones, meaning that limited or split proprietary rights must be spelled out in an existing context.[57] Thus, instead of a general flexible system of trusts, civil law systems must develop specific statutory mechanisms or legal doctrines to deal with particular instances of split rights, in which a person holds or manages an asset for the benefit of another. Such trustlike legal instruments include the German *Treuhand*, and in particular the *fiduziarische Treuhand*, and the French *fiducie*.[58]

1.3.7 New Property

The concept of *new property*, which gained popularity in academic discourse as of the 1960s following an influential law review article bearing this title,[59] refers to the argument by which in modern society, private property should be expanded to include also state largess – namely, social-security benefits and other transfer payments, government services, licenses and so forth – such that a person receiving it has some sort of a property right.[60] Over time, despite the fact that such interests are not covered by the conventional *numerus clausus* lists of national property law systems, this concept gained traction in constitutional property jurisprudence, with national courts increasingly willing to identify such interests as falling under the definition of *property* in constitutional property clauses.[61] Importantly for the global context, supranational courts, such as the European Court of Human Rights (ECHR), have also shown more inclination to recognize these interests, such as by referring to social-security benefits as *possessions* in Article 1 of the First Protocol to the European Convention for the Protection of Human Rights and Fundamental Freedoms.[62] This view was then

57 Ibid., p. 505.

58 van Erp and Akkermans, *Cases on Property Law*, pp. 551–580.

59 C. A. Reich, "The New Property," *Yale Law Journal*, 73 (1964), pp. 733–787.

60 F. McCarthy, "Protection of Property and the European Convention on Human Rights," *Brigham-Kanner Property Rights Conference Journal*, 6 (2017), pp. 299–328 at 320.

61 An early example is the US Supreme Court's decision in *Goldberg* v. *Kelly*, 397 US 254, 262 n.8 (1970) (nothing that "it may be realistic today to regard welfare entitlements as more like 'property' than a 'gratuity'").

62 European Convention for the Protection of Human Rights and Fundamental Freedoms, November 4, 1950, 213 UNTS 221, Protocol 1, Art. 1

expanded by the ECHR to incorporate both contributory and non-contributory state benefit schemes.[63] As Chapter 2 will show, licenses, franchises, and other types of state-based entitlements in business contexts have also become part of property jurisprudence due to their protection as investments in bilateral investment treaties and similar cross-border instruments.[64] This means that various types of new property gradually become part of the landscape of property rights on both the national and cross-border levels.

1.4 Why Interstate Differences Linger in Property Law

While market forces, interpersonal networks, and technology increasingly push toward the dissemination, use, and trade of assets across borders, property law has not moved similarly in a clear-cut path of convergence or another mode of unification. The potential tension between legal systems and decentralized forces of markets, networks, and technology applies also to other fields of law. In the present context, it is noteworthy to highlight the particular features of property law in order to illustrate why devising globalization strategies may prove to be particularly essential.

One set of considerations that explains the lingering differences between national property law systems is that of historical trajectories. Thus, for example, the system of estates in land developed in medieval England as a manifestation of the feudal system, in which possession and use of land were intertwined with a broader political system of power, provision of services, and other contingencies, flowing from the King down the multiple steps in the feudal ladder.[65] While the system of estates developed over time, such that the fee simple absolute gradually became an inheritable, tradable, and essentially indefinite right, the traces of history were not simply deleted. Accordingly, unlike the comprehensive, full-fledged nature of ownership in civil law systems,

[63] App. No. 10373/05, *Moskal* v. *Poland* (Eur. Ct. H.R., Fourth Section, September 15, 2009) para. 38 (holding that the "mere fact that a property right is subject to revocation in certain circumstances does not prevent it from being a 'possession' within the meaning of Article 1 of Protocol No. 1, at least until it is revoked").

[64] See Chapter 2, Section 2.3.4.5.

[65] Dukeminier et al., *Property*, pp. 249-253.

many common law countries still maintain particular arrangements for property rights in land.[66]

Another historical development, which still characterizes common law systems, concerns the role of equity, which emerged during the late Middle Ages as a tool to provide new types of remedies where common law had proven inadequate and limited in its ability to develop due to internal conflicts between royal common law courts and the courts lower down the feudal chain.[67]

The Court of Chancery, which emerged as a new type of royal court that assumed the authority to grant new discretionary remedies and develop new doctrines, played a major role in the development of property law. Equity was initially dominant in land law, where it considered and defined new types of uses and entitlements that were not within the traditional common law system of estates, such as custody arrangements in the case of absentee estate holders.[68] Equity also proved essential in developing the doctrine of *equitable redemption* of mortgages, with mortgages originally structured in common law as a (conditioned) transfer of rights in the land.[69] Equity played a subsequent role in creating new types of limited proprietary rights in chattels and then in intangibles, such as equitable interests emerging from trust relations, conditional and temporary ownership rights, and floating charges.[70] More generally, equity has a historic role in the evolution of property law as a relatively more flexible system of rights as compared with civil law systems.

The modern property systems in civil law countries developed in a very different fashion, albeit with significant divergences among the major systems. Thus, for example, the French Civil Code of 1804 (Code Napoléon) reflected the ideology of the French Revolution and the 1789 Declaration of the Rights of Man and of the Citizen. The French Civil Code sought to create a new legal order, repealing all prior law, and in particular the feudal features that had served mostly the landed aristocracy. The reconceptualization and definition of the right to private ownership under the French civil code were considered part of this

[66] This is also the case in the United States, in which feudalism was never part of the political system. One exception is the fee tail (an estate passed only to lineal descendants), which was abolished in most US States. Ibid., pp. 261–265.

[67] van Erp and Akkermans, *Cases on Property Law*, p. 9.

[68] Dalhuisen, Vol. II, p. 366.

[69] C. M. Rose, *Property and Persuasion: Essays on the History, Theory and Rhetoric of Ownership* (Boulder, San Francisco, Oxford: Westview Press, 1994), pp. 203–205.

[70] Dalhuisen, Vol. II, p. 368.

revolutionary agenda.[71] The German Civil Code of 1896 (*Bürgerliches Gesetzbuch*), which became effective in 1900, developed in a different manner, focusing on a historical study of the origins of civil law in Germany, including Roman law and old Germanic law, as well as of more recent elements. Thus, the definition of ownership in the German Civil Code, and property law in general, relied also on concepts of Roman law, as solidified in the *Corpus Juris Civilis* published as a series of books as of 533 AD (including the book "on things").[72] The strong and abstract nature of ownership relied, therefore, in part on Roman law antecedents. Path-dependency thus proves to be a dominant force, particularly in property law.[73] Accordingly, historical origins still play a major role in explaining the lingering differences in property law.

Moreover, methodological principles and intellectual styles may also play a prominent role in substantiating local idiosyncrasies in property law. Thus, as Chapter 6 will show, legal systems exhibit different approaches along the functional–formal spectrum in regard to reservation of title or transfer of ownership for security purposes, as falling or not under the general framework of security interests, with divisions running not only across the common law/civil law taxonomy.[74]

Obviously, differences in property law are not only the result of history or methodology. Social, economic, and political considerations have played, and continue to play, a crucial role in crafting national property law doctrines and may thus pose challenges to a smooth transition to globalism.

The more evident aspect of property law which is prone to be influenced by social, economic, and political considerations is that of public or constitutional law, and the protection of private property from government intervention in particular. A comprehensive comparative analysis of constitutional property clauses and related doctrines is obviously outside the scope of this book.[75]

[71] J. H. Merryman and R. Pérez-Perdomo, *The Civil Law Tradition: An Introduction to the Legal Systems of Europe and Latin America*, 3d ed. (Stanford: Stanford University Press, 2007), pp. 15–17, 28–31.

[72] Ibid., pp. 6–8, 31–32.

[73] Y. C. Chang and H. E. Smith, "An Economic Analysis of Civil versus Common Law Property," *Notre Dame Law Review*, 88 (2012), pp. 1–55 at 9 (noting that the delineation of rights tends to be more resistant to change in property law than in contract law, and that *in rem* aspects of property remain particularly stable).

[74] See Chapter 6, Section 6.2.2.

[75] See, generally, A. J. Van der Walt, *Constitutional Property Clauses* (Cambridge, MA: Kluwer Law International, 1999).

By way of illustration, the defining feature of German constitutional property law, which distinguishes it from other prominent constitutional property clauses, is the social-obligation norm. Article 14(2) of the German Basic Law (*Grundgesetz*) reads: "Property entails obligations. Its use shall also serve the public good."[76] The social-obligation norm requires that the legislature and the courts maintain a proper balance between the owner's individual interests and the well-being of the community, with the principle of proportionality (*Verhältnismäßigkeit*) playing a key role.[77]

While the promotion of public interests may serve as a constraint on the right to private property also in legal systems whose constitutions do not include such an explicit principle – as is the case, for example, with the property clauses in the Fifth Amendment to the US Constitution[78] – the underlying normative choice made in the German Constitution carries substantive consequences.[79]

Another prominent example, which will be discussed in more detail in Chapter 3, concerns the change in the South African Constitution after the fall of the Apartheid regime. Section 25 of the 1996 Constitution explicitly considers, for purposes of identifying the public interest that justifies expropriation of land, the "nation's commitment to land reform, and to reforms to bring about equitable access to all South Africa's natural resources." Moreover, in determining the compensation to be paid for such expropriation, Section 25 of the South African Constitution opts for a multifactor test, in which the market value is but one component, and that is aimed at achieving "an equitable balance between the public interest and the interests of those affected."[80]

That said, the implications of social, economic, and political normative choices go also to the heart of the private law aspects of national property laws, such that different agendas lead to different doctrines. As already

76 Federal Ministry of Justice and Consumer Protection, Basic Law for the Federal Republic of Germany, Art. 14(2), available at www.gesetze-im-internet.de/englisch_gg/englisch_gg.html#p0090 (accessed on March 1, 2018).

77 G. S. Alexander, *The Global Debate over Constitutional Property: Lessons for American Takings Jurisprudence* (Chicago and London: University of Chicago Press, 2006).

78 "No person . . . shall be deprived of life, liberty, or property, without due process of law; nor shall private property be taken for public use, without just compensation." The Constitution of the United States of America, Amend. V.

79 Alexander, *The Global Debate*, pp. 199–211.

80 Constitution of the Republic of South Africa No. 108 of 1996 (as amended), s. 25. See Chapter 3, Section 3.2.

suggested, private law played a key role in state-making in continental Europe during the eighteenth and nineteenth centuries, particularly in Napoleonic France.[81] The emphasis on private law codification explicitly sought not only to protect individual freedom and private property, but also to establish legislative and administrative superiority over courts and other institutions. More recently, the state-making function of private law, and property law in particular, has been also evident in post-Soviet countries and other economies in transition.[82]

Current comparative empirical literature supports the argument by which private law aspects of property law derive from deeply embedded normative considerations. These grounds may explain how national legal systems differ, for example, in protecting minority shareholders and creditors in business corporations,[83] judicially enforcing debt contracts,[84] and constraining landlords' ability to evict defaulting tenants.[85]

Rafael La Porta, Florencio López-de-Silanes, and Andrei Shleifer offer a consolidating theory as to the interrelations between social and political institutions, legal rules, and financial and economic outcomes of countries.[86] They argue that what explains differences in private and commercial laws – which in turn account for disparities in economic and financial outcomes – are legal origins (applying not only to origin countries but also to former colonies and other countries following these systems), with the English common law, French civil law, and German civil law constituting the chief origins.[87] More precisely, the term *legal origins* refers to the ways in which countries "have developed very different styles of social control of business, and institutions supporting these styles."[88] Regardless of whether they can be traced back to medieval or revolutionary periods, these styles have since proven quite persistent even in the face of regulatory or legal changes. The English common law

81 D. Caruso, "Private Law and State-Making in the Age of Globalization," *NYU Journal of International Law and Politics*, 39 (2006), pp. 1–74 at 24–26.

82 Ibid., p. 26. See also Chapter 3, Section 3.2.

83 R. La Porta et al., "Law and Finance," *Journal of Political Economics*, 106 (1998), pp. 1113–1155; S. Djankov et al., "Private Credit in 129 Countries," *Journal of Financial Economics*, 84 (2007), pp. 299–329.

84 R. La Porta et al., "Judicial Checks and Balances," *Journal of Political Economics*, 112 (2004), pp. 445–470.

85 S. Djankov et al., "Courts," *Quarterly Journal of Economics*, 118 (2003), pp. 453–517.

86 R. La Porta et al., "The Economic Consequences of Legal Origins," *Journal of Economic Literature*, 46 (2008), pp. 285–332.

87 Ibid., pp. 287–91.

88 Ibid., p. 307.

system is said to advocate a general hands-off approach with only specific interventions by the state. In contrast, the German and French civil law systems give the state a key role in ordering social and legal relations and in providing top-down solutions to economic challenges.[89]

Other writers have focused on even more fundamental and slow-moving institutions, such as culture.[90] Amir Licht, Chanan Goldschmidt, and Shalom Schwartz offer a classification of culture based on three axes of value orientations: embeddedness versus autonomy, hierarchy versus egalitarianism, and mastery versus harmony, and the causal influence of these cultural attributes on national legal norms.[91] Amir Licht and this author examined empirically the relationship between the degree of cultural embeddedness/autonomy and property rights, using a comparative dataset on property rights protection compiled by the Property Rights Alliance.[92] The analysis found a clear association between the two variables: the more a country's culture emphasizes embeddedness and de-emphasizes autonomy, the less likely it is to protect private property rights in tangible goods, and even more so intellectual property rights, as captured by these datasets.[93]

Giuseppe Dari-Mattiacci and Carmine Guerriero explore the dependency of private-law property doctrines on cultural attributes in their study of the good-faith purchaser doctrine.[94] They attribute the significant differences among the 126 surveyed countries to a cultural notion of

[89] Ibid., pp. 309–310.

[90] For this conceptualization of culture and similar institutions, see G. Roland, "Understanding Institutional Change: Fast-Moving and Slow-Moving Institutions," *Nanjing Business Review*, 2 (2005), pp. 1–34.

[91] A. N. Licht et al., "Culture Rules: The Foundations of the Rule of Law and Other Norms of Governance," *Journal of Comparative Economics*, 35 (2007), pp. 659–688 at 662–663.

[92] A. Lehavi and A. N. Licht, "BITs and Pieces of Property," *Yale Journal of International Law*, 36 (2011), pp. 115–166 at 120. The property rights data came from the 2009 version of the International Property Rights Index (IPRI) Report, which is published on an annual basis, and is available at www.internationalpropertyrightsindex.org (accessed on March 1, 2018). The IPRI is a cross-country, comparative, and composite index comprising three subindices, each of which is also composite. These subindices cover the following subjects: legal and political environment (LP), physical property rights (PPR), and intellectual property rights (IPR). It is a long-term project that seeks to improve property rights systems around the world by showing the relationship between a strong property rights system and a country's economic well-being.

[93] To address the issue of causality among the variables, we ran a regression analysis in which cultural embeddedness emerged as a clear negative explanatory variable for property rights protection. Lehavi and Licht, "BITs and Pieces," pp. 139–148.

[94] G. Dari-Mattiacci and C. Guerriero, "Law and Culture: A Theory of Comparative Variation in Bona Fide Purchase Rules," *Oxford Journal of Legal Studies*, 35 (2015), pp. 543–574.

self-reliance, defining it along two dimensions: regard for hierarchy and emphasis on the individual.[95] They view self-reliant cultures as being characterized by egalitarianism (or a low regard for hierarchy) and individualism, and find that the corresponding legal systems exhibit strong owner protection, meaning that the good-faith purchaser never acquires ownership of a stolen good. Consequently, countries with cultures characterized by low self-reliance strongly protect the buyer, meaning that the *bona fide* purchaser of a stolen good immediately acquires ownership. Cultures with an intermediate level of self-reliance provide an intermediate level of protection to the buyer, meaning that the purchaser acquires ownership only upon the passage of a number of years.[96]

While the methodology of these empirical cross-country studies has been debated,[97] it seems safe to conclude that the way in which a certain national legal system designs its private-law property doctrines is neither a technical matter nor merely the result of different analytical approaches by jurists. To a considerable degree, these doctrines are embedded in long-lasting cultural orientations, social perceptions, and political structures. Any significant change in such doctrines must be initiated, or at the least supported, by the same basic societal institutions that crafted existing legal norms. Accordingly, any attempt at devising globalization strategies for either private law or public law aspects of property must confront the parameters by which some underlying national norms and institutions may be more of less apt for change than others.

1.5 Different Strategies for the Globalization of Property

The lingering differences in property law principles and doctrines, analyzed above, suggest that any move toward globalization will not take place as a natural seamless phenomenon, and it requires rather a careful consideration of the potential venues for globalization and their likelihood of success. Accordingly, the abundance of cross-border property scenarios involving distant parties who have no privity of contract or another preset legal mechanism for resolving potential disputes, as

95 Ibid., p. 550.

96 Ibid., pp. 557–558, 563–566. The doctrinal aspects of the research on *bona fide* purchasers are discussed further in Chapter 4, Section 4.5.1.

97 See, e.g., H. Spamann, "Large Sample, Quantitative Research Designs for Comparative Law," *American Journal of Comparative Law*, 57 (2009), pp. 797–810.

illustrated in Section 1.1, calls for a systematic evaluation of property law in a globalizing world.

I suggest that just as processes of globalization do not take a single route, so the appropriate legal strategy for addressing the various cross-border scenarios should not take a single form.

This book examines four legal strategies that could be employed to decrease the gap between property law and the cross-border nature of markets, interpersonal networks, and technology:

1. Adopting nonbinding principles or institutions, which aim to serve as potential legislative and administrative templates, guides to best practices, tools of interpretation and so forth, in order to promote the prospects of cross-border collaboration on property law (*soft law strategy*).[98] Although such principles or institutions are not directly binding on states, and accordingly, are not enforceable by domestic and supranational institutions – unlike hard law – soft law or private ordering mechanisms can influence practically the ways in which both states and private actors design and administer arrangements that pertain to property law across borders.
2. Advancing new or improved interstate agreements on rules concerning conflict of laws or private international law (*conflict of laws strategy*). This relatively modest strategy aims at improving certainty about the national forum that would have jurisdiction and the law that would apply, while leaving the mainstay of property ordering to the respective domestic systems. One example, mentioned in Section 1.1, is the choice recently made by eighteen EU Member States regarding matrimonial property. This framework of "enhanced cooperation" seeks to unify conflict of laws rules, while also defining the scope of party autonomy in making such choices, but without requiring Member States to amend or approximate their substantive laws on the distribution of matrimonial property or the legal standing of third parties regarding such assets.
3. Requiring states to approximate their substantive and procedural property norms (*approximation strategy*). This is normally done through treaties or conventions that introduce "minimum standards of protection" in a certain field of law, while leaving to states and their courts the chief power of lawmaking and enforcement of such norms. A prominent

[98] For the general distinction between hard law and soft law in the international setting, see K. W. Abbott and D. Snidal, "Hard and Soft Law in International Governance," *International Organization*, 54 (2000), pp. 421–456.

example of the approximation strategy is the Agreement on the Trade-Related Aspects of Intellectual Property Rights (TRIPS).[99] While TRIPS requires all signatory states to introduce certain minimum standards for the protection of patents, copyrights, trademarks, and other intellectual property rights, and it vests some authority for interstate dispute resolution with a panel of the World Trade Organization (WTO), the TRIPS mechanism still leaves the operation and enforcement of intellectual property rights mostly to domestic law. Not only do state legislatures have the authority to go beyond the minimum standards, but more broadly, intellectual property rights are enforced and interpersonal disputes are litigated by national courts that apply their domestic laws. The intermediate approach of the approximation strategy thus goes beyond the conflict of laws strategy, because it intervenes in domestic legal ordering by requiring states to approximate their laws, such as by establishing minimum standards. At the same time, the approximation strategy stops short of directly preempting local lawmaking and enforcement.

4. Establishing supranational norms and institutions with binding lawmaking and enforcement powers (*supranationalism strategy*). Such supranational norms enjoy some type of a superior legal status over national norms in case of conflict, even if the application of such supranational provisions may be tempered or limited by adopting principles that defer to domestic rules in some cases. Leading examples are the property clauses included in binding human rights treaties, such as Article 1 of the First Protocol of the European Convention on Human Rights.[100] In reviewing the conformity of local lawmaking to the binding provisions of this supranational property clause, the European Court of Human Rights has gradually developed a set of supranational criteria for interpreting and applying this clause. The court has thus established *fair balance, proportionality,* and other principles as supranational standards for reviewing the validity of local lawmaking, while subjecting such review to some level of deference by introducing a "margin of appreciation" for local norms. Other manifestations of the supranational strategy may include the introduction of a supranational registry of property rights, one that has direct applicability in all countries that ratify the

[99] Agreement on Trade-Related Aspects of Intellectual Property Rights, April 15, 1994 (Marrakesh Agreement Establishing the World Trade Organization, Annex 1C, 1869 UNTS 299).

[100] European Convention for the Protection of Human Rights and Fundamental Freedoms, November 4, 1950, 213 UNTS 221, Protocol 1, Art. 1

underlying convention creating the registry. A prominent example is the Cape Town Convention on International Interests in Mobile Equipment and the Protocols to the Convention, studied in Chapters 2 and 6,[101] which create an international registry of security interests in aircrafts. This mechanism therefore seeks to resolve the legal fragmentation that would otherwise take place when assets, which are by definition constantly in transition across borders, become subjected to insolvency proceedings or other legal actions.

Considering both normative and practical considerations, this book argues that no single strategy could serve as a panacea for all types of challenges that property law faces in an age of increasing globalization. The choice among the strategies may depend, inter alia, on the specific attributes of the assets that are the object of cross-border property scenarios; relative weight of cross-border versus domestic traffic for a certain market, network, or technology; existence of genuine normative differences in the underlying features of domestic legal ordering; and *realpolitik* considerations of setting up supranational bodies with binding enforcement power. These parameters may thus lead to choosing different strategies in various property law settings.

1.6 Choosing Globalization Strategies: Methodological Principles

Having laid out four potential globalization strategies for property law, this section offers some fundamental methodological principles for studying the features and potential prospects of such strategies. These principles will serve as the basis for the analysis offered throughout the book.

1.6.1 Quantitative versus Qualitative Analysis

Any evaluation of the actual weight of cross-border transfer of capital, goods, services, and persons, and the consequential need to move away from traditional domestic ordering of property relations, must be anchored in a current empirical analysis of the relevant market, interpersonal network, or technology. Alongside official data provided by states or intergovernmental organizations – such as the United Nations

[101] See, respectively, Chapter 2, Section 2.3.4.7; Chapter 6, Section 6.3.4.

Conference on Trade and Development (UNCTAD), International Monetary Fund (IMF), or the World Bank – nonprofit organizations, private companies, and academic research may also offer invaluable data on cross-border activities. Thus, for example, as Chapter 3 shows, Land Matrix,[102] a nonprofit monitoring initiative, is publishing data on cross-border land deals – especially in developing countries – in which foreign investors purchase property rights in huge tracts of land either for the extraction of biofuels, agricultural products, and minerals, or simply as an investment. The direct parties to the transaction often look to preserve the opacity of the deal, especially in host countries that do not otherwise excel in public transparency or adherence to the rule of law. Therefore, such data not only sheds light on normative concerns over potential "land grabs" – which may often come at the expense of indigenous groups holding only customary rights in land – but it more broadly shows how land is increasingly becoming a cross-border commodity.

At the same time, a quantitative analysis of the current cross-border scope of markets, networks, and technology cannot serve as the sole criterion for deciding on the appropriate strategy for the local/global balance in property law. Qualitative criteria that deal, inter alia, with the underlying premises of property law – whether grounded in universal moral considerations or in contextual features of sovereignty and adherence to cultural values – must always play a prominent role. As suggested above, the resolution of such a quantitative/qualitative trade-off need not always arrive at the same point. Thus, for example, the local-to-global governance of intellectual property rights may prove to be very different from that of land, investment securities, or monetary claims.

1.6.2 Need for an Interdisciplinary Approach

A related principle is that the study of property law in an era of globalization must be based on a full-fledged interdisciplinary analysis that accounts for the dynamic relations between law, politics, economics, and society. While such an analysis may be useful in principle for any type of legal pursuit, it holds special merit during times of legal change, and especially when the prospective move toward cross-border legal

[102] Land Matrix, "The Online Public Database on Land Deals," available at www.landmatrix.org (accessed on March 1, 2018).

ordering impacts core attributes of nation-states. On the one hand, legal change is almost always driven by exogenous forces, with property law often playing a key role in facilitating the implementation of the exogenous drivers of change. Thus, as already mentioned in Section 1.4, one cannot understand the reconstruction of land law in South Africa as of the 1990s, dealing with aspects of both public law (e.g., expropriation) and private law (e.g., adverse possession) without underscoring the political and social changes embedded in the abolition of the Apartheid regime. The same applies to the rewriting of Russia's civil code in the aftermath of the Soviet Union's collapse and Russia's initial desire to make its market attractive for international investment.[103] And the list could go on.

At the same time, however, any legal reform must be evaluated for its congruence, or lack thereof, with slowly changing social systems, such as culture. As this book shows, the dynamic relations between law, economics, society, and culture play a dominant role in any attempt to employ one of the strategies for cross-border property ordering, from soft law to the conflict of laws strategy, through the approximation strategy, and up to supranationalism. Countries' resistance to a certain cross-border property initiative could derive from political opposition to yielding their sovereignty to a supranational institution; an economic cost-benefit calculation; or a genuine conflict of values with predominant social or cultural concepts. Intellectual property has been a hotbed for such value conflicts, which go beyond mere opportunism by some developing economies. One example, discussed in Chapter 5, concerns a 2013 decision by the Supreme Court of India, which offers a narrow interpretation of the provisions concerning the renewing of patents for enhanced pharmaceutical products.[104] Although India's patent law was amended as part of the country's commitment under the TRIPS Agreement, the Court reasoned that overbroad patent protection would put "life-saving medicines beyond the reach of a very large section of people" and run counter to the state's commitment to promote public health. The approximation strategy promoted by TRIPS was thus seen as conflicting with the country's core values.

[103] A. Lehavi, "The Culture of Private Law," *Real Estate Law Journal*, 45 (2016), pp. 35–91 at 47–49.

[104] *Novartis AG* v. *Union of India* (2013) 6 S.C.C. 1 (India). See Chapter 5, Section 5.2.4.

1.6.3 Key Role of Institutions

As noted above, property law is based on creating a set of rules for the *in rem* ranking of rights, powers, and priorities in regard to assets. This calls for a dominant role for the legislative and judicial branches in devising the list of recognized property rights, establishing formalities for their validation (e.g., through registration), and setting the ranking of proprietary interests in case of conflicting claims. The key role that such top-down institutions play, while not entirely dismissing the role of mechanisms of private ordering and party autonomy with third-party effects, proves highly challenging in the cross-border context. Especially as far as the supranationalism strategy is concerned, the current fragmentation and incompleteness of supranational institutions that deal with property issues may place limits on the ability to create and enforce a comprehensive cross-border ranking of rights in assets. The problem of limited competence and jurisdiction can be exemplified by the European Union, probably the world's most expansive supranational institution. The EU treaties go a long way in providing for negative harmonization, such as by placing limits on domestic law's hindrance of free movement of capital, goods, services, and persons within the internal market. But the jurisdiction of the EU's legislative bodies falls short of being able to impose comprehensive positive harmonization – e.g., by requiring all Member States to adopt a single blueprint for property law. The same considerations are at play for evaluating the prospects of supranational courts/tribunals and administrative bodies in promoting cross-border legal ordering. The institutional dimension of globalization strategies is studied in detail in Chapter 2.

1.6.4 Normative-Functional Trade-Off

At the end of the day, the choice of the appropriate strategy for narrowing the gap between property law and global markets, interpersonal networks, and technology hinges to a large extent on the potential trade-off between the *normative* and *functional* considerations for staying local, going global, or moving anywhere in between.

The functional component seems straightforward enough. Thus, when a certain market is dominated by a cross-border activity, rather than by a domestic one, and is liable to regularly implicate distant parties who have no privity of contract or another preset system of rules to adjudicate disputes, the functional need to create an *in rem* ranking of rights might justify the costs of moving to a substantial supranational system. Consider the role of registries. Intellectual property, or security interests in certain consumer goods or intangible rights, may be considered particularly appropriate for making the effort toward some sort of a supranational registry, or at least, toward better coordination among national registries. Land might have been considered up until a few years ago as not justifying the effort to move to a supranational registration system because of the dominance of domestic transactions, but this state of affairs may be also changing.

The normative grounding may be, however, more complex and would not always align with the functional consideration. Normative reasons for scaling down supranational pressures posed by functional forces may be multiple and can go beyond general considerations of sovereignty, national pride, or cultural idiosyncrasy. National-security considerations could justify, for example, some limits on the applicability of cross-border norms or on the jurisdiction of supranational tribunals in regard to assets clearly impacted by national-security concerns. Somewhat counterintuitively, protection of human rights or promotion of public health may at times cast doubts on the desirability of introducing a single set of supranational norms.

One oft-discussed example concerns the tension between a cross-border enforcement of patents in pharmaceutical products and the affordability of medicines for life-threatening diseases in developing countries. Obviously, an international property regime should optimally strike an internal balance between incentives to innovate and commitment to saving as many human lives as possible. But to the extent that the international system of patents is practically captured by one side, such as by patent owners, then the normative case for allowing individual states some leeway in how to enforce these patents, while promoting local public health, is not entirely senseless.

More generally, the functional/normative trade-off is also instructive in showing that the terms *global* or *processes of globalization* are not synonymous with the notion of *universalism*. The fact that a certain economic activity that implicates property rights is constantly crossing borders may mandate a reevaluation of traditional domestic legal systems, but it does not necessarily require an unequivocal move toward an all-inclusive supranational unity of property law.

2

Local to Global

An Institutional Analysis

2.1 The Complete Nature of Domestic Institutions

Under well-established rules of international law, one of the inherent features of a state is the existence of an effective "government."[1] This term should be understood as going beyond the ability to identify some sort of a sovereign power that is generally recognized by persons located inside the state's territory and by other states outside of it. Securing a "general habit of obedience"[2] to a person or collective body identified as the sovereign is the first step in moving away from an anarchic state of nature, but it must be complemented by establishing an orderly system of government. For a state to properly function, it needs to have a complete set of institutions that are formally authorized and capable of making, administering, and enforcing an entire set of legal norms that would apply within the state's territory.

Scholarly accounts of legal systems have traditionally sought to identify the types of fundamental legal norms that define a legal system but have also realized that such rules cannot be detached from the institutions that make and enforce them. Hans Kelsen focused on the hierarchy of norms in a legal system, by identifying the *basic norm* (*Grundnorm*) as the ultimate authoritative source that legitimizes subsequent lawmaking, and on which the "validity of all the norms of our legal systems depends."[3] Such a basic norm does not necessarily hinge, however, on possessing some sort of moral superiority or other substantive virtue. It may be simply the result of

[1] Montevideo Convention on Rights and Duties of States, December 26, 1933, 49 Stat. 3097, 165 UNTS 19. Under Article 1, the other features of the state are a permanent population, a defined territory, and the capacity to enter into relations with the other states.

[2] H. L. A. Hart, *The Concept of Law*, 2d ed. (Oxford: Oxford University Press, 1994), pp. 23–24 (identifying the general traits of a sovereign power based on the works of British legal theorist John Austin).

[3] H. Kelsen, *General Theory of Law and State*, A. Wedberg, trans. (Cambridge, MA: Harvard University Press, 1945), p. 115.

identifying the first link in a chain of norms or authoritative acts. The basic norm may come down to the postulation by which "one ought to behave as the individual, or the individuals, who laid down the first constitution have ordained."[4] Thus, according to Kelsen, the fundamental features of a legal system rely on identifying not only certain core norms, but also the institutions that crafted them.

H. L. A. Hart mapped the varieties of rules that typify a legal system.[5] Alongside primary rules that impose certain obligations or duties on norm-bearers (associated with John Austin's view of legal norms as "orders backed by threats"),[6] legal systems also include types of secondary norms that are essential for their operation.[7] One such set of norms concerns *power-conferring rules*, which grant persons certain powers to "mould their legal relations with others by contracts, wills, marriages" and so forth.[8] Another set of norms includes *rules of recognition*, which help to identify the types of norms considered legally valid and included, therefore, as items in the "authoritative list of rules."[9] The identifying criteria under such rules of recognition for viewing certain norms as legally binding may include, *inter alia*, "the fact of their having been enacted by a specific body."[10] Finally, *rules of change* empower "an individual or body of persons to introduce new primary rules for the conduct of the life of the group."[11] The variety of secondary norms identified by Hart thus emphasizes the essential role of institutions in a legal system and shows how the identity of a certain institution may implicate the validity of substantive norms.

It is furthermore essential to distinguish between the identity and authority of the sovereign in a certain state and the formal capacity of institutions in charge of lawmaking and enforcement. This distinction is especially essential in view of the growing dominance, at least among

[4] Ibid.

[5] Hart, *Concept of Law*, pp. 79–99.

[6] J. Austin, *The Province of Jurisprudence Determined* (London: John Murray, 1832), pp. 199–200 (noting that one of the features of a sovereign is that "the *bulk* of a given society are in a *habit* of obedience or submission to a determinate and common superior: let that common superior be a certain individual person, or a certain body or aggregate of individual persons").

[7] Hart, *Concept of Law*, p. 78 (portraying Austin's theory as insufficient to account for the variety of legal norms).

[8] Ibid., pp. 27–28.

[9] Ibid., pp. 94–99.

[10] Ibid., p. 95.

[11] Ibid.

democratic societies, of the idea of popular sovereignty, by which the People at large or the electorate body of citizens is considered to be the ultimate sovereign within the state.[12] The capacity for lawmaking thus hinges on the authority granted by the sovereign, explicitly or implicitly, not only to elected institutions – particularly the legislature – but also to nonelected branches of government, most notably courts, administrative agencies, and other public officials.

As Hart notes, according to this perspective on sovereignty, "the difference between a legal system in which the ordinary legislature is free from legal limitations, and one where the legislature is subject to them, appears merely as the difference between the manner [sic] in which the sovereign electorate chooses to exercise its sovereign powers."[13] Thus, the lesser limits imposed on the British Parliament in its lawmaking capacity as compared with the US Congress – which is constrained both by the limits of federalism and the superior status of the US Constitution over regular lawmaking – can be attributed to the different scope of authority granted by the sovereign electorate to the various types of institutions operating within the legal system.[14]

In a representative democracy, the fact that we identify the People or the electorate body as the "sovereign free from all legal limitations" tells only part of the story about how the system of governance and its legal system operate. It is the way in which a lawmaking power is transferred from the sovereign to various governmental institutions that truly defines a state's legal system.

For a state and its legal system to function properly, one needs to identify the (1) authority of each institution to make, revise, or enforce legally binding norms, (2) capability of the state's institutions as a whole to completely cover all themes considered to be ones that should be governed by legal norms or authoritative acts, and (3) inter-institutional allocation of power, including resolution of conflicts or other frictions among such institutions. This latter component may require elements of hierarchy within the same governmental branch – such as the capacity of a court of appeals to review and overturn decisions made by courts of first instance,[15] or the decision-making hierarchy that exists within the

[12] K. Anderson, "Through Our Glass Darkly: Does Comparative Law Counsel the Use of Foreign Law in U.S. Constitutional Adjudication?" *Duquesne Law Review*, 52 (2014), pp. 115–149 at 122–125.

[13] Hart, *Concept of Law*, p. 74.

[14] Ibid.

[15] See P. S. Atiyah and R. S. Summers, *Form and Substance in Anglo-American Law* (Oxford: Oxford University Press, 1987), pp. 267–297 (discussing the respective roles of lower and upper courts in the Anglo-American system).

executive branch.[16] Moreover, any legal system must have rules on the potential hierarchy, or any other type of resolution mechanism for potential conflicts, among different branches of government. These mechanisms may obviously be very controversial at times, both legally and politically, with judicial review of legislative acts being a particularly contested issue.[17] Federal systems also exhibit tensions between state and federal institutions.[18] Difficult as these issues may be, every legal system must establish a set of rules for resolving potential frictions among governmental branches about lawmaking powers.

To sum up, in well-functioning states, a legal system must include generally acceptable and comprehensive rules that cover (1) authority of institutions for lawmaking and enforcement; (2) capability of complete coverage, such that no issue worthy of legal ordering would remain in a vacuum, with no institution authorized to act in the matter; and (3) resolution of potential conflicts among governmental institutions. When this is the case, we can speak of the state's domestic institutions as being authorized, complete, and coordinated among themselves.[19]

2.2 The Global Setting: Incomplete Institutions and Normative Fragmentation

Unlike individual states, the international setting is largely lacking in all three institutional parameters that were identified in Section 2.1, namely (1) authority to act on an international scale; (2) capability of complete coverage of all legal norms that are relevant for cross-border legal ordering; (3) inter-institutional mechanisms for resolving potential conflicts

[16] See K. M. Stack, "An Administrative Jurisprudence: The Rule of Law in the Administrative State," *Columbia Law Review*, 115 (2015), pp. 1985–2018 at 1994–2002.

[17] R. A. Posner, "The Rise and Fall of Judicial Self-Restraint," *California Law Review*, 100 (2012), pp. 519–556 (examining the history of judicial review of legislative and administrative decisions in the United States); J. H. Merryman and R. Pérez-Perdomo, *The Civil Law Tradition*, 3d ed. (Stanford: Stanford University Press, 2007), pp. 137–140 (examining the concept of judicial review across civil law systems).

[18] See G. Anderson, *Federalism: An Introduction* (Oxford: Oxford University Press, 2008), pp. 21–29.

[19] See R. S. Summers, *Form and Function in a Legal System: A General Study* (Cambridge, UK: Cambridge University Press, 2006), pp. 307–308 (identifying how "second-level systematizing devices" unify diverse institutions "into the coherent whole of an operational legal system" based on ideas such as hierarchy, priorital relations, coordination and so forth).

both between international and domestic institutions, and among different types of supranational institutions.

These gaps, generally dubbed here as problems of *incomplete institutions* and *normative fragmentation*, pose a significant challenge for the ability of any field of law, and property law in particular, to move from the domestic level to an effective system of global governance.

As Section 2.3 will show, the potential implications of these institutional deficiencies hinge on the type of strategy that is adopted to handle a certain cross-border aspect of property law. A soft law strategy does not require, by definition, the establishment of binding supranational institutions. It would benefit, however, from the existence of cross-border professional or intergovernmental bodies that engage in drafting the soft law norms or in voluntarily implementing such norms in different jurisdictions. Moving to the various hard law strategies, a conflict of laws strategy is generally the most modest in its need for establishing supranational institutions, because it relies on states agreeing only about the authorized national forum and the law that would apply. Once this choice has been made, domestic institutions will engage in lawmaking and its enforcement. An approximation strategy requires a more extensive array of international institutions, which would establish the scope and content of the norms that would then serve as a benchmark for state lawmakers tasked with adjusting their local laws. The supranationalism strategy calls for the most comprehensive set of institutions and lawmaking on the supranational level, because by its nature, it relies on the preeminence of such norms for lawmaking, administration of the laws, and their adjudicative interpretation and enforcement. Section 2.3 will map out the institutional landscape, and the deficiencies of the current state of incomplete institutions and normative fragmentation, based on these different strategies for globalization.

Prior to doing so, this section highlights a few basic points concerning the (1) interface of sovereignty and institutional capacity in the international arena; (2) interplay between bottom-up and top-down forces in driving cross-border activities that implicate property law; and (3) unique features of property law that require both institutional completeness and normative coherence.

2.2.1 Sovereignty and Institutions: An International Perspective

Under the conventional account of international law, it is a body of law that exists “between states recognizing common principles and ways of doing things."[20] Unlike the hierarchal or otherwise-coordinated structure of domestic institutions and norms, the international system is viewed in principle as horizontal, meaning that all states are sovereign and equal, and no entity has superior authority over them. This means, therefore, that there is no such thing as global or supranational sovereignty that, by definition, supersedes the sovereignty of individual states.[21]

That said, the mechanisms of international law do establish institutions and norms with an international validity, or some sort of a supranational reach, binding more than one country.

Treaty-based international law is the chief mechanism by which both institutions and norms are established and are binding on states that have approved and ratified the treaty.[22] As such, however, these sources of law do not bind states that have not joined the treaty, or states that decide to retract their membership in the treaty at a later stage.[23] As Section 2.3 will show, many treaties not only devise norms that apply to a certain cross-border matter, but also establish institutions in charge of consequent lawmaking and enforcement. The supranational institutions thus become authorized to act and bind states by virtue of the treaty.

The other main source of international law, i.e., custom, refers to certain practices and other forms of conduct that have been broadly accepted by states over time and that can be attributed to a sense of legal obligation – known as *opinio juris* (acceptance of law) – that states feel toward abiding by such a norm.[24] While such a customary norm, once identified, can be attributed in principle to all states across the globe, it is also more limited in the sense that by its customary nature, it does not in itself establish institutions authorized to enforce such customary norms, and it might also not apply to states that have persistently objected to applying such a custom.[25] The custom's enforcement would have to rely

[20] M. N. Shaw, *International Law*, 7th ed. (Cambridge, UK: Cambridge University Press, 2014), pp. 4–5.

[21] Ibid.

[22] Ibid., pp. 66–68.

[23] J. Klabbers, *International Law* (Cambridge, UK: Cambridge University Press, 2013), pp. 41–43.

[24] Ibid., pp. 28–30.

[25] For the long-standing debate in international law about the "persistent objector rule" as exempting states from abiding by norms that have been otherwise identified as being part of customary international law, see International Law Association, Committee on the Formation of Customary (General) International Law, "Statement of Principles Applicable to the Formation of General Customary International Law" (2000), pp. 27–29, available at https://ruwanthikagunaratne.files.wordpress.com/2011/04/ila-customary-law-study.pdf (accessed on March 1, 2018).

either on domestic institutions, such as local courts, reaffirming the custom, or on pre-existing supranational institutions, formed by a past treaty, whose authority is viewed as extending to apply and enforce customary international law.

The key lesson that should be derived about the interface between sovereignty and lawmaking institutions in the international setting is that the general concept of sovereignty does relatively little work in explaining the scope of international law, when it is viewed in isolation from the institutional perspective. This state of affairs is even more manifested than the domestic setting, in which the sovereign entity – the People or electorate body – has effective channels, such as general elections or referenda to directly decide normative matters, if needed. The sovereign electorate in a state can thus resolve potential conflicts among government entities and ensure that there is no legal vacuum because no institution has the capacity to act. In the international or supranational arena, there is no global or supranational sovereign electorate that can act directly. This means that cross-border legal ordering will simply not exist without clearly authorized institutions and a normative framework that is both coherent and comprehensive enough.

2.2.2 Top-Down and Bottom-Up Institutions

Processes of globalization may be driven by top-down forces, i.e., states working together to promote a certain cross-border agenda. Alternatively, such processes can be led by bottom-up drivers, such as corporations or individuals engaging in cross-border market activity, development of technology, interpersonal networks, and so forth. In some cases, these two types of forces may work in the same direction, such as when states promote free-trade measures that follow up on decentralized cross-border trade. In other cases, these forces may work at cross-purposes, such as when states impose trade barriers that undermine commerce.

The identity of the driving force for a certain process of globalization has clear institutional implications for the legal ordering of such a process. When states collaborate to facilitate the movement of capital, goods, services or persons, or to otherwise promote some type of cross-border activity, they are likely to create a top-down institutional arrangement, especially if the scheme is based on an approximation strategy or a supranationalism strategy. For example, the World Trade Organization (WTO), presented in Section 2.3.3.1, deals with the rules of trade between nations. It is a "rules-based, member-driven organization – all decisions are made by the member governments, and the rules are the outcome of negotiations among governments."[26] The institutional structure of the WTO and its dispute-settlement mechanism are clearly typified by a top-down approach, wherein Member States make trade policy as well as take part in the dispute-settlement process through an array of international institutions.

Oppositely, when a process of globalization is driven largely by an aggregation of decentralized actions taken by individuals and corporations, these forces would have to rely at the outset on private-ordering mechanisms, mostly through contracts and other types of bottom-up mechanisms for interpersonal coordination. Gunther Teubner points to the spontaneous, grassroots development of a new body of law that "emerges from various globalization processes in multiple sectors of civil society independently of the laws of the nation states."[27] Teubner notes in particular the emergence of the contemporary *lex mercatoria* – the transnational law of economic transactions – alongside other practices of private global norm-production, including the internal legal regimes of multinational corporations, private lawmaking by labor unions, technical standardization, Internet arrangements or international rules on sports.[28] A notable international institution that is privately organized is the International Chamber of Commerce (ICC), which seeks to promote "international trade, services and investment."[29] While the ICC has no general binding force on states or individuals, its professional prominence often leads contractual parties to adopt terms of reference crafted by it, and in many cases parties agree to arbitrate contractual disputes before the ICC's International Court of Arbitration.[30] Therefore, while there is debate about whether we can truly identify a comprehensive contemporary *lex mercatoria* that allows merchants to bridge gaps created

[26] World Trade Organization, "The WTO," available at www.wto.org/english/thewto_e/thewto_e.htm (accessed on March 1, 2018).

[27] G. Teubner, "'Global Bukowina': Legal Pluralism in the World Society," in G. Teubner (ed.), *Global Law without a State* (London: Dartmouth Pub. Co., 1996), pp. 3–4.

[28] G. Teubner, "Breaking Frames: The Global Interplay of Legal and Social Systems," *American Journal of Comparative Law*, 45 (1997), pp. 149–169 at 156–159.

[29] S. Cassese, *The Global Polity: Global Dimensions of Democracy and the Rule of Law* (Sevilla: Global Law Press, 2012), p. 19.

[30] International Chamber of Commerce, "ICC's International Court of Arbitration," available at www.iccwbo.org/about-icc/organization/dispute-resolution-services/icc-international-court-of-arbitration/ (accessed on March 1, 2018).

by national norms,[31] privately organized institutions, such as the ICC, definitely capture a growing role in the international arena.[32]

However, these bottom-up institutions have their inherent limits, especially in the context of property law. Contractual parties, including those located across borders, can engage in private ordering if they are displeased with the general laws of contracts in their respective countries or with the default conflict of laws rules governing international contracts. In so doing, parties can resort to privately organized international institutions, such as the ICC, not only by adopting their terms of reference in drafting the contract but, moreover, by resolving potential disputes before its court of arbitration, while agreeing on the substantive and procedural rules that would apply.

But such an agreement, and the subsequent work of institutions such as the ICC in implementing the parties' contractual freedom, is generally binding only on these parties. The lawmaking and adjudication capacities of such institutions do not generally bind third parties, which may have competing legal claims or causes of action, and that have not been a party to the underlying contract or to the mechanisms for dispute resolution. As Section 2.2.3 highlights, the structure of property law is different, particularly because it purports to set up legal priorities and ranking of property interests that have an *in rem* effect. As such, property law also orders legal relations among parties that have no contractual privity or another preset mechanism for private ordering. This feature of property law places a limit on the power of bottom-up institutions that derive their authority from the explicit consent of the parties. To bind also parties that have not engaged in such private ordering, institutions must derive their authority from the coercive and general legal power of top-down institutions. What this means in the international context is that the power to legislate broadly binding property norms and to resolve conflicts with an *in rem* effect is vested in institutions that derive their authority from the conventional sources of international law. This refers mostly to top-down institutions authorized by international treaties.

[31] E. Kadens, "The Myth of the Customary Law Merchant," *Texas Law Review*, 90 (2012), pp. 1153–1206.

[32] Cassese, *The Global Polity*, p. 19.

2.2.3 In Rem *Effect of Property Law: Institutional Implications*

As Chapter 1 showed, property legal interests, such as ownership, leases, security interests, and servitudes, possess a qualitative trait of general applicability toward a broad class of stakeholders in establishing the set of legal rights, powers, and priorities in regard to assets. This *in rem* feature of property law places, therefore, practical limits on the ability of parties to engage in private ordering to circumvent potential problems of legal uncertainty or of procedural and substantive incongruence of norms in cross-border legal settings. Legal scenarios such as cross-border conflicting sale transactions, good-faith purchase of voidable or void title to assets, and insolvencies with multiple creditors fighting over priority to a limited pool of the debtor's assets, highlight how property law must decide conflicts between parties that have no contractual privity and/or a preset arrangement about the forum for dispute resolution and the law that would apply.

Due to the considerable disparities between the substantive and procedural property norms of different nations – including the list and content of the *numerus clausus* of property rights in each system – attempts at facilitating some level of globalization cannot settle for bottom-up institutions for lawmaking and enforcement. The cross-border ordering of property requires at least some kind of an interstate agreement about the identity and authority of legal institutions.

Moreover, due to the *in rem* feature of property rights, and the respective need for sufficient clarity, comprehensiveness, and predictability of property rights, the field of property law calls for a considerable degree of legislative lawmaking, even in traditionally common law systems.[33] The role of legislative institutions is no less crucial in the international setting, where the need to bridge disparities requires a coordinated effort to provide a comprehensive set of rules, whether providing for joint rules on jurisdiction and applicable law in cross-border settings (conflict of laws strategy), a minimal level of similarity among national systems (approximation strategy), or direct establishment of supranational binding norms (supranationalism strategy). At the

[33] T. W. Merrill and H. E. Smith, "Optimal Standardization in the Law of Property: The Numerus Clausus Principle," *Yale Law Journal*, 110 (2000), pp. 1–70 at 60–66.

same time, the subjection of state lawmaking powers to supranational authority may be particularly sensitive due to the specific association of legislatures with national sovereignty.

Alongside legislative institutions, cross-border property law, under any of the strategies for globalization, requires significant collaboration among executive or administrative agencies and at times also the establishment of an interstate executive body. This is particularly so when a cross-border activity requires the registration, administration, or regulation of property interests. This is demonstrated, for example, in Section 2.3.4.7, which deals with the international registration of security interests in aircrafts and their equipment.

Finally, any cross-border property regime requires adjudicative institutions, such as courts or tribunals, with authority and practical ability to decide property disputes, while also considering, in appropriate cases, the potential property interests of third parties beyond the litigating parties. As with other types of institutions, the appropriate level (state or supranational) and nature of adjudicative institutions hinge on the type of strategy chosen for globalizing property norms. A conflict of laws strategy focuses on national courts. An approximation strategy, and moreover, a supranationalism strategy, require some type of a cross-border adjudicative institution, whether it is operating alongside domestic courts, or is explicitly authorized to preempt national case law. This breakdown of adjudicative institutions will be featured throughout Section 2.3 below.

A final note about the general institutional implications of the *in rem* nature of property law has to do with interface between private law and public law aspects. As Chapter 1 has shown, property law deals both with public law issues (such as the scope of permissible governmental intervention with private property rights) and with private law issues (having to do with the entire array of interpersonal legal relations regarding assets). Domestic legal institutions generally address both aspects, even if in diverging settings or by distinctive institutions, so that there are normally no legal vacuums or no lack of institutions authorized to act on both fronts.

The situation may be different, however, in the international arena. Because the authority of cross-border institutions, be they legislative, administrative, or adjudicative ones, hinges on identifying an underlying source, the result can be one in which legal norms and respective institutions deal with only one aspect (public or private) of a property law issue. As Section 2.3 shows, this deficiency may at times lead to normative fragmentation and incomplete institutions, which could be detrimental to designing property norms with *in rem* validity in a global context.

2.3 Institutional Analysis of Cross-Border Property Norms

This section offers an institutional analysis of the current landscape of cross-border property norms. The delineation of these norms is based on the different strategies for globalization, starting with soft law templates, such as model laws, and moving to the hard law strategies: conflict of laws strategy, approximation strategy, and supranationalism strategy. The main argument cutting through the analysis is that the type of hard law strategy chosen for a certain theme in property law should be correlated with the level (local or supranational) and scope of authority of the institutions tasked with making, administering, and enforcing the norms. A conflict of laws strategy generally requires a treaty that establishes rules on jurisdiction and applicable law, but otherwise relies on domestic judicial institutions. An approximation strategy necessitates a treaty or convention, which establishes the substantive and procedural norms that need to be equated or approximated. Administration of these norms would usually be carried out by local institutions. Judicial interpretation and interstate dispute resolution of the treaty might require a supranational court or tribunal, while adjudication among private parties would usually be done by local courts. Finally, a supranationalism strategy would usually require granting some sort of preemptive authority to various types of supranational institutions – legislative, administrative, or judicial – while establishing the general allocation of powers among local and supranational institutions.

2.3.1 Soft Law Strategy

While much of the focus of this book lies in identifying hard law norms and the institutions that make and enforce them, it is also essential to underscore the significant role of soft law or private-ordering mechanisms in the promotion of cross-border property norms and practices.[34]

[34] For the general distinction between hard law and soft law in the international setting, see K. W. Abbott and D. Snidal, "Hard and Soft Law in International Governance," *International Organization*, 54 (2000), pp. 421–456.

Although such norms are not directly binding on states, and accordingly, are not enforceable by domestic and supranational institutions as part of such hard commitments, soft law or private-ordering mechanisms can practically influence the ways in which both states and private actors across borders design and administer arrangements that pertain to property law. The following paragraphs briefly discuss the work of some top-down and bottom-up institutions in this context.

2.3.1.1 Declarative International Instruments

One of the most prominent institutions that promote soft law mechanisms, touching also on property law, is the quintessential top-down international institution: the United Nations and its various agencies. Section 2.3.1.2 will discuss some of the work done by UN agencies in drafting model laws, legislative guides, and practice guides, which are then offered as a model for the different nations of the world. But to start with, it is worth considering the role of the UN General Assembly in adopting a number of non-binding declarations or resolutions that have a bearing on property law, and which in some cases have influenced property law concepts in various national legal systems. In this sense, these UN declarative instruments can be seen as soft law mechanisms, which nevertheless have had an impact on the global legal landscape.

The most prominent example is the 1948 Universal Declaration of Human Rights.[35] Article 17 reads: "(1) Everyone has the right to own property alone as well as in association with others; (2) No one shall be arbitrarily deprived of his property."[36] As with all other rights included in the Declaration, the right to property is subject to the provision of Article 29(2) that enables states to limit the right to property in order to respect the rights and freedoms of others or to promote "just requirements of morality, public order and the general welfare in a democratic society."[37]

The somewhat exceptional conception of property, which includes not only private property, but also property held "in association with others," can be attributed to pressures levied by the Soviet Union and its allies prior to adopting the Declaration.[38] The same kind of resistance to

[35] Universal Declaration of Human Rights, December 10, 1948, G. A. Res. 217 (III)A, UN Doc. A/RES/217(III).

[36] Ibid., Art. 17.

[37] Ibid., Art. 29(2).

[38] J. G. Sprankling, *The International Law of Property* (Oxford: Oxford University Press, 2014), p. 10.

recognizing the special status of private property led the Soviet bloc to veto later attempts to enshrine the right to property in international instruments, such as in the 1966 International Covenant on Economic, Social and Cultural Rights,[39] and the 1966 International Covenant on Civil and Political Rights.[40] Article 17 of the Universal Declaration of Human Rights has therefore remained part of a declaratory instrument, which was not followed by subsequent binding international treaties. As such, the special status of the right to property remains a matter of soft law on the universal scale.

That said, Article 17 has proven to be significant, at least in the sense that it was embraced by various courts around the world in giving content to the right to property on the domestic level. Although courts around the world stress that the Declaration in general has no binding force, some national courts – such as those of India or Sri Lanka – do resort to the various provisions of the Declaration as a tool for interpretation of domestic constitutional provisions.[41] Some writers go further to argue that the provisions of Article 17 in particular are now part of international customary law, albeit on a limited scale, and although this right is not universally recognized.[42]

Another declarative international instrument that has gained some prominence and which touches on property law is the 2007 UN Declaration on the Rights of Indigenous Peoples.[43] Article 26 of the Declaration refers specifically to the protection of property interests, by providing, inter alia, that "indigenous peoples have the right to the lands, territories and resources which they have traditionally owned, occupied or otherwise used or acquired."[44] It further calls on states to "give legal recognition to these lands, territories, and resources."[45]

[39] G. A. Res. 2200A (XXI), International Covenant on Economic, Social and Cultural Rights, December 16, 1966, 993 UNTS 3.

[40] G. A. Res. 2200A (XXI), International Covenant on Civil and Political Rights, December 16, 1966, 999 UNTS 171.

[41] H. Hannum, "The Status of the Universal Declaration of Human Rights in National and International Law III: The Status and Future of the Customary International Law of Human Rights," *Georgia Journal of International and Comparative Law*, 25 (1995–1996), pp. 287–397 at 299–300.

[42] Ibid., p. 347.

[43] United Nations Declaration on the Rights of Indigenous Peoples, September 13, 2007, UN GAR 61/295, UN Doc A/res61/295.

[44] Ibid., Art. 26(1).

[45] "Update Paper: United Nations Declaration on the Rights of Indigenous Peoples," January 10, 2008, cited in: S. J. Frantzman, H. Yahel, and R. Kark, "Contested Indigeneity:

The Declaration on Indigenous Peoples initially received a cool reception from countries that might be particularly affected by the call to actively validate customary interests. Canada initially rejected the Declaration by arguing that the provisions were "overly broad" and "not balanced" in that it suggested that "indigenous rights prevail over the rights of others."[46] Later, however, Canada reframed its position by supporting the Declaration, with the understanding that its provisions were vague enough to allow for various interpretations. The vagueness of the provisions, alongside the soft law nature of the Declaration, therefore, allowed states such as Canada, Australia, and New Zealand to somehow get along with the Declaration. The Declaration currently serves mostly as a symbolic international instrument, and as such, it proves particularly dominant in political campaigns launched by various indigenous and tribal groups around the world, without formally binding the property laws of the respective states.[47]

2.3.1.2 Collaboration on Best Practices, Guidelines, and Model Laws

Numerous international institutions, including UN Agencies and other interstate entities, engage in collaboration and coordination with the purpose of promoting "best practices," guidelines, or suggested blueprints for domestic law and regulation, including in matters dealing with property law. Therefore, while these international institutions are essentially top-down organizations, the products of their labor are soft law measures that do not immediately bind states or any of their governance organs. At the same time, these suggested guidelines or model laws are not entirely powerless. This is so, for example, because the adoption of such measures by a particular state may confer concrete benefits to it, such as when financial support granted by bodies like the World Bank or the International Monetary Fund (IMF) is explicitly or implicitly conditioned on reforming domestic systems, based on such model laws or guidelines.[48]

The Development of an Indigenous Discourse on the Bedouin of the Negev, Israel," *Israel Studies*, 17 (2012), pp. 78–104 at 81.

46 The Government of Canada, "Canada's Statement of Support of the U.N. Declaration on the Rights of Indigenous Peoples," November 12, 2010, available at www.aadnc-aandc.gc.ca/eng/1309374239861/1309374546142 (accessed on March 1, 2018).

47 Frantzman, Yahel, and Kark, "Contested Indigeneity," pp. 81–84.

48 P. Gupta, R. Kleinfeld, and G. Salinas, World Bank Operations Evaluation Department (OED), "Legal and Judicial Reform in Europe and Central Asia" (2002), available at http://documents.worldbank.org/curated/en/761991468021642749/pdf/11200278110Legal.pdf (accessed on March 1, 2018).

The following paragraphs highlight the work of some of these international institutions in promoting best-practice mechanisms, guidelines, and model laws in matters pertaining to property law. The list of institutions and the depiction of their work are obviously nonexhaustive. Further elaboration will be offered in following chapters in the context of specific types of assets.

The Basel Committee on Banking Supervision, an international institution tasked with overseeing banks and other significant financial institutions, is one of the most prominent intergovernmental entities in charge of setting professional standards.[49] The Basel Committee's suggested practices operate initially as soft law, but may then be embraced by states, via their central banks, as binding domestic policy. Created in the mid-1970s, in the aftermath of several cross-border crises involving the banking industry, the Basel Committee currently comprises members of G-20 countries, but its professional standards also resonate among, and are often embraced by, nonmember states.[50] In so doing, the Basel Committee also sets the tone for other international institutions engaged in standard-setting, such as the International Organization of Securities Commissions,[51] and the International Association of Insurance Supervisors.[52]

From its inception, the Basel Committee has been occupied not only with promoting general "best practices" across the banking industry, but also with controlling the potential cross-border effects of inadequate standards, such as when the failure of local branches of foreign banks impacts the relevant domestic market.[53] Accordingly, the capital adequacy requirements adopted in the 1988 Basel I Accord,[54] and revised in subsequent accords, were driven to a large extent by concerns over

[49] For the underlying features of the Basel Committee, see Bank for International Settlements, "About the Basel Committee," available at www.bis.org/bcbs/about.htm (accessed on March 1, 2018).

[50] C. Brummer, *Soft Law and the Global Financial System* (New York: Cambridge University Press, 2015), pp. 77–78.

[51] International Organization of Securities Commission, "The Global Standard Setter for Securities Markets Regulation," available at www.iosco.org/ (accessed on March 1, 2018).

[52] International Association of Insurance Supervisors (IAIS), "About the IAIS," available at www.iaisweb.org/home (accessed on March 1, 2018).

[53] Brummer, *Soft Law*, p. 77.

[54] Basel Committee on Banking Supervision, "International Convergence of Capital Measurements and Standards" (1998), available at: www.bis.org/publ/bcbsc111.pdf (accessed on March 1, 2018).

the arbitrage or differences in regulatory approaches across national boundaries.[55] Furthermore, more recent accords have sought to close the gaps that still existed in the Basel I Accord, particularly about the criteria for assessing risks. Capital reforms under the Basel II[56] and Basel III[57] frameworks seek to more closely coordinate the standards for capital adequacy.[58]

A recent measure taken by the Basel Committee, which has a direct bearing on property law, is the revised Basel III document on "Revisions to the Securitisation Framework" published in July 2016.[59] Securitization, the process by which loans or other claims to monetary rewards are bundled, packaged, and sold off to investors, played a major role in the 2007 subprime fiasco, which led to a global financial crisis.[60] The process of removing risk from the original borrowers, and creating different tranches of securities and derivatives generated from bundled loans, allowed securities markets' speculators to collude with credit-rating agencies in selling high-risk securities to dispersed and practically ignorant investors across the globe. When interest rates began to rise in 2006–2007, and house values fell below outstanding balances on home mortgages, the chain reaction of over-exposure to risk quickly unfolded across borders.[61] Further, the over-fragmentation of property interests among the various stockholders made it extremely difficult to restructure the underlying debts so as to decrease the devastating effects of the massive foreclosure of underwater assets.[62] Therefore, the need to monitor against the hazards of irresponsible securitization of mortgage-backed assets concerns not only the financial risk of steep decreases in the price

55 Brummer, *Soft Law*, p. 235.

56 Basel Committee on Banking Supervision, "International Convergence of Capital Measurements and Standards: A Revised Framework" (2004), available at www.bis.org/publ/bcbs107.pdf (accessed on March 1, 2018).

57 The Basel III framework is made up of a number of regulatory instruments regarding capital adequacy and related risk-management measures. Bank for International Settlements, "Basel III: International Regulatory Framework for Banks," available at www.bis.org/bcbs/basel3.htm?m=3%7C14%7C572 (accessed on March 1, 2018).

58 Brummer, *Soft Law*, pp. 243–245.

59 Basel Committee on Banking Supervision, "Basel III Document: Revisions to the Securitisation Framework" (revised, July 2016), available at www.bis.org/bcbs/publ/d374.pdf (accessed on March 1, 2018).

60 Brummer, *Soft Law*, pp. 219–221.

61 Ibid.

62 D. Dana, "The Foreclosure Crisis and the Anti-Fragmentation Principle in State Property Law," *University of Chicago Law Review*, 77 (2010), pp. 97–120 at 118–120.

of investment securities across global markets, but also the legal risk of inefficient over-fragmentation of the property regime that governs the underlying assets.

The Basel III framework for assessing risks, establishing credit ratings, and constructing the hierarchy of entitlements, thus serves the important goal of decreasing the regulatory arbitrage among different national systems – dealing with both property and securities regulation aspects. While the work of the Basel Committee is principally a soft law mechanism, the Committee's prominence creates an effective mechanism that decreases the risks of uncontrolled cross-border securities trade and allows for the development of shared property concepts about securitization.

The United Nations Conference on Trade and Development (UNCTAD), a permanent intergovernmental body established by the UN General Assembly in 1964, is a prominent body in advancing soft law mechanisms tying economic development and international investment.[63] These instruments have a direct bearing on property law on both the national and supranational levels. This is so because the suggested blueprints for law and regulation concerning economic development may incentivize countries to reform their property law, and land law in particular, especially when UNCTAD's financial support is somehow conditioned on such a legal reform.[64]

Moreover, international investment, by its nature, has a cross-border effect on property law, especially when investors seek, via an international investment agreement (IIA), to protect their property rights beyond the application of the "national treatment" standard by the host country.[65]

A recent example for such a soft law instrument designed by UNCTAD is the 2015 Investment Policy Framework for Sustainable Development.[66] It is aimed at serving as a "point of reference for policy-makers in formulating national investment policies, in negotiating or reviewing IIAs, and in designing concrete policy initiatives to promote

[63] United Nations Conference on Trade and Development (UNCTAD), "About," available at http://unctad.org/en/Pages/aboutus.aspx (accessed on March 1, 2018).

[64] UNCTAD, "Projects," available at http://unctad.org/en/Pages/technicalcooperation.aspx (accessed on March 1, 2018).

[65] See, for example, the discussion of the property effects of BITs in Section 2.3.4.5 below.

[66] UNCTAD, "Investment Policy Framework for Sustainable Development" (2015), available at http://investmentpolicyhub.unctad.org/Upload/Documents/INVESTMENT%20POLICY%20FRAMEWORK%202015%20WEB_VERSION.pdf (accessed on March 1, 2018).

investment in priority sectors for sustainable development."[67] This document identifies, *inter alia*, strategic and normative goals that states should pursue in promoting investment, balancing state commitments to investors with maintaining the state's regulatory space for development, and launching regional initiatives to promote sustainability-driven investment, especially for cross-border infrastructure development and regional clusters of sector-specific firms.[68] This soft law mechanism thus seeks to shore up national property laws to promote UNCTAD's goals of sustainable development and to alleviate property-related tensions over cross-border investment.

The United Nations Commission on International Trade Law (UNCITRAL), another UN-based intergovernmental institution, concerns itself with the "modernization and harmonization of rules on international business."[69] UNCITRAL drafts convention texts, model laws, legislative guides, and practice guides in various legal fields touching on commercial law, with the purpose of enhancing interstate coordination and streamlining international trade and investment.[70] Therefore, alongside the facilitation of hard law instruments, such as the 1980 UN Convention on Contracts for the International Sale of Goods,[71] or the 1988 UN Convention on International Bills of Exchange and International Promissory Notes,[72] UNCITRAL has proven to be a key institution in promoting soft law mechanisms, including in the context of property law.

A prominent soft law mechanism dealing with property law is the UNCITRAL Legislative Guide on Insolvency Law. Published in three parts, between 2004 and 2013,[73] this legislative guide is intended to

[67] Ibid., p. 6.

[68] Ibid., pp. 4–6.

[69] United Nations Commission on International Trade Law (UNCITRAL), "About UNCITRAL," available at www.uncitral.org/uncitral/en/about_us.html (accessed on March 1, 2018).

[70] UNCITRAL, "A Guide to UNCITRAL: Basic Facts about the United Nations Commission on International Trade Law" (2013), p. 1, available at www.uncitral.org/pdf/english/texts/general/12-57491-Guide-to-UNCITRAL-e.pdf (accessed on March 1, 2018).

[71] United Nations Convention on Contracts for the International Sale of Goods, April 11, 1980, 1489 UNTS 25567.

[72] G. A. Res. 43/165, United Nations Convention on International Bills of Exchange and International Promissory Notes, December 9, 1988.

[73] UNCITRAL, "Legislative Guide on Insolvency Law, Parts One and Two" (2004), available at www.uncitral.org/pdf/english/texts/insolven/05-80722_Ebook.pdf; UNCITRAL, "Legislative Guide on Insolvency Law, Part Three" (2010), available at www.uncitral.org/pdf/english/texts/insolven/Leg-Guide-Insol-Part3-ebook-E.pdf (accessed on March 1, 2018); UNCITRAL, "Legislative Guide on Insolvency Law, Part Four" (2013),

"inform and assist insolvency law reform around the world, providing a reference tool for national authorities and legislative bodies when preparing new laws and regulations or reviewing the adequacy of existing laws and regulations."[74] Interestingly, the legislative guide purports to present "different approaches and solutions available" for balancing the interests of debtors, creditors, other stakeholders, and the public at large, so that each legal system would be able to "choose the one most suitable to the local context."[75]

That said, UNCITRAL's work on insolvency law is definitely concerned with cross-border effects and the need to better coordinate among legal systems, even if states preserve power over their domestic law. This is particularly so with UNCITRAL's 1997 Model Law on Cross-Border Insolvency, revised in 2013 to include a "Guide to Enactment and Interpretation."[76] The model law refers to situations in which the "insolvent debtor has assets in more than one State or where some of the creditors of the debtor are not from the State where the insolvency proceeding is taking place."[77] While the model law suggests that "in incorporating the text of a model law into its system, a state may modify or leave out some of its provisions,"[78] it also provides that "in order to achieve a satisfactory degree of harmonization and certainty, it is recommended that States make as few changes as possible in incorporating the Model Law into their legal systems."[79] UNCITRAL thus sees the model law as a "vehicle for the harmonization of laws."[80]

Finally, a significant role in devising soft law mechanisms dealing also with property law lies with the International Institute for the Unification of Private Law (UNIDROIT), an intergovernmental organization set up

available at www.uncitral.org/pdf/english/texts/insolven/Leg-Guide-Insol-Part4-ebook-E.pdf (accessed on March 1, 2018).

74 UNCITRAL, "UNCITRAL Legislative Guide on Insolvency Law," available at: www.uncitral.org/uncitral/en/uncitral_texts/insolvency/2004Guide.html (accessed on March 1, 2018).

75 Ibid.

76 UNCITRAL, "Model Law on Cross-Border Insolvency with Guide to Enactment and Interpretation" (2013), available at www.uncitral.org/pdf/english/texts/insolven/1997-Model-Law-Insol-2013-Guide-Enactment-e.pdf (accessed on March 1, 2018).

77 UNCITRAL, "UNCITRAL Model Law on Cross-Border Insolvency" (1997), available at www.uncitral.org/uncitral/en/uncitral_texts/insolvency/1997Model.html (accessed on March 1, 2018).

78 UNCITRAL, Model Law on Cross-Border Insolvency with Guide to Enactment and Interpretation, p. 25.

79 Ibid.

80 Ibid., p. 24.

in 1926 by the League of Nations and re-established in 1940 on the basis of a multilateral agreement, the Statute of UNIDROIT.[81]

UNIDROIT's purpose is to modernize, harmonize, and coordinate "private and in particular commercial law as between States and groups of States and to formulate uniform law instruments, principles and rules to achieve those objectives."[82] It drafts conventions, model laws, principles, and legal and contractual guides. In the context of property law, one of its prominent soft law instruments is the 2011 UNESCO - UNIDROIT Model Legislative Provisions on State Ownership of Undiscovered Cultural Objects.[83] This model law identifies the underlying commitment of the state to "take all necessary and appropriate measures to protect undiscovered cultural objects and to preserve them for present and future generations."[84]

Although the model law focuses on national lawmaking, the theme of cultural objects cannot be understood outside of its cross-border context. The model law should be seen as intertwined with a number of international and regional conventions – dealing with instances of the border-crossing of cultural objects due to armed conflicts, thefts, or unauthorized international sales – such as the 1995 UNIDROIT Convention on Stolen or Illegally Imported Cultural Objects.[85] The soft law mechanism embedded in the model law on state ownership of undiscovered cultural objects is intended, inter alia, to facilitate the ability of states to request restitution of cultural objects that end up in another country. The model law is therefore intended to put states on equal footing as both sovereigns and property owners in remedying illegal cross-border transfers.[86] The cross-border body of law on artwork and cultural objects is taken up further in Chapter 4.[87]

81 International Institute for the Unification of Private Law (UNIDROIT), "Statute" (1940, revised in 1993), available at www.unidroit.org/about-unidroit/institutional-documents/statute (accessed on March 1, 2018).

82 Ibid.

83 UNESCO – UNIDROIT Model Legislative Provisions on State Ownership of Undiscovered Cultural Objects (2011), available at www.unidroit.org/instruments/cultural-property/model-provisions.

84 Ibid., Provision 1 – "General Duty."

85 International Institute for the Unification of Private Law (UNIDROIT), Convention on Stolen or Illegally Exported Cultural Objects, June 24, 1995, available at www.unidroit.org/instruments/cultural-property/1995-convention (accessed on March 1, 2018).

86 UNESCO – UNIDROIT Model Legislative Provisions, "Introduction."

87 See Chapter 4, Section 4.5.2.

2.3.2 *Conflict of Laws Strategy*

Moving to hard law strategies, this section focuses on institutions that play a prominent role in bridging inter-jurisdictional disparities by employing the conflict of laws strategy. Therefore, the legal instruments produced by such institutions seek, in dealing with cross-border property cases, to improve coordination and certainty about the domestic judicial forum that would have jurisdiction to decide the cross-border case, the substantive and procedural laws that would apply to it, and the extent to which judgements would be enforced in other jurisdictions.

At the same time, the conflict of laws strategy refrains from establishing supranational norms regarding the substance of property law doctrines, or from requiring states to approximate such substantive rules. The mainstay of property law ordering is thus reserved to the respective domestic institutions. This section exemplifies how such institutions work to implement the conflict of laws strategy in the contexts of (a) matrimonial property and succession and (b) insolvency law.

2.3.2.1 Treaties on Matrimonial Property and Succession

The following paragraphs highlight two types of intergovernmental institutions that have proven dominant in crafting conflict of laws instruments on matrimonial property and succession.

The Hague Conference on Private International Law (HCCH) is an intergovernmental organization, currently comprising eighty-two members,[88] with other countries also becoming parties to some of its conventions and other legal instruments.[89] The key goal of the HCCH is to facilitate a "progressive unification" of the rules of private international law.[90] The various conventions facilitated by HCCH since its establishment in 1893 thus embrace the conflict of laws strategy.

The thirty-eight conventions adopted to date cover a broad array of private law, commercial law, and civil procedure issues.[91] In the context

[88] Hague Conference on Private International Law (HCCH), "The Kingdom of Saudi Arabia Becomes the 82nd Member of the Hague Conference," October 19, 2016, available at www.hcch.net/en/news-archive/details/?varevent=525 (accessed on March 1, 2018).

[89] Hague Conference on Private International Law (HCCH), "About HCCH – A World Organization," available at www.hcch.net/en/about (accessed on March 1, 2018).

[90] Ibid.

[91] For a full list of HCCH conventions, see Hague Conference on Private International Law, "Conventions, Protocols and Principles," available at www.hcch.net/en/instruments/con ventions (accessed on March 1, 2018).

of property, one might observe the lack of conventions dealing generally with *in rem* rights pertaining to land, chattels, and other assets. Property law issues do receive treatment, however, in the context of matrimonial property and succession.

The Convention of 14 March 1978 on the Law Applicable to Matrimonial Property Regimes, which entered into force in 1992, focuses on the applicable laws that pertain to matrimonial assets.[92] Under Article 3, the parties may designate, before their marriage, the law that would apply to their assets, with special provisions pertaining to the designation of the law for all or some of the spouses' immovable property. Articles 6 to 8 detail the options available to spouses to establish the governance of an applicable law at a later stage. Article 4 lists the criteria based on which the applicable law would be determined, where no agreement exists between the parties. The chief criterion established in Article 4 provides that the matrimonial property regime would be governed by the law of the state in which "both spouses establish their first habitual residence after marriage."[93] Under any of these scenarios, and with respect to the *in rem* effect of the laws that apply to the matrimonial property, Article 9 establishes the general principle by which "the effects of the matrimonial property regime on the legal relations between a spouse and a third party are governed by the law applicable to the matrimonial property regime in accordance with the Convention," with some exceptions to this rule detailed in Article 9.[94]

The Convention of 1 August 1989 on the Law Applicable to Succession to the Estates of Deceased Persons – which is not (yet) in force – offers rules on succession that generally validate the choice of applicable laws made by a person in regard to his or her estate, while establishing criteria for determining the applicable law that would apply where no such choice was made.[95]

Other HCCH conventions touch on issues that have a bearing on property interests in similar contexts. Such is the Convention of

[92] Hague Conference on Private International Law (HCCH), Convention on the Law Applicable to Matrimonial Property Regimes, March 14, 1978, available at www.hcch.net/en/instruments/conventions/full-text/?cid=87 (accessed on March 1, 2018).

[93] Ibid., Art. 4.

[94] Ibid., Art. 9.

[95] Hague Conference on Private International Law (HCCH), Convention on the Law Applicable to the Succession to the Estates of Deceased Persons, August 1, 1989, available at www.hcch.net/en/instruments/conventions/full-text/?cid=62 (accessed on March 1, 2018).

13 January 2000 on the International Protection of Adults, in force as of 2009, which deals, inter alia, with conflict of laws rules about the property of adult persons who are unable, due to physical or mental disabilities, to take care of their interests.[96]

The HCCH conventions provide the most prominent international framework for the employment of the conflict of laws strategy in the context of property law. Given the fact that legal fields such as marital property and succession are often embedded in locally determined moral, social, or religious aspects, the work of an intergovernmental institution such as HCCH and its facilitation of a conflict of laws strategy is no small feat. It allows for a significant degree of certainty and predictability in identifying the national laws that would apply to the matrimonial property or succession. This strategy may also enable third parties outside of the marital household or immediate relatives to reasonably plan their actions regarding such assets.

A different supranational institution that has largely embraced a conflict of laws strategy in the case of matrimonial property and succession is the European Union (EU). As shown throughout the chapter, the EU employs all types of strategies for globalization – or more exactly, regionalization – with respect to property matters. This means that alongside the embracement of the conflict of laws strategy for matrimonial property and succession, the EU also employs the approximation strategy and the supranationalism strategy in other contexts of property law.

Prior to discussing the use of the conflict of laws strategy for matrimonial property and succession, the following paragraphs identify the EU's general structure and competences.

The EU, comprising twenty-eight Member States,[97] and featuring seven major institutions,[98] is the most extensive supranational framework in

[96] Hague Conference on Private International Law (HCCH), Convention on the International Protection of Adults, January 13, 2003, available at www.hcch.net/en/instruments/conventions/full-text/?cid=71 (accessed on March 1, 2018).

[97] The count still includes the United Kingdom, which has not yet withdrawn from the European Union following the results of the June 23, 2016 referendum in favor of leaving the European Union.

[98] The seven main EU institutions are the European Parliament, European Council, Council of the European Union, European Commission, Court of Justice of the EU, European Central Bank, and European Court of Auditors. The list is available at http://eur-lex.europa.eu/summary/glossary/eu_institutions.html (accessed on March 1, 2018).

the world.[99] The new Treaty on European Union (TEU),[100] Treaty on the Functioning of the European Union (TFEU),[101] and Charter of Fundamental Rights of the European Union (EU Charter),[102] cover more thematic ground than ever before. At the same time, the EU still falls short of being a full-fledged federal entity.[103]

Article 2 of the TFEU identifies three distinct categories of EU competence: exclusive, supporting, and shared.[104] *Exclusive* competence entrusts legislative powers only to the EU, unless members are empowered to act by the EU or work to implement the acts of the Union. The scope of exclusive competence is defined in Article 3(1) of the TFEU, which refers to customs union, competition rules, Euro monetary policy, marine conservation, common commercial policy, and some aspects of external relations addressed in Article 3(2).[105]

Supporting competence enables the EU to support, coordinate, and supplement the actions of Member States without superseding their actions in these areas. This competence applies to matters such as protection of human health, industry, culture, tourism, and education.[106]

The most intricate type of competence, which is also understood to serve as a residual category, is that of a *shared* competence. Article 2(2) of the TFEU provides that Member States "shall exercise their

99 For a study of these post-Lisbon institutions, see L. Pech, "The Institutional Development of the EU Post-Lisbon: A Case of Plus ça Change . . .?" in D. Ashiagbor, N. Countouris, and I. Lianos (eds.), *The European Union after the Treaty of Lisbon* (Cambridge, UK: Cambridge University Press, 2012), pp. 7–46 at 22–32.

100 Consolidated Version of the Treaty on European Union, signed on December 13, 2007, OJ (C 326/13), October 26, 2012, available at http://eur-lex.europa.eu/legal-content/EN/TXT/PDF/?uri=OJ:C:2012:326:FULL&from=EN (accessed on March 1, 2018).

101 Consolidated Version of the Treaty on the Functioning of the European Union, signed on December 13, 2007, OJ (C 326/47), October 26, 2012, available at http://eur-lex.europa.eu/legal-content/EN/TXT/PDF/?uri=OJ:C:2012:326:FULL&from=EN (accessed on March 1, 2018).

102 Charter of Fundamental Rights of the European Union, adopted on December 13, 2007, OJ (C 326/02), October 26, 2012, available at http://eur-lex.europa.eu/legal-content/EN/TXT/?uri=CELEX:12012P/TXT (accessed on March 1, 2018).

103 Thus, the EU has some state-like features, such as an autonomous legal order; rules addressed directly to Member States; power to legislate; a system of democratic governance; judicial controls; and economic and monetary union. But it also has some significant nonstate features, such as reservation of core elements of national sovereignty in matters such as security and defense or taxation; and the lack of concepts such as territory and population. A. Roses and L. Armati, *EU Constitutional Law: An Introduction*, 2d ed. (Oxford: Hart Publishing, 2012), pp. 15–19.

104 TFEU, Art. 2.

105 Ibid., Art. 3.

106 Ibid., Art. 6.

competence to the extent that the Union has not exercised its competence" or "has decided to cease exercising its competence."[107] The principal (though unclosed) list of areas of shared competences in Article 4 (2) of the TFEU includes eleven items, the most notable of which for the property context is the "internal market."[108] The concept of the internal market, which has been a mainstay of the European economic community from the EU's inception and that still serves as its major pillar, is articulated in Article 26(2) of the TFEU: "[t]he internal market shall comprise an area without internal frontiers in which the free movement of goods, persons, services and capital is ensured in accordance with the provisions of this Treaty."[109]

It is in the context of the EU's shared competence to promote the internal market that one should consider the use of the conflict of laws strategy for matrimonial property and succession.

To start with, Regulation No 650/2012 on Jurisdiction, Applicable Law, and Enforcement of Decisions in Matters of Succession ("Succession Regulation") is intended to ensure that a "given succession is treated coherently, by one single court applying one single law."[110] At the same time, it "in no way alters the substantive national rules on succession."[111] The Succession Regulation therefore clearly embraces the conflict of laws strategy.

The Succession Regulation generally establishes the deceased's habitual residence at the time of death as the basis for both national jurisdiction and the law that applies to the succession as a whole.[112] While allowing for some flexibility regarding both jurisdiction and applicable law, especially when a person chooses to apply the law of his or her nationality to the succession – if different from the place of habitual residence – the Succession Regulation principally promotes the concept of the unity of the succession.[113] This has obvious implications for the ranking of cross-border property interests. The entire pool of assets included in the estate is to

[107] Ibid., Art. 2(2).

[108] Ibid., Art. 4(2).

[109] Ibid., Art. 26(2).

[110] Regulation (EU) No 650/2012 of the European Parliament and of the Council of 4 July 2012 on Jurisdiction, Applicable Law, Recognition and Enforcement of Decisions and Acceptance and Enforcement of Authentic Instruments in Matters of Succession and on the Creation of a European Certificate of Succession, OJ (L 201/107), July 4, 2012.

[111] European Commission, "Succession and Wills," available at http://ec.europa.eu/justice/civil/family-matters/successions/index_en.htm (accessed on March 1, 2018).

[112] Regulation (EU) No 650/2012, Art 2.

[113] J. von Hein, "Conflicts between International Property, Family and Succession Law: Interfaces and Regulatory Techniques," *European Property Law Journal*, 6 (2017), pp. 142–157.

be governed by a single law. This means that the recognition and prioritization of property interests in regard to assets, including those located outside of the respective territory, are subjected to the unity concept.

In those cases in which there is a divergence between the jurisdiction and applicable law, and the two legal systems differ on the recognition of a certain type of an *in rem* right, Article 31 of the Succession Regulation provides that: "[w]here a person invokes a right in rem to which he is entitled under the law applicable to the succession and the law of the Member State in which the right is invoked does not know the right in rem in question, that right shall, if necessary and to the extent possible, be adapted to the closest equivalent right in rem under the law of that State. . ."[114]

The Succession Regulation establishes a European Certificate of Succession, which is issued by the authorized national court and is recognized in all EU countries without any special procedure.[115] This mechanism allows for an effective enforcement of this type of a conflict of laws strategy.

In June 2016, the EU adopted regulations for implementing enhanced cooperation in the area of jurisdiction, applicable law, and enforcement of decisions in property matters concerning both married couples (Council Regulation (EU) 2016/1103)[116] and registered partners (Council Regulation (EU) 2016/1104).[117] Agreed to by eighteen EU Member States, this enhanced cooperation[118] follows a conflict of laws strategy in property matters upon the dissolution of spousal relations with a cross-border

[114] Regulation (EU) No 650/2012, Art. 31.

[115] Ibid., Arts. 62–73; Commission Implementing Regulation (EU) No 1329/2014 of 9 December 2014 Establishing the Forms Referred to in Regulation (EU) No 650/2012 of the European Parliament and of the Council on Jurisdiction, Applicable Law, Recognition and Enforcement of Decisions and Acceptance and Enforcement of Authentic Instruments in Matters of Succession and on the Creation of a European Certificate of Succession, OJ (L 359/30), December 16, 2014.

[116] Council Regulation (EU) 2016/1103 of 24 June 2016 Implementing Enhanced Cooperation in the Area of Jurisdiction, Applicable Law and the Recognition and Enforcement of Decisions in Matters of Matrimonial Property Regimes, OJ (L 183/1), July 8, 2016.

[117] Council Regulation (EU) 2016/1104 of 24 June 2016 Implementing Enhanced Cooperation in the Area of Jurisdiction, Applicable Law and the Recognition and Enforcement of Decisions in Matters of the Property Consequences of Registered Partnerships, OJ (L 183/30), July 8, 2016.

[118] Under Article 31 of TFEU, enhanced cooperation allows a group of at least nine Member States to implement measures if all twenty-eight Member States fail to reach an agreement. Other EU countries keep the right to join the enhanced cooperation framework at a later time.

dimension. In so doing, the enhanced cooperation seeks to increase certainty about rules on jurisdiction, applicable law, and enforcement in an area of law otherwise marked by considerable substantive differences among various states. In particular, it seeks to "end parallel proceedings – costing around €1.1bn annually – in various Member States whose courts have to settle such property disputes."[119]

Moreover, embracing the concept of the unity of the matrimonial property, as is the case with the regulation on succession, the matrimonial property regulations emphasize that the "law applicable to a matrimonial property regime... shall apply to all assets falling under that regime, regardless of where the assets are located."[120]

2.3.2.2 Treaties on Insolvency

The European Union is also employing the conflict of laws strategy in another prominent field that has a major bearing on property interests: insolvency law. The essence of an insolvency proceeding, and bankruptcy in particular, can be essentially conceptualized as a property law setting: the bankruptcy court must rank competing legal interests in deciding how and to whom to allocate priority over a limited pool of assets.[121] With the ever-growing increase in the number of insolvency proceedings that have a significant cross-border dimension, in the sense that a certain person or corporation has creditors and/or assets in many jurisdictions, the EU has engaged in legislation aimed at providing rules on jurisdiction, applicable law, and enforcement.

Thus, according to Council Regulation (EC) No 1346/2000,[122] which was recast in 2015 in Regulation (EU) 2015/848 ("Insolvency Regulation"),[123] the debtor's "centre of main interests" is identified as the basis

[119] European Parliament, "International Divorces: New Rules on Whose Courts Settle Property Disputes" (June 23, 2016), available at www.europarl.europa.eu/news/en/news-room/20160622IPR33203/international-divorces-new-rules-on-whose-courts-settle-property-disputes (accessed on March 1, 2018).

[120] Council Regulation (EU) 2016/1103, Art. 21.

[121] B. E. Adler, "Bankruptcy as Property Law," in K. Ayotte and H. E. Smith (eds.), *Research Handbook on the Economics of Property Law* (Cheltenham, UK: Edward Elgar, 2011), pp. 206–220.

[122] Council Regulation (EC) No 1346/2000 of 29 May 2000 on Insolvency Proceedings, OJ (L 160/1), June 30, 2000.

[123] Regulation (EU) 2015/848 of the European Parliament and the Council of 20 May 2015 on Insolvency Proceedings, OJ (L 141/19), June 5, 2015.

for establishing the territory whose national courts are authorized to open insolvency proceedings.[124]

The law of the Member State in whose jurisdiction the insolvency proceedings are opened is generally the applicable law that governs the proceedings.[125] At the same time, according to Article 8 of the Insolvency Regulation, which deals with third parties' rights *in rem*: "[t]he opening of insolvency proceedings shall not affect the rights *in rem* of creditors or third parties in respect of tangible or intangible, moveable or immoveable assets . . . belonging to the debtor which are situated within the territory of another Member State at the time of the opening of proceedings."[126] Article 8 thus seeks to balance the role for a unified settlement of insolvency proceedings with the need to respect and validate *in rem* rights in favor of third parties where certain assets are located.

The essentiality of providing an effective solution for insolvency proceedings with a cross-border element has led to efforts for a similar conflict of laws strategy on a broader scale. As Section 2.3.1.2 showed, UNCITRAL has been promoting soft law mechanisms, comprising a legislative guide on insolvency law and a model law on cross-border insolvency. At the same time, UNCITRAL is currently considering the possibility of developing a binding international convention on selected aspects of international bankruptcy law.[127] This shift seems essential especially because, as of the end of 2016, only forty states had adopted some version of the model law on cross-border insolvency. It may be the case that UNCITRAL's soft law mechanisms have reached their limits of effectiveness, so that a binding convention would now be required.[128] The current agenda, though still in early consideration, seems to focus on a conflict of laws strategy, establishing rules on jurisdiction, law, and enforcement of cross-border bankruptcy proceedings. The cross-border body of insolvency law and institutional setup is analyzed in detail in Chapter 6.

[124] Ibid., Art. 3.
[125] Ibid., Art. 7(1).
[126] Ibid.
[127] United Nations Commission on International Trade Law (UNCITRAL), "Annotated Provisional Agenda for the Fifteenth Session of Working Group V (Insolvency Law)," available at https://documents-dds-ny.un.org/doc/UNDOC/LTD/V16/083/58/PDF/V1608358.pdf?OpenElement (accessed on March 1, 2018).
[128] B. Vessels, Leiden Law Blog, "Towards a Worldwide International Insolvency Convention?" (May 24, 2016), available at http://leidenlawblog.nl/articles/towards-a-worldwide-international-insolvency-convention (accessed on March 1, 2018).

2.3.3 *Approximation Strategy*

This section examines how cross-border institutions implement the approximation strategy, by which binding supranational instruments such as conventions require states to approximate their substantive and procedural norms on a certain theme. Some of the institutions featured below were presented in the contexts of soft law mechanisms and the conflict of laws strategy. The discussion will start, however, with introducing the World Trade Organization (WTO) and its role in the Trade-Related Aspects of Intellectual Property Rights (TRIPS) Agreement.

2.3.3.1 Intellectual Property Conventions

The World Trade Organization (WTO), established in 1994,[129] is the successor of the 1948 General Agreement on Tariffs and Trade (GATT) as the chief international institution for trade issues. Designed to streamline cross-border trade, the WTO serves as a negotiation forum for resolving trade problems, and specifically for crafting binding international instruments.[130]

The WTO Agreement is actually made up of about sixty agreements, falling into six main parts: an umbrella agreement that sets up, *inter alia*, the WTO organization and its different organs; three agreements, each covering one key area of trade addressed by the WTO: goods, services, and intellectual property; dispute settlements; and reviews of governments' trade policies.[131]

Prior to introducing the Trade-Related Aspects of Intellectual Property Rights (TRIPS) Agreement and its use of the approximation strategy in the context of intellectual property, one should take note of a significant institutional feature of the WTO: its binding dispute-settlement mechanism. In many ways, it is the existence of this institutional feature that enables the WTO to promote and enforce an approximation strategy in the context of intellectual property.

The WTO's dispute settlement mechanism is administered by its Dispute Settlement Body (DSB), which is part of the WTO's General

[129] The Marrakesh Agreement Establishing the World Trade Organization, April 15, 1994, 1867 UNTS 154, 33 ILM 1144.

[130] World Trade Organization, "Understanding the WTO: Who We Are," available at www.wto.org/english/thewto_e/whatis_e/who_we_are_e.htm (accessed on March 1, 2018).

[131] H. B. Pauwelyn, A. T. Guzman, and J. A. Hillman, *International Trade Law*, 3d ed. (New York: Wolters Kluwer, 2016), p. 100.

Council, so that all WTO members are members in it and may participate in the DSB.[132] The DSB sets up panels to adjudicate specific disputes among states. The panel's final report is referred to the DSB for formal adoption, which takes place within sixty days unless there is a consensus among Member States *not* to adopt it, or that an appeal has been filed to the WTO Appellate Body.[133]

This institutional structure has a direct bearing on property. This is so because the Trade-Related Aspects of Intellectual Property Rights (TRIPS) Agreement[134] was tied to the WTO from its inception as part of a package, and accordingly, the DSB has jurisdiction to adjudicate interstate conflicts in matters of intellectual property under the TRIPS Agreement.[135]

The TRIPS Agreement, discussed in detail in Chapter 5, advances the approximation strategy for intellectual property rights – such as patents, copyrights, trademarks, geographical indications, industrial designs, and layout designs of integrated circuits – in a number of ways.[136]

First, TRIPS sets out minimum substantive standards of protection to be provided by each national system of the signatory states. Beyond reiterating the binding commitments set forth in the Paris Convention on Patents and Trademarks[137] and the Berne Convention on Copyrights,[138] the TRIPS Agreement goes on to establish additional minimum standards for the different rights.[139]

Second, it requires national legal systems to strengthen their enforcement mechanisms, prescribing both civil and criminal procedures.[140] This facet of the approximation strategy thus underscores the institutional role that national bodies must play in ensuring that the

[132] Ibid., pp. 128–131.

[133] Ibid., p. 135. The negative consensus rule is a fundamental change from the previous dispute-settlement system under GATT, where a positive consensus was required to adopt a final report, thus permitting a dissatisfied losing party to block any action on the report.

[134] Agreement on Trade-Related Aspects of Intellectual Property Rights, April 15, 1994, 1869 UNTS 299, 33 ILM 1197. The TRIPS Agreement is Annex IC to the Marrakesh Agreement Establishing the World Trade Organization.

[135] Pauwelyn et al., *International Trade Law*, pp. 708–719.

[136] Ibid.

[137] Paris Convention for the Protection of Industrial Property, adopted March 20, 1883, as amended on September 29, 1979, 828 UNTS 305.

[138] Berne Convention for the Protection of Literary and Artistic Works, adopted September 9, 1886, as amended on July 24, 1971, 828 UNTS 221.

[139] Pauwelyn et al., *International Trade Law*, p. 708.

[140] Ibid., p. 709.

cross-border substantive commitments undertaken by signatory states would be credible and effective.

Third, TRIPS seeks to ensure the international enforcement of intellectual property rights by subjecting the agreement to the WTO's binding dispute-settlement mechanism, operating through the DSB, and backed up by the possibility of trade sanctions in the case of systematic non-compliance. This aspect of TRIPS therefore relies on the general institutional mechanisms that proved essential in making the WTO work.[141] For the approximation strategy to be effectively applied, cross-border and domestic institutions must be mutually reinforcing in meeting the minimum standards set up by TRIPS. This institutional dimension is also what sets TRIPS apart from the earlier generations of intellectual property conventions, which were lacking in domestic and international enforcement. These and other features of TRIPS are analyzed in Chapter 5.

2.3.3.2 Cultural Property

UNIDROIT, the international organization whose work in promoting soft law mechanisms was depicted in Section 2.3.1.2, has also facilitated several binding international instruments.

One such example, employing an approximation strategy, is the 1995 UNIDROIT Convention on Stolen or Illegally Exported Cultural Objects.[142] The UNIDROIT Convention, aimed at aiding the "fight against illicit trade in cultural objects," does so by "establishing common, minimal legal rules for the restitution and return of cultural objects between Contracting States."[143]

The Convention's use of the approximation strategy in regard to national legal systems concerns two different types of scenarios: (1) the stealing of cultural objects, whether such an act remains within the territory of a certain state or if it involves the crossing of national borders, and (2) the unlawful removal of cultural objects from their state of origin and their transfer to another contracting state.[144] The UNIDROIT Convention sets substantial standards for claims of restitution and the right

141 Ibid.

142 International Institute for the Unification of Private Law (UNIDROIT), Convention on Stolen or Illegally Exported Cultural Objects, June 24, 1995, 34 ILM 1330.

143 Ibid., Preamble, para. 4.

144 S. van Erp and B. Akkermans, *Cases, Materials and Text on Property Law* (Oxford: Hart Publishing, 2012), pp. 1121–1122.

of the possessor, under certain circumstances, to compensation upon such restitution. It gives additional instructions to national courts on how to balance the interests of the different parties – concerning both disputes between private parties and those between a possessor and a foreign government in the case of an unauthorized transfer of a cultural object to another state.[145]

The Convention provides that "[n]othing in this Convention shall prevent a Contracting State from applying any rules more favourable to the restitution or the return of stolen or illegally exported cultural objects than provided for by this Convention."[146] It could be therefore seen as setting minimum standards for the protection of cultural objects, somewhat similar to the TRIPS Agreement discussed in Section 2.3.3.1. Moreover, the fact that the Convention relies on national courts for the enforcement of its substantive and procedural provisions, rather than establishing a supranational tribunal for adjudication of disputes over cross-border transfers of cultural objects, further shows how the UNIDROIT Convention generally opts for an approximation strategy. The role of the Convention and its institutional implications are discussed further in Chapter 4.[147]

2.3.4 Supranationalism Strategy

This section highlights the institutional aspects of the supranationalism strategy, which establishes supranational norms and entrusts supranational institutions with binding lawmaking and enforcement powers. These supranational norms enjoy some type of a superior legal status over national norms in case of conflict, even if the application of such norms may be tempered or limited by adopting certain principles that defer to domestic rules in some cases. As demonstrated below, the supranationalism strategy for property law relies on the existence of binding and effective supranational institutions – be they legislative, administrative, or adjudicative. This state of affairs demonstrates that as we move up the ladder of the strategies for globalization from the more constrained ones of soft law mechanisms or the conflict of laws strategy, to the midlevel approximation strategy, and up to the most ambitious

145 Ibid.
146 UNIDROIT, Convention on Stolen or Illegally Exported Cultural Objects, Art. 9(1).
147 See Chapter 4, Section 4.5.2.

supranationalism strategy, there is greater need for effective supranational institutions that may preempt national laws in appropriate cases.

2.3.4.1 The European Union: Negative/Positive Harmonization

As Section 2.3.2.1 has shown, the European Union is the most comprehensive international organization in the world, and its different institutions carry out legislative, administrative, and adjudicative roles based on the division of competences between the EU and the Member States.

In some cases, such as in matrimonial property and succession, the EU settles for a conflict of laws strategy, which leaves to the states the power to legislate substantive legal norms. In other cases, the EU may opt for a more ambitious strategy, such as the supranationalism one. In such instances, EU institutions seek to create EU law that could supersede conflicting national norms.

The move toward supranational norms in the EU is depicted as comprising negative and positive components.[148] The negative feature relates mostly to the protection of substantive principles set forth in EU treaties, such as those relating to the freedom of movement of capital, goods, services, and persons within the internal market, enshrined in Article 26 of the TFEU.

The Court of Justice of the European Union (CJEU) is entrusted with ensuring that countries and EU institutions abide by EU law, and that it would be interpreted the same way in every country,[149] while granting states some leeway through principles such as proportionality.[150]

Another major setting of negative harmonization through treaty law, enforced by the CJEU, concerns the Charter of Fundamental Rights of the European Union, which went into force in 2009.[151] The right to property is explicitly articulated in Article 17 of the Charter.[152] The CJEU

[148] van Erp and Akkermans, *Cases on Property Law*, pp. 1024–1025.

[149] European Union, "Court of Justice of the European Union," available at https://europa.eu/european-union/about-eu/institutions-bodies/court-justice_en (accessed on March 1, 2018).

[150] T. Tridimas, "Competence after Lisbon: The Elusive Search for Bright Lines," in D. Ashiagbor et al. (eds.), *The European Union after the Treaty of Lisbon* (Cambridge, UK: Cambridge University Press, 2012), pp. 47–77 at 49–55.

[151] Charter of the Fundamental Rights of the European Union, approved on December 13, 2007, OJ (C 326/391), October 26, 2012.

[152] Article 17 reads: "1. everyone has the right to own, use, dispose of and bequeath his or her lawfully acquired possessions. No one may be deprived of his or her possessions, except in the public interest and in the cases and under the conditions provided for by

is thus tasked both with ensuring that state law does not violate the right to property in the Charter, and that other EU law – regulations, directives, etc. – does not contradict this and other rights.[153]

Alongside the negative component, legislative EU institutions also engage in positive harmonization, i.e., promulgating regulations, directives, and other legislative acts that seek to equate or otherwise harmonize private law doctrines, including in matters of property law.

The competence of EU institutions to do so is a highly complicated matter. This is particularly so with respect to Article 114 of the TFEU, which reads, inter alia, that EU institutions shall "adopt the measures for the approximation of the provisions laid down by law, regulation or administrative action in Member States which have as their object the establishment and functioning of the internal market."[154] While this provision could have been interpreted as an open-ended mandate for EU institutions to engage in supranational norm-making, the CJEU has held in *Germany* v. *Parliament and Council* (the *Tobacco Advertising* case)[155] that the EU legislature does not have a "general power to regulate the internal market" and that a "mere finding of disparities between national rules and of the abstract risk of obstacles to the exercise of fundamental freedoms or of distortions of competition" forms an insufficient basis to establish EU competence to act.[156] However, later CJEU cases seem to have opted for a less stringent approach,[157] approving in one case the use of minimum harmonization contract legislation adopted

law, subject to fair compensation being paid in good time for their loss. The use of property may be regulated by law in so far as is necessary for the general interest. 2. Intellectual property shall be protected." Ibid., Art. 17.

[153] For example, in its 2013 *Trabelsi* decision, the CJEU invalidated the Council of the EU's decision to freeze the assets of one of the petitioners, finding it violative of the petitioner's right to property. Holding that a limitation on the exercise of the right of property must (1) "have a legal basis;" (2) "refer to an objective of public interest, recognized as such by the EU;" and (3) "not be excessive" – meaning that it "must be necessary and proportional to the aim sought" without impairing the "essential content" of the right – the CJEU held that the Council failed to meet this test in the specific circumstances. Case T-187/11, *Trabelsi* v. *Council of the European Union* (CJEU, Third Chamber, May 28, 2013), paras. 74–117.

[154] TFEU, Art. 114(1).

[155] Case C-376/98, *Germany* v. *Parliament and Council* [2000] ECR I-8419.

[156] Ibid., paras. 83–84.

[157] L. Miller, "European Contract Law after Lisbon," in D. Ashiagbor et al. (eds.), *The European Union after the Treaty of Lisbon* (Cambridge, UK: Cambridge University Press, 2012), pp. 227–251 at 247–249.

under the former version of Article 114 of the TFEU.[158] In the context of property, one could mention the 2014 directive on cultural property;[159] a 2011 directive on late payments addressing the issue of retention of title;[160] and the regulation on insolvency proceedings.[161] More ambitious efforts, such as designing an EU-level single system of security rights through a European Security Right in movables,[162] or a Eurohypothec for real estate,[163] have so far not come to fruition. The most significant achievement so far in the context of EU positive harmonization on property law – the EU Patent Package – will be discussed in Section 2.3.4.6.

2.3.4.2 European Convention on Human Rights

The evolution of the European Convention for the Protection of Human Rights and Fundamental Freedoms ("European Convention")[164] and the European Court of Human Rights (ECHR) is often depicted as one of the most incredible phenomena in the history of international law.[165] The European Convention, signed by forty-seven Member States of the Council of Europe,[166] establishes the right to property in Article 1 of the First Protocol.[167] As the following paragraphs show, the increasing role of the

158 Case C-205/07, *Lodewijk Gysbrechts and Santurel Inter BVBA* [2008] ECR I-9947.

159 Directive 2014/60/EU of the European Parliament and of the Council of 15 May 2014 on the Return of Cultural Objects Unlawfully Removed from the Territory of a Member State (Recast), OJ (L 159/1), May 25, 2014.

160 Directive 2011/7/EU on Combating Late Payments in Commercial Transactions, OJ (L 48/1), February 23, 2011.

161 Regulation (EU) 2015/848 of the European Parliament and the Council of 20 May 2015 on Insolvency Proceedings, OJ (L 141/19), June 5, 2015,

162 E. M. Kieninger, "Introduction: Security Rights in Movable Property within the Common Market and the Approach of This Study," in E. M. Kieninger (ed.), *Security Rights in Movable Property in European Private Law* (Cambridge, UK: Cambridge University Press, 2009), pp. 6–37.

163 O. Stöcker, "The Eurohypothec," in B. Akkermans, A. F. Salomons, and J. H. M. van Erp (eds.), *The Future of European Property Law* (Munich: Sellier, 2012), pp. 65–77.

164 Convention for the Protection of Human Rights and Fundamental Freedoms, November 4, 1950, 213 UNTS 221.

165 M. O'Boyle, "On Reforming the Operation of the European Court of Human Rights," *European Human Rights Law Review*, 1 (2008), pp. 1–11.

166 For a list of the forty-seven members, see Council of Europe, "Our Member States," available at: www.coe.int/en/web/about-us/our-member-states (accessed on March 1, 2018).

167 The first paragraph reads: "Every natural or legal person is entitled to the peaceful enjoyment of his possessions. No one shall be deprived of his possessions except in the public interest and subject to the conditions provided for by law and by the general principles of international law." The second paragraph states: "The preceding provisions shall not, however, in any way impair the right of a State to enforce such laws as it deems

ECHR in interpreting the scope of the right to property, by applying substantive principles such as "fair balance" and "proportionality," has resulted in a thick body of case law that employs a supranationalism strategy in property law across Europe.

The property jurisprudence of ECHR had initially opted for a relatively narrow review of the deprivation or regulation of property, focusing on lawfulness or a quality of law principle, under which states had only to demonstrate that they complied with the formal requirements of their legal system and that such rules were sufficiently accessible, precise, and foreseeable. This early approach has thus served as a procedural check, focusing on formalities and due process, rather than on constructing a set of supranational substantive concepts.[168] This approach changed in the 1982 *Sporrung* v. *Sweden*[169] and 1986 *James* v. *United Kingdom*[170] cases, which will be surveyed in detail in Chapter 3.[171] In these cases, the ECHR developed self-standing criteria of fair balance and proportionality for reviewing domestic legislation or regulation. These supranational criteria now cover the entire array of rights in the European Convention.[172]

Therefore, while leaving states with a "margin of appreciation" in defining both the public purpose and the means required to achieve it,[173] the ECHR's review of state legislation, administrative actions, and state court decisions has in many cases resulted in the ECHR overturning or otherwise preempting national property law. Property issues are featured prominently in the ECHR's docket. Between 1959 and 2016, twelve percent of the entire cases in which the ECHR found a violation of the European Convention dealt with the right to property.[174]

necessary to control the use of property in accordance with the general interest or to secure the payment of taxes or other contributions or penalties." European Convention, Protocol 1, Art. 1.

168 T. Allen, "Compensation for Property under the European Convention on Human Rights," *Michigan Journal of International Law*, 28 (2007), pp. 287–335.

169 *Sporrung and Lönnroth* v. *Sweden*, 52 Eur. Ct. H.R. (ser. A) (1982).

170 *James* v. *United Kingdom*, 8 Eur. H.R. Rep. 123 (1986).

171 See Chapter 3, Section 3.3.

172 E. Bates, *The Evolution of the European Convention on Human Rights: From Its Inception to the Creation of a Permanent Court of Human Rights* (Oxford: Oxford University Press, 2010), pp. 5–8.

173 Y. Arai-Takahashi, *The Margin of Appreciation Doctrine and the Principle of Proportionality in the Jurisprudence of the ECHR* (Antwerp: Intersentia, 2002).

174 Council of Europe, "ECHR: Overview 1959–2016," p. 6, available at www.echr.coe.int/Documents/Overview_19592016_ENG.pdf (accessed on March 1, 2018).

It should be noted, however, that there is a difference between the scope of the margin of appreciation granted in cases said to implicate the deprivation of property under the first paragraph of Article 1 of the First Protocol and in those dealing with regulation that works to control the use of property under Article 1's second paragraph.[175] The first type of case is usually subject to a higher level of scrutiny and stricter application of supranational standards, such as fair balance and proportionality.[176] On the other hand, when evaluating a regulation that controls the use of property without expropriating it de facto or de jure, the ECHR has granted states a particularly wide margin of appreciation to design an underlying policy, choose the means to achieve the public goal, and evaluate the effects such means have on property.[177]

With this differentiation in mind, the jurisprudence of the ECHR currently serves as probably the most extensive application of the supranationalism strategy in property law. This is made possible first and foremost by the institutional power granted to the ECHR and its expansive right of standing.[178] The ECHR serves, therefore, as a clear example of how a supranationalism strategy in property law hinges to a large extent on effective supranational institutions.

2.3.4.3 American Convention on Human Rights

The American continent is home to a regional supranational ordering that has a bearing on property law, although the scope and authority of the Organization of American States (OAS) and its various institutions, presented in the following paragraphs, is significantly narrower than in the European context.

The OAS, established in 1948 and currently comprising all of the continent's thirty-five states, has adopted a series of instruments, including ones intended for the protection of human rights.[179] The key binding instrument adopted by OAS is the American Convention on Human

[175] See the text of Article 1 to the First protocol in *supra* note 167.

[176] Arai-Takahashi, *Margin of Appreciation*, pp. 149–150.

[177] *AGOSI* v. *U.K.*, 108 Eur. Ct. H.R. (ser. A) (1986), para. 52 ("the State enjoys a wide margin of appreciation with regard both to choosing the means of enforcement and to ascertaining whether the consequences of enforcement are justified in the general interest for the purpose of achieving the object of the law in question").

[178] Bates, *Evolution of the European Convention*, pp. 319–349.

[179] Inter-American Commission on Human Rights (IACHR), "Introduction," available at www.oas.org/en/iachr/mandate/basic_documents.asp (accessed on March 1, 2018).

Rights, which was signed in 1969 and went into force in 1978.[180] So far, twenty-five OAS Member States have ratified the American Convention.[181] Notably, the United States and Canada have not done so.[182]

The two key OAS institutions operating under the American Convention are the Inter-American Commission on Human Rights, tasked, among other things, with submitting petitions for alleged violations of human rights,[183] and the Inter-American Court of Human Rights, authorized to apply and interpret the American Convention following such petitions.[184] The work of these institutions plays a significant role in the ability of the American Convention to allow for some kind of a supranationalism strategy in human rights, including under Article 21, which articulates the right to property.[185] In fact, while serving as a regional supranational court, the Inter-American Court of Human Rights also aspires to exert influence outside of the American continent by offering innovative interpretations of human rights and by identifying norms as *jus cogens*.[186]

As Chapter 3 will show, the most prominent cases handed down by the Court, according to Article 21 on the right to property, have dealt with indigenous tribes' rights to land. These cases also demonstrate the complex relations between the public/constitutional law aspects of land law – which are clearly within the mandate of the Inter-American Court in dealing with human rights – and the private law aspects of land law that are practically implicated by such case law.

[180] Organization of American States, American Convention on Human Rights, November 22, 1969, OASTS No. 36, 1144 UNTS 143.

[181] For a list of the signatories and the current status of ratifications, see Organization of American States, "Multinational Treaties, American Convention on Human Rights," available at www.oas.org/dil/treaties_B-32_American_Convention_on_Human_Rights_sign.htm (accessed on March 1, 2018).

[182] Ibid.

[183] Inter-American Commission on Human Rights, "What is IACHR?" available at www.oas.org/en/iachr/mandate/what.asp (accessed on March 1, 2018).

[184] Inter-American Court of Human Rights, available at www.corteidh.or.cr/corte/index.cfm?lang=en (accessed on March 1, 2018).

[185] Article 21 reads: "1. Everyone has the right to the use and enjoyment of his property. The law may subordinate such use and enjoyment to the interest of society. 2. No one shall be deprived of his property except upon payment of just compensation, for reasons of public utility or social interest, and in the cases and according to the forms established by law. 3. Usury and any other form of exploitation of man by man shall be prohibited by law." American Convention on Human Rights, Art. 21.

[186] G. L. Neuman, "Import, Export, and Regional Consent in the Inter-American Court of Human Rights," *European Journal of International Law*, 19 (2008), pp. 101–123.

2.3.4.4 OHADA and the Harmonization of Business Law in Africa

Another significant regional set of institutions, which has substantial implications also for cross-border features of property law, is shared by seventeen countries in West and Central sub-Saharan Africa, who belong mostly to the African Franc Zone (being former French colonies).[187]

After a lengthy process dating back to the 1960s, the Organization for the Harmonization of Business Law in Africa (OHADA) (French: *Organisation pour l'Harmonisation en Afrique du Droit des Affaires*) was established in 1993, when fourteen states adopted the Treaty on the Harmonization of Business Law in Africa ("OHADA Treaty").[188] The original treaty went into force in 1995.[189] It was revised in 2008, and the amendments went into force in 2011.[190]

The driving force for the establishment of OHADA was to create a friendlier environment for investment, implicating both African investors and international ones. The economic recession that hit the region as of the 1980s, alongside other economic and political concerns, significantly slowed down the flow of capital into the region.[191] In addition, the fragmentation of legal systems within the region was also a point of concern. Although most of the states shared a French colonial past, and generally adhered during colonial times to the French Commercial Code

[187] Organization for the Harmonization of Business Law in Africa (OHADA), "General Overview," available at www.ohada.org/index.php/en/ohada-in-a-nutshell/general-overview (accessed on March 1, 2018).

[188] *Traité Relatif à l'Harmonisation du Droit des Affaires En Afrique* (Treaty on the Harmonization of Business Law in Africa), signed October 17, 1993, in Abidjan, Ivory Coast. The original treaty is available (in French) at www.ohada.org/index.php/fr/traite-relatif-a-l-harmonisation-du-droit-des-affaires-en-afrique/preambule (accessed on March 1, 2018).

[189] On September 18, 1995, OHADA received the instruments of ratification of Niger, fulfilling the number of ratifications required for the treaty to enter into force. See A. Mouloul, "Understanding the Organization for the Harmonization of Business Laws in Africa (O.H.A.D.A.)," 2d ed., June 2009, p. 20, available at www.ohada.com/content/newsletters/1403/Comprendre-l-Ohada-en.pdf (accessed on March 1, 2018).

[190] *Traité Portant Révision du Traité Relatif à l'Harmonisation du Droit des Affairs en Afrique* (Treaty for the Revision of the Treaty on the Harmonization of Business Law in Africa), signed October 17, 2008, Québec, Canada. The revised treaty in French is available at the OHADA Official Journal No. 26 (December 1, 2011), 3. An English translation of the revised treaty is available at http://juriafrique.com/eng/wp-content/uploads/sites/2/2017/08/TRAITE-REVISE-OHADA-en.pdf (accessed on March 1, 2018). Further references to the OHADA Treaty will be made to the revised version.

[191] Mouloul, "Understanding OHADA," p. 8.

of 1807, upon their independence each of these countries engaged in a piecemeal legislation that either followed developments in France in awkward ways or simply became obsolete in the face of changing circumstances. The result was one of 'legal balkanization' within the region. In addition, inadequate training of judges in these countries also brought about judicial insecurity in the sense that business law lacked predictability and proper enforcement.[192]

The leaders of the region realized that the fragmentation of business law, alongside the malfunctioning of the national judicial systems, put the region at a significant disadvantage. Legal harmonization was thus required to generate trust, predictability, and a sense of security both among the Member States and vis-à-vis investors. To facilitate such legal harmonization, the OHADA Treaty established a number of institutions: Conference of Heads of State and Government (bringing together the seventeen leaders of the states as the supreme institution of OHADA); the Council of Ministers (composed of the Ministers of Justice and Finance Ministers of the Member States, and serving as the legislative body of OHADA); the Permanent Secretariat (which serves as the executive body of OHADA and also prepares the draft legislation); and the Common Court of Justice and Arbitration (CCJA) (which is the court of cassation for all disputes related to the uniform body of law created by OHADA).[193] According to Article 14 of the OHADA Treaty, the CCJA "shall rule on decisions taken by appellate courts of the States Parties in all matters raising issues to the application of the uniform Acts and to the regulations contemplated by the Treaty..."[194] In addition to its judicial capacity, the CCJA also facilitates arbitration under Title IV of the OHADA Treaty, initiated either by private parties or by referring domestic courts.[195]

The heart of the OHADA harmonization strategy lies in the Uniform Acts, a series of legislative acts that deal with different aspects of business law. As of 2017, OHADA enacted eight Uniform Acts, with several draft laws being in the process of approval.[196] Of particular interest in the

192 Ibid. pp. 9–17.

193 For a review of these institutions, see OHADA, "Presentation," then "Our Institutions," available at www.ohada.org/index.php/en/ (accessed on March 1, 2018); Mouloul, "Understanding OHADA," pp. 30–47.

194 OHADA Treaty, Art. 14, para. 3.

195 Ibid., Title IV (Arts. 21–26).

196 For the list of Uniform Acts in force and in preparation, see OHADA, "Presentation," then "Uniform Acts," available at www.ohada.org/index.php/en/ (accessed on March 1, 2018).

context of property law is the Uniform Act on Bankruptcy Proceedings, which went into force in 2015.[197] This law deals not only with procedural aspects of bankruptcy proceedings, but also with the substantive principles of insolvency and the ranking of priorities to assets among creditors.[198] As such, it creates a single system of *in rem* rights and priorities to assets upon insolvency. In addition, the Uniform Act on Organizing Securities, which went into force in 2011, determines the types of security interests, recognized across OHADA Member States, and their legal features.[199]

The insolvency law, like the other Uniform Acts, has direct applicability in all Member States and it supersedes any conflicting provisions in the respective domestic systems. As such, OHADA's Uniform Acts exemplify a globalization strategy that can be depicted as located midway between an approximation strategy and a supranationalism strategy. On the one hand, the Uniform Acts are incorporated in the domestic legal systems. Each country has its own statute. The national courts are entrusted with adjudicating cases and interpreting the (now domestic) pieces of legislation. Accordingly, domestic courts run bankruptcy proceedings and other commercial law matters addressed by the Uniform Acts. This means that the national legal layer of both security interests and bankruptcy laws remains intact and is operated routinely by national courts. At the same time, however, the CCJA serves as the final authority on interpreting the Uniform Acts. Given the broad right of appeal to the CCJA as a court of cassation both by litigants themselves, as well by referring domestic courts, the CCJA has significant institutional capacity to ensure that the Uniform Acts are interpreted and applied in a similar manner across all Member States, especially in view of the CCJA's power to "hear and decide points of fact" when sitting as a court of final appeal.[200] This has obvious implications for the Uniform Acts that deal

197 Uniform Act on Bankruptcy Proceedings, OHADA Official Gazette, September 25, 2017. An English translation is available at www.ohada.org/index.php/en/aupc-insolvency-law/presentation-and-innovations (accessed on March 1, 2018).

198 See OHADA, "Uniform Act on Bankruptcy Proceedings: Presentation and Innovations," available at www.ohada.org/index.php/en/aupc-insolvency-law/presentation-and-innovations (accessed on March 1, 2018).

199 *Acte Uniforme Portant Organisation des Sûretés* (Uniform Act on Organizing Securities), OHADA Official Journal No. 22, February 15, 2011, 3, text available at http://biblio.ohada.org/pmb/opac_css/doc_num.php?explnum_id=483 (accessed on March 1, 2018) (in French).

200 OHADA Treaty, Art. 14, para. 5. The only key issue left outside the scope of the CCJA's authority on appeal is that of criminal sanctions imposed by national courts by virtue of a Uniform Act. Ibid., Art. 14, para. 3.

with property law and the ranking of rights and priorities to assets, as it purports to provide both local and international investors a single system of *in rem* interests across the seventeen Member States. As such, OHADA is a significant variety of a hybrid of an approximation strategy and a supranationalism strategy on both the legislative and adjudicative levels.

2.3.4.5 Bilateral Investment Treaties

International investment treaties, prominently taking the form of bilateral investment treaties (BITs), are a burgeoning phenomenon. As of 2017, BITs number over 2,950 worldwide, following a dramatic rise in the early 1990s, with about 370 other treaties – such as those dealing with free trade – including special provisions about the protection of investments.[201] BITs tie together not only developed-developing country dyads, but also pairs of developing countries as well as developed country dyads. Just about every country is party to at least one such treaty.[202] As the following paragraphs show, BITs prove to be a significant force in the implementation of a supranationalism strategy (albeit in the form of bilateral treaties), due to the focus of the term *investment* on property rights and the institutional role of independent arbitration tribunals.

To put things in historical context, the first BIT is commonly traced to the agreement signed in 1959 between Germany and Pakistan in the aftermath of the end of colonialism and the decline of customary international law norms on the protection of foreign investments.[203]

During the 1950s, a number of newly independent countries embarked on a series of massive expropriations of properties and enterprises controlled by foreign investors from Western economies. Nationalizations and expropriations have been a recurring theme in international investment, reaching another peak during the 1970s, and never truly disappearing.[204]

Despite the slow start, the number of BITs grew from a handful to a few dozen each year following a series of key events – notably, the debt

201 United Nations Conference on Trade and Development (UNCTAD), "World Investment Report 2017 – Investment and the Digital Economy," pp. 111–112, available at unctad.org/en/PublicationsLibrary/wir2017_en.pdf (accessed on March 1, 2018).

202 For a list of international investment treaties, see UNCTAD, Investment Policy Hub, "International Investment Agreements Navigator," available at http://investmentpolicyhub.unctad.org/IIA (accessed on March 1, 2018).

203 K. J. Vandevelde, "A Brief History of International Investment Agreements," *UC Davis Journal of International Law and Policy*, 12 (2005), pp. 157–409.

204 A. Lehavi and A. N. Licht, "BITs and Pieces of Property," *Yale Journal of International Law*, 36 (2011), pp. 115–166.

crisis of developing countries in the 1980s and the collapse of the Soviet bloc – and in response to the advancement of a neoliberal policy by the World Bank and the International Monetary Fund. The current scope of BITs extends, however, well beyond the paradigm of a developed, capital-exporting country conditioning the flow of investments into a capital-dependent developing country on signing a BIT. Capital is currently flowing also from South to North through sovereign wealth funds, government subsidiaries, and private corporations based in China, Russia, the Persian Gulf, and elsewhere.[205]

From a legal and institutional perspective, BITs typically implement three related measures: (1) commitment by host countries to a certain set of substantive standards of treatment for foreign investment; (2) direct right of action for investors against host countries for an alleged breach of these commitments; and (3) resolution of disputes by international arbitration, most often by the International Centre for Settlement of Investment Disputes (ICSID), which is affiliated with the World Bank.[206] The substantive commitments that states undertake in BITs typically include the duties of national treatment, most-favored-nation treatment, fair and equitable treatment, and guarantees of compensation with respect to expropriation (direct or indirect). An investment is typically defined as comprising a list of rights in various assets, with immovable property featured regularly in such lists alongside tangible and intangible goods. The types of property rights covered in BITs include not only ownership but also leases, pledges, and so forth.

Consequently, BIT jurisprudence has gradually shifted toward a property discourse, focusing on investors' property rights as the object of legal protection, and balancing these rights against states' legislative and regulatory powers, while also borrowing from the property jurisprudence of the European Convention, the US Constitution, and other legal instruments.[207]

Recent years have also seen a dramatic growth in the number of arbitration cases. By the end of 2016, the total number of known treaty-based cases stood at 767, with 62 new disputes filed during 2016. So far, 109 countries have been sued at least once for an alleged breach of

[205] UNCTAD, "World Investment Report 2017," pp. 13–20.

[206] See International Centre for Settlement of Investment Disputes (ICSID)'s website at https://icsid.worldbank.org/apps/ICSIDWEB/Pages/default.aspx (accessed on March 1, 2018).

[207] Lehavi and Licht, "BITs and Pieces," pp. 128–136.

a BIT.[208] Moreover, the success rate of investors in such arbitrations has been significant. Out of all the decisions made on the merits of the case up until the end of 2016, a majority of the cases – 60 percent – has been decided in favor of the investor.[209] This means that the interpretation of BITs and the consequent protection of investments go well beyond the application of host governments' laws, and this body of law thus implements a supranationalism strategy.

2.3.4.6 European Unified Patent

The European Union is currently in the process of introducing a unitary patent package, which will include an EU-wide registry for patents and a Unified Patent Court. The patent package will introduce a significant supranationalism strategy for this type of intellectual property, going well beyond the current approximation strategy embedded in TRIPS. This scheme serves as yet another vivid example of the centrality of authorized institutions – here, the current institutions of the EU and the new court – for the supranationalism strategy. The following paragraphs briefly depict the concept of a unified patent, the regulations that establish it, and the new institution – the Unified Patent Court – in charge of implementing it.

The unitary patent is the first piece of the EU patent package.[210] It is based on two EU regulations that went into force in 2013. Regulation (EU) No 1257/2012 on Implementing Enhanced Cooperation in the Creation of Unitary Patent Protection[211] lays the foundations for a unitary patent, which would be granted by the European Patent Office,[212] and to which a unitary effect for the territories of the twenty-five participating states (all EU countries except for Spain, Poland, and Croatia) would be given after its grant.[213] Council Regulation (EU) No 1260/2016

208 UNCTAD, "World Investment Report 2017," pp. 114–116.

209 Ibid., pp. 117–118.

210 European Patent Office, "Unitary Patent & Unified Patent Court," available at www.epo.org/law-practice/unitary.html (accessed on March 1, 2018).

211 Regulation (EU) No 1257/2012 of the European Parliament and of the Council of 17 December 2012 Implementing Enhanced Cooperation in the Area of the Creation of Unitary Patent Protection, OJ (L 361/1), December 31, 2012.

212 The European Patent Office is one of the two bodies of the European Patent Organization (alongside the Administrative Council). EPO has thirty-eight Member States across Europe. European Patent Office, "European Patent Organization," available at www.epo.org/about-us/organisation.html (accessed on March 1, 2018).

213 European Patent Office, "Unitary Patent," available at www.epo.org/law-practice/unitary/unitary-patent.html (accessed on March 1, 2018).

on Applicable Translation Arrangements[214] sets out the translation arrangements required for such unitary protection across the twenty-five participating states.

Both regulations will be applicable once the Agreement on a Unified Patent Court,[215] signed by Member States on February 2013, will have been properly ratified. One threshold has already been met with more than half of the signatories – fifteen states as of early 2018 – ratifying the agreement.[216] In addition, the agreement has to be specifically ratified by Germany, France, and the United Kingdom, comprising the three Member States in which the highest number of European patents had effect in the year preceding the signature of the agreement.[217] As of May 2018, France had done so, as did the United Kingdom,[218] despite the uncertainty brought about by the 2016 Brexit referendum.[219] Germany has not yet ratified the agreement.

Once launched, the Unified Patent Court will have exclusive jurisdiction for litigation over European patents with unitary effect. It will include a Court of First Instance, a Registry, and a Court of Appeal.[220] The Unified Patent Court will thus become the second EU-level supranational court, after CJEU. Chapter 5 will elaborate further on the EU patent package.[221]

2.3.4.7 International Registry of Interests in Mobile Equipment

Aircrafts are probably the quintessential example of assets that constantly defy national borders in the age of globalization. With about 50,000

[214] Council Regulation (EU) No 1260/2012 of 17 December 2012 Implementing Enhanced Cooperation in the Area of the Creation of Unitary Patent Protection with regard to the Applicable Translation Arrangements, OJ (L 361/89), December 31, 2012.

[215] For the full text of the Agreement on a Unified Patent Court, see http://documents.epo.org/projects/babylon/eponet.nsf/0/A1080B83447CB9DDC1257B36005AAAB8/$File/upc_agreement_en.pdf (accessed on March 1, 2018).

[216] For a list of the current state of ratifications, see European Council, "Agreement on a Unified Patent Court (UPC)," available at www.consilium.europa.eu/en/documents-publications/treaties-agreements/agreement/?id=2013001 (accessed on May 31, 2018).

[217] European Patent Office (EPO), "When Will the Unitary Patent System Start?" available at www.epo.org/law-practice/unitary/unitary-patent/start.html (accessed on March 1, 2018).

[218] European Council, "Agreement on a Unified Patent Court (UPC)."

[219] T. Jaeger, "Reset and Go: The Unitary Patent System Post-Brexit," *International Review of Intellectual Property and Competition Law*, 48 (2017), pp. 254–285.

[220] European Patent Office, "Unified Patent Court," available at www.epo.org/law-practice/unitary/patent-court.html (accessed on March 1, 2018).

[221] Chapter 5, Section 5.2.3.1.

routes being served globally and 100,000 flights per day,[222] the movement of aircrafts across national borders is a trivial matter, but its legal implications are not. This is especially so with respect to security interests in aircrafts and their equipment, and the enormous difficulties that financiers/creditors might face in enforcing their property rights in view of such a constant movement of the underlying asset.[223] When a security interest over the aircraft is registered in one country, but the vehicle is located in the territory of another country when foreclosure is required, conflict of laws rules and the *lex rei sitae* principle may prove particularly problematic for the creditors and other stakeholders. This problem is even more acute than in the case of conventional commercial goods, in which the financier/creditor may have some advance knowledge about the cross-border destination of the goods. In the case of an aircraft, the underlying asset may be found at any point in the world at any given time.

The property strategy that has been devised to address this problem presents what may be considered the most ambitious version of a supranationalism strategy today: a global registry of security interests, known as *international interests.*

The UNIDROIT Convention on International Interests in Mobile Equipment ("Cape Town Convention"),[224] and the Protocol to the Convention on International Interests in Mobile Equipment on Matters Specific to Aircraft Equipment,[225] ratified so far by seventy-three countries,[226] establish this unified registry system.[227] From an institutional perspective, the Cape Town Convention and the Protocol establish the Registrar, as well as the Supervisory Authority that is charged, *inter alia*, with establishing administrative procedures, supervising the Registrar,

222 The overall number of flights relates to both domestic and international flights. G. Garfors, "Globetrotting Galore: 100,000 Flights a Day" (June 2, 2014), available at www.garfors.com/2014/06/100000-flights-day.html (accessed on March 1, 2018).

223 van Erp and Akkermans, *Cases on Property Law*, pp. 1109–1110.

224 International Institute for the Unification of Private Law (UNIDROIT), Convention on International Interests in Mobile Equipment, November 16, 2001, 2307 UNTS 285.

225 Protocol to the Convention on International Interests in Mobile Equipment on Matters Specific to Aircraft Equipment, November 16, 2001, 2307 UNTS 517.

226 In some cases, the Cape Town Convention has been ratified but has not yet gone into force in that state. For the current status of the Cape Town Convention, see UNIDROIT, "Convention on International Interests in Mobile Equipment," available at www.unidroit.org/status-2001capetown (accessed on March 1, 2018).

227 Additional Convention protocols on railway equipment and space assets are not yet in force. Sprankling, *International Law of Property*, p. 60.

setting fees to be charged for the services, and reporting to the contracting states.[228] The Cape Town Convention provides, therefore, the administrative institutional framework required to operate the international registry and to register the international interests.

At the same time, the Cape Town Convention does not establish a supranational court or another adjudicative body in charge with interpreting and applying the Convention , or with enforcing the international interests. In this aspect, the Convention's institutional structure is still fragmented.

Chapter 6 will look in more detail into the Cape Town Convention and the Protocol, and the ways in which international security interests are created, perfected, and enforced.[229] The analysis will show that the Cape Town Convention is truly innovative in its particular application of the supranationalism strategy for property law. It is the first global registry system for any form of property rights. In the sense of defining a genuine international property right, it is the most ambitious manifestation of the supranationalism strategy. In particular, the institutional facets of the Cape Town Convention show the prospects, but also the limits, of bypassing the national systems. The existence of the Registrar and the Supervising Authority allow for a truly universal registration of security interests and a single ranking of priorities of property interests to the underlying asset. At the same time, the lack of a supranational court or adjudicative body may allow for locally based arbitrage in interpreting the Cape Town Convention and its application. Moreover, the reliance of the Cape Town Convention's rules, regarding both jurisdiction and applicable law, on the domestic conflict of laws rules of the forum state allows for some uncertainty among the various stakeholders. This somewhat undermines the ability of the international registry of security interests in aircrafts to be truly detached from national rules.

2.4 Conclusion: Aligning Cross-Border Property Strategies with Institutions

Institutions play a key role in the ability of top-down or bottom-up forces to promote the various strategies for globalization. The challenge of establishing authorized and coordinated institutions is particularly acute in the case of property law. Property rights are based on an *in rem*

[228] Cape Town Convention, Art. 17.
[229] See Chapter 6, Section 6.3.4.

principle, which should optimally provide a single ranking of property interests for different types of assets through structural and legal features, such as some version of a closed list principle, registries and other forms of publicity, and principles for prioritization of certain interests over others.

In a global context, this feature of property law requires a cross-border legal ordering by an array of domestic and supranational institutions: legislative, administrative, and adjudicative.

Whereas soft law instruments or a conflict of laws strategy may not require binding supranational institutions, the establishment of such bodies may prove critical for an approximation strategy, and even more so for a supranationalism strategy. Currently, the framework of such supranational institutions is still fragmented and incomplete, and this in turn entails challenges for the ability of bottom-up or top-down forces to move closer to a supranational ordering in various contexts of property law. The following chapters will discuss these institutional aspects for different types of assets, while resorting to the other methodological principles guiding this book: quantitative versus qualitative analysis; interdisciplinary approach; and the normative-functional trade-off.

3

Land

3.1 Cross-Border Land Deals: Global Market or Land Grabbing?

Since the beginning of the twenty-first century, and especially the 2007–2008 steep increase in food prices, an unprecedented wave of large-scale land transactions has been taking place in developing countries rich in arable lands, mostly in Africa, Latin America, and parts of Asia. Investors, both public and private entities, come mostly from capital-rich countries in the West, Gulf States, and emerging economies with fast-growing populations – and consequently, with rapidly increasing needs for food and sources of energy – such as China, India, and South Korea.[1]

Statistics are often hard to compile because many of these deals are kept private by both investors and host countries. Critics attribute this to the fact that many of the host countries are plagued by weak governance, poor records of formally recognizing rural or tribal land tenure, and lack of accountability and access to information, often resulting in alleged cases of corruption.[2] *Land Matrix*, an independent initiative led by the International Land Coalition, presents data, as of early 2018, about more than 50 million hectares in which land deals have been concluded, more than 20 million hectares for which negotiations are currently underway, and nearly 8 million hectares in which negotiations failed. Four of the top-ten target countries for concluded deals are located in Africa. The Democratic Republic of Congo (DRC) leads the list with recorded cross-border deals in more than 7 million hectares. Other developing or transitional economies are also featured prominently, such as the second-ranked Papua New Guinea (with recorded deals in nearly 3.8

[1] S. Narula, "The Global Land Rush: Markets, Rights, and the Politics of Food," *Stanford Journal of International Law*, 49 (2013), pp. 101–175.

[2] S. Borras, Jr. and J. Franco, "Global Land Grabbing and Trajectories of Agrarian Change: A Preliminary Analysis," *Journal of Agrarian Change*, 12 (2012), pp. 34–59.

million hectares). The United States leads the top-ten investor list, followed by Malaysia, Singapore, China, Brazil, and Arab Emirates.[3] These figures correlate roughly with earlier estimates made by the World Bank, according to which in the period between 2010 and 2011, foreign investors expressed interest in around 56 million hectares globally, with over half of it (29 million hectares) located in sub-Saharan Africa.[4]

This intriguing phenomenon, explored further below, highlights the unique challenges that land law faces in an age that increasingly defies physical and legal borders. Studied together with other major developments surveyed in this chapter, the influx of cross-border mega land deals requires a comprehensive inquiry, based on the methodological principles set out in the Introduction. These cross-border land deals therefore mandate an analysis of quantitative and qualitative parameters pertaining to them; an interdisciplinary account of the social, economic, and cultural factors that drive or, rather, seek to hinder these deals; the role of legislative, regulatory, and judicial institutions in guiding these cross-border transfer mechanisms; and the trade-off between functional and normative considerations in evaluating whether such land deals should be governed by national law principles or, alternatively, by a supranational body of property norms.

Looking more closely at such cross-border mega land deals, the first point to be explored is one of identifying the drivers of this phenomenon, and whether these indicators point to the emergence of a genuine global market or, rather, to "land grabbing" in the guise of market mechanisms.[5]

Food supply is one such driver. Triggered to a large extent by the above-mentioned food price boom, import-dependent countries such as the Gulf States, China, and South Korea are looking to control supply and prices more directly by taking control of agricultural lands in Africa and elsewhere.[6] Moreover, the World Bank, responding to social unrest

[3] Land Matrix, The Online Public Database on Land Deals, available at http://landmatrix.org/en/ (accessed on March 1, 2018).

[4] World Bank, "Rising Global Interest in Farmland: Can It Yield Sustainable and Equitable Benefits?" (2011), available at http://siteresources.worldbank.org/INTARD/Resources/ESW_Sept7_final_final.pdf (accessed on March 1, 2018).

[5] Transnational Institute, "The Global Land Grab: A Primer" (2013), pp. 2–3, available at http://reliefweb.int/sites/reliefweb.int/files/resources/landgrabbingprimer.pdf (accessed on March 1, 2018).

[6] L. Brilmayer and W. J. Moon, "Regulating Land Grabs: Social Activism, Third Party States, and International Law," in N. C. S Lambek et al. (eds.), *Rethinking Food Systems: Structural Challenges, New Strategies and the Law* (Heidelberg, New York, London: Springer, 2014), pp. 123–146. See also J. Wigginton, "Large-Scale Land Investment in

across many countries because of the food price crisis, seeks to encourage foreign direct investment (FDI) in agriculture so as to provide capital and technical expertise to developing countries and works with host governments to provide a more hospitable regulatory climate for FDI. As a result, both foreign government subsidiaries and private investors – including institutional investors who viewed this type of investment as relatively safe in the aftermath of the 2007 global financial crisis – are increasingly pursuing long-term deals for agricultural lands.[7]

Biofuel is another major driving force for massive foreign investment in lands. Seeking to generate alternative sources of energy due to the volatility of oil prices, and often required to do so by governmental policies mandating the blending of agro-fuel in petrol and diesel fuels in the United States and the European Union, corporations increasingly look to produce biofuels.[8] Moreover, recent years have seen the emergence of flex crops – crops such as soya, sugarcane, oil palm, and corn, which have multiple uses (food, animal feed, fuel, industrial materials) and can be quite feasibly interchanged.[9] In fact, the majority of agricultural land which is the object of these cross-border mega deals currently serves for flex crops or multiple agricultural uses.[10]

A related driving force for the massive foreign investment in agricultural and forest land is the global and regional set of policies aimed at responding to gas emissions and climate change. In addition to the advancement of biofuels and other forms of green or carbon-neutral energies, the Kyoto Protocol's Clean Development Mechanism (CDM) incentivizes corporations in Western countries to meet their emission-reduction compliance requirements by planting forests in developing countries, further driving demand for large-scale land acquisitions.[11]

Other reasons prompting massive foreign investment in land include demand for timber and other raw materials, mineral extraction,

Africa: An Issue of Self-Help and Self-Determination," *UC Davis Journal of International Law and Policy*, 20 (2013), pp. 105–138.

[7] D. S. Bettwy, "The Human Rights and Wrongs of Foreign Direct Investment: Addressing the Need for an Analytical Framework," *Richmond Journal of Global Law and Business*, 11 (2012), pp. 239–272.

[8] S. Smis, D. Cambou, and G. Ngende, "The Question of Land Grab in Africa and the Indigenous Peoples' Right to Traditional Lands, Territories and Resources," *Loyola of Los Angeles International and Comparative Law Review*, 35 (2013), pp. 493–535.

[9] Transnational Institute, "The Global Land Grab," pp. 17–19.

[10] Land Matrix, "Agricultural Drivers," available at http://landmatrix.org/en/get-the-idea/agricultural-drivers/ (accessed on March 1, 2018).

[11] Narula, "Global Land Rush," pp. 106–112.

industrial development, and tourism.[12] Finally, mere land speculation cannot be ruled out as a driving force for the acquisition of millions of hectares of land across the developing world.[13] Consequently, critics of these transactions argue that the harvesting of such "cash crops" comes clearly at the expense of the residents of developing countries, and rural communities in particular, with foreign investors and self-serving host governments aligning to benefit from such speculation.[14] Some authors go further to tie land grabbing to a broader ambition by capital-rich governments and corporations for control grabbing over an entire array of resources in the developing world.[15] Interestingly, this discourse about neocolonialism is not limited to critical studies by scholars or human rights groups. In a visit to Africa in June 2011, then US Secretary of State Hillary Clinton warned Africa against Chinese "new colonialism" in the continent.[16] Reports indeed attest to growing uneasiness of host governments with Chinese investments, work practices, and dominance in trade and infrastructure projects, including in Brazil – itself one of the Southern countries that increasingly invest in land and natural resources abroad.[17] A 2016 report by *The Economist* goes further to suggest that Chinese investment in Africa is practically conditioned on host countries voting with China in international forums, thus having to yield a core attribute of their sovereignty.[18] At the same time, Western investors are also criticized for similar practices. For example, media reports show how the signing of a fifty-year lease on 40,000 hectares in Sierra Leone to a Swiss company to grow biofuels for Europe has left the local farmers of Makeni with loss of control over the land, only fifty new jobs, and severe damages to nearby swampland.[19] Moreover, one should also note that in many countries, such as in Russia or across Latin America, "land grabs"

[12] W. Anseeuw et al., "Transnational Land Deals for Agriculture in the Global South" (2012), available at www.landcoalition.org/sites/default/files/publication/1254/Analytical%20Report%20Web.pdf (accessed on March 1, 2018).

[13] O. De Schutter, "The Green Rush: The Global Race for Farmland and the Rights of Land Users," *Harvard International Law Journal*, 52 (2011), pp. 503–559.

[14] Anseeuw et al., "Transnational Land Deals," pp. 26–29; Wigginton, "Large-Scale Land Investment," pp. 107–108.

[15] Transnational Institute, "Global Land Grab," p. 3.

[16] "Clinton Warns against 'New Colonialism' in Africa," *Reuters*, June 11, 2011.

[17] A. Barrionuevo, "China's Farming Pursuits Make Brazil Uneasy," *The New York Times*, May 27, 2011.

[18] "A Despot's Guide to Foreign Aid: Want More Money? Vote with China in the United Nations," *The Economist*, April 16, 2016.

[19] "When Others Are Grabbing Their Land," *The Economist*, May 5, 2011.

may be carried out chiefly by powerful domestic or intraregional economic actors, who collaborate with the government at the expense of disenfranchised stakeholders in their home country/region.[20]

The debate about the benefits and harms of these cross-border land deals is lingering, involving different international institutions and agencies with diverse views on the matter. On the one hand, the World Bank and affiliated bodies may be viewed as supporting a *market-plus* approach to land.[21] This approach views agricultural land as a resource that could be used more productively through capital investment, technology, and human capital that is located outside of the host country. It sees the formalization of property rights in land as essential for both increasing the security of tenure and enabling efficient allocation.[22] This approach identifies the potential local benefits of cross-border land commodification in infrastructure development, increased tax revenues, creation of new jobs, advancement of human capital and technology, and attraction of other investments to the host country.[23] Being aware of potential social costs that may fall largely on local communities, the market-plus approach seeks to supplement such transactions with procedural and substantive guarantees that would respect existing rights of local communities, increase food security, and promote good governance and accountability.[24]

In many cases, however, the anticipated advantages have not yet come to fruition. Moreover, academic research, studies by nonprofit organizations, and media reports point to numerous problems, leading critics to deep skepticism about the cross-border commodification of land.

Probably most acute is the problem of displacement of tribal or rural communities whose customary use and tenure of the land are not formally entrenched in the local legal system. The host government's interest in luring foreign investment may often cause it to evict or

[20] S. M. Borras, Jr., et al., "'Land Grabbing in Latin America and the Caribbean," in B. White et al. (eds.), *The New Enclosures: Critical Perspectives on Corporate Land Deals* (London and New York: Routledge, 2013), pp. 1–30. See also O. Visser, N. Mamonova, and M. Spoor, "Oligarchs, Megafarms and Land Reserves: Understanding Land Grabbing in Russia," *in* B. White et al. (eds.), *The New Enclosures: Critical Perspectives on Corporate Land Deals* (London and New York: Routledge, 2013), pp. 281–314.

[21] Narula, "Global Land Rush," pp. 121–123.

[22] World Bank, "Rising Global Interest in Farmland," pp. 102–104.

[23] L. Cotula, *The Great African Land Grab? Agricultural Investments and the Global Food System* (London: Zen Books, 2013).

[24] World Bank, "Rising Global Interest," pp. 102–104, 139.

otherwise disregard the local farmers' interests, leading to decreased food, water, and tenure security for the latter.[25] The recent wave of transactions is far from implicating only idle lands: about forty-five percent of the deals target lands already in use by local farmers.[26] Moreover, even when interests of local communities are being considered, members may be undercompensated in the allocation of lands or other benefits, with compensation ending up in the hands of the local elite. Women are particularly vulnerable in this respect.[27]

More generally, the process of formalizing property rights to conform to Western-type titling systems, which has been strongly supported by organizations such as the World Bank and the International Monetary Fund, especially in the context of incentivizing FDI in land, is not clean of dilemmas. Studies on property rights reforms in sub-Saharan Africa, and other developing countries, point to political struggles, tensions between central governments and local communities, and other forms of governance crises.[28] Other writers focus on the often-hidden costs of formalization, including not only general concerns over social unrest or transition costs, but also the undermining of otherwise functioning informal mechanisms of tenure and resource use.[29] Such tension may be particularly acute when a property-rights reform ends up in an inefficient deadlock between the new formal regime and preexisting informal modes of control.[30]

Critics of cross-border land deals also point to other potential harms to domestic markets and ecosystems, loss of public revenue due to excessive tax exemptions and minimal lease fees, and lengthy delays in the materialization of the agricultural development.[31] The general approach taken by such commentators and organizations is a rights-based one, which looks to the control and use of lands as a way to prioritize the affirmative

25 De Schutter, "The Green Rush," pp. 508–519.

26 Anseeuw et al., "Transnational Land Deals," p. vii.

27 Wigginton, "Large-Scale Land Investment," pp. 112–114.

28 S. F. Joireman, *Where There Is No Government: Enforcing Property Rights in Common Law Africa* (Oxford: Oxford University Press, 2011); A. K. Onoma, *The Politics of Property Rights Institutions in Africa* (Cambridge, UK: Cambridge University Press, 2010).

29 M. Trebilcock and P. E. Veel, "Property Rights and Development: The Contingent Case for Formalization," *University of Pennsylvania Journal of International Law*, 30 (2008), pp. 397–481.

30 D. Fitzpatrick, "Evolution and Chaos in Property Rights Systems: The Third World Tragedy of Contested Resources," *Yale Law Journal*, 115 (2006), pp. 996–1048.

31 Anseeuw et al., "Transnational Land Deals," pp. ix–x.

fulfillment of human rights for local communities, including the rights to food, water, housing, health, and adequate standards of living.[32] This view is shared by some international agencies and office holders, such as the UN Special Rapporteur on the Right to Food. It manifests in a policy document entitled "Minimum Human Rights Principles Applicable to Large-Scale Land Acquisitions or Leases," setting forth eleven principles for such deals, including the enactment and enforcement of legislation that "safeguards the rights of host communities."[33] Thus, while not entirely antagonistic to cross-border land deals, the rights-based approach goes beyond the prevention of harms to local communities as compared with the *status quo ante* to require that all such transactions would affirmatively pursue the realization of human rights of local communities.[34]

This approach should also be viewed in the context of the broader debate in the international law literature about the potential identification of a universal human right to land. Advocates of this idea try to anchor it, inter alia, in current international instruments and guidelines addressing the right to food, the right against forceful evictions, and the right to security of tenure.[35]

The policy debate about the moral, economic, and societal consequences of cross-border land transactions is likely to continue in years to come. But regardless of the specific normative position that one takes, this state of events challenges the traditional tenets of land law. As the following sections show, institutions on both the national and supranational levels must reevaluate the tension between overlapping, and at times conflicting, sets of land law norms. One such aspect has to do with the disparity between customary tenure regimes and formally registered rights in view of the mass reallocations of land in such large-scale transactions, especially when such potential conflicts implicate supranational legal instruments or international law norms, including relevant human rights provisions. Further, the dramatically growing presence of nonlocal stakeholders in land, mostly private and public investors

[32] Narula, "Global Land Rush," pp. 124–127.

[33] Special Rapporteur on the Right to Food, Addendum to Report of the Special Rapporteur on the Right to Food, "Large-scale Land Acquisitions and Leases: A Set of Minimum Principles and Measures to Address the Human Rights Challenge" (2009), UN Doc. A/HRC/13/33/add.2.

[34] De Schutter, "The Green Rush," pp. 548–556.

[35] J. G. Sprankling, *The International Law of Property* (Oxford: Oxford University Press, 2014), pp. 123–132.

alongside credit institutions, introduces yet another set of legal instruments and norms that may not simply adhere to the traditional rule of *lex rei sitae*. Such provisions, from bilateral investment treaties designated to protect the interests of foreign investors, to other supranational instruments such as those applying in the European Union, may implicate the various stakeholders and their respective legal interests in the same piece of land.

3.2 Land Law as a National Construct

Chapter 1 identified the key reasons why property law has a longstanding domestic nature, and why differences among legal systems linger despite exogenous pressures toward globalization.[36] Land law has a particular place in this context. Therefore, prior to engaging in the current cross-border challenges of land law, it is essential to underscore the conventional local features of land law, and to emphasize why an interdisciplinary account, connecting politics, economics, culture and law, is essential to identify the core traits of national land systems. In fact, disregarding the municipal essence of land law is liable to undermine the feasibility of institutional and normative endeavors of shoring up legal systems to the growing pressures of globalization. This section presents a few examples of how local land laws across the world have been reflecting political, economic, and cultural features of societies, and how land law systems are responding to short- or long-term changes along these various dimensions.

The control of land and the socio-political construction of communities and nations have traditionally gone hand in hand. For many centuries, land was considered not only the most essential source of independent economic livelihood, but moreover a chief indicator of a person's social and political status.[37] A vivid illustration of this interconnectivity is the evolution of the land tenure system in England. As Pollock and Maitland suggest in their *History of English Law*: "[i]n so far as feudalism is mere property law, England is of all countries the most perfectly feudalized."[38] Indeed, one cannot truly understand the way land

[36] See Chapter 1, Sections 1.3–1.4.

[37] C. M. Rose, "Property as the Keystone Right?," *Notre Dame Law Review*, 71 (1996), pp. 329–365.

[38] F. Pollock and F. W. Maitland, *The History of English Law before the Time of Edward I*, 2d ed., Vol. I. (Cambridge, UK: Cambridge University Press, 1899), p. 235.

law has evolved in England since the Norman Conquest without coming to terms with the socio-political developments in this country from that time onwards.[39] In modern times, the changing landscape of land law in England has both reflected and exacerbated the centralization of political power, shifting focus from the family to the individual as the subject of law, and expansion of the market economy.[40]

Contemporary illustrations of the dynamic ties between the design of land law and a nation's political, economic, and social characteristics are abundant. Consider, for example, the way in which land tenure systems were transformed in the former Soviet republics and in Central and Eastern European countries in the aftermath of the collapse of the Soviet bloc. Notably, each such country followed a different path in its transition from a socialist society to some type of a market economy and a corresponding legal system, touching on both public law and private law aspects. These differences reflect both geopolitical decisions (e.g., whether to seek admission to the European Union, as was the case with some Central and Eastern European countries); economic features (with Russia and the Ukraine originally seeking to reform their private law systems mainly to attract domestic and foreign investments); and moral attitudes (such as the decision of most Caucasus and Central Asian republics to combine European legal models with traditional law – in many cases, Islamic law).[41] These differences find particular expression in these countries' respective land laws. Whereas some countries, including Russia and Ukraine, gradually recognized and validated private ownership,[42] other countries followed a different path, reflecting their distinctive ideological stance. Thus, for example, Tajikistan and Uzbekistan retained full state ownership of land in their state constitutions.[43]

39 K. Gray and S. F. Gray, *Elements of Land Law*, 5th ed. (Oxford: Oxford University Press, 2009); T. F. T. Plucknett, *A Concise History of the Common Law*, 5th ed. (Boston: Little, Brown, 1956), pp. 506–623.

40 A. Lehavi, "The Global Law of the Land," *University of Colorado Law Review*, 81 (2010), pp. 425–471.

41 P. Cserne, "The Recodification of Private Law in Central and Eastern Europe," in P. Larousche and P. Cserne (eds.), *National Legal Systems and Globalization: New Role, Continuing Relevance* (The Hague: T. M. C. Asser Press, 2013), pp. 45–88.

42 This is not to say that the formal switch to a private property regime may not have been abused by the Russian government to promote the financial interests of political allies. K. Davisha, *Putin's Kleptocracy: Who Owns Russia?* (New York: Simon & Schuster, 2015).

43 Z. Lerman, C. Csaki, and G. Feder, *Agriculture in Transition: Land Policies and Evolving Farm Structures in Post-Soviet Countries* (Oxford: Lexington Books, 2004).

As already noted in Chapter 1, South Africa presents another instance of land law that has changed dramatically as a result of its political and social restructuring.[44] In pledging to correct the wrongs of Apartheid and to create a more just and egalitarian society, South Africa focuses much attention on planning for a comprehensive land reform. The state's constitution and other government measures embrace an affirmative commitment to such a reform. This includes not only the restitution of lands to the pre-Apartheid stakeholders, but also measures such as a planned mass-scale expropriation of privately owned lands for the purpose of equitable wide-scale redistribution, and an explicit constitutional right to have "access to adequate housing."[45]

Accordingly, Section 25 of the 1996 South African Constitution explicitly considers, in the context of identifying the public interest that justifies expropriation of land, the "nation's commitment to land reform, and to reforms to bring about equitable access to all South Africa's natural resources." Moreover, in determining the compensation to be paid for such expropriation, the South African Constitution opts for a multifactor test, in which the market value is but one component, and that is aimed at achieving "an equitable balance between the public interest and the interests of those affected."[46] While courts have only recently started to systematically deal with compensation disputes over expropriation for land reform, there is already a heated debate about the desirable extent of using expropriation for land reform, the proper compensation to be paid, and the adequateness of referring to foreign constitutional property clauses.[47]

China provides yet another fascinating example of land law's embeddedness in political, economic, and cultural characteristics, alongside its response to changes along these features, including China's self-driven interest in adjusting its system to international developments.

Since the 1980s, the Chinese government has gradually embraced the concept of private property, entrenching it in distinctively Chinese yet significant ways in the state's constitution, legislation, and administrative

[44] See Chapter 1, Section 1.4.

[45] See, generally, A. J. Van der Walt, *Property in the Margins* (Portland, Oregon: Hart Publishing, 2009).

[46] Constitution of the Republic of South Africa No. 108 of 1996 (as amended), s. 25.

[47] J. Zimmerman, "Property on the Line: Is an Expropriation-Centered Land Reform Constitutionally Permissible?" *South African Law Journal*, 122 (2005), pp. 378–418.

regulations.[48] This process culminated in the enactment of the 2007 Property Law of the People's Republic of China.[49] This development should also be seen in conjunction with the 1999 enactment of the Uniform Contract Law.[50] The latter reform took place after decades in which contract law effectively did not exist in China as a private law field. It was motivated, at least partly, by the 1981 accession of China to the Convention on Contracts for the International Sale of Goods (CISG),[51] as well as by China's then-pending negotiations to join the World Trade Organization.[52]

In the context of urban land, China has introduced, as of 1994, a comprehensive national housing reform policy.[53] It moved to establish a planned market, one that retains the formal ownership of the land with the state, but creates and protects long-term property rights of individuals. Urban lands and real estate developments have thus become a market commodity, in which private interests and rights play a substantial role.[54] A key part of the housing reform has to do with employing privatization and commercialization in the housing market not only to shift much of the new development to the private sector, but also to

[48] M. D. Kielsgard and L. Chen, "The Emergence of Private Property Law in China and Its Impact on Human Rights," *Asian-Pacific Law and Policy Journal*, 96 (2013), pp. 94–134; M. Zhang, "From Public to Private: The Newly Enacted Chinese Property Law and the Protection of Property Rights in China," *Berkeley Business Law Journal*, 5 (2008), pp. 317–363.

[49] Property Rights Law of the People's Republic of China, promulgated by the National People's Congress, March 16, 2007, effective October 1, 2007, 2007 Standing Committee National People's Congress Gazette 291. An unofficial English version is available at www.lehmanlaw.com/resource-centre/laws-and-regulations/general/property-rightslaw-of-the-peoples-republic-of-china.html (accessed on March 1, 2018).

[50] Uniform Contract Law, promulgated by the National People's Congress, March 15, 1999, effective October 1, 1999. An unofficial English translation is available at www.novexcn.com/contract_law_99.html (accessed on March 1, 2018).

[51] United Nations Convention on Contracts for the International Sales of Goods, Art. 9(2), UN Doc. A/CONF.97/18, Annex I (1980), reprinted in 19 ILM 671.

[52] S. Han, "A Snapshot of Chinese Contract Law from an Historical and Comparative Perspective," in L. Chen and C. H. (Remco) von Rhee (eds.), *Towards a Chinese Civil Code: Comparative and Historical Perspectives* (Leiden: Martinus Nijhoff Publishers, 2012), pp. 235–256.

[53] J. Lee, "From Welfare Housing to Home Ownership: The Dilemma of China's Housing Reform," *Housing Studies*, 15 (2000), pp. 61–76.

[54] L. Chen and M. D. Kielsgard, "Evolving Property Rights in China: Patterns and Dynamics of Condominium Governance," *Chinese Journal of Comparative Law*, 2 (2014), pp. 21–42.

gradually relieve the government of the responsibility for maintaining and managing residential buildings that had been originally built by the state. Accordingly, in a series of government regulations promulgated in the early 2000s alongside scattered provisions in the 2007 Property Law, China created the legal infrastructure for condominiums and their internal governance and maintenance, chiefly through the establishment of homeowner associations.[55] In fact, condominiums now represent the main type of tenure in China's urban areas.[56]

These legal changes should be evaluated against yet another dramatic process that is currently taking place in China, and which is likely to influence land law's future trajectory. In 2014, China unveiled its first-ever official plan for urbanization. The plan views urbanization as a necessary step for modernization, one that would shift the focus of the Chinese economy from continued reliance on export to an expansion of domestic demand for products and services as an engine for "sustainable and healthy" growth.[57] The plan sets out an incredibly ambitious goal of moving 100 million villagers to cities, while also granting formal urban status (*hukou*) to another 100 million rural migrant workers already living in cities but hitherto denied access to public services such as schools and healthcare.[58] The dramatic change to China's land tenure system is thus tied to the introduction of condominiums and homeowner associations as the default organizational mechanism that facilitates urban living: both reforms should work together to meet the top-down plan for mass migration to cities. Land law is therefore tasked with responding to, and further mobilizing, an incredible social change.

The interconnectivity between social, economic, and political changes and land law also impacts the feasibility of promoting changes in domestic land law to accommodate changes related to cross-border transactions and the evolution of a global market. To the extent that the absorption and implementation of new legal norms require also a correlative shift in cultural traits that guide the ways in which people transact and collaborate with others, one must consider the fact that culture tends to be a

55 F. Wang, H. Yin, and Z. Zhou, "The Adoption of Bottom-Up Governance in China's Homeowner Associations," *Management and Organization Review*, 8 (2012), pp. 559–583.

56 L. Chen, *The Making of Chinese Condominium Law* (Antwerp: Intersentia, 2010).

57 Xhingua, "China Unveils Landmark Urbanization Plan," *People's Daily Online*, March 17, 2014.

58 I. Johnson, "China Releases Plan to Incorporate Farmers into Cities," *The New York Times*, March 18, 2014.

"slow-moving institution" as opposed to politics or law that can change more rapidly.[59] Accordingly, the challenge of reconstructing national land laws lies not only in motivating states to opt into supranational institutions and norms through top-down reforms, but also in facilitating grassroots absorption of such changes.

3.3 Land Law and Supranational Constitutionalism

The 1948 Universal Declaration of Human Rights includes in its Article 17 the right to property.[60] While the Declaration envisions the right to property as one which is vested in private actors and that could be asserted against the state, its nonbinding nature failed to contribute significantly to the development of supranational property norms, including in land law. Subsequent attempts to incorporate property clauses into binding universal treaties did not materialize.[61] Thus, a strong version of the supranationalism strategy, in the sense of a single universal norm, has never come to fruition in the context of property and land law in particular. What has emerged, however, is a number of regional human rights treaties that include the right to property and which have each facilitated some type of supranational constitutional jurisprudence on property, with land law playing a particularly dominant role. This section analyzes the supranational effects of the European Convention for the Protection of Human Rights and Fundamental Freedoms ("European Convention")[62] on national land laws, touching on both public law and private law aspects. Section 3.6, dealing with the interplay between national land laws, customary land tenures, and supranational human rights provisions, will discuss the role of the American Convention on Human Rights ("American Convention") in the context of land.[63]

As Chapter 2 showed, the evolution of the European Convention and the European Court of Human Rights (ECHR) is often depicted as one of

[59] G. Roland, "Understanding Institutional Change: Fast-Moving and Slow-Moving Institutions," *Nanjing Business Review*, 2 (2005), pp. 1–34.
[60] Universal Declaration of Human Rights, Art. 17, December 10, 1948, G.A. Res. 217 (III) A, UN Doc. A/RES/217(III).
[61] Sprankling, *International Law of Property*, pp. 9–11.
[62] Convention for the Protection of Human Rights and Fundamental Freedoms, November 4, 1950, 213 UNTS 221.
[63] Organization of American States, American Convention on Human Rights, November 22, 1969, OASTS No. 36, 1144 UNTS 143.

the most incredible phenomena in the history of international law.[64] While the original vision of the European Convention, enacted in the aftermath of the Second World War, was one of a pan-European safeguard against large-scale, flagrant violations of human rights, this concept changed over time. The ECHR began to develop a European bill of rights with regard to the types of civil-liberty issues regularly adjudicated by national courts, and many states amended their laws in response to ECHR rulings.[65] As Chapter 2 demonstrated, while the ECHR's approach initially focused on the procedural principle of the domestic quality of law principle, the Court's attitude changed in the 1982 *Sporrung* v. *Sweden*[66] and 1986 *James* v. *United Kingdom*[67] cases, in which the ECHR developed self-standing criteria of fair balance and proportionality for reviewing domestic legislation or regulation, criteria that now cover the entire array of rights under the European Convention. Importantly, both disputes arose in the context of land law. *Sporrung* dealt with the validity of an expropriation order for multiple land plots in central Stockholm; *James* with a statute in the United Kingdom that conferred on tenants residing in certain types of houses on long leases the right to purchase the freehold of the property from the owners at below market rates. Land law thus became the bellwether for the potential subjection of domestic law to the Convention's supranational norms.

This supranational set of standards, however, is far from creating a uniform blueprint for the domestic ordering of land law. As is the case throughout the ECHR jurisprudence, the review of national law is subject to the margin of appreciation principle. Briefly, this doctrine goes beyond the general deference that courts award to legislative or administrative bodies in reviewing their actions, tying it to the European Convention's subsidiarity principle that divides powers among supranational and national institutions.[68] In the property context, the argument for the margin of appreciation has relied on the need to defer to the "more democratically accountable national legislature in pursuing social, economic, and fiscal policies," assuming that "domestic authorities are better

[64] See Chapter 2, Section 2.3.4.2.

[65] See, generally, E. Bates, *The Evolution of the European Convention on Human Rights: From its Inception to the Creation of a Permanent Court* (Oxford: Oxford university Press, 2010).

[66] *Sporrong* v. *Sweden*, 52 Eur. Ct. H.R. (ser. A) (1982).

[67] *James* v. *United Kingdom*, 8 Eur. H.R. Rep. 123 (1986).

[68] J. A. Sweeney, *The European Court of Human Rights in the Post-Cold War Era: Universality in Transition* (Abingdon: Routledge, 2013).

placed to evaluate the complex and technical nature of such policies and their specific implementing measures."[69]

There is, however, a difference between the scope of the margin in cases said to implicate the "deprivation" of property under the European Convention's first paragraph of Article 1 of the First Protocol and those dealing with regulation that works to "control the use of property" under the second paragraph.[70] The first type of case is usually subject to a higher level of scrutiny in applying principles of fair balance and proportionality, such as in determining due compensation for the deprivation of property. This may be due to the fact that *deprivation* – i.e., permanent dispossession or compulsory transfer of title – is easier to identify, typically considered a more serious injury to property, and may be easier to quantify for purposes of the fair market value standard, even if this value does not account for the overall impact on the condemnee's economic security.[71] Thus, for example, between January 1992 and March 2003, 354 cases regarding expropriation of lands were filed against Turkey, more than 25 percent of all cases (1,357) submitted against Turkey to the ECHR during that period. The overwhelming majority of these cases dealt with the rate of compensation aimed at adjusting for inflation for the lengthy periods between the valuation of compensation and its actual payment. The ECHR intervened extensively, awarding overall damages amounting to nearly 20 million Euros. Subsequently, Turkey revised its domestic expropriation law.[72]

In contrast, in evaluating domestic regulation that controls the use of lands without expropriating it, the ECHR has granted states a particularly wide margin of appreciation to design an underlying policy, choose the most appropriate means to achieve such legitimate social ends, and

[69] Y. Arai-Takahashi, *The Margin of Appreciation Doctrine and the Principle of Proportionality in the Jurisprudence of the ECHR* (Antwerp: Intersentia, 2002).

[70] The first paragraph reads: "Every natural or legal person is entitled to the peaceful enjoyment of his possessions. No one shall be deprived of his possessions except in the public interest and subject to the conditions provided for by law and by the general principles of international law." The second paragraph states: "The preceding provisions shall not, however, in any way impair the right of a State to enforce such laws as it deems necessary to control the use of property in accordance with the general interest or to secure the payment of taxes or other contributions of penalties." European Convention, Article 1 of the First Protocol.

[71] T. Allen, "Compensation for Property under the European Convention on Human Rights," *Michigan Journal of International Law*, 28 (2007), pp. 287–335.

[72] T. Yomralioglu, B. Uzun, and R. Nisanci, "Land Valuation Issues of Expropriation Application in Turkey," *Land Reform*, 1 (2008), pp. 80–90.

evaluate the effects that such means have on property interests. This approach has been criticized as reducing the proportionality criterion to a minimum degree.[73]

The analysis so far has dealt with the European Convention's supranational effects on the public law aspects of land law, i.e. those dealing chiefly with vertical legal relations between the state and private parties, embedded in various forms of regulation and other top-down measures. In some cases, however, the ECHR addressed petitions that alleged a breach of Article 1 in what was essentially a private law dispute. Plaintiffs in such cases have sought to challenge the underlying legislatively or judicially created national land law that governs private legal relations.

A prominent example is *J. A. Pye (Oxford) Ltd* v. *United Kingdom*.[74] The case dealt with adverse possession of registered private land. The applicants, the land's former owners who had lost their case before the national courts, argued that the then-in-force English adverse possession law, based on the Land Registration Act of 1925, was in violation of Article 1. The ECHR's Section 4 Chamber ruled that the case did engage the first paragraph of Article 1, and that although English adverse possession law may be deemed as serving a genuine public interest, the interference with the registered owners' rights was disproportionate and thus in violation of Article 1. The Grand Chamber reversed. It noted that "the margin of appreciation available to the legislature in implementing social and economic policies should be a wide one" and that this deferential approach is "particularly true in cases such as the present one where what is at stake is a long-standing and complex area of law which regulates private law matters between individuals." Moreover, the Grand Chamber held that "it is characteristic of property that different countries regulate its use and transfer in a variety of ways. The relevant rules reflect social policies against the background of the local conception of the importance and role of property."[75]

A somewhat different approach has been taken by the ECHR in its 2012 *Lindheim* v. *Norway* decision.[76] The court reviewed a 2004 amendment to

[73] Arai-Takahashi, *Margin of Appreciation.*

[74] App. No. 44302/02, *J. A. Pye (Oxford) Ltd.* v. *United Kingdom* (ECHR, Grand Chamber, August 30, 2007), 46 Eur. Hum. R. Rep. 45 (2008).

[75] Ibid., para 74.

[76] Apps. Nos. 13321/08 and 2139/10, *Lindheim* v. *Norway* (ECHR, Fourth Section, October 22, 2012).

Norway's Ground Lease Act of 1975, which subjected the leasing of lands for permanent homes or holiday homes to special statutory regulation, entitling lessees to demand an unlimited extension of the contracts on the same conditions as applied previously once the agreed term of the lease has expired. The ECHR referred to its previous case law about "the margin of appreciation available to the legislature in implementing social and economic policies." But it nevertheless held that the statutory intervention in lease contracts, even if looking to address the growing pressure on real estate prices, placed its social and financial burden solely on the applicant lessors, not striking a "fair balance between the general interest of the community and the property rights of the applicants."[77]

What can be made of the overall effect of the European Convention on national land laws? On the one hand, the ECHR has been particularly careful in intervening with the private law aspects of land law doctrines, granting domestic lawmaking institutions a manifestly wide margin of appreciation in defining both the ends and the means set forth against the background of the local conception of the role of land law in allocating interpersonal property rights, duties, and powers.

On the other hand, The ECHR has found more room to intervene through its general doctrines of fair balance and proportionality in matters relating to both procedural adequacy of legislative or judicial actions and substantive forms of governmental power exerted against individuals. At the same time, going beyond a strict formalistic distinction between private law and public law, the ECHR more closely scrutinizes domestic land law doctrines that are practically exercised by private parties but driven by broader social justice or other redistributive considerations. This was the case with both the *James* v. *United Kingdom* and *Lindheim* v. *Norway* decisions, both of which dealt with a substantial realignment of landlord-tenant legal relations aimed at serving a broader housing policy reform, viewed by the ECHR as placing an essentially public burden on a distinctive group of landowners. However, the final results reached by the ECHR diverged. While the court intervened in the *Lindheim* case, in the earlier *James* case it legitimized the below-market rate reimbursement to landowners "designed to achieve greater social justice."[78]

[77] Ibid., para. 134.
[78] *James* v. *United Kingdom*, para. 54.

3.4 The European Union and Degrees of Land Law Synchronization

As noted in Chapter 2, the European Union, presently comprising twenty-eight Member States,[79] and featuring various EU-level institutions, is the most extensive transnational framework in the world, with the current Treaty on European Union (TEU),[80] Treaty on the Functioning of the European Union (TFEU),[81] and Charter of the Fundamental Rights of the European Union ("EU Charter")[82] covering more thematic ground than ever before.[83] At the same time, the EU still falls short of being a full-fledged federal entity, relying rather on a complex web of "competences" in various areas of activity, some of which being "exclusive" to EU institutions, others merely "supporting" those of national governments, and yet other competences "shared" by EU institutions and Member States.[84] To concisely illustrate the implications that EU law-making may have on national land laws, this section identifies the main areas of EU competences that implicate land law; the interplay between public law and private law aspects; and the distinction that has emerged between negative and positive harmonization, reflecting substantive differences of degree in the synchronization of national land law regimes.

To start with, consider the centrality of one of the items included in the "shared competences" list of Article 4(2) of the TFEU, that which addresses "the internal market." This concept, also known as the "four freedoms," is articulated in Article 26(2) of the TFEU, which reads: "[t]he internal market shall comprise an area without internal frontiers in which the free movement of goods, persons, services and capital is ensured in accordance with the provisions of this Treaty."

The Court of Justice of the European Union (CJEU) has invoked these guarantees to scrutinize national legislation limiting the acquisition of

[79] The count still includes the United Kingdom, which has not yet formally withdrawn from the EU following the results of the June 23, 2016, referendum in favor of leaving the EU.

[80] Consolidated Version of the Treaty on European Union, signed on December 13, 2007, OJ (C 326/13), October 26, 2012.

[81] Consolidated Version of the Treaty on the Functioning of the European Union, signed on December 13, 2007, OJ (C 326/47), October 26, 2012.

[82] Charter of Fundamental Rights of the European Union, approved on December 13, 2007, OJ (C 326/02), October 26, 2012.

[83] L. Pech, "The Institutional Development of the EU Post-Lisbon: A Case of Plus ça Change. . .?" in D. Ashiagbor, N. Countouris, and I. Lianos (eds.), *The European Union after the Treaty of Lisbon* (Cambridge, UK: Cambridge University Press, 2012), pp. 7–46 at 22–32.

[84] A. Rosas and L. Armati, *EU Constitutional Law: An Introduction*, 2d ed. (Oxford: Hart Publishing, 2012).

land within the internal market. In *Konle* v. *Republic of Austria*,[85] the CJEU invalidated an Austrian legislative provision by which foreigners wishing to purchase land in the Tyrol region had first to obtain administrative authorization. Konle, a German citizen, was denied such authorization by the Austrian court under a policy limiting the purchase of second homes in order to preserve the Alpine environment. The CJEU ruled that restrictions on cross-border land acquisition generally amount to restraints on the free movement of capital. As for the specific Austrian legislation, the Court ruled that while "the aims of securing land management and environmental protection are imperative requirements in the general interest," national legislation based on such aims must be applied in a nondiscriminatory manner. Furthermore, any such restrictions must also meet the test of proportionality. This means that such restrictions would be valid only when the regulatory aims are imperative and cannot be pursued by measures that are less restrictive,[86] a condition not met for this specific provision.

In a subsequent case, *Reisch* v. *Mayor of Salzburg*,[87] the CJEU reviewed a local law that, for certain types of transactions, required potential acquirers of land in Salzburg to declare, first, that they are nationals of Austria or another EU Member State, and second, that the land will be used as a principal residence or will meet a commercial need. Based on such a declaration, the local Austrian land commission would then issue a confirmation of the transaction but could refuse to do so if it had reason to suspect either that the land would not be used for the declared goal or that the transaction was otherwise inconsistent with the local law. The CJEU held that the applicant's status as an Austrian national did not make interpretation of EU law unnecessary, given the potential application of the law to residents of other Member States. It then invalidated the local ordinance, holding that the specific statutory scheme was cumbersome and not "strictly indispensable" to achieve the admittedly legitimate goal of preventing tourist colonies.

This is, of course, not to say that preemption of local land laws has become the convention under the negative harmonization jurisprudence of the CJEU – i.e., that which is tasked with guaranteeing that national laws would not disproportionately hinder the EU's "four freedoms."

[85] Case C-302/97, *Konle* v. *Republic of Austria*, June 1, 1999, 1999 E.C.R. I-3099.
[86] Ibid., para. 40.
[87] Joined Cases C-515, C-519–C-524 & C-526–C-540/99, *Reisch* v. *Bürgermeister der Landeshauptstadt Salzburg* (Court of Justice, Sixth Chamber, March 5, 2002), 2002 E.C.R. I-2157.

The powers of EU institutions, including those of the CJEU, are still governed by principles of conferral and subsidiarity operating in favor of Member States.[88] Moreover, one should also consider Article 345 of the TFEU, by which "[t]he Treaties shall in no way prejudice the rules in Member States governing the system of property ownership." A literal interpretation of this provision would suggest that property law, and land law in particular, lies entirely outside the competence of EU institutions, but the CJEU rejected this approach in the *Commission* v. *Kingdom of Belgium* case,[89] holding that Article 345 "does not have the effect of exempting the Member States' systems of property ownership from the fundamental rules of the Treaty." Notwithstanding this statement, the CJEU must still run a delicate balance between entrenching the four freedoms and respecting the authority of Member States to design land law and policy.

The other major setting in which the negative harmonization of property law, and land law in particular, plays out in the CJEU's review of domestic lawmaking is in the context of the EU Charter, which formally went into force in 2009 alongside the Lisbon Treaty. The EU Charter protects the right to property in Article 17.[90] The EU Charter is presently considered to apply only vertically – that is, to EU institutions or national lawmakers, but not to private actors.

At the same time, the application of the EU Charter to Member States is construed in a relatively broad manner. This means that the EU Charter would apply not only when states specifically act as agents of the Union in applying EU law, but also when the substance of the domestic law falls within the general scope of EU norms embodied in treaties, directives, and regulations.[91] According to Article 52(3) of the

[88] See, generally, P. Sparkes, *European Land Law* (Oxford: Hart Publishing, 2007); T. Tridimas, "Competence after Lisbon: The Elusive Search for Bright Lines," in D. Ashiagbor, N. Countouris, and I. Lianos (eds.), *The European Union after the Treaty of Lisbon* (Cambridge, UK: Cambridge University Press, 2012), pp. 47–76.

[89] Case C-503/99, *Commission* v. *Kingdom of Belgium* (Court of Justice, June 4, 2002), 2002 E.C.R. I-4809.

[90] Charter of Fundamental Rights of the European Union, Art. 17. It reads: "(1) Everyone has the right to own, use, dispose of and bequeath his or her lawfully acquired possessions. No one may be deprived of his or her possessions, except in the public interest and in the cases and under the conditions provided for by law, subject to fair compensation being paid in good time for their loss. The use of property may be regulated by law in so far as is necessary for the general interest; (2) Intellectual property shall be protected."

[91] P. P. Craig, "The Charter, the ECJ and National Courts," in D. Ashiagbor, N. Countouris, and I. Lianos (eds.), *The European Union after the Treaty of Lisbon* (Cambridge, UK: Cambridge University Press, 2012), pp. 78–108.

Charter, and an Explanatory Memorandum accompanying the Charter,[92] the right to property under the EU Charter is enumerated as one of the rights that correspond to the rights included in the European Convention. Under Article 52(3), such correspondence does not prevent EU law from "providing more extensive protection." It remains to be seen how the CJEU will develop its jurisprudence on land law in the context of the negative harmonization potentially derived from the supranational provisions of the Charter's Article 17.

Consider next the positive harmonization component, which refers to the scope and content of EU lawmaking – through regulations, directives, and other legislative acts – designated to affirmatively synchronize or at the least approximate national legal regimes. Leaving aside complex questions of the EU institutions' competence or authority to do so – as discussed briefly in Chapter 2 – one should ask which specific features of land law should be considered as particularly befitting, or even essential, for EU norms to more fully facilitate the internal market.

On the one hand, the geographical fixity of real estate makes the traditional *lex rei sitae* rule apparently appealing as a legal focal point, even in an age of cross-border land markets. In this respect, land law diverges from the law of movable goods. In the latter case, the physical movement of chattels across jurisdictions creates potential legal complications, implicating the *in rem* rights and duties of parties who may not be otherwise governed by contract and that *ex post facto* compete for priority over the movable asset, especially in cases of insolvency, good-faith purchase of stolen goods, etc. As Chapters 4 and 6 will show, for chattels, recognition of these legal complexities has resulted in certain practices of professional merchants, aimed at detaching the bulks of financial gains and risks of the cross-border flow of goods from the legal priorities over specific assets,[93] or in calls to introduce a European Security Right for movable goods.[94]

[92] Explanations Relating to the Charter of Fundamental Rights, 2007 OJ (C 303/17), December 14, 2007.

[93] See J. Dalhuisen, *Dalhuisen on Transnational, Comparative, Commercial, Financial and Trade Law, Vol. II: Contract and Movable Property Law* (Oxford: Hart, 2016), pp. 623–625.

[94] See E. M. Kieninger, "Introduction: Security Rights in Movable Property within the Common Market and the Approach of this Study," in E. M. Kieninger (ed.), *Security Rights in Movable Property in European Private Law* (Cambridge, UK: Cambridge University Press, 2009), pp. 6–37.

This is not to say, however, that cross-border land transactions within the EU do not result in legal frictions or in other institutional or financial obstacles that may hinder such a market. One such obstacle has to do with the information costs involved with becoming acquainted with a national system for registering titles and finding out which types of other interests may affect it. Title registration systems across Europe differ substantially, with many systems not excelling in being transparent to potential buyers.[95] The problem of information costs may justify at least some level of standardization,[96] although efforts to do so in land registries across the EU have so far not materialized.[97]

Issues of information costs and coordination in cross-border land transactions, which are particularly acute given the *in rem* nature of property rights, may affect not only buyers, but also lending institutions. Identifying this problem has led to discussions in Europe, going back several decades, about the introduction of a Eurohypothec – a common European mortgage.[98] The need for a unified system of mortgages for the real-estate market becomes more pressing not only quantitatively, but also qualitatively, due to the changing nature of the credit market. Moving away from the old paradigms of a single bank granting a customer a loan that is secured by a charge on a specific piece of real estate, financial institutions increasingly engage in practices of portfolio finance, syndication (both primary and secondary), and securitization of mortgage-based loans.[99]

Maintaining the *in rem* nature of security interests in land across a pan-European market, even when most actors are professional repeat-play institutions – while bearing in mind local tax and statutory liens and

[95] H. Ploeger and B. van Loenen, "The European Real Estate Market – Transparency, Security and Certainty through Registration by Eurotitle," in B. Akkermans, A. F. Salomons, and J. H. M. van Erp (eds.), *The Future of European Property Law* (Munich: Sellier, 2012), pp. 183–198.

[96] T. W. Merrill and H. E. Smith, "Optimal Standardization in the Law of Property: The Numerus Clausus Principle," *Yale Law Journal*, 110 (2000), pp. 1–70.

[97] See, generally, B. Arruñada, *Institutional Foundations of Impersonal Exchange: The Theory and Policy of Contractual Registries* (Chicago: University of Chicago Press, 2012).

[98] S. Nasarre-Aznar, "The Need for the Integration of the Mortgage Market in Europe," in B. Akkermans, A. F. Salomons, and J. H. M. van Erp (eds.), *The Future of European Property Law* (Munich: Sellier, 2012), pp. 79–121.

[99] O. Stöcker, "The Eurohypothec," in B. Akkermans, A. F. Salomons, and J. H. M. van Erp (eds.), *The Future of European Property Law* (Munich: Sellier, 2012), pp. 65–77. See also Chapter 6, Section 6.1.

diverse interests of private stakeholders – increasingly calls for a flexible, standardized system of mortgages, one that cannot simply fall back on the *lex rei sitae* rule. What this means is that a conflict of laws strategy cannot suffice in order to facilitate land transactions with an *in rem* effect within an internal market. To the extent that a straightforward supra-nationalism strategy (i.e., enacting a single EU regulation controlling all contractual and proprietary aspects of land systems) is impractical due to formal issues of competence or political pushback, then some type of an approximation strategy would be most likely needed to alleviate the information costs for the legal governance of lands within the internal market.

3.5 Bilateral Investment Treaties and Foreign Investment in Land

Another front that has put pressure on national land laws is the massive growth of foreign investment in real estate – even outside the context of alleged "land grabs" discussed in Section 3.1 – and the increasing reliance of foreign investors on bilateral investment treaties (BITs) and similar instruments as an additional layer of legal protection vis-à-vis host governments. As Chapter 2 showed, BITs are proving to be a significant force in the implementation of a supranationalism strategy for property norms, due to the focus of the term *investment* in BITs on protecting property rights and to the institutional role of independent arbitration tribunals.[100]

Land law matters have been clearly featured in such cases. In the oft-cited *Metalclad Corp.* v. *United Mexican States* case,[101] the plaintiff, a US corporation, received from the Mexican federal government a permit to construct a hazardous waste landfill in the city of Guadalcazar, but a few months after construction had begun, it was notified by the local government that a municipal permit was also required. Metalclad applied for a local permit, while at the same time completing construction of the landfill, but the application was denied by the local government. The governor of the state of San Luis Potosi then issued an Ecological Decree declaring a protected natural area that included the designated landfill site, permanently closing the project.

[100] See Chapter 2, Section 2.3.4.5.

[101] ICSID Case No. ARB(AF)/97/1, *Metalclad Corporation* v. *United Mexican States* (Award, August 30, 2000), reviewed by *United Mexican States* v. *Metalclad Corp.*, [2001] 2001 BCSC 664 (Canada).

The ICSID tribunal accepted the claimant's argument that it was denied "fair and equitable treatment" in view of the municipality's lack of authority to deny the permit on environmental grounds and its nontransparent conduct in the application proceedings. It further held that the denial amounts to indirect expropriation and the Ecological Decree results in full expropriation.

The British Columbia Supreme Court, reviewing the arbitration proceedings that had taken place in Canada, reversed the ICSID tribunal's ruling on the violation of the "fair and equitable treatment" standard, reasoning that an independent commitment of transparency cannot be read into Chapter 11 of the North American Free Trade Agreement (NAFTA).[102] It agreed, however, with the ICSID tribunal that the Ecological Decree amounts to an expropriation of the land.[103]

A 2015 ICSID decision, *Von Pezold* v. *Republic of Zimbabwe*,[104] highlights the complexity of the "full protection and security" standard in controlling land law and policy and underscores the intricate interface between state action and private action for purposes of BIT protection.

The case dealt with land policy reforms in Zimbabwe, aimed at "acquiring" land owned by white farmers and redistributing it to black Zimbabweans. One of the issues that arose was whether the acts of the "settlers" (or "war veterans"), who moved onto the claimants' land, could be attributed to the respondent government, and thus considered a violation by the government of the relevant BITs (the BITs with Germany and Switzerland, of which the claimants were nationals).

The claimants argued that the government actively encouraged and assisted the "settlers." The tribunal concluded, however, that Article 8 of the International Law Commission's Articles on Responsibility of States for Internationally Wrongful Acts (on Conduct Directed or Controlled by a State)[105] called for "direction and control" on the part of the government, a fact not sufficiently proven in this case.[106] However, the relevant state conduct – including the inaction of the police once approached by the landowners in response to the invasion by the "settlers," as opposed to the actions of the "settlers" themselves – was

[102] North American Free Trade Agreement, Ch. 11, December 17, 1992, 32 ILM 605 (1993).

[103] *Metalclad* v. *United Mexican States*, paras. 102–112.

[104] ICSID Case No. ARB/10/15, *Bernhard von Pezold and* v. *Republic of Zimbabwe* (Award, July 28, 2015).

[105] International Law Commission's Articles on Responsibility of States for Internationally Wrongful Acts (2001), UN Doc A/56/10.

[106] *Von Pezond* v. *Republic of Zimbabwe*, para. 448.

subsequently considered by the tribunal on the merits and ultimately found to be in breach of the applicable BITs.[107] Therefore, state *inaction* in enforcing property rights in land was considered sufficient to constitute a breach of the BIT.

What does this growing body of jurisprudence mean for the balance between domestic lawmaking and supranational norms in constructing and reforming land law? It seems that the sheer scope of arbitration proceedings, as well as numerous judgments awarded by tribunals, place increasing pressure on host governments. This growing body of jurisprudence does not formally follow a *stare decisis* principle and otherwise falls short of offering a single universal interpretation to key terms such as *expropriation* or *fair and equitable treatment*. But it does work to significantly scrutinize local land laws, alongside other areas of domestic legislation and regulation, at least to the extent of subjecting national laws to minimum extraterritorial standards of property protection. Moreover, the application of state action to inaction in the *Von Pezold v. Zimbabwe* case, if followed in subsequent cases, could serve to practically insert private law disputes into BIT jurisprudence, whenever the state, serving as umpire in private law disputes, fails to enforce BIT-protected property rights.

A recent development that may further place pressure on local land law, this time with Western countries being inherently on both sides of the equation, has to do with the advanced process of ratification of the Comprehensive Economic and Trade Agreement (CETA) between Canada and the European Union,[108] and the lingering (and largely secret) negotiations between the United States and the EU about the Transatlantic Trade and Investment Partnership (TTIP).[109] These two mechanisms are already creating much controversy, especially across the European Union, where opponents feel that the pacts are biased in favor

107 Ibid., paras. 592–596.

108 The negotiations between the parties were concluded in 2014. In July 2016, the European Commission adopted the resulting texts and proposed them to the Council of the EU. On September 21, 2017, CETA entered into force provisionally. CETA will fully enter into force only upon the completion of the national ratification process by all EU Member States. European Commission, "EU-Canada Comprehensive Economic and Trade Agreement (CETA)," available at http://ec.europa.eu/trade/policy/in-focus/ceta/ (accessed on March 1, 2018).

109 European Commission, "The Transatlantic Trade Investment Partnership: Making Trade Work for You," available at http://ec.europa.eu/trade/policy/in-focus/ttip/ (accessed on March 1, 2018).

of North American corporations, while undermining the ability of governments within Europe to make new policy choices.[110] The provisions of CETA (and most likely, those of TTIP) generally follow, in the part dealing with the protection of investments, the standards and terminology adopted by BITs (such as *fair and equitable treatment* and *indirect expropriation*) and are intended to eventually replace the eight existing BITs between Canada and EU Member States.[111] CETA seeks to balance between protecting investments and preserving a clear right for countries to engage in regulation. But it will eventually be up for the international arbitration panels to fine-tune, through interpretation of CETA's provisions, the extent to which a supranationalism strategy would come to control local lawmaking with regard to different types of assets, and land in particular.[112]

Finally, it should be noted that although BITs commit states to protecting present and future investments made, not all treaties necessarily include an affirmative obligation to liberalization of domestic markets, including, for that matter, fully opening up the real-estate market to foreign acquisitions. In this respect, BITs may still fall short of the internal-market essence of the EU. Interestingly, in the finalized version of CETA, while the agreement generally curtails the ability of Canada and the EU Member States to limit market access to investors of the other party, it is explicitly stated that a measure concerning "zoning and planning regulations affecting the development or use of land, or another analogous measure" would be considered as conforming with the parties' obligations under the agreement.[113] Therefore, while market access is the

[110] N. Dearden, "Think TTIP Is a Threat to Democracy? There's Another Trade Deal That Is Already Signed," *The Guardian*, May 30, 2016.

[111] European Commission, "CETA – Summary of the Final Negotiation Results," February 2016, pp. 11–12, available at http://trade.ec.europa.eu/doclib/docs/2014/december/tradoc_152982.pdf (accessed on March 1, 2018).

[112] For the potential implications of CETA on domestic land law and regulation, see F. Thiel, "The Comprehensive Economic and Trade Agreement between Canada and the European Union (CETA) and its Impact on Property and Zoning in Germany," in A. Lehavi (ed.), *100 Years of Zoning and the Future of Cities* (New York: Springer, 2018), pp. 151–173.

[113] European Commission, Annex to the Proposal for a Council Decision on the Conclusion of a Comprehensive Economic and Trade Agreement between Canada of the One Part, and the European Union and Its Member States, of the other Part, July 5, 2016, COM (2016) 443 Final, Section B, Article 8B, sub-para. 2(a), available at http://eur-lex.europa.eu/resource.html?uri=cellar:1fcbd7d1-4356-11e6-9c64-01aa75ed71a1.0001.02/DOC_2&format=PDF (accessed on March 1, 2018).

norm, some types of measures pertaining to the regulation of land remain fully within local discretion.

Moreover, legal restrictions on the acquisition of land by aliens have a substantial pedigree in many legal systems, including in highly industrialized, democratic nations.[114] These limits have been grounded not only in social and economic reasons (e.g., fear of rising prices or the undermining of agriculture) but also in security, national, and ethnic concerns – with such measures backed not only by domestic courts but also by international law.[115] While pressed by current trends of globalization, as well as by some international investment agreements, such rules have not necessarily lost currency and may even be currently introduced or reintroduced in response to the very same pressures, often deviating from the conventional North-South dynamics.

Thus, for example, in November 2014, an Australian parliamentary committee recommended strengthening rules on foreign investment in the country's booming real-estate market. Although the inquiry did not explicitly focus on investors from any particular country, wealthy buyers from mainland China have been largely blamed for "ramping up home prices" in Australian key cities.[116] Thus, the tension between global markets and land policy constantly takes on new dimensions, with clear implications for the choice of legal strategy for property norms: supranationalism, approximation, or reliance on the *lex rei sitae* rule as the traditionally prevailing conflict of laws rule for resolution of *in rem* conflicts concerning land.[117]

3.6 Traditional Land Tenure, Globalization, and the Human Rights Discourse

As noted in Section 3.1, in the context of the current debate about land grabs, one of the main challenges of land law in the age of globalization has to do with the need to accommodate traditional, often informal, land tenure systems to the country's official land law system and to further

[114] J. Weisman, "Restrictions on the Acquisition of Land by Aliens," *American Journal of Comparative Law*, 28 (1980), pp. 39–66.

[115] Sparkes, *European Land Law*, p. 64.

[116] "Australia Set to Tighten Rules for Foreign Property Buyers," *South China Morning Post*, November 28, 2014.

[117] S. van Erp, "*Lex Rei Sitae*: The Territorial Side of Classical Property Law," in C. Godt (ed.), *Regulatory Property Rights: The Transforming Notion of Property in Transnational Business Regulation* (Leiden and Boston: Brill Nijhoff, 2016), pp. 61–81.

coordinate such legal ordering with cross-border commitments resulting from international investment treaties, and the potential implication of human rights conventions.

In the context of indigenous and tribal groups, a growing body of international instruments has sought to address the question of entitlement to the possession and use of ancestral lands. The 1966 International Covenant on Economic, Social, and Cultural Rights[118] and 1966 International Covenant on Civil and Political Rights,[119] which both recognize the rights of all peoples to "freely dispose of their natural rights and resources," have been interpreted in subsequent instruments as protecting the land rights of indigenous and tribal peoples. The 1989 Convention Concerning Indigenous and Tribal Peoples in Independent Countries,[120] and 2007 UN Declaration on the Rights of Indigenous Peoples,[121] go further to explicitly recognize the right of indigenous peoples to own, use, develop, and control lands they had traditionally occupied.[122]

An intriguing example of the complex and multilayered features of land law, implicating tribal norms, domestic law, international investment commitments, and human rights provisions, is the petition filed by the Sawhoyamaxa Indigenous Community of the Enxet People to the Inter-American Commission on Human Rights, alleging that the government of Paraguay violated the American Convention on Human Rights, including the right to property.[123]

The tribe argued that the government had failed to complete its own initiative to recover part of the ancestral lands of the tribe of over 14,000 hectares in the Chaco region, even though Paraguayan constitutional law recognizes the right of indigenous peoples to preserve their way of life in their habitat and to protect the claimed lands. As a result, community members had to live in inhumane conditions, resulting in a number of deaths due to lack of food and medical care. The government contended

[118] G.A. Res. 2200A (XXI), International Covenant on Economic, Social and Cultural Rights, December 16, 1966, 993 UNTS 3.

[119] G.A. Res. 2200A (XXI), International Covenant on Civil and Political Rights, December 16, 1966, 999 UNTS 171.

[120] Convention concerning Indigenous and Tribal Peoples in Independent Countries, June 27, 1989, 1650 UNTS 383.

[121] United Nations Declaration on the Rights of Indigenous Peoples, September 13, 2007, UN GAR 61/295, UN Doc A/res61/295.

[122] Sprankling, *International Law of Property*, pp. 132–136.

[123] *Sawhoyamaxa Indigenous Community* v. *Paraguay*, 2006 Inter-Am. Ct. H.R. (ser. C.), No. 146, March 29, 2006.

that, although it was committed to solving the matter, the lands in question had been formally purchased by a German investor, who used the land for beef production. Consequently, the executive branch's efforts to expropriate the land had been met with staunch resistance by the legislature in view of the provisions of the 1993 BIT between Germany and Paraguay.

In March 2006, ruling in favor of the tribe, the Inter-American Court reasoned that the enforcement of bilateral investment treaties may not allow a state to infringe its obligations under the American Convention. As for the problem of conflicting rights to the land, the Court reasoned that although it is "not a domestic judicial authority with jurisdiction to decide disputes among private parties," it is nevertheless competent to "analyze whether the State ensured the human rights of the members of the Sawhoyamaxa Community." According to the Court, the government's recognition of the tribe's rights to traditional lands remains "meaningless in practice if the lands have not been physically . . . surrendered because the adequate domestic measures necessary to secure effective use and enjoyment of said right . . . are lacking."[124] The court ordered Paraguay to adopt measures to return the land to the Sawhoyamaxa Community.

In June 2014, after many delays, and two other rulings by the Inter-American Court in favor of indigenous tribes in Paraguay, President Horacio Cartes signed into law a bill that orders the expropriation of the land from the German owner and its return to the tribe.[125]

Considered a historic victory, and a tour de force of the Inter-American Court, the case nevertheless demonstrates the structural, institutional, and normative quandaries of land law in the age of globalization. It shows how private actors, corporations, states, and supranational bodies must carefully navigate through a highly fragmented system of norms and institutions, while still accounting for the inherent *in rem* nature of property rights in land. The concluding section highlights some of these challenges by invoking the methodological principles that guide this book and offers potential guidelines for choosing a legal strategy for land in a global setting.

124 Ibid., paras. 136–143.

125 G. Constantine, "Paraguay: Indigenous Community Records Rare Land Rights Victory," *Eye on Latin America*, June 20, 2014, available at https://eyeonlatinamerica.wordpress.com/2014/06/20/paraguay-indigenous-land-rights-victory/ (accessed on March 1, 2018).

3.7 Policy Analysis: Adopting Strategies for Land Law in a Global Setting

The *Sawhoyamaxa* case vividly illustrates the challenges of a multilayered land law scheme involving supranational, national, and subnational norms and institutions. This is so because it entails (1) an international human rights convention (American Convention) and a respective international tribunal; (2) a supranational investment treaty (Germany-Paraguay BIT) with its distinctive potential arbitration forum; (3) general provisions in Paraguay's constitution and national legislation about the recognition of traditional tribal rights and commitment to land restitution; (4) land law of Paraguay with its land titling system and the property rights that emanate from it; and (5) tribal norms, institutions, and practices of sub-society groups – all of which are tied up in this case to the same piece of land.

What is even more intriguing in this case is the lack of a clear-cut hierarchy among the different sets of norms applying in the matter. In fact, one could argue for a circular pattern (maybe even a vicious circle) that is driving the structure of legal norms, while constantly tilting the balance of legal interests back and forth among the different parties. Figure 3.1 illustrates this point.

To start with, national land law would regularly trump any nonconforming forms of subnational traditional land tenure (thus supporting the position of the investor, formally registered as owner). However, national constitutional law provisions, committed to land restitution, might supersede national land law, especially if constitutional rights are viewed as implicating also horizontal relations among persons and not only vertical ones (i.e., state v. persons). Then, the BIT, including commitments by the state against certain acts of expropriation, denial of fair and equitable treatment, and so on, may make the case in favor of the foreign investor, who would argue that these commitments should serve as a *lex specialis* in protecting the investment. Then, the American Convention on Human Rights is viewed by the court as prevailing, in case of conflict, over other commitments that the state has undertaken in a bilateral investment agreement – thus moving the pendulum again toward the side of the indigenous tribe in its conflict with the German landowner (even though the latter was not a formal party to the proceeding before the Inter-American Court, and Germany is obviously not a signatory to the American Convention). Moving one step further, the very recognition of the tribe's human right under the American

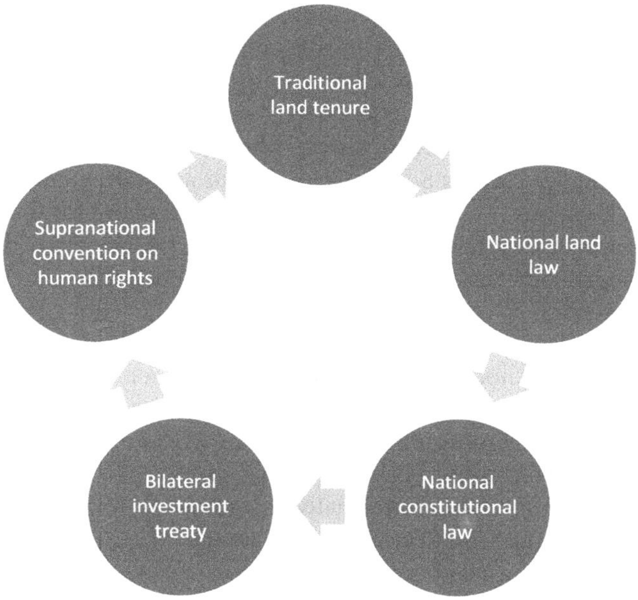

Figure 3.1 Structure of Land Law Layers in the *Sawhoyamaxa* Case

Convention by the Inter-American Court is based on the customary land tenure – the same subnational norm superseded by Paraguay's national land law – thus coming a full circle. The result is, therefore, one in which we encounter a multitude of legal norms that have no clear hierarchy among them, featuring a genuine normative fragmentation.

The difficulty incurred here is not only one of normative fragmentation, but also one of institutional incompleteness. Recall the Inter-American Court of Human Rights' statement, by which it is "not a domestic judicial authority with jurisdiction to decide disputes among private parties."[126] But when a court or tribunal decides on the superiority of some property rights or interests over others, granting them an *in rem* effect in regard to competing claims over the same asset, it cannot simply disregard the broader implications of its decision. Therefore, even though the Court is allegedly concerned only with the public law aspect, that is to say, constitutional or human rights aspect with respect to indigenous tribes, it in fact implicates also the private law aspect of the dispute and the entire array of *in rem* rights.

[126] *Sawhoyamaxa* case, para. 136.

Obviously, when a dispute concerning both public law and private law facets of land rights is argued before a national court in a pure domestic matter, the court cannot look selectively only at some of the legal norms that have a bearing on the case. Moreover, if a certain national constitution is understood as having also a "horizontal" dimension – as is the case in countries such as South Africa and to a lesser extent in jurisdictions like Germany[127] – the court would have to account for the entire set of legal norms that grant *in rem* priority to some parties over others. This is a responsibility that cannot be entirely avoided also in the supranational setting.

The Inter-American Court may have been absolutely sincere in its account that it is not a domestic court with power to decide a private dispute, but this is exactly the gap that is currently making property jurisprudence even more burdensome than it should be in a world of incomplete globalization. For a system of property to make any sense, even in the current state of normative fragmentation, courts and tribunals asked to decide in effect on *in rem* aspects of rights to land cannot simply overlook the existence of other legal norms that might govern the entire set of rights, powers, and priorities in regard to the asset. A state of events in which each judicial forum could simply disregard relevant norms as it chooses is not a viable legal strategy for land law (and property law more generally, as the following chapters will show in regard to other assets).

How to come up with an inter-institutional system of coordination is not an easy task, very much so because the respective legislative institutions – from national legislatures to collective bodies of counterparts to certain supranational conventions – are not themselves coordinated. This dilemma highlights the essential role of authorized and effective institutions in implementing a strategy chosen for the globalization of property, as Chapter 2 demonstrated in detail. One could theoretically think about some sort of a referral system, such as the process of *preliminary ruling* by the Court of Justice of the European Union in matters referred to it by national courts, whenever a domestic norm may find itself in conflict with EU conventions or legislation.[128] Until such a (formal or

[127] See, generally, G. A. Alexander, *The Global Debate Over Constitutional Property: Lessons for American Takings Jurisprudence* (Chicago: University of Chicago Press, 2006).

[128] See, generally, Court of Justice of the European Union, "Recommendations to National Courts in Relation to the Initiation of Preliminary Ruling Proceedings," OJ (C 338/1), November 6, 2012.

informal) system emerges, courts and tribunals must exercise particular caution in considering the potential implications of norms that might implicate the *in rem* setup of rights.

The analysis above leads to the following potential guidelines for legal strategies that should be employed in constructing, interpreting, and enforcing cross-border rights in regard to land:

a. At the most basic level, the conflict of laws strategy should continue to adhere to the general dominance of the *lex rei sitae* rule, governing both the jurisdiction that has power to adjudicate a conflict pertaining to *in rem* ordering of rights, powers, and priorities and the substantive law that would apply to the matter. The *lex rei sitae* continues to prove dominant not only because of mere legal path-dependence or logic, but also because it has cultural and political merit given the longtime affiliation between land and sovereignty.
b. The *lex rei sitae* should be, however, modified or at least more liberally interpreted, when the asset at stake and the legal regime that applies to it cannot be viewed in isolation from a broader normative or jurisdictional setting that a certain country is part of. As Sjef van Erp suggests, in the context of a cross-border dispute within the European Union, a better understanding of applying the *lex rei sitae* rule, at least in regard to the substantive law that should apply, could inherently relate also to the relevant body of EU law.[129] This means that even a private law dispute cannot entirely disregard the potential relevance of EU treaties or legislation, so that the process of referral or preliminary rulings should be consistently viewed as applying the *lex rei sitae* rule on both local and EU dimensions. A more ambitious, and probably politically charged move, would be to apply such a broad perspective on the *lex rei sitae* rule to other regional treaties, especially those based on free trade and movement of capital, such as under the NAFTA or Mercosur[130] treaties.

[129] van Erp, "*Lex Rei Sitae*," pp. 64–69.

[130] Mercosur was established as a regional trade zone in the Treaty of Asunción signed between Argentina, Brazil, Paraguay, and Uruguay in 1991. Article 1 of the Treaty provides that a Common Market shall be formed by the end of 1994. Treaty Establishing a Common Market, Art. 1, March 26, 1991, 1041 ILM. 1044. The Common Market was set up with the signature of the Ouro Preto Protocol in 1994. Mercosur has not resorted, however, to supranational institutions that create binding rules immediately enforceable in Member States. Instead, Mercosur's Member States (and associate countries) have opted for an institutional arrangement that relies heavily on the existence of functional domestic regulatory institutions. Commentators argue that Mercosur's reliance on

c. The approximation strategy could prove particularly useful when transaction costs or information costs are substantial, but a supranationalism strategy leading to a single set of norms is impracticable, due to international politics, lobby groups, or technical issues. Registries are a good example. It seems unlikely that we will move to a global registry of land anytime soon, for the above-mentioned reasons and others. A more practical solution could be to introduce a new treaty that would establish certain minimum standards for national registries, or at the least, a soft law mechanism of best practices, which will introduce at least some level of uniformity or common practices across jurisdictions.
d. The supranationalism strategy will continue to gain currency in land law via the constantly increasing number of supranational instruments, from property provisions in regional human rights treaties (such as the European Convention, EU Charter, and American Convention), and up to the nearly 3,500 international investment agreements, including both BITs and chapters on investment in bilateral and multilateral free-trade agreements. All such treaties have an explicit effect on the public law aspect of domestic land laws. This is so although the various supranational commitments may go in different, even conflicting routes, by which some of these instruments seek primarily to protect the interests of foreign investors, while other mechanisms look to protect members of vulnerable groups, as vividly demonstrated in the *Sawhoyamaxa* case. Such potential conflicts call, therefore, for the future development of property jurisprudence that goes beyond the need to resolve the already familiar tension between the alleged superiority of supranational norms and the margin of appreciation reserved to countries in making domestic land policy. Such conflicts also call for a body of jurisprudence that addresses the potential hierarchy – or another type of interrelation – among provisions across various supranational instruments.
e. The growing influence of the supranationalism strategy also necessitates the development of general principles about the effect of supranational property provisions on the private law aspect of land law. Importantly, a general statement by which such provisions are only meant to bind the relevant host government and not private parties

domestic institutions proves to be an obstacle to the harmonization process. M. M. Prado and V. Bertrand, "Regulatory Cooperation in Latin America: The Case of Mercosur," *Law and Contemporary Problems*, 78 (2015), pp. 205–230 at 208–209.

cannot truly resolve the inherent *in rem* implications that such supranational norms would practically have also on interested private parties. This peculiarity of property law, and land law in particular, calls for a normative policy that always takes into account the potential implications, even if indirect, on private parties. In many cases, such implications could lead supranational courts or tribunals to take a more restrained approach toward upsetting local land law. As demonstrated in the *J. A. Pye Oxford* case, analyzed in Section 3.3, the ECHR exercised particular caution in reviewing English land law when it implicated mostly private parties.

f. Against the backdrop of the constantly growing number of cross-border land transactions and supranational property provisions, on the one hand, and lack of a clear institutional hierarchy among different types of lawmakers, on the other, it is really up to courts and tribunals to do their best to alleviate the potential tensions rather than increasing them. While ideally, a global system of intercourt referrals, consultations, and coordination to deal with potential frictions among different sets of norms would have truly taken us forward in making sense of land law in a globalized context, there is much that can be done by individual courts and tribunals as a matter of judicial policy. To start with, obliviousness to the very existence of normative fragmentation is not a viable option for the judiciary. True, courts and tribunals may run the risk of overstepping their authority if they become too "inventive" in stretching the rules on party standing, evidentiary rules, and interpretation of legislative instruments in regard to which they have no formal capacity. At the very least, however, judges should pay attention to cases in which employing a treaty-specific supranational strategy would carry *in rem* effects for parties who are not represented. In some cases, such third-party effects may justify a renewed focus on the *lex rei sitae* as the overarching norm that governs the entire *in rem* structure of property rights in land.

4

Tangible Goods, Monetary Claims, and Investment Securities

4.1 The Challenge of Cross-Border Movement of Tangible and Intangible Goods

As an economic phenomenon, globalization is most clearly identified with the ever-increasing growth in the cross-border movement of goods (both tangible and intangible ones), services, and capital. The new global markets for trade, investment, and provision of services are driven largely by decentralized forces, such as individuals and corporations, and are impacted on both the demand and supply sides by macro- and micro-economic changes, technological developments (such as digital platforms), immigration patterns, cultural preferences, and many other considerations.[1]

Governments, on their end, play a central role in facilitating – or hindering – such global markets through their public-policy and law-making capacities, and by their willingness or lack thereof to collaborate at the international level to set common rules for the global economy. Thus, for example, the term *liberalization* is increasingly used to describe the willingness of a certain national government not only to open up a centrally operated or highly regulated domestic market, but even more, to enable international actors to invest, own, and control assets in its territory.[2]

At the international level, the World Trade Organization (WTO) is probably the most prominent intergovernmental mechanism that

[1] See, e.g., M. King, *The End of Alchemy: Money, Banking, and the Future of the Global Economy* (New York: W. W. Norton & Company, 2016), pp. 290–332 (studying the current features and drivers of the world economy).

[2] See United Nations Conference on Trade and Development (UNCTAD), "World Investment Report 2017: Investment and the Digital Economy" (2017), pp. 99–110 (discussing current trends in national investment policies, and specifically those relating to the "liberalization" of domestic markets for international investment), available at http://unctad.org/en/PublicationsLibrary/wir2017_en.pdf (accessed on March 1, 2018).

coordinates the regulatory and legal regimes concerning cross-border trade in goods and services. It serves as the main mechanism for dealing with tariffs, quantitative restrictions, standards of "national treatment" for domestic taxation, and so forth.[3]

This chapter focuses on the challenges that property law faces in view of the cross-border movement of various types of physical goods, intangible goods that represent monetary claims (such as receivables), negotiable instruments, and investment securities (such as stocks or bonds).

4.2 Current Scope of Cross-Border Transfer of Movable Assets

To get a general sense of the scope of cross-border movements of tangible and intangible goods, consider the following data. According to the World Bank, between 2005 and 2016, annual merchandise exports grew on a global scale from $10,580 billion to $16,055 billion, with manufactures (representing a broad plethora of physical assets, from manufactured goods for personal consumption to machinery and transport equipment) constituting 68.8% of the volume of cross-border exports. Fuels represented 12.7% of merchandise exports, food – 9.1%, ores and metals – 4.4%, and agricultural raw materials 1.5% in 2016.[4] Data by the European Commission shows that as of 2017, the EU's 28 Member States combined hold a 15.1% share of the world trade in goods, China has a 14.8% world share, and the United States a 14.4% share.[5]

As for international investment, the annual global inflows of foreign direct investment (FDI) rose from €284 billion in 2005 to €1,263 billion in 2015.[6] The global FDI inward stock (i.e., the overall value of foreign investment) grew from €4,977 billion to €15,184 billion during the same period.[7] This rate of growth is particularly significant because during the period between 2005 and 2015, world GDP grew from €40,982 billion to

[3] See, generally, H. B. Pauwelyn, A. T. Guzman, and J. A. Hillman, *International Trade Law*, 3d ed. (New York: Wolters Kluwer, 2016).
[4] World Bank, World Development Indicators, Economy, 4.4: Structure of Merchandise Exports (last updated on July 1, 2017), available at http://wdi.worldbank.org/tables (accessed on March 1, 2018).
[5] European Commission, "DG Trade Statistical Guide" (June 2017), Sect. 1, Share in World Trade of Goods, p. 20, available at http://trade.ec.europa.eu/doclib/docs/2013/may/tradoc_151348.pdf (accessed on March 1, 2018).
[6] Ibid., Sect. 2, Global FDI Inflows (billion EUR), p. 26.
[7] Ibid., Sect. 2, Global FDI Inward Stocks (billion EUR), p. 28.

€68,008 billion.[8] This means that the shifting of investment toward global markets grew at a relatively higher rate than the general growth of GDP, such that capital investments are increasingly international in nature.

The volume of cross-border movement of capital and financial assets is also manifested in the constant growth of multinational corporations' issuance of securities in foreign stock exchange markets. According to data by the World Federation of Exchanges, as of early 2018, foreign corporations are increasingly being listed in stock exchange markets across all five continents, with certain markets featuring a particularly dominant portion of foreign corporations.[9] In addition to the well familiar presence of foreign corporations in the New York Stock Exchange (NYSE) and Nasdaq in the United States,[10] or in the London Stock Exchange,[11] other stock exchange markets have also become attractive to international (or at least, regional) corporations. Thus, for example, as of January 2018, the Singapore Exchange trades in securities of 269 foreign corporations alongside 480 domestic ones; the Austrian Wiener Borse has 467 foreign companies listed versus 67 domestic ones; and Bolsa de Comercio de Santiago in Chile trades in securities of 81 foreign corporations alongside 214 domestic firms.[12]

The choice by a corporation to issue securities in a foreign exchange market as a substitute to the corporation's domestic market, or as a supplement to domestic listing (typically referred to as *cross-listing* or *dual-listing*), is inherently driven by a number of economic and financial considerations beyond the general trend toward globalization, such that empirical research points to "waves" in the scope and geography of foreign listing or cross-listing.[13] The 1990s saw more cross-listings than

[8] Ibid., Support Statistics, GDP (current price, billion EUR), p. 66.

[9] World Federation of Exchanges, Focus, Market Statistics – January 2018, "Listed Companies," available at www.world-exchanges.org/focus/index.php/in-every-issue/statistics/market-statistics/260-domestic-market-capitalisation-jan-18 (accessed on March 1, 2018).

[10] As of January 2018, NYSE trades in securities of 494 foreign corporations versus 1,797 domestic ones; Nasdaq has 404 foreign corporations versus 2,553 ones. Ibid.

[11] In the London Stock Exchange, as of February 28, 2018, 290 foreign corporations are traded versus 1,739 UK ones. London Stock Exchange, Statistics, "Companies and Securities," then "Company List," available at www.londonstockexchange.com/statistics/companies-and-issuers/companies-and-issuers.htm (accessed on March 1, 2018).

[12] World Federation of Exchanges, "Listed Companies."

[13] S. Sarkissian and M. J. Schill, "Cross-Listing Waves," *Journal of Financial and Quantitative Analysis*, 51 (2016), pp. 259–306.

the previous and subsequent decades.[14] Legal considerations, such as the extent of investor protection in the host jurisdiction, also play a major role in deciding on foreign listing.[15] This in mind, the data clearly points to a significant growth in foreign stock issuance over time.[16]

The cross-border nature of securities and other forms of stakeholding in business corporations goes well beyond the cross-listing of firms in foreign exchange markets, or the setting up of private (nonlisted) affiliate corporations in foreign countries to enable business activities in these jurisdictions. As a 2016 report by UNCTAD shows, firms, and particularly affiliates of multinational corporations (MNCs), are increasingly controlled by hierarchal webs of ownership involving a multitude of entities. More than forty percent of foreign affiliates are owned through complex chains with multiple cross-border links involving on average three jurisdictions.[17] Such schemes are driven by a number of considerations, most prominently tax benefits (especially in offshore financial centers), and the pursuit of favorable regulation on corporate governance.[18]

In addition, this cross-border forum shopping is also driven by the pursuit of increased investor protection by registering in countries that are signatories to a broad array of international investment agreements (IIAs) or free-trade agreements (FTAs) with an investment chapter. Investors registering in such host countries seek to enjoy the benefits that nationals of these countries enjoy in making investments abroad. Thus, for example, a 2015 UNCTAD study, commissioned by the Dutch Ministry of Foreign Affairs, shows how Dutch companies are disproportionately represented as claimants in investor-state dispute settlement (ISDS) cases, which implicate BITs and other treaties to which the Netherlands is a counterpart.[19] Cases initiated by Dutch companies represent ten percent of the global number of known ISDS cases and

[14] Ibid., pp. 265–268.

[15] N. Fernandes and M. Giannetti, "On the Fortunes of Stock Exchanges and Reversals: Evidence from Foreign Listings," *Journal of Financial Intermediation*, 23 (2014), pp. 157–176.

[16] Ibid., pp. 163–168.

[17] UNCTAD, "World Investment Report 2016 – Investor Nationality: Policy Challenges," p. 124, available at http://unctad.org/en/pages/PublicationWebflyer.aspx?publicationid=1555 (accessed on March 1, 2018).

[18] Ibid.

[19] UNCTAD, "Treaty-Based ISDS Cases Brought under Dutch IIAs: An Overview" (June 30, 2015), p. 1, available at http://investmentpolicyhub.unctad.org/Publications/Details/135 (accessed on March 1, 2018).

account for twenty percent of claims filed by investors from the EU. However, in around three-quarters of Dutch cases, the ultimate owners of the claimant corporations are not Dutch. In two-thirds of these cases, the relevant foreign-owned group of companies does not appear to engage in substantial business activities in the Netherlands.[20] This means that investors strategically register companies in the Netherlands to enjoy the improved protection of property rights that Dutch investors enjoy through BITs and FTAs to which the Netherlands is a party. From a legal perspective, this practice highlights the complexity of identifying an investor's "true" nationality. From an economic perspective, this state of events shows that the scope of cross-border movement of capital and intangible assets exceeds the mere issuance of securities in foreign markets or the purchase thereof.

Other types of financial assets, such as monetary claims, are also increasingly the object of cross-border movements. Such transfers of financial assets involve not only the original parties to the transaction (thus chiefly implicating contractual issues), but also third-party stakeholders, such as assignees of the monetary claims, parties holding a security interest in the monetary claim (e.g., when a creditor of a monetary claim due at a future date uses it as collateral for credit he or she currently receives from a financial institution), or tax authorities that demand legal priority to financial assets upon default. Financial assets thus have also a cross-border proprietary aspect.

To get a sense of the scope of cross-border movements of financial assets, consider the following data by the Bank of International Settlements (BIS), an international financial organization owned by more than sixty central banks, representing countries that together make up ninety-five percent of the world GDP.[21] In particular, the locational bank statistics (LBS) of BIS provides information about the currency composition of bank balances and the geographical boundaries of their counterparties. Banking offices located in 46 countries report the LBS, capturing outstanding claims and liabilities of internationally active banks in these countries vis-à-vis counterparties residing in more than 200 countries, and reflecting around ninety-three percent of all cross-border interbank

[20] Ibid.

[21] Bank of International Settlements, "About the BIS – Overview," available at www.bis.org/about/index.htm?m=1%7C1 (accessed on March 1, 2018).

business in the world.[22] As of end-June 2017, cross-border positions[23] in claims across all banks stand at $28,285 billion, out of which $19,153 billion comprise loan instruments, $5,988 billion – debt securities, and $3,144 billion – other/unallocated instruments.[24] The international counterparts come from both the bank sector (i.e., banks in other countries – $15,067 billion in total claims) and nonbank sector (referring collectively to the nonbank financial sector, nonfinancial corporations, general government, and households – $12,772 billion).[25]

Interestingly, the growth of the digital economy has diverse effects on the scope and nature of the cross-border transfer of goods, including physical and intangible ones. According to a 2017 report by UNCTAD, digitization tends to break the operational nexus between foreign sales and foreign assets, and as the following paragraphs will show, this has obvious implications for cross-border property law issues, as well as for other legal issues, such as taxation of MNCs.[26]

To explain the particular international footprint of the digital economy vis-à-vis other types of business and industry, the UNCTAD report divides digital MNCs into two groups: *purely digital actors* (including both internet platforms, such as search engines or social networks, and digital solutions, such as digital payment operators and cloud players), and *mixed digital players* that combine a prominent digital dimension with a physical one (including both e-commerce, such as Internet retailers and online travel agencies, and providers of digital content, which produce and distribute goods such as music or movies in digital format).[27] Digital MNCs are then compared to MNCs dealing with information and communications technology (ICT) – which are in turn composed of information technology (IT) or tech companies, such as manufactures of hardware or software developers, and telecom

[22] Bank for International Settlements, "BIS Statistical Bulletin – December 2017," p. 1, available at www.bis.org/statistics/bulletin1712.htm (accessed on March 1, 2018).

[23] A cross-border position is defined as a "position on a non-resident – for example, claim on or liability to a counterparty located in a country other than the country where the banking office that books the position is located." Ibid., p. 342 (under "Glossary").

[24] Ibid., p. 6. (Table A1.1: Summary of Locational Statistics, by Currency, Instrument, and Residence and Sector of Counterparty).

[25] "Unallocated sector" makes up the remainder of $446 billion. Ibid. For the definitions of the various terms in the database, see ibid., pp. 340–349 (Glossary).

[26] UNCTAD, "World Investment Report 2017 – Investment and the Digital Economy," p. 172 (hereinafter: UNCTAD, 2017), available at http://unctad.org/en/pages/PublicationWebflyer.aspx?publicationid=1782 (accessed on March 1, 2018).

[27] Ibid., p. 165. Digital assets will be discussed separately in Chapter 5.

companies that provide telecommunications infrastructure and connectivity.[28] Digital MNCs have a very different international footprint than ICT companies or other, more traditional types of MNCs (e.g., those corporations operating in the food and beverages industry, automotive and aircraft, or chemicals and pharmaceuticals).[29]

For digital MNCs, because of the ways in which operating and delivery models rely on a high level of digitization, the share of foreign tangible assets (e.g., land and offices, manufacturing equipment, and inventory located outside of the company's home jurisdiction) is small relative to their foreign business as measured by the share of foreign sales. For digital or tech MNCs, physical presence in a foreign market is less critical for sales than is the case with telecom MNCs or other types of MNCs.[30] This means that the international profile of digital/tech MNCs is highly skewed toward foreign sales over foreign assets, resulting in a higher ratio between the share of foreign sales and the share of foreign assets (defined by UNCTAD as a "foreign assets lightness ratio").[31] In contrast, for traditional MNCs, the two components have a roughly equal weight, whereas the ratio is lowest for telecom MNCs, reflecting the asset-heavy nature of this industry.

Accordingly, as of the end of 2015, the share of foreign *sales* of all sales is 73% for top tech MNCs, 57% for telecom MNCs, and 64% for other MNCs. In contrast, the share of foreign *assets* for tech MNCs is only 41%, as compared with a 66% share for telecom MNCs and a 65% share for other MNCs.[32] Therefore, while digital/tech MNCs rely mostly on international markets in term of sales, their international footprint is much lighter with respect to owning tangible assets in foreign countries. This state of affairs has consequent implications for other issues, such that, for example, most employees of these MNCs work in the home jurisdiction of the corporation.[33]

At the same time, despite holding limited tangible assets abroad, foreign affiliates of tech and digital MNCs retain a sizable part of their foreign earnings overseas, mainly in the form of cash and cash equivalents. A significant part of this cash consists of unremitted foreign earnings, retained abroad for tax optimization purposes. Thus, tech mega-corporations from the United States included in UNCTAD's 2015 ranking of the top 100 MNCs kept 62% of their total foreign earnings unremitted, a share almost three times higher than that of other

28 Ibid.
29 Ibid., pp. 171–172.
30 Ibid., p. 172.
31 Ibid., p. 169.
32 Ibid., pp. 169–170.
33 Ibid., p. 164.

American MNCs.[34] For these corporations, unremitted foreign earnings are equivalent to about six times the estimated value of foreign tangible assets, suggesting that these financial resources are only in small part used to finance foreign productive capacity in these countries. The main objective in holding on to these enormous cash earnings outside of the United States is, therefore, to (indefinitely) defer payment of the tax adjustment upon repatriation of these foreign earnings to the United States.[35] This turn of events has led, however, foreign governments to pressure these US tech and digital MNCs – Google being a notable example – to pay taxes on revenues made inside their territory.[36]

As Chapter 5 will further show, the exponential growth of the tech and digital economy has distinctive implications for the cross-border movement of digital assets or certain other types of intangible goods such as intellectual property, data, or know-how (discussed also in Chapter 5), as compared with the nature and scope of cross-border movement of physical goods, monetary claims, and investment securities, discussed in this chapter.

As already indicated, while some types of assets move across borders more intensely in the age of the global economy, other types of assets may actually become re-concentrated in the relevant home jurisdiction of a multinational corporation. These economic and technological complexities, and the need for an asset-specific analysis to understand the distinctive effects these have on the cross-border movement of assets, also shed light on the need to accurately identify the actual types of property law challenges that are especially pertinent for different types of assets. The rest of this chapter seeks to do so in the context of physical goods, monetary claims, negotiable instruments, and investment securities. Chapter 5 will discuss the distinctive ways in which intellectual property, data, and digital assets move across jurisdictions, and it will accordingly identify the unique challenges that such patterns of cross-border transfer pose for property law.

4.3 National Laws on Movable Assets: Similarities and Differences

This section explores the key differences and similarities among national systems in regard to the proprietary aspects of the three main types of

[34] Ibid., p. 173.

[35] Ibid., p, 174.

[36] See, e.g., A. Petroff, “Italy Gets Google to Pay $335 million in Tax Arrears,” *CNN Tech*, May 4, 2017 (reporting also a similar deal with the United Kingdom in 2016 handing over $185 million to British tax authorities), available at http://money.cnn.com/2017/05/04/technology/google-italy-tax-payment/index.html (accessed on March 1, 2018).

assets explored in this chapter: tangible goods, intangible financial assets in the form of monetary claims, and investment securities.

4.3.1 *Tangible Goods*

Tangible goods, also referred to as *chattels*, exhibit a number of lingering differences between national legal systems, alongside some functional attributes that may alleviate potential jurisprudential conflicts in the case of a cross-border transfer of such assets, or of a proprietary dispute that otherwise implicates parties from multiple jurisdictions. The following points of comparison will focus on the overarching disparities between the common law and civil law traditions, although, as will be shown below, there may also be substantial differences within each such legal family, due mostly to recent statutory developments in various countries.

Generally speaking, in contemporary markets, the value and importance of chattels in terms of industrial equipment and stocks, commercial receivables, or consumer holdings – and particularly, the use of chattels as security for the extension of commercial credit – has become very considerable. This means that legal systems across the world must reconsider their property laws on chattels not only in the conventional sense of the transfer of ownership in goods, but also in regard to the creation of limited proprietary rights in them, so that goods could be used as security.

4.3.1.1 Openness of the System

As Chapter 1 has shown, the civil law system abides more strictly by the *numerus clausus* principle, by which the national property law recognizes a limited number of proprietary rights, thus limiting party autonomy in designing tailor-made arrangements, outside of these set forms, which would be binding on third parties. In the context of goods, this means that alongside ownership, civil law systems also recognize a fairly narrow list of limited proprietary rights, including security interests such as possessory and nonpossessory pledges, charges, and liens.[37] In fact, security interests is one area in which civil law countries have been willing to show more openness in their property law systems, in view of the contemporary need to streamline the provision of financing for both professional traders and end-consumers.

[37] S. van Erp and B. Akkermans, *Cases, Materials and Text on Property Law* (Oxford: Hart Publishing, 2012), pp. 253–264, 426–427.

Accordingly, proprietary mechanisms such as reservation of title, in which the seller preserves ownership of the asset until payment is made in full, while possession is already surrendered to the buyer, is becoming more developed and sophisticated in civil law systems. In many civil law countries, reservation of title in a specific asset may be used not only to secure payment for the secured good itself, but also to secure future claims that the seller may have against the buyer.[38]

Traditionally, the common law recognized ownership and possession/bailment (i.e., possession granted by the owner to another party as part of a lending/letting arrangement or to perform a custodial function by the bailee) as the only legal rights in chattels.[39] However, in equity, the types of proprietary interests that can be created by parties are practically limitless. Trusts, conditional and temporary ownership, and floating charges are now conventional mechanisms developed through equity in common law countries. Rather than limiting the number of proprietary rights, equity instead limits the scope of their effect, and does not generally uphold these rights against *bona fide* third parties who acquire a legal interest (ownership or bailment) in these assets for value.[40] The proprietary effects of such equitable interests with respect to goods will be further explored in Chapter 6 in the context of security interests and priorities in cases of insolvency.

Accordingly, common law systems – including their equity components – do not have a unitary theoretical basis for proprietary rights in chattels. Concepts and rules tend to change according to the nature of the underlying asset. This state of affairs dictates not only substantial differences between the proprietary aspects of real estate, chattels, and intangibles, but also disparities between different types of products or legal structures such as sales, leases, and security interests.[41]

4.3.1.2 The Role of Physical Possession

The common law and civil law traditions diverge on the role of possession, and on the essentiality of physical possession for the transfer of rights in chattels.

[38] Ibid., pp. 480–484.

[39] J. Dalhuisen, *Dalhuisen on Transnational, Comparative, Commercial, Financial and Trade Law, Vol. II: Contract and Movable Property Law* (Oxford: Hart, 2016), pp. 344–346.

[40] Ibid., pp. 350–352.

[41] Ibid., p. 365.

In civil law, the role of possession is considered ancillary to the underlying proprietary right, primarily ownership. Possession expresses the will of the owner to maintain his or her physical control over the asset. In the case of holdership, i.e., when someone else physically holds the asset lawfully, the legal significance of possession derives from the underlying proprietary right that enables the holder to do so, be it a lease, possessory pledge, or other limited proprietary right. Because the focus of civil law systems lies in the self-standing recognition (and protection) of the underlying proprietary right, most typically ownership, possession of the good can be constructive, assuming some form of control over the underlying asset but not necessarily physical holding.[42] Accordingly, the rules on the protection of possession in the civil law have primarily the function of enhancing the preservation of peace rather than of establishing substantive proprietary rights.[43]

In contrast, in common law, possession in chattels is not merely a manifestation of an underlying right but is itself a proprietary interest. It is in principle physical. While delivery of physical possession is no longer necessary in England for the sale of goods,[44] it still matters in other proprietary contexts. This is particularly so in the case of the voluntary handing over of an asset by the owner, which often happens in the case of custody, hire-purchase, lending, or a pledge. These are indeed the most common forms of bailment or possession in this sense, although there are forms of custody that are not considered bailment, for example, when representatives or employees handle the owner's goods.[45] Accordingly, in common law systems, anyone who voluntarily surrenders possession of chattels, including the owner, is in a vulnerable position. Thus, for example, in case of bankruptcy of the bailee, the bailor cannot simply rely on his or her ownership right to retrieve the asset, but the bailment must be unowned first in the bankruptcy estate.[46]

Matters may be different in the case of limited or derivative proprietary rights created in equity. Such equitable rights or interests operate quite independently from the legal interests of ownership and possession. As the following paragraphs will show, this would be particularly

[42] Ibid., pp. 368–371.

[43] van Erp and Akkermans, p. 206.

[44] Sale of Goods Act 1979 (UK), Sect. 17(1): "Where there is a contract for the sale of specific or ascertained goods the property in them is transferred to the buyer at such time as the parties to the contract intend it to be transferred."

[45] Dalhuisen, Vol. II, p. 370.

[46] Ibid., p. 374.

important in the case of nonpossessory security interests, such as floating charges or bulk transfers of such assets. The protection of such nonpossessory equitable interests is valid against third parties, including in the case of bankruptcy, but it is extinguished by a transfer of title by the legal owner or possessor (bailee) to a *bona fide* purchaser for value. Moreover, no delivery of possession is required for the protection of the *bona fide* purchaser against holders of such nonpossessory equitable interests.[47]

4.3.1.3 Floating Charges, Bulk Transfers, and Future Assets

As a general rule, in order for an asset to be the object of proprietary rights in a private law sense, it must have a certain economic value and, at least in civil law, since the nineteenth century, some specificity in the sense that it is at the least identifiable. The latter notion has traditionally limited, at least from a civil law perspective, bulk transfers of both chattels and intangible claims, and it may also limit the transferability of future assets, or their use as a collateral for obligations.[48] That said, statutory reforms in some civil law countries are creating functional equivalents to those in operation in common law jurisdictions, thus facilitating, at least partially, the extension of commercial credit.

To start with, the floating charge is a mechanism developed in equity to secure business credit, and it is relevant in England to corporations.[49] Such a charge covers all or most present and future assets of a debtor, but at least in England, it does not attach to the assets until a certain event happens, typically crystallizing upon default of the debtor, in which case it becomes a fixed charge on then-existing assets.[50] The English floating charge has a low rank in bankruptcy proceedings, ranking not only below originally fixed charges but also below preferential creditors.[51] The situation is different in the United States, at least according to the Uniform Commercial Code (UCC),[52] in the sense that the floating lien (as it is known in the United States) crystallizes upon the date of notice-filing of the security interest, while also allowing for the inclusion of future assets in such a lien. This also seems to be the case in other common law

47 Ibid., p. 372.
48 Ibid., pp. 321–322.
49 D. Sheehan, *The Principles of Personal Property Law*, 2nd ed. (Oxford: Hart Publishing, 2017), p. 345.
50 van Erp and Akkermans, p. 454.
51 Sheehan, *Principles of Personal Property Law*, p. 354.
52 Uniform Commercial Code (UCC), Article 9 (Secured Transactions), § 9–204 (American Law Institute, 2012).

countries, such as the common law provinces in Canada, as well as Australia and New Zealand, which have followed the UCC model.[53] At the same time, until the debtor, secured creditors, or another party starts insolvency proceedings, a floating charge does not prevent the charger from disposing of the assets, thus protecting *bona fide* purchasers as well as buyers in the ordinary course of business, who are aware of the floating lien/charge.

As suggested, civil law has been much slower in developing a functionally equivalent system of floating charges/liens, requiring in many cases statutory intervention. Generally speaking, civil law countries are more willing to recognize a lien on future assets when these assets are replacement or equivalent assets. This is provided for statutorily in Article 2343 of the French Civil Code, and it has also been recognized in case law in Germany and the Netherlands.[54] In Germany, the mechanisms for securing debts through future assets can also be achieved through an extended reservation of title, namely, a reservation of title that shifts into replacement goods.[55]

A related issue has to do with the possibility of a transfer/sale of assets in bulk, such as libraries, inventories, portfolios of receivables, and the like.[56] The key jurisprudential issue is whether these assets can be transferred, and moreover, whether they are sufficiently specific to have owner, possessor, or user rights in them transferred in bulk, with common law countries generally exhibiting a more flexible approach, at least theoretically, than civil law jurisdictions.[57] Beyond the conceptual account of bulk assets, such a bulk transfer may raise practical concerns, especially when a seller may seek to secretly sell his or her entire business and flee with the money to avoid paying the business's creditors. The American UCC provides a detailed arrangement in its Article 6 to monitor such bulk transfers, while not flatly prohibiting them.[58] Article 6 imposes duties not only on the seller but also on the buyer, requiring the buyer to give a notice to the seller's claimants.[59]

[53] Sheehan, *Principles of Personal Property Law*, pp. 372–388.

[54] van Erp and Akkermans, pp. 454–465.

[55] Dalhuisen, Vol. II, pp. 413–414.

[56] Ibid., pp. 323–324.

[57] Ibid.

[58] According to UCC § 6–102, a bulk sale is typically "a sale not in the ordinary course of the seller's business of more than half of the seller's inventory, as measured by value on the date of the bulk-sale agreement."

[59] See UCC § 6–105.

4.3.1.4 Remedies

The two legal traditions diverge also in the ways in which proprietary rights in chattels are protected. Based on Roman law, the civil law systems provide specific claims for the protection of ownership and other proprietary rights. The *res vindicatio* gives the asset's owner the right to assert his or her proprietary right and claim the return of the object from any third party who holds the object without sufficient entitlement.[60] At the same time, a defendant may invoke the owner's right as a defense against anyone else claiming ownership. This means that rights to possession or repossession rely on proving the underlying proprietary right of the affected party.[61]

In common law, possessory protection of chattels is regularly obtained through tort law, particularly by traditional actions in trespass, detinue, conversion, trover, or replevin. At the same time, such causes of action are very different from the modern tort of negligence, or the civil law tort action which is purely personal.[62] In England today, much of the protection of assets is statutory, such as by the Torts (Interference with Goods Act) 1977,[63] which applies to all personal property other than money in choses in action.[64] Tort actions in common law systems also include the right to ask for an injunction, an equitable remedy which lies at the discretion of the court.[65]

4.3.2 Intangible Financial Assets: Monetary Claims

As Section 4.2 has shown, intangible financial assets are taking an increasing role in world economy, so that the need for transnational legal frameworks, or at the least, for the mitigation of disparities across national legal systems, becomes ever more essential. The following paragraphs highlight some of the major proprietary features of intangible assets in common law and civil law. The focus of the analysis here is on the monetary claim, a legal obligation of a debtor to pay a creditor a certain amount of money. When the monetary claim results from a sale, it is often called a *receivable* or an *account*.[66] Obviously, there are

[60] van Erp and Akkermans, pp. 207–208.
[61] Dalhuisen, Vol. II, p. 377.
[62] Ibid., pp. 373–375.
[63] Torts (Interference with Goods Act) 1977.
[64] Sheehan, p. 183.
[65] van Erp and Akkermans, pp. 208–209.
[66] Dalhuisen, Vol. II, p. 314.

many other settings in which a monetary claim emerges. A bank has monetary claims against its borrowers for the return of the principal and payment of interest. Respectively, depositors have monetary claims against their banks.[67]

4.3.2.1 Proprietary Status

A monetary claim is in essence a personal right against a counterparty. In its internal aspect, that is, between the parties to the contract or the underlying obligation, it can be enforced through an *in personam* claim. But as a matter of practice, a monetary claim also has an external aspect vis-à-vis third parties in a variety of situations. This is so, for example, in the case of insolvency of the debtor, in conflicting assignments of the monetary claim, or when the creditor of a monetary claim that is not yet due to be paid (including in the case of future installments) wishes to use this entitlement as a security for a current line of credit he or she receives from a third party such as a bank. Once third parties become stakeholders in the monetary claim, legal systems must develop mechanisms to establish *in rem* rights and priorities in monetary claims.

In common law systems, the development of proprietary concepts for intangibles and their assignment has been done mainly through equity.[68] Especially in terms of future and temporary interests, equity became less physical in nature – as opposed to the traditional common law concepts on chattels – and consequently, it was flexible enough to enable the development of equitable proprietary rights in intangibles, which are based on a proper conceptual description of the asset (or class of assets) rather than on its physicality.[69] Moreover, the proprietary system developed via equity tends to be product specific, allowing also for different approaches according to different uses of monetary claims and the contexts in which such assets are used, most prominently when the assignment of monetary claims, or their use as security, is required to facilitate financing for businesses. This practical approach saves much of the need for a unified theoretical analysis on whether ownership can exist in monetary claims, or choses in action in English law terminology.[70] Further, a more recent development in common law systems seeks to practically grant monetary claims a status which is similar to negotiable

[67] Ibid.
[68] Ibid, pp. 327–328.
[69] Ibid.
[70] van Erp and Akkermans, pp. 382–383.

instruments, such as bills of exchange,[71] thus making the assignment or use of the claim as a security independent of the underlying contract that created the monetary claim. Such an approach, to the extent it will be validated by courts on the national and maybe also supranational levels, would further increase the liquidity of monetary claims when they are deployed outside the context of the original contract.[72]

Civil law jurisdictions differ on the question whether intangibles, and monetary claims in particular, can be the object of ownership, with French law being viewed as offering a more liberal approach in reading monetary claims into the types of assets that can be objects of ownership.[73] In other systems, such as in Germany, in which the Civil Code explicitly limits ownership to tangible assets,[74] the solution has been to recognize limited proprietary rights in intangibles, including the right of usufruct and the right of pledge on claims.[75] Because under civil law, possession can be purely constructive, the employment of such mechanisms for intangibles does not create particular difficulties. Practically speaking, the pragmatic approach followed in civil law allows for the types of proprietary structures that facilitate financing and commercial practices, such as the assignment of monetary claims and their use as a security for extension of credits, finance sales, and so forth.[76]

4.3.2.2 Assignment and Notification

Assignment is the term commonly used for the transfer of intangible assets, including monetary claims. The particular mode of transfer or assignment of the monetary claim is determined in each legal system, and it is usually affected by a contract that transfers the right of ownership (or other proprietary right) over the claim.[77] Notice is typically a constitutive requirement for the validity of the assignment vis-a-vis the debtor. The debtor's consent is generally not required – only notice – which in itself illustrates the proprietary nature of the right to the claim.[78] In some civil law countries, such as in France, the notice to the debtor may also be

[71] For the role of negotiable instruments, and bills of exchange in particular, as objects of property, see Dalhuisen, Vol. II, pp. 646–663.
[72] Ibid., pp. 460–461.
[73] van Erp and Akkermans, pp. 378–379.
[74] Section 90 of the German Civil Code reads: "Sachen im Sinne des Gesetzes sind nur körperliche Gegenstände" ("things in the context of this law are only material objects").
[75] van Erp and Akkermans, p. 422.
[76] Dalhuisen, Vol. II, p. 444.
[77] van Erp and Akkermans, p. 387.
[78] Dalhuisen, Vol. II, pp. 444–446.

constitutive in the sense of binding third parties.[79] In equity, neither documentation nor notification were a formal or constitutive requirement for the equitable assignment of legal or equitable claims, but notification may otherwise be significant, such as in the case of conflicting assignments.[80] Different jurisdictions in the United States have diverging approaches for the notice requirement.[81] A notice to the debtor may prove, however, essential in some cases under US law. First, under UCC Section 9–406(a), it puts the account debtor on the hook for ensuring that payments are actually made to, and received by, the assignee.[82] Moreover, an "authenticated" assignment by the assignor or assignee to the debtor is required to block any defenses or claims made by the debtor that do not originate from the terms of the underlying transaction between creditor and debtor.[83]

The civil law and common law traditions do not have a single approach to the validity of contractual limits on the assignment of monetary claims agreed to by the original parties to the transaction. In the Netherlands, for example, while generally it is not possible to prohibit or limit the assignability or transferability of the rights of ownership or limited proprietary rights, it is possible to prohibit or limit the assignability of claims.[84] In France, however, a nonassignability clause is considered as violating the principle of free circulation of objects, which underlies the French Civil Code.[85] Differences occur also within common law systems. In England, a nonassignability clause is considered valid and is not contrary to public policy.[86] US courts have a different approach, being more adverse toward binding third parties by nonassignability limits.[87]

[79] van Erp and Akkermans, p. 389.
[80] Dalhuisen, Vol. II, pp. 451–452.
[81] Ibid., pp. 484–488.
[82] S. D. Chait, "The Critical Need to Give Proper Notice of Assignment," *Equipment Finance Advisor*, May 6, 2015, available at www.equipmentfa.com/blogs/4248/the-critical-need-to-give-proper-notice-of-assignment (accessed on March 1, 2018).
[83] UCC § 9–404(a)(2).
[84] van Erp and Akkermans, pp. 410–411.
[85] Ibid., pp. 405–406.
[86] Ibid., pp. 412–415.
[87] Dalhuisen, Vol. II, pp. 458–460. For a comparative analysis of statutory or contractual limits on the assignability of claims, see G. Rasche, "Prohibitions on Assignment, a European Civil Code, and Business Financing," *The European Legal Forum*, 3 (2002), pp. 133–140, available at www.simons-law.com/library/pdf/e/284.pdf (accessed on March 1, 2018).

4.3.2.3 Future Monetary Claims

With respect to the assignability of future claims, and their validity versus third parties, differences linger both across the civil law and common law traditions. The most common situation in which assignment of future claims arises is under an extended reservation of title or a floating charge. In Germany, an extended reservation of title means that all future goods and receivables may automatically be included in the charge as replacement property. In France, there is a restriction on the assignment of absolutely future claims (meaning, for example, that an author cannot assign royalties from a book he or she intends to write in the future).[88]

The English approach to equitable assignments, which does not require notification as a constitutive requirement, is similar to the German approach, yet the date of transfer may be different. This is so because the proprietary right of the assignee is in principle only established at the day the claim is materialized. Once that happens, the crystallization of the property right is automatic and an intervening bankruptcy of the assignor will therefore have no impeding effect on the transfer.[89] In the United States, the approach toward assignability of future claims is more mixed. However, UCC Section 9–110 accepts for security assignments any financing statement of the collateral, whether or not it is specific, as long as it reasonably identifies the assets that it covers.[90]

4.3.3 Investment Securities

The term *investment securities* refers to shares, bonds, derivatives, and other tradable financial assets regularly used by commercial enterprises to raise capital from investors, mostly through stock exchange markets. The proprietary aspects of such assets operate along several dimensions.

4.3.3.1 Security Owners as Stakeholders in the Corporation

The key proprietary aspect involving investment securities has to do with the array of rights, powers, and priorities in regard to the value stemming from assets owned or controlled by the corporation – that is, allocation of

88 Dalhuisen, Vol. II, p. 464.

89 Ibid., pp. 462–463.

90 UCC § 9–110. For the essential features of a financing statement, or security notice, filed pursuant to the UCC, see Lien Solutions, UCC Back-to-Basics, "Your Questions Answered – What's a UCC?," June 2017, available at www.liensolutions.com/blog/2017/06/your-questions-answered-whats-a-ucc/ (commercial website) (accessed on March 1, 2018).

rights among shareholders, secured and preferred creditors (bond holders), and other stakeholders in regard to such assets. Such questions are particularly pertinent upon insolvency or reorganization of the corporation.

While the conventional account of the corporation is one of a "nexus of contracts,"[91] this author has elsewhere argued that a more systematic way to conceptualize the corporation would be one of a property microcosm or a "nexus of property."[92] This means that the legal structure of the corporation defines a set of rights, powers, and priorities. Some of these entitlements are based on contractual arrangements, such as the articles of incorporation, executive employment agreements, or debt covenants. But other rights, powers, and priorities are based on top-down norms in corporate law and related legal fields such as bankruptcy or equity. These norms also serve to order legal relations between stakeholders that do not otherwise have contractual privity – such as relations among different creditors or between individual shareholders or directors and creditors.[93] Thus, for example, while shareholders are entitled in principle to receive periodic dividends when the firm is profitable, in the case of insolvency, shareholders will be typically ranked after secured creditors (bond holders) and other preferred creditors in the distribution of the bankruptcy estate.[94]

The chief legal mechanism that facilitates the construction of the firm's nexus of property is the corporation's separate legal entity. The separate entity defines the boundaries of both the assets located within this socio-economic organization and those of the organization itself. It allows for the conceptual and formal carving out of assets and the setting up of a system of rights, powers, and priorities that also apply to third parties outside the firm, and thus have an *in rem* feature.[95]

A key concept in this respect is *asset portioning*,[96] which has two components. First is designating a separated pool of assets that are associated with the firm and are distinct from the personal assets of the firm's

91 See M. C. Jensen and W. H. Meckling, "Theory of the Firm: Managerial Behavior, Agency Costs, and Ownership Structure," 3 (1976) *Journal of Financial Economics*, pp. 305–360.

92 A. Lehavi, *The Construction of Property: Norms, Institutions, Challenges* (Cambridge, UK: Cambridge University Press, 2013), p. 212.

93 Ibid., p. 208.

94 P. R. Wood, "The Bankruptcy Ladder of Priorities," *Business Law International*, 14 (2013), pp. 209–244 at 210.

95 Lehavi, *The Construction of Property*, pp. 208–209.

96 H. Hansmann and R. Kraakman, "The Essential Role of Organizational Law," *Yale Law Journal*, 110 (2000), pp. 387–440 at 340.

owners (shareholders) and managers. Second is assigning creditors (such as bond holders) with priorities in the distinct pools of assets that result from the formation of the legal entity. The assignment of such priorities can take two forms: (1) *affirmative* asset portioning, which assigns to the firm's creditors a claim on the firm's assets that is categorically prior to the claims of the personal creditors of the firm's owners, and (2) *defensive* asset portioning, which does the opposite: granting to the owners' (shareholders') personal creditors a claim on the owners' personal assets that is prior to the claim of the firm's creditors. The latter type of asset portioning is regularly achieved through the limited liability corporation.[97]

The essence of corporations lies in affirmative asset portioning. This portioning could not be achieved effectively by contract or through a standard application of the proprietary mechanism of secured transactions. This is so because given the default rules of obligations law – by which all creditors have an equal-priority claim to the entire pool of assets in case of default – an entrepreneur would be practically unwilling and unable to credibly promise to business creditors a priority over the business assets. The entrepreneur would be unwilling to do so because the costs of obtaining such consent from past and future personal creditors would be prohibitive, and he or she would be unable to do so because this compliance could not be monitored or bonded: any contractual promise for priority would be valueless when the entrepreneur is insolvent and assets are distributed under bankruptcy rules. Needless to say, the credibility problem is exacerbated when the enterprise is made up of multiple owners. To ensure their priority, business creditors would have had to constantly reassess the personal creditworthiness of each one of the owners.[98]

It is here that mechanism of establishing a separate legal entity comes into play. Permitting the firm itself to be the owner of assets, while issuing to investors investment securities such as shares or bonds, provides a simple means for identifying which assets are considered business assets as opposed to personal assets. It also enables to distinguish business creditors from personal creditors: the former are those whose dealings are with a formally organized firm rather than with an individual.[99] Affirmative asset portioning grants a discernible group of shareholders and creditors – especially those holding secured bonds – a categorical priority with regard to a discernible group of resources (present and

[97] Ibid., pp. 393–394.
[98] Ibid., pp. 401–403.
[99] Ibid., pp. 408–409.

future). It thus becomes clear why the core of the business corporation, and the issuance of investment securities in it, lies in proprietary concepts.

4.3.3.2 Investment Security as a Tradable Asset

The investment security itself is an asset that can be freely traded – in fact, the key attribute of the investment security lies in its market value and its inherent liquidity and transferability.[100] The investment security may also be pledged as a security, in the sense of a security interest.[101] As such, it is an intangible asset, which is the object of proprietary rights across both civil law and common law systems, with alienability being supported by corporate and securities laws. These laws also define any unique traits that investment securities may have as objects of property, such in cases of selling or buying controlling shares in the firm, with different legal systems diverging on the nature and scope of regulating such transactions.[102]

4.3.3.3 Proprietary Rights versus Intermediaries and Brokers

Contemporary systems of trading also highlight the set of proprietary entitlements in investment securities, which implicate intermediaries such as brokers and financial institutions, especially in view of the paperless, electronic system of book-entry.[103] Typically, in a book-entry system, a depository function is created under which the issuer places all securities with a depository, or a number of depositories, who thereby become legal owners of all the issued securities. Investors will hold security entitlements against these depositories expressed in security accounts that they keep with them. End-investors will hold entitlements against their brokers in this manner, meaning that they have securities accounts with them only. In fact, there could be more intermediaries (or subcustodians) in the chain, holding accounts with each other. The result

100 J. Armour et al., "Introduction" in R. Kraakman et al. (eds.), *The Anatomy of Corporate Law: A Comparative and Functional Approach*, 3d ed. (Oxford: Oxford University Press, 2017), pp. 1–20 at 10–11.

101 D. Larcker and B. Tayan, "Pledge (and Hedge) Allegiance to the Company," *Stanford Closer Look Series* (October 11, 2010), available at www.gsb.stanford.edu/sites/default/files/documents/CGRP11-HedgingandPledging_0.pdf/ (accessed on March 1, 2018).

102 P. Davies, K. Hopt and, W. G. Ringe, "Control Transactions," in R. Kraakman et al. (eds.), *The Anatomy of Corporate Law: A Comparative and Functional Approach*, 3d ed. (Oxford: Oxford University Press, 2017), pp. 205–242.

103 US Securities and Exchange Commission, "Holding Your Securities – Get the Facts," March 4, 2003, available at www.sec.gov/reportspubs/investor-publications/investorpubsholdsechtm.html (accessed on March 1, 2018) (distinguishing between "street name" registration and "direct" registration as two varieities of the US book-entry paperless record system).

is one of a tiered system in which there are layers or tiers of ownership rights.[104] Investors will thus have security accounts with their brokers, who in turn have them with the depository either directly or via other subcustodians in a system of layers and tiers.[105] The beneficial ownership rights of investors against the depository are thus held through a tiered system of security entitlements, in which these beneficial rights may in principle be exercised only against the most immediate tier.[106]

This proprietary structure may become meaningful especially in an insolvency of a subcustodian or broker who is part of this system on behalf of its clients/end-investors.[107] While the nature of the proprietary rights of the end-investors may remain somewhat obscure even in common law countries, upon insolvency of the immediate intermediary the investor may shift his or her entitlement to another broker with the duty of the bankruptcy trustee to shift also the back-up entitlement.[108] That said, there are still operational or collateral risks in this system of depository and custodial arrangements via brokers and other intermediaries. While the assumption is that the investments can be segregated from those of the intermediary, there is still the potentially serious problem of commingling and lack of segregation.[109] The result may be that investors as beneficial owners of the investment securities will only get the *pro rata* share in the liquidation proceeds of their bankrupt broker. That said, modern clearing systems may guard against default by the broker.[110] Moreover, in the United States, the Securities Investor Protection Corporation (SIPC),[111] created by US Congress under the Securities Investors Protection Act,[112] protects customers against the loss of securities or cash when a brokerage firm which is a SIPC member is in financial trouble, although such protection is far from covering all potential losses of investors.[113]

104 Dalhuisen, Vol. II, p. 677.
105 Ibid., p. 678.
106 Ibid., pp. 679–680.
107 Ibid., p. 677.
108 Ibid., pp. 680–681.
109 Ibid., p. 691.
110 Ibid., pp. 694–695.
111 Securities Investor Protection Corporation, "SIPC Mission," at www.sipc.org/about-sipc/sipc-mission (accessed on March 1, 2018).
112 Securities Investor Protection Act of 1970 (as amended through P.L. 112–90, approved on January 3, 2012).
113 P. Bajpai, "What Happens when a Stock Broker Goes Bust?" *Investopedia*, May 5, 2015, available at www.investopedia.com/articles/investing/050515/what-happens-when-stock-broker-goes-bust.asp (accessed on March 1, 2018).

4.4 The Limited Role of the *Lex Rei Sitae* Rule for Movable Assets

As Chapter 3 showed, the *lex rei sitae* rule preserves much of its gravity in cross-border disputes implicating real estate even in the age of globalization. This is so especially in regard to the private law aspects of property, in view of the immovable trait of the asset, and the nature of land registries as nationally based systems for administering property rights.[114] The public law aspect of property rights to land, which implicates the limits of the regulation and expropriation powers of governments toward domestic and international right-holders may be, however, affected by supranational mechanisms, such as investment treaties and binding human rights conventions.[115]

This state of affairs is manifestly different for chattels, intangible assets such as monetary claims, and investment securities. The ever-growing movement of tangible goods across borders means that jurisdiction may change over time, with potential implications for the applicable law and the enforcement of proprietary rights made by previous jurisdictions. In the case of intangible assets, the identification of the locus requires a legal construct, rather than mere observation of the asset's physical presence. Such a construction may actually facilitate the use of legal fictions that could be useful in creating cross-border arrangements. This requires, however, the establishment of common rules on conflicts of laws, and more so, the creation of a shared baseline of substantive priority rules, especially for insolvencies involving assets or creditors across different jurisdictions. Moreover, once the asset at question has no "real" situs in the sense of a clear physical location – as is the case with intangible assets – it becomes clear that questions of jurisdiction, applicable law, and enforcement embody normative considerations of control and competing interests of different countries, rather than merely hinging on identifying an "objective" locus.[116] This section presents the current state of conflict of laws rules for different types of movable assets: tangible goods, monetary claims, negotiable instruments, and investment securities.

[114] Z. Akhtar, "Land Registry, Electronic Conveyancing and Harmonisation: A Review of Current Practice," *The Conveyancer and Property Lawyer*, 2 (2014), pp. 106–122 at 107.

[115] See Chapter 3, Sections 3.3–3.4.

[116] See S. van Erp, "Lex Rei Sitae: The Territorial Side of Classical Property Law," in C. Godt (ed.), *Regulatory Property Rights: The Transforming Notion of Property in Transnational Business Regulation* (Leiden and Boston: Brill Nijhoff, 2016), pp. 59–81 (noting the particular relevance of the American realist approach to *lex rei sitae* for assets with no "real" situs).

4.4.1 Tangible Assets

In proprietary matters relating to physical goods, the mere reference to the *lex rei situs* does not in itself produce a choice of law solution when it matters most, namely when the asset moves across borders. In such a case, the question is whether the applicable law would be the law of the situs of origin, or of the situs of the destination of the asset.[117] A prevailing notion in this respect is that the rules of the place of the origin of the asset determine the extent of the proprietary rights created in it, but that upon the asset's movement, the recognition and operation of such rights in other countries is determined by the law of the destination country. The potential disparity among national systems may be especially prevalent in cases involving secured transactions or finance sales, or in those cases featuring reservation of title or retention rights.[118]

Problems may arise even when no asset moves. This would be so, for example, in the case of a transfer in bulk, either outright or conditionally, or of the pledging of such a bulk of chattels located in different countries. These scenarios present particular problems of applicable property law because of the different approaches to bulk transfers across countries, with many countries not explicitly recognizing or otherwise referring to the possibility of such transfers.[119] While it is possible to attribute the location of the bulk to the locus of its current owner or to that of the assignee, such a fiction would make more sense for intangible assets than it would for chattels.[120]

Moreover, in the case of insolvency, jurisdiction is not necessarily based on the location of the assets, but often on the location or place of major activities of the debtor, as Chapter 6 will show. When the debtor's assets are located in different jurisdictions, the court of a jurisdiction in which a certain asset (or class of assets) is located might be approached by a foreign bankruptcy trustee, claiming the asset or requiring the recognition of a certain proprietary right (e.g., reservation of title over a good sold in a credit transaction, or a floating lien over inventory located in that jurisdiction), which is not identically recognized, if at all, in the jurisdiction in which the physical asset is located.

Accordingly, modern conflict of laws rules in many countries consider the question of the discretion of its judiciary for both (a) recognition of foreign proprietary charges or security interest/finance sales in respect to

117 Dalhuisen, Vol. II, p. 545.
118 Ibid.
119 See Section 4.3.1.
120 Dalhuisen, Vol. II, p. 545.

assets that move to such countries (or their closest equivalent in the designated jurisdiction), and (b) recognition of foreign enforcement and collection power, at least in a foreign bankruptcy, in respect of assets within the jurisdictions of these countries.[121] Generally speaking, rights of *bona fide* purchasers of an asset are also determined initially by the law of the asset's location at the time of the title transfer, therefore by the *lex situs* of the origin.[122]

The recognition of proprietary rights in goods that were created in a different jurisdiction than that of the jurisdiction in which the assets are currently located requires the court, first, to make a principled normative decision whether to respect the provisions of the foreign property law in the first place – usually framed around the public-policy exception that national conflict of laws statutes contain – and second, to find the closest equivalent property law concept in domestic law.

The term *public policy* (*ordre public*) is regularly understood as referring to a small number of core values and fundamental principles of the local forum.[123] While most such values are usually associated with constitutional law values, they could also be applied in private law, and property law in particular, for example, in protecting certain vulnerable stakeholder groups in bankruptcy.[124]

The problem of finding the closest equivalent concept in domestic law and adapting the foreign property law concept to the domestic setting remains intact even if a certain legal concept, such as a reservation of title, is recognized in two countries, but has different substantive and procedural features (for example, if it is considered in one of them as a security interest and therefore requires filing to overcome third-party interests).[125] Accordingly, the adjustment and conversion of the foreign proprietary right requires a determination of its relative priority vis-à-vis other proprietary rights in the law of the recognizing country. In common law countries, the recognition of foreign proprietary rights may give them the status of equitable proprietary interests as nearest equivalents, subject to the protection of *bona fide* purchasers in the recognizing common law country.[126]

121 Ibid., p. 546.
122 Ibid., p. 551.
123 G. Cuniberti, *Conflict of Laws: A Comparative Approach, Text and Cases* (Cheltenham, UK: Edward Elgar, 2017), pp. 136–137.
124 Ibid.
125 Dalhuisen, Vol. II, 556–557.
126 Ibid.

In the case of trusts, central in common law systems but underdeveloped in civil law ones, the approach of the Hague Convention on the Law Applicable to Trusts and on Their Recognition[127] is to recognize trusts that are created according to the applicable law under the conflict of laws rules of the convention, assuming that the applicable law provides for trusts.[128] The contractual aspects of the trust may be governed by the law chosen by the parties, but such a private choice of law does not govern proprietary aspects of the trust. The latter aspects are still covered by the law applicable to the conflict of laws rules of the forum, which, in the case of tangible assets, largely focuses on the *lex rei situs*.[129]

4.4.2 *Monetary Claims*

The international aspects of proprietary rights in monetary claims remain very much underdeveloped, including in identifying the location of the asset.[130] As the following paragraphs show, these dilemmas have particular importance in international financing, arising in the context of bulk transfers, or in the assignment of claims vis-à-vis debtors in various countries to support a single funding transaction, that is, a security transfer of a portfolio of receivables.[131]

For purposes of identifying the prevailing conflict of laws rules, a distinction has to be made between the contractual, proprietary, and enforcement aspects of the monetary claim. Different countries have diverging approaches to the question of whether the forum and law that apply to the contractual dimension of the monetary claim – which would regularly be a matter of party autonomy – could also govern at least some of the proprietary aspects of the claim. In Germany, established opinion is that the law of the contract out of which the receivable arises determines also its proprietary regime, as is the case in France.[132] In England, there is a preference, at least in matters of validity of the assignment, to apply the law of the assignment, while a clear distinction between the contractual and proprietary aspects is not made. In any event, in

[127] Hague Conference on Private International Law, Convention of 1 July 1985 on the Law Applicable to Trusts and on Their Recognition, Arts. 6–10, concluded on July 1, 1985, entered into force on January 1, 1992, available at www.hcch.net/en/instruments/conventions/full-text/?cid=59 (accessed on March 1, 2018).

[128] Ibid., Art. 5.

[129] Dalhuisen, Vol. II, pp. 560–561.

[130] Ibid., pp. 565–566.

[131] Ibid.

[132] Ibid., pp. 576–577.

England, party autonomy, including the choice of a foreign law in these matters, leads only to equitable rights and is balanced by an adequate protection for *bona fide* purchasers or collectors of the underlying debt. Assignments governed by foreign law may be accepted but converted into equitable rights. US law may also rely on the law of assignment and party autonomy, probably also subject to the recharacterization of the ensuing interests as equitable proprietary rights (as nearest equivalents), leading to *bona fide* purchaser protection of third parties.[133] Generally speaking, the UCC opts for applying the personal law of the borrower/debtor who offers the receivables as security, therefore of the assignor, at least in matters of protection of security interests or the transfer of receivables under UCC Article 9 and its effects.[134] This is in line with chattels, in which the UCC prefers the personal law of the debtor/assignor of the security interest over the *lex situs* of the chattels.[135]

A bigger challenge emerges with respect to bulk transfers of monetary claims, especially those used as security or conditional assignments for funding purposes and/or assignments of monetary claims for payment for services and goods that may be recoverable in different countries.[136] The underlying issue is whether a measure of unity of the entire portfolio of receivables that are assigned may be legally assumed or construed at the transnational level, even if debtors come from different countries, and if so, which laws would govern the bulk of the receivables.[137] Differences in formalities, time of effectiveness, assignability, and defenses might make such a unified theory hard to implement. It may therefore be essential to move away from traditional conflict of laws rules to some type of supranational ordering through international custom or a binding treaty.[138]

4.4.3 Negotiable Instruments

Bills of exchange or promissory notes can obviously be drawn by a seller or debtor, respectively, in one country, to a buyer or creditor in another,

[133] Ibid., p. 579.

[134] UCC § 9-301(1)(a) reads: "Except as otherwise provided in this section, while a debtor is located in a jurisdiction, the local law of that jurisdiction governs perfection, the effect of perfection or nonperfection, and the priority of a security interest in collateral." The following subsections contain exceptions that apply the collateral's *lex situs*.

[135] Dalhuisen, Vol. II, pp. 580–581.

[136] Ibid., pp. 568–569.

[137] Ibid., p. 570.

[138] Ibid., p. 570.

who is likely to accept the bill in his or her own country.[139] Moreover, the negotiable instrument may subsequently circulate in yet more countries and be delivered and endorsed in any of them. This may result in a potential conflict of laws regarding the creation of the instrument in terms of formalities, capacity, and validity; any subsequent transfer of the same asset; acceptance and effect of the instrument elsewhere when ultimately presented for payment; or payment and discharge under the instrument. The basic rule, at least in England, is that the creation and transfer are complete when the instrument is delivered to the party concerned – that is, its handing over to the payee. It is therefore not the place of the signatures but rather the law of the place where the instrument is sent to after it. *Acceptance* means its return by the drawee to the payee, and *transfer* means the delivery to the subsequent holder. In all instances, upon circulation in other countries, it is likely that the new *lex situs* will adjust rights acquired earlier under the instrument to its own system as a matter of the nearest equivalent, so as to respond best to the purposes for which the instrument is used.[140]

4.4.4 Investment Securities

The conflict of laws rules, which govern the proprietary rights of holders of investment securities in a corporation with a cross-border dimension, operate along several fronts.

The first aspect concerns the applicable law for the corporation itself (*lex societatis*), when the corporation has factors connecting it to various countries, for example, when it is registered in one country, but its headquarters are physically located in another country. According to the *incorporation theory* (known also as the *place of incorporation* rule), the deciding factor for determining the applicable law for the corporation is the jurisdiction in which the company was incorporated, regardless of where the firm's principal place of business or other assets and activities are located.[141] This is the conflict of laws rule that prevails in the United States, both within its own federal system, and internationally vis-à-vis other countries, and it is also the case in the United Kingdom.[142] In

139 Ibid., pp. 658–659.

140 Ibid.

141 Armour et al., "Introduction," pp. 21–22.

142 C. Gerner-Beuerle et al., "Why Do Businesses Incorporate in Other EU Member States? An Empirical Analysis of the Role of Conflict of Laws Rules," European Corporate Governance Institute (ECJI) Law Working Paper No. 361/2017, July 2017, p. 18, available at http://ssrn.com/abstract_id-=3010133 (accessed on March 1, 2018).

contrast, under the *real-seat theory*, which originally prevailed in many continental European countries, firms are required to incorporate under the law of the state where the firm has its actual headquarters and/or its principal place of business, and, accordingly, the applicable law for the firm would be that of the jurisdiction of its "real seat."[143]

Within the European Union, the principle of the freedom of establishment, currently embedded in Article 54 of the Treaty on the Functioning of the European Union (TFEU),[144] and in a corresponding set of decisions by the Court of Justice of the European Union (CJEU),[145] has led to a gradual shift from the real-seat theory to the incorporation theory's rule across EU Member States. However, the CJEU case law leaves EU Member States with the power to take certain measures designated to prevent potential abuse of the principle of freedom of establishment in regard to their own nationals as well as to foreign corporations registering in their jurisdictions. As a result, EU Member States diverge from one another in the scope of embracing the incorporation theory, with some EU Member States preserving elements of the real-seat theory.[146]

143 Armour et al., "Introduction," p. 22.

144 Consolidated Version of the Treaty on the Functioning of the European Union, signed on December 13, 2007, OJ (C 326/47), October 26, 2012, available at http://eur-lex.europa.eu/legal-content/EN/TXT/PDF/?uri=OJ:C:2012:326:FULL&from=EN (accessed on March 1, 2018).

145 For a review of this case law, and its implications for the applicable conflict of laws rule in the EU Member States, see J. Meeusen, "Freedom of Establishment, Conflict of Laws and the Transfer of a Company's Registered Office: Towards Full Cross-Border Corporate Mobility in the Internal Market," *Journal of Private International Law*, 13 (2017), pp. 294–323 at 300–304.

146 Gerner-Beuerle et al., pp. 3–4, 17–18. This diversity in mind, a 2017 empirical analysis shows that a clear "place of incorporation" rule adopted by a Member State makes it more attractive for incorporation by nonresidents. The United Kingdom, with its long-standing place of incorporation rule, is home to more than half of all businesses incorporated by residents of other Member States across the European Union. It has over 227,000 companies registered by nonresidents from other Member States, out of 420,000 such companies across the EU countries. Ibid., pp. 9–21. Obviously, the adoption of the place of incorporation rule makes it easier for corporations, and MNCs in particular, to engage in forum shopping that builds on the regulatory arbitrage between countries in their corporate laws (in addition to other elements that are not discussed here, such as tax and labor laws). A. Riles, "Managing Regulatory Arbitrage: A Conflict of Laws Approach," *Cornell International Law Journal*, 47 (2014), pp. 63–119 at 96–102. This is particularly so in the case of corporate groups, which are able to split their legal location across various jurisdictions to enjoy different aspects of such arbitrages. V. Harper Ho, "Theories of Corporate Groups: Corporate Identity Reconceived," *Seton Hall Law Review*, 42 (2012), pp. 879–951 at 935.

Under either of these options for identifying the applicable law for the corporation, the *lex societatis* governs the various aspects that deal with the governance of the corporation, including potential conflicts among shareholders (e.g., between controlling and minority shareholders), and between shareholders and the corporation and its management (board of directors and/or executive management). It thus controls the proprietary aspects of shareholding as comprising the residual claim to the stream of benefits from the corporation's assets (e.g., dividends) and participation in its decision-making (through voting).[147]

The second aspect deals with the forum and choice of law in matters of securities law, impacting mostly investors' litigation concerning securities of public corporations traded in stock exchange markets. As Section 4.2 has shown, corporations are increasingly listed in stock exchange markets in other countries, through either a foreign-listing or dual-listing setup. Moreover, sellers and buyers of stocks, bonds, derivatives, and other security instruments in prominent stock exchange markets come from all over the world, such that cross-border issues may also impact, for example, a US corporation that sells bonds in the US stock exchange market, with individual investors, brokers, and institutional investors coming from all over the world (one may recall the worldwide effects on investors of the 2007 US subprime crisis).[148] Questions of extraterritoriality, and in particular jurisdiction and choice of law in cross-border disputes, are thus currently highly prevalent in establishing the property rights of securities' holders.

A major development in this regard has been the 2010 US Supreme Court decision in the matter of *Morrison* v. *National Australia Bank Ltd.*[149] In *Morrison*, Australians who purchased shares of National Australia Bank (NAB) in the Australian market claimed that the bank officials misled them about the performance of a US mortgage subsidiary and sought to invoke the antifraud provisions of Section 10(b) of the Securities Exchange Act of 1934. Rejecting a context-specific "conduct and effects" test that had been developed for decades by the lower federal courts, the US Supreme Court held that these antifraud provisions do not extend to securities' transactions outside of the United States. According to the Court, "the focus of the

[147] Lehavi, *The Construction of Property*, pp. 208–213.

[148] M. Landler, "U.S. Credit Crisis Adds to Gloom in Norway," *The New York Times*, December 2, 2007 (describing the financial distress of Norwegian villages who lost millions in purchasing real-estate based securities in US markets).

[149] *Morrison* v. *National Australia Bank Ltd.*, 130 S. Ct. 2869 (2010).

Exchange Act is not on the place where the deception originated, but upon purchases and sales of securities in the United States."[150]

Morrison thus significantly clips the wings of holders of investment securities, who seek to bring securities litigation, and class actions in particular, to US courts. Therefore, for private lawsuits, securities litigation would be primarily litigated by the national courts of the jurisdictions in whose territory the exchange transactions were made. This is so although investors may be on the lookout for other jurisdictions that might be willing to expand their territorial reach to adjudicate such cases and to offer a more stringent protection to owners of investment securities.[151]

The third aspect deals with questions of jurisdiction and choice of law, which arise in the context of the tiered system of entitlements to investment securities that implicate brokers and intermediaries alongside issuers/sellers and end-consumers, as discussed in Section 4.3.3. This could be so, for example, when a broker or another intermediary, located in a different jurisdiction than that of the seller and/or the beneficial owner, becomes insolvent or engages in a conflicting transaction. As long as such proprietary relationships are not explicitly governed by a transnational legal regime that addresses the particular features of professional traders and financial institutions,[152] such cross-border conflicts would be based on a conflict of laws approach, with several options presenting themselves for the proper law to be applied in such cases.

The Convention on the Law Applicable to Certain Rights in Respect of Securities Held with an Intermediary, which went into force on April 1, 2017 (ratified so far only by the United States, Switzerland, and Mauritius),[153] establishes in Article 4 a "primary rule" on the applicable law concerning the various matters covered under the convention. According to this primary rule, "[t]he law applicable to all the issues . . . is the law in force in the State expressly agreed in the account agreement as the State whose law governs

150 Ibid., p. 2884.

151 W. A. Kaal and R. W. Painter, "Forum Competition and Choice of Law Competition in Securities Law after Morrison v. National Australia Bank," *Minnesota Law Review*, 97 (2012), pp. 132–205 at 138–139 (pointing to other countries, such as the Netherlands, which show signs of expanding their jurisdiction to cover such securities litigation).

152 Dalhuisen, Vol. II, pp. 586–601 (calling to apply a new *lex mercatoria* that would also cover proprietary aspects).

153 Hague Conference on Private International Law, Convention on the Law Applicable to Certain Rights in Respect of Securities Held with an Intermediary, concluded on July 5, 2006, entered into force on April 1, 2017, available at www.hcch.net/en/instruments/conventions/full-text/?cid=72 (accessed on March 1, 2018).

the account agreement or, if the account agreement expressly provides that another law is applicable to all such issues, that other law."[154] When no such agreements exists, the convention establishes in Article 5 a number of fallback rules, including the application of the law of the state "in which the relevant intermediary has its place of business."[155]

The fourth and final aspect deals with the proprietary status of investment securities with a cross-border dimension in case of the corporation's insolvency. It is then that the relative priority of different security investments, mainly shares and bonds, is determined vis-à-vis competing interests, such as those of other secured and nonsecured creditors, in allocating the limited pool of the corporation's assets, or in reorganizing the corporation and the respective entitlements to it. Questions of jurisdiction, applicable law, and extraterritorial enforcement thus become pertinent. This dimension of cross-border property rights in investment securities will be discussed in Chapter 6.[156]

4.5 Cross-Border Norms on Conflicting Transactions and Bona Fide Purchases

4.5.1 Scope of the Problem and Lingering Differences across Borders

The nature and scope of the *in rem* applicability of proprietary rights in movable assets finds a vivid expression in the various situations in which parties, not in contractual privity themselves, assert simultaneous, conflicting claims of rights over the same asset, which are the result of the wrongdoing of an intermediary party. Property law is called upon to resolve this "legal accident" and to settle the proprietary priorities in regard to the asset between the distant parties.[157]

One such instance is the conflicting transaction. A is the owner of a good or an intangible asset. A undertakes to sell or assign the right in the asset to B, but before the transfer of the right is completed, A undertakes to transfer or assign a conflicting right in the same asset to C.[158] Another prominent setting is that of theft: A is the owner of certain goods. B steals A's goods and then (typically, through a chain of intermediaries) "sells"

[154] Ibid., Art. 4.
[155] Ibid. Art. 5(3).
[156] See Chapter 6, Section 6.4.
[157] M. Mautner, "'The Eternal Triangles of the Law': Toward a Theory of Priorities in Conflicts Involving Remote Parties" *Michigan Law Review*, 90 (1991), pp. 95–154.
[158] Ibid., pp. 134–135.

them to C. A demands reclamation of the goods from C. The law must determine which of the two competing parties has priority over the goods. Such an instance invokes the principle of *nemo dat quod non habet* ("he who does not have cannot give") and the question is whether, and under what conditions, the buyer of the goods could nevertheless prevail.[159] A related, though a different scenario, is that of entrustment or embezzlement: A is the owner of a movable asset, which he or she willingly entrusts in the hands of B as bailee. B sells the good to C and disappears. C, a good-faith purchaser of the good for value, claims priority to the asset over A.[160]

While many of these scenarios remain within domestic borders, the growing cross-border transfer of tangible and intangible assets in contemporary economy also increases the likelihood that such legal scenarios would implicate more than one legal system. As Section 4.5.2 shows, one set of cases in which the transnational component is particularly present has to do with an artwork that is stolen in one country and then ends up being traded in another, or with antiquities or other cultural objects that are illegally excavated and then illicitly traded across borders. Yet problems of conflicting transactions, theft, or embezzlement can cross borders in many other cases.

A database of 126 legal systems, published in 2017 by Giuseppe Dari-Mattiacci and Carmine Guerriero, studies the lingering differences between national doctrines pertaining to various types of such proprietary disputes.[161] One such comparative analysis deals with the national rules referring to the purchase of a stolen movable good. The database's indicators gauge the number of years after which the buyer acquires ownership, if at all, through either a private sale, public market, an auction, or from a professional seller. Another set of variables deals with the purchase of a movable good that was embezzled, that is, traded by someone to whom the good was entrusted to be held or used for specific purposes. Similar to the variables on theft, national law indicators gauge the number of years after which the buyer, if at all, acquires ownership of an embezzled good purchased within either a private sale, public market, auction, or from a professional seller.[162]

159 Ibid., pp. 149–150.
160 Ibid., pp. 129–131.
161 G. Dari-Mattiacci and C. Guerriero, "A Novel Dataset on Horizontal Property Rights in 126 Jurisdictions," *Data in Brief* 11 (2017), pp. 557–561.
162 Ibid.

The differences between the national systems, for these two sets of variables, are significant and also cut through the common law and civil law traditions. Thus, for example, under US law, the original owner in principle almost always prevails over a subsequent buyer in each one of these scenarios (theft and embezzlement/entrustment),[163] whereas in England the purchaser would prevail over the original owner after a period of six years in the case of theft (based on the general provisions of the Limitation Act 1980),[164] and a good-faith buyer would under certain circumstances prevail over the original owner in case of a purchase from an agent to whom the owner voluntarily surrendered possession of the good (including in the case of embezzlement).[165]

Differences also exist within the civil law system, in which the protection of a good-faith purchaser as an exception to the *nemo dat* rule is more pervasive. Thus, for example, in Germany, the purchaser would prevail over the original owner after a period of ten years in the case of theft, and would triumph as a good-faith buyer immediately in the case of embezzlement.[166] In comparison, in France, a good-faith buyer would prevail over the original owner after a period of three years in both scenarios: theft and embezzlement/entrustment.[167]

Differences between national law norms, cutting through both the common law and civil law systems, exist also in other types of proprietary conflicts over tangible or intangible goods, including in the case of conflicting transactions. In France, for example, where an act of delivery is not generally required for transfer of ownership in chattels, a second-in-time buyer would prevail in a conflicting transaction scenario only if he or she received possession while acting in good faith. In Germany, where delivery is in principle required to transfer ownership in a tangible good, the second-in-time party may prevail upon receipt of possession even if he or she is not in good faith, although such a buyer could be liable in torts to the first-in-time party in appropriate cases.[168]

Accordingly, a property dispute among distant parties, involving a cross-border dimension, might be decided differently based on the identity of the jurisdiction and applicable law in the matter. Thus, for

[163] Ibid., Appendix A, Supplementary Material.

[164] Limitation Act 1980, s. 3.

[165] Dari-Mattiacci and Guerriero, Appendix A, Supplementary Material; Sheehan, *The Principles of Personal Property Law*, pp. 60–66.

[166] Dari-Mattiacci and Guerriero, Appendix A, Supplementary Material.

[167] Ibid.

[168] Dalhuisen, Vol. II, pp. 400–405.

example, when a precious stone is stolen in one country and ends up being sold to a good-faith buyer in a different country, the specific conflict of laws rules that apply to such a proprietary dispute may have a crucial bearing on its substantive outcome.

The conflict of laws rules for property disputes over goods with a cross-border dimension diverge among countries. Some follow the *lex situs* of the asset at the time of acquisition of the good by the buyer, with other countries embracing the *lex originis* (country of origin in which the theft from the true owner took place), or the principle of the "law of the closest connection."[169] With no international convention covering the conflict of laws rules in such settings, this additional disparity among national rules on jurisdiction may lead to uncertainty and forum shopping.

4.5.2 *The Special Case of Artwork and Cultural Artifacts*

In some cases, national legal systems may establish special jurisdiction and applicable law rules, beyond merely opting for the *lex situs*, *lex originis*, or the law of the closest connection.

A prominent example is discussed in the 2004 US Supreme Court case, *Republic of Austria* v. *Altmann*,[170] which dealt with the high-profile proceedings initiated by Maria Altmann, niece and sole surviving heir of Jewish businessman and art patron Ferdinand Bloch-Bauer, to recover six paintings by Gustav Klimt, including two portraits of his wife Adele Bloch-Bauer, which had been looted by the Nazis and were eventually placed in the Austrian state gallery in Vienna.[171]

Altmann initially announced that she would file a lawsuit in Austria to recover the paintings under Austrian law. Because Austrian court costs are proportional to the value of the recovery sought – and in this case, would have totaled several million dollars, an amount far beyond Altmann's means – she requested a waiver. The Austrian court granted this request in part but still would have required Altmann to pay approximately $350,000. When the Austrian government appealed the partial

[169] For an analysis of these different conflict of laws rules, see M. Wantuch-Thole, *Cultural Property in Cross-Border Litigation: Turning Rights into Claims* (Berlin: Walter de Gruyter, 2015), pp. 234–251.

[170] *Republic of Austria* v. *Altmann*, 124 S. Ct. 2240 (2004).

[171] This case was featured in numerous books and films, such as the 2015 drama movie *Woman in Gold* (BBC Films).

waiver, Altmann voluntarily dismissed her suit and filed a suit in the United States District Court for the Central District of California (her place of residency).[172]

Altmann asserted jurisdiction under Section 2 of the Foreign Sovereign Immunities Act of 1976 (FSIA),[173] which authorizes federal "civil suits for relief in personam with respect to which the foreign state is not entitled to immunity" under other sections of the FSIA. She further asserted that the Republic of Austria and the gallery were not entitled to immunity under FSIA's "expropriation exception."[174] This exception expressly exempts from sovereign immunity certain cases involving "rights in property taken in violation of international law," provided that the property has a commercial connection to the United States, or that the agency or instrumentality which owns the property is engaged in commercial activity in the United States.[175]

The US Supreme Court held in favor of Altmann, ruling that FSIA has retroactive force to cover past violations of international law in taking property, such as those committed by the Nazis.[176] Accordingly, and because the lower federal courts determined that the gallery, being state-owned, qualifies as an "agency or instrumentality" of Austria, and that the gallery's publishing and advertising activities in the United States amount to "commercial activity" under FSIA,[177] the Supreme Court allowed the case to move forward.[178]

Interestingly, following this ruling, both parties agreed to arbitration in Austria, at the end of which the tribunal held in favor of Altmann, relying on the provisions of the 1998 Austrian Federal Act Regarding the Restitution of Artworks from Austrian Federal Museums and Collections.[179] The tribunal ordered the gallery to return the paintings without remuneration to Ms. Altmann as the sole heir of Bloch-Bauer.[180] Upon

[172] 124 S. Ct. 2240, at 2245.
[173] 28 U.S.C. § 1330(a).
[174] 28 U.S.C. § 1605(a)(3).
[175] 124 S. Ct. 2240, at 2245–2246.
[176] Ibid., at 2252–2254.
[177] Ibid., at 2258 (Breyer J., concurring).
[178] Ibid., at 2256 (Stevents, J.).
[179] Federal Law Gazzette 1 No. 18111998, December 4, 1998 (in German).
[180] Arbitral case *Maria V. Altmann et al.* v. *The Republic of Austria*, decided on January 15, 2006, available at www.unodc.org/res/cld/case-law-doc/traffickingcul turalpropertycrimetype/aut/maria_altmann_vs__republic_of_austria_html/Arbitral_ Award_-_5_Klimt_paintings_Maria_V._Altmann_and_others_v._Republic_of_Aus tria-_15_January_2004.pdf (accessed on March 1, 2018).

return of the paintings, Ms. Altmann sold one of the paintings, *Adele Bloch-Bauer I* (known as "The Woman in Gold") in a private sale for $135 million, and the other paintings at an auction for a total of over $327 million.[181]

Reflecting on the US Supreme Court decision, Donald Burris and Randol Schoenberg, who represented Ms. Altmann, as well as other heirs of Jewish owners of artworks looted by the Nazis, attributed the willingness of US courts to assert jurisdiction in such cross-border cases to two factors.[182] First, the fact that under US law, a thief cannot convey good title to a *bona fida* purchaser, such that good-faith purchasers are required to return stolen property to their prior owners. Second, the strong public-policy interest of US governmental institutions, state and federal, in seeking the return of Nazi-looted art.[183] It may be reasonably assumed that this high-profile decision resonated in other jurisdictions internationally, concerning both the process and substance of deciding such stolen artwork cases.[184] This is so although no international convention generally governs the conflict of laws rules or substantive doctrine on disputes over stolen assets.

The one setting concerning proprietary disputes over movable property, in which a thick body of both soft law and hard law instruments has emerged internationally, has to do with the cross-border return of cultural artifacts, which have been illegally excavated, stolen, or otherwise illicitly moved away from one country and that end up in the hands of museums, private collectors, or other purchasers in another country. In fact, in following the development of supranational mechanisms dealing with the cross-border return of cultural artifacts during the past few decades, one can discern the concurrent employment of the four strategies for globalization identified in this book: soft law, conflicts of laws, approximation, and supranationalism. As the following paragraphs will show, while the development of supranational instruments has been slow, and its trajectory is often haphazard, the combination of these

181 C. Michaud, "Christie's Stages Record Art Sale," *Reuters*, January 19, 2007, available at http://uk.reuters.com/article/uk-britain-mcdonalds/mcdonalds-workers-stage-com panys-first-strike-in-britain-idUKKCN1BF1AS (accessed on March 1, 2018).

182 D. S. Burris and E. R. Schoenberg, "Reflections on Litigating Holocaust Stolen Art Cases," *Vanderbildt Journal of Transantional Law*, 38 (2005), pp. 1041–1050.

183 Ibid., p. 1043.

184 S. T. Shapiro, "How Republic of Austria v. Altmann and United States v. Portrait of Wally Relay the Past and Forecast the Future of Nazi Looted Art Restitution Litigation," *William Mitchell Law Review*, 34 (2008), pp. 1147–1176.

various strategies seems to become more effective, with the norms now more directly addressing the private law relations between original owners and purchasers of cultural artifacts, superseding national private law norms in the matter.

The first major milestone is the 1970 UNESCO Convention on the Means of Prohibiting and Preventing the Illicit Import, Export and Transfer of Ownership of Cultural Property ("1970 UNESCO Convention"),[185] which went into force in 1972 and has been adopted by 133 states.[186]

According to Article 1, an asset is classified as *cultural property* only if it is "specifically designated by each State as being of importance for archaeology, prehistory, history, literature, art or science," and it must also fall within one of twelve general categories included in Article 1. The general categories identified in the 1970 UNESCO Convention are thus a necessary but insufficient condition for identifying an asset as cultural property. Each state must designate and publicize in its national laws the types of assets it wishes to protect as cultural property.[187] In this respect, the convention may be seen as adopting an approximation strategy, rather than embracing a uniform supranational norm. Moreover, the 1970 UNESCO Convention places the main onus on potentially origin states to set the terms for exporting cultural artifacts, accompanied by an appropriate certificate, such that any cross-border transfer violating such norms established by the state of origin would be considered illicit.[188] Absent such specific norms promulgated by the state of origin, the export or transfer of cultural artifacts is not per se prohibited.[189]

In contrast, the affirmative duties imposed on potentially destination states are narrower. Most importantly, the duty of a state to return a cultural artifact to its state of origin arises only when the cultural property has been stolen from a "museum or secular public monument

[185] United Nations Educational, Scientific and Cultural Organization (UNSECO), Convention on the Means of Prohibiting and Preventing the Illicit Import, Export, and Transfer of Ownership of Cultural Property, November 14, 1970, 823 UNTS 231.

[186] For a current list of the Member States, see the 1970 UNESCO Convention website at www.unesco.org/eri/la/convention.asp?KO=13039&language=E&order=alpha (accessed on March 1, 2018).

[187] A. Tasdelen, *The Return of Cultural Artefacts: Hard and Soft Law Approaches* (New York: Springer, 2016), p. 20.

[188] J. G. Sprankling, *The International Law of Property* (Oxford: Oxford University Press, 2014), pp. 54–55.

[189] Tasdelen, *The Return of Cultural Artefacts*, p. 23.

or similar institution,"[190] and upon the specific request of the state of origin to the destination state, made through "diplomatic offices." The 1970 UNESCO Convention thus applies only among states and requires them to actively engage in executing it.

The one dimension in which the convention establishes a clear supranational norm, which supersedes any national norm, it that upon a valid request for return made by the origin state, it "shall pay just compensation to an innocent purchaser or to a person who has valid title to that property."[191] This requirement holds valid regardless of the local rules of either the origin state or the destination state on proprietary conflicts among original owners and *bona fide* purchasers.[192] This means, for example, that if a cultural artifact ends up in the hands of a buyer in the United States, after being stolen from a museum or similar institution in another country, its return would require the payment of just compensation to the good-faith buyer. This is although under a domestic US scenario, such a good-faith buyer would not have been entitled to such compensation.

A different strategy is followed by the 1995 UNIDROIT Convention on Stolen or Illegally Exported Cultural Objects ("1995 UNIDROIT Convention").[193] This convention, aimed at aiding the "fight against illicit trade in cultural objects," seeks to do so by "establishing common, minimal legal rules for the restitution and return of cultural objects between Contracting States."[194]

Compared with the 1970 UNESCO Convention, the 1995 UNIDROIT Convention creates a broader system for compelling the return of an illegally exported or stolen cultural artifact. At the same time, the 1995 UNIDROIT Convention is so far ratified by a much smaller number of states – 42 members as of the early 2018 – most of them potential "exporters" of cultural artifacts.[195]

The 1995 UNIDROIT Convention creates a uniform definition of cultural objects, unlike the 1970 UNESCO Convention, which allowed

190 1970 UNESCO Convention, Art. 7(b)(i).

191 Ibid., Art. 7(b)(ii).

192 Tasdelen, *The Return of Cultural Artefacts*, pp. 30–31.

193 International Institute for the Unification of Private Law (UNIDROIT), Convention on Stolen or Illegally Exported Cultural Objects, June 24, 1995, 34 ILM 1330.

194 Ibid., at Preamble, para. 4.

195 For the current status of signatory states, see UNIDROIT's website at www.unidroit.org/status-cp (accessed on March 1, 2018).

each state to establish its scope.[196] In this sense, it applies a supranationalism strategy in identifying the types of assets governed by the convention. Applying to "claims of an international character" it is designed as a self-executing convention that addresses the prospective proprietary rights of distant parties to a dispute over such assets.[197]

As for the illegal export of cultural objects, the 1995 UNIDROIT Convention provides that a court or another competent authority in the destination state must order the return of the object from a buyer, if the state of origin establishes that the removal of the object from its territory "significantly impairs" the physical preservation, integrity of a complex object, preservation of information of a scientific or historical character, or the traditional or ritual use of the object.[198] The requesting state may alternatively show that "the object is of significant cultural importance" to it. In such case, the person who acquired the object after its illegal export and "neither knew nor ought reasonably to have known at the time of acquisition that the object had been illegally exported" is entitled to payment of reasonable compensation by the requesting state.[199]

In the case of a stolen object (the definition of *stolen* covering also cases of illegal excavation of a cultural artifact from an archeological site in the origin state),[200] the 1995 UNIDROIT Convention addresses directly the prospective rights of the possessor and the claimant.

According to Article 3(1), "the possessor of a cultural object which has been stolen shall return it." The claim for restitution may be brought within a period of three years from the time when the claimant knew the location of the cultural object and the identity of its possessor, and in any case within a period of fifty years from the time of the theft.[201] Article 3(1) does not, however, specify the claimant. Since the object has been stolen, it is obvious that the original owner is a legitimate claimant, regardless of his or her nationality. This means that in the spirit of the convention, even citizens of countries that are not party to the convention may invoke the rights provided by it. In addition, the provisions can also be invoked by the contracting state itself if it is the rightful owner.[202]

[196] Sprankling, *International Law of Property*, p. 55.
[197] Tasdelen, *The Return of Cultural Artefacts*, pp. 77–78.
[198] Sprankling, *International Law of Property*, pp. 55–56.
[199] 1995 UNIDROIT Convention, Art. 6(1).
[200] Ibid., Art. 3(2).
[201] Ibid., Art. 3(3).
[202] Tasdelen, *The Return of Cultural Artefacts*, p. 87.

According to Article 4(1), "the possessor of a stolen cultural object required to return it shall be entitled, at the time of its restitution, to payment of fair and reasonable compensation provided that the possessor neither knew nor ought reasonably to have known that the object was stolen and can prove that it exercised due diligence when acquiring the object."[203] The convention therefore adopts a uniform substantive rule for deciding proprietary disputes between original owners (claimants) and buyers (possessors), superseding any national norms that govern in the matter.

As mentioned above, the number of signatories to the 1995 UNIDROIT Convention is still limited, representing almost exclusively countries that are normally origin states. However, a number of concurrent soft law and hard law mechanisms has increased the effective influence of this convention so that it is not simply ignored by countries who are not formal counterparts to it.

One such measure is the 2014 European Directive on the Return of Cultural Objects Unlawfully Removed from the Territory of a Member State.[204] The directive enables Member States to secure the return of cultural objects, which are classified as "national treasures" within the meaning of Article 36 of the Treaty on the European Union (which grants the right to identify such national treasures to the Member States) and that have been removed from their territory in breach of national provisions or the 2009 Council Regulation on the Export of Cultural Goods.[205]

While restricted to the illegal cross-border transfers of cultural objects within the Member States of the European Union, the directive nevertheless binds countries that are regularly destination states, adding yet another layer of binding supranational norms in regard to such movable goods.

According to Article 3 of the 2014 Directive, "cultural objects which have been unlawfully removed from the territory of a Member State shall be returned in accordance with the procedure and in the circumstances provided for in this Directive." Article 10 provides that "where return of

203 1995 UNIDROIT Convention, Art. 4(1).

204 Directive 2014/60/EU of the European Parliament and of the Council of 15 May 2014 on the Return of Cultural Objects Unlawfully Removed from the Territory of a Member State (Recast), OJ (L 159/1), May 25, 2014.

205 Council Regulation (EC) No 116/2009 of 18 December 2008 on the Export of Cultural Goods, OJ (L 39/1), February 10, 2009.

the object is ordered, the competent court in the requested Member State shall award the possessor fair compensation according to the circumstances of the case, provided that the possessor demonstrates that he exercised due care and attention in acquiring the object." These supranational norms therefore supersede national norms on proprietary conflicts among distant parties, which, as shown above, may vary significantly among the Member States. The Directive also includes conflict of laws rules pertaining to various proprietary aspects. Thus, for example, under Article 13, "ownership of the cultural object after return shall be governed by that law of the requesting Member State."[206]

Moving to soft law mechanisms, attention should be paid to the 2011 UNESCO - UNIDROIT Model Legislative Provisions on State Ownership of Undiscovered Cultural Objects.[207] This model law is aimed at giving further substance to the 1970 UNESCO Convention and 1995 UNIDROIT Convention, by aiding countries, which are typically origin states, to formalize their ownership of archeological findings and other types of undiscovered cultural objects, thus granting them standing as both requesting states and owners under the respective provisions of these conventions.

Yet another set of soft law provisions, reflecting a more decentralized approach that seeks to bring in private actors, such as museums or collectors, together with national governments, in creating rules against the illicit cross-border transfer of cultural artifacts, is comprised of a number of ethical codes and principles. These instruments include the ICOM Code of Ethics for Museums,[208] the UNESCO International Code of Ethics for Dealers in Cultural Property,[209] and the ILA Principles for Cooperation in the Mutual Protection and Transfer of Cultural Material.[210]

The ICOM Code of Ethics, for instance, dictates minimum standards of professional conduct carrying the spirit of the conventions to museums in 136 countries and territories, thus reaching many more actors than the 1995 UNIDROIT Convention, including all the major destination states.[211] Moreover, in recent years, the various hard law and soft law mechanisms increasingly adopt rules of procedure for mediation

206 Directive 2014/60/EU, Art. 13.

207 UNESCO – UNIDROIT Model Legislative Provisions on State Ownership of Undiscovered Cultural Objects (2011), available at www.unidroit.org/instruments/cultural-property/model-provisions (accessed on March 1, 2018).

208 See Tasdelen, *The Return of Cultural Artefacts*, pp. 155–168.

209 Ibid., pp. 168–178.

210 Ibid., pp. 178–184.

211 Ibid., p. 225.

and conciliation. Even though these provisions are not mandatory, they establish a regulated framework to resolve such complex proprietary disputes.[212] Recent years have also seen mounting pressure on museums and collectors to avoid clandestine transactions, and on Western governments – to recognize their role in preventing looting.[213]

A vivid example of the changing landscape of proprietary disputes over high-value artworks and cultural artifacts, and the growing prominence of supranational norms and procedures, is a warrant issued in July 2017 to the Metropolitan Museum of Art in New York by prosecutors at the district attorney's office in Manhattan, to hand over a 2,300 year-old vase exhibited in the Met's Greco-Roman Galleries.[214] The warrant came after an international investigation found evidence indicating that the vase had been looted by tomb raiders in Italy in the late 1970s, then going through the hands of an Italian art dealer, Giacomo Medici, convicted in 2004 of conspiracy to traffic in antiquities, and bought by the Met at auction at Sotheby's in 1989 for $90,000.[215]

The case closely echoes the removal of another terra-cotta wine vessel, the Euphronios Krater, from the Met in 2008, following an international dispute that spanned over three decades. The museum had acquired the krater in 1972 from an American dealer with ties to Medici for $1 million – a record-breaking price for antiquities at the time. But by 2006, it had become clear that the krater had been looted from an Etruscan tomb northwest of Rome in 1971.[216]

In the current case, however, it seems that the vase will make its way back to Italy much more quickly.[217] The entrenchment of supranational norms covering such proprietary disputes, alongside the growing role of soft law mechanisms and public pressure, highlight how the combination of globalization strategies may be effective in governing the cross-border transfer of such high-value movable assets despite long-standing national differences in both substantive and procedural rules.

[212] Ibid.
[213] A. Efrat, "A Major Musuem Has to Return Another Looted Artifact. Welcome to the Dark Side of the Art World," *The Washington Post*, August 7, 2017.
[214] T. Mashberg, "Ancient Vase Seized from Met Museum on Suspicion It Was Looted," *The New York Times*, July 31, 2017.
[215] Ibid.
[216] Ibid.
[217] Ibid.

4.6 Policy Analysis: Old Paradigms and New Challenges for Movable Assets

The need to establish globalization strategies for cross-border conflicts involving proprietary aspects of movable assets must account for both the quantitative and qualitative features of the contemporary world economy, and for the implications this has for potential proprietary disputes.

The exponential growth in trade, investment, and other forms of economic activities that increasingly move tangible and intangible assets across borders generally increases the likelihood of proprietary conflicts implicating more than one jurisdiction or a single set of national rules. But this general, almost self-evident statement of facts is far from being helpful in identifying the particular kinds of legal challenges that require attention in designing cross-border mechanisms.

Thus, the case of artworks and cultural artifacts, analyzed in Section 4.5.2, should be seen as an exception rather than the rule. Cross-border disputes over such assets generate public attention because of the high-value of a single object, and the ways in which proprietary issues become intermingled with questions of international politics, history, and culture. But these cases do not represent the typical legal challenges of current international trade and investment. Major cross-border quarrels over ownership of a single tangible asset are truly reserved for exceptional cases.

In contrast, proprietary conflicts may arise more prominently in cross-border settings when bulks of chattels (such as inventories) or intangible financial assets, such as portfolios of monetary claims, are assigned or being used as a security in financing transactions. When such assets – in the case of chattels – or the creditors or debtors of monetary claims are located in different jurisdictions, proprietary issues may implicate multiple jurisdictions or national rules. Conflicting assignments, disputes over priorities between holders of security interests in such assets versus subsequent purchasers, or rules of distribution in case of insolvency are matters that may come up very frequently in the contemporary world of commerce. Chapter 6 addresses specifically the issues of security interests and proprietary priorities in case of cross-border insolvency. But in the context of this chapter, a number of general conclusions can be drawn.

(a) The focus on devising cross-border mechanisms, dealing with the coordination of conflict of laws rules, approximation of substantive rules, or setting up supranational norms on such proprietary conflicts, must lie in understanding the role that bulks of chattels or portfolios of monetary claims play in facilitating credit through their use as a security. This state of affairs may call for establishing a set of procedural and substantive norms that would apply to multinational corporations, professional traders, and financiers that engage in cross-border commerce and financing as a daily routine. This may require distinguishing a potential "new lex mercatoria" from the need to establish a more general set of rules that would apply broadly to individuals or corporations.[218]

(b) The prominence of bulks of chattels, such as inventories, or portfolios of monetary claims, undermines the effectiveness of the traditional *lex rei sitae* rule, including, for that matter, attempts to clearly identify between scenarios in which the law of the origin state would apply and ones in which the law of the destination state should prevail. The latter strategy may be relevant for the (exceptional) case of artworks and cultural artifacts, where it makes sense to track the particular physical route of the object (because this also bears on tracking the legal chain of title), but it is much less relevant for inventories or monetary claims. In the case of intangible assets, identifying the locus of the asset is inherently a conceptual, rather than a physical endeavor. What this means is that in reconsidering conflict of laws rules, and particularly in case of future attempts at devising international conventions that would set uniform conflict of laws rules, it may make sense to focus on the personal law of the most relevant party (creditor, debtor, assignor, assignee, etc., as the case may be) in the typical scenarios involving transfer or pledging of movable assets *en masse*. While this is very much the case with bankruptcy, as Chapter 6 will show, there are many other scenarios in which identifying a single jurisdiction or set of applicable laws to govern the bulk or portfolio in its entirety may prove useful. Thus, for example, as Chapter 2 has shown in regard to matrimonial property and succession,[219] the current approach that typifies European regulations is one of *unity* of the matrimonial property or the estate, by identifying the appropriate personal law of the most relevant parties, rather than tracking each specific asset and applying a distinctive jurisdiction and applicable law to such an asset.

(c) In the case of investment securities in corporations, and especially in regard to proprietary relations among different holders of investment securities within the corporation, the strategy should be one of

[218] Dalhuisen, Vol. II, pp. 593–601.

[219] See Chapter 2, Section 2.3.2.1.

identifying the most effective set of jurisdictional and substantive rules that bring together all interested stakeholders within a single process. This is why proprietary disputes entangled with corporate governance are probably best decided by the incorporation theory rule, whereas proprietary disputes about securities in public corporations, traded in stock exchange markets, would be best resolved by the securities laws of the jurisdiction in which the stock exchange market is located. In the case of proprietary disputes over investment securities, preserving the unity of the pool of assets should be closely intertwined with the idea of the separate legal entity of the corporation.

(d) Globalization strategies that go beyond coordinating conflict of laws, and which seek to move toward approximation of national laws or outright supranationalism, should be fine-tuned to address the particular features of the class of assets and its cross-border dimensions. There is not much point in establishing a single international convention that would seek to establish a unified set of supranational norms for all types of movable assets: chattels, monetary claims, negotiable instruments, investment securities, and so forth. There is very little in common between the settings in which a proprietary conflict emerges in regard to a cultural artifact and the typical case in which a proprietary dispute arises over a portfolio of monetary claims. To the extent that future international conventions will indeed be developed to govern each one of these inherently different classes of assets, such legal instruments should truly account for the particular role of these assets in today's economy.

(e) Finally, because of the highly decentralized nature of the current global economy and international trade, and investments in particular, any international convention or other interstate legal instrument must be accompanied by complementary soft law mechanisms – whether these are best practices, guidelines, or ethical codes. These should seek to directly involve the relevant private actors that drive the cross-border trade of the particular class of assets, such as financial institutions, multinational corporations, traders, consumer-protection NGOs, and providers of digital platforms through which trade is carried out.

5

Intellectual Property, Data, and Digital Assets

5.1 How Intellectual Property, Innovation, and Digitization Defy National Borders

Intellectual property has long raised cross-border issues, well before the current technological and digital age. It is thus no wonder that intellectual property law has developed, both within and across national jurisdictions, with an eye toward transnational legal governance.

The concern over the inherent ease at which knowledge-intensive goods (from books and musical works to pharmaceuticals) cross national borders, and the disparities between legal systems in protecting the underlying knowledge, played a key role in the stages leading to the drafting and adoption of the 1883 Paris Convention for the Protection of Industrial Property ("Paris Convention"),[1] and the 1886 Berne Convention for the Protection of Literary and Artistic Works ("Berne Convention"),[2] considered the founding stones of international intellectual property law.[3]

Events such as the Vienna International Exhibition in 1873 and the Paris Universal Exhibition of 1878 served as platforms for calls to establish a multilateral agreement on patents, trademarks, and designs,

1 Paris Convention for the Protection of Industrial Property, adopted March 20, 1883, as amended on September 29, 1979, 828 UNTS 305. As of early 2018, the Paris Convention has 177 contracting parties. WIPO, "Administered Treaties," then "Contracting Parties," then "Paris Convention," available at www.wipo.int/treaties/en/ShowResults.jsp?lang=en&treaty_id=2 (accessed on March 1, 2018).

2 Berne Convention for the Protection of Literary and Artistic Works, adopted September 9, 1886, as amended on July 24, 1971, 828 UNTS 221. As of early 2018, the Berne Convention has 175 contracting parties. WIPO, "Administered Treaties," then "Contracting Parties," then "Berne Convention," available at www.wipo.int/treaties/en/ShowResults.jsp?lang=en&treaty_id=15 (accessed on March 1, 2018).

3 S. Ricketson and J. Ginsburg, "The Berne Convention: Historical and Institutional Aspects," in D. J. Gervais (ed.), *International Intellectual Property: A Handbook of Contemporary Research* (Cheltenham, UK: Edward Elgar Publishing, 2015), pp. 3–36 at 6–16.

whereas international literary gatherings such as the congress presided over by Victor Hugo in Paris in parallel to the 1878 Exhibition prompted calls to enhance protection of authors' rights. Problems of *free riding* of knowledge among countries with a common language typified not only Britain and the United States, but were also present among French- and German-speaking countries, with bilateral treaties granting only limited protection to authors and publishers.[4]

At the core, it was the interdependence of nations in the production of knowledge and extensive trade in knowledge-intensive goods that instigated the move to international law mechanisms.[5] While the Paris Convention and Berne Convention included relatively few substantive norms on protection, and were thus far off from the ideal of a universal codification of intellectual property law, the conventions did address some of the concerns about the inherent border-crossing of knowledge. Such was the binding principle of *national treatment,* securing the same level of protection for foreign and local claimants in each Member State.[6] Freeing foreign authors or innovators from formalities other than those imposed in the country of origin allowed creators to enter foreign markets and protect their rights under equal terms to those of local right-holders.[7]

The intertwining of the ease of cross-border movement of knowledge-intensive goods, the internationalization of markets, and the need to alleviate problems of arbitrage in property laws is clearly a defining feature of the current state of intellectual property, data, and digital assets. Intellectual property is now embedded not only in physical objects, but also in digital assets. More broadly, the need to address proprietary aspects of knowledge, innovation, and digitization cannot be separated from the challenge of devising globalization strategies for data and digital assets.

Practically all types of multinational corporations (MNCs) that sell their products worldwide are concerned with the need to protect intellectual property components embedded in their products. Thus, for example, global pharmaceutical revenues in 2016 reached over

[4] Ibid., pp. 7–11.

[5] G. B. Dinwoodie and R. C. Dreyfuss, "An International *Acquis*: Integrating Regimes and Restoring Balance," in D. J. Gervais (ed.), *International Intellectual Property: A Handbook of Contemporary Research* (Cheltenham, UK: Edward Elgar Publishing, 2015), pp. 121–164 at 123.

[6] Ricketson and Ginsburg, "The Berne Convention," pp. 11–13.

[7] Ibid.

$1.1 trillion, out of which 49% were made in North America, 21.5% in Europe, 16.4% in Africa, Asia (excluding Japan) and Australia, 8.3% in Japan, and 4.7% in Latin America.[8] Worldwide revenues of pharmaceutical giants Novartis and Pfizer stood at $48.5 billion and $52.8 billion, respectively.[9] Patent-protected pharmaceutical products make up a large segment of the market, which explains the worldwide corporate spending of $157 billion on research and development in 2016,[10] and the crucial role of protecting patents.

Tech MNCs face the particular challenge of cross-border legal protection of intellectual property alongside other proprietary aspects of digital assets. As Chapter 4 showed, international markets are increasingly dominated by digital MNCs, which are either purely digital actors (including both Internet platforms and digital solutions) or mixed digital players that combine a prominent digital dimension with a physical one (such as in e-commerce of physical goods) or that provide digital content, such as music or movies in digital format.[11]

The cross-border distribution of sales and revenues of Apple, the world's largest tech company,[12] vividly illustrates the proprietary aspects of knowledge and innovation in a global market, and how the need to protect intellectual property increasingly extends beyond physical goods also to digital assets. During the last quarter of 2017, Apple's overall revenues stood at $52.58 billion.[13] During this quarter, 43.93% of revenues were made in North America, 24.74% in Europe, 18.64% in Greater China, 7.34% in Japan, and 5.35% in the rest of Asia Pacific.[14] Most of Apple's sales are still those of knowledge-intensive physical goods, such as iPhones, iPads, and Macs, with revenue shares of

[8] Statista, "Dossier: Global Pharmaceutical Industry" (2018), pp. 7–8, report available at www.statista.com/topics/1764/global-pharmaceutical-industry/ (accessed on March 1, 2018).

[9] Ibid., pp. 23–26.

[10] Ibid., p. 30.

[11] UNCTAD, "World Investment Report 2017 – Investment and the Digital Economy," p. 165 (hereinafter: UNCTAD, 2017), available at http://unctad.org/en/pages/PublicationWebflyer.aspx?publicationid=1782 (accessed on March 1, 2018).

[12] K. Stoller, "The World's Largest Tech Companies in 2017: Apple and Samsung Lead, Facebook Rises," *Forbes*, May 24, 2017.

[13] Statista, "Apple's Global Revenue from 1st Quarter 2005 to 4th Quarter 2017 (in Billion U.S. Dollars)," available at www.statista.com/statistics/263426/apples-global-revenue-since-1st-quarter-2005/ (accessed on March 1, 2018).

[14] Statista, "Share of Apple's Revenue by Geographical Region from the First Quarter of 2012 to the Fourth Quarter of 2017," available at www.statista.com/statistics/382288/geographical-region-share-of-revenue-of-apple/ (accessed on March 1, 2018).

54.86%, 9.19% and 13.64%, respectively, during the fourth quarter of 2017.[15] At the same time, Apple App Store sales – by which Apple sells digital assets that embed the intellectual property of the content's creators – are rising steadily. Thus, the annual Apple App Store's revenues were $29 billion in 2016, as compared with $20 billion in 2015.[16]

The global digital media market generated a revenue of over $100 billion in 2017.[17] Video games accounted for $52.54 billion; video-on-demand, $19.82 billion; e-publishing, $16.64 billion; and digital music, $11.25 billion.[18] The worldwide distribution of revenues for all digital media points to a dominance of the US market, which generated $36.3 billion in revenue, as compared with Europe, $21.5 billion; China, $15.1 billion; and rest of the world, $27.4 billion.[19]

As of 2018, probably the most high-profile digital assets, which also exemplify how technology and globalization require a reconsideration of markets, governance, and property law, are cryptocurrencies, and most prominently Bitcoin.[20] As Section 5.3.1 shows, Bitcoin and other digital coins are currently conceptualized by regulators and lawmakers as property rather than as currency, thus raising complex new issues about the proprietary features of these digital assets and their governance in view of the inherently decentralized and cross-border system for trading.

This chapter examines various globalization strategies for the protection of intellectual property, data, and digital assets. Prior to doing so, one should consider the ways in which market actors seek to protect their property by acting within country-based systems of legal governance, and how the current distribution of such action across multiple countries emphasizes the challenges of narrowing the gaps between cross-border markets and national legal disparities.

According to a report by the World Intellectual Property Organization (WIPO), the year 2016 saw a substantial growth in the number of worldwide

15 Statista, "Share of Apple's Revenue by Product Category from the First Quarter of 2012 to the Third [sic] Quarter of 2017," available at www.statista.com/statistics/382260/segments-share-revenue-of-apple/ (accessed on March 1, 2018).

16 Statista, "Annual Apple App Store Revenue from 2013 to 2016 (in Billion U.S. Dollars)," available at www.statista.com/statistics/296226/annual-apple-app-store-revenue/ (accessed on March 1, 2018).

17 Statista, "Digital Media Report 2017," p. 5, available at www.statista.com/study/44526/digital-media-report/ (accessed on March 1, 2018).

18 Ibid., p. 5.

19 Ibid., p. 6.

20 C. Kline, "Five Reasons Bitcoin Will Be Your Best High-Growth Investment for 2018," *Forbes*, November 27, 2017.

applications for registration of intellectual property rights in national and regional registries: 3,127,900 for patents, 9,768,200 for trademarks, and 1,240,600 for industrial designs.[21] The largest number of applications for all categories – patents, trademarks, and industrial designs – was filed in China.[22] Thus, the State Intellectual Property Office of the People's Republic of China received 1.3 million patent applications in 2016, more than the combined total for the United States Patent and Trademark Office (605,571), the Japan Patent Office (318,381), the Korean Intellectual Property Office (208,830), and the European Patent Office (159,358).[23]

Most patent applications in China were filed by residents, and the rest by nonresidents (although it should be noted that "residents" for this purpose consist also of local subsidiaries of foreign parent corporations).[24] Chinese residents filed the overwhelming majority of their patent applications (96%) in China, such that only 4% of applications were filed abroad. In sharp contrast, US residents have the highest number of filing applications in foreign patent registries (215,918 in 2016), followed by Japan (191,819) and Germany (75,378).[25] This means that innovators, who seek to act globally and protect their intellectual property across borders, must apply for foreign protection, particularly in countries that could otherwise play a dominant role in free riding on locally unprotected intellectual property and then in distributing such copied physical and digital assets also to other countries. This is clearly the reason why China leads the pack in the number of applications submitted to it for the protection of patents, trademarks, and industrial designs.

In some cases, the motive for filing for protection of intellectual property rights in a certain foreign registry stems not so much from the fear that the foreign country would serve as a source of (worldwide) free riding and copying, but rather from the wish to enter a certain dominant market. In the case of economies that are rich in intellectual and human capital but have small domestic markets in which to extract returns on such capital, resident corporations are motivated to file for

21 World Intellectual Property Organization (WIPO), "World Intellectual Property Indicators 2017," p. 7, available at www.wipo.int/edocs/pubdocs/en/wipo_pub_941_2017.pdf (accessed on March 1, 2018). In addition, 1,553,300 applications were filed for utility models, and 16,510 for plant varieties. For a brief analysis of these two latter categories, see ibid., pp. 209–211.

22 Ibid., pp. 8–9.

23 Ibid., p. 29.

24 Ibid., p. 30.

25 Ibid., pp. 33–34.

patents in other economies that excel in production and distribution capacities required to reach markets.[26] This is why small, research and development (R&D)-intensive countries, such as South Korea, Taiwan, and Israel, apply often for patents in the United States. This allows innovators from such countries to transact safely with production/distribution American partners, leading to an economic and legal system that relies on comparative advantages across borders.[27] In such cases, market and legal arbitrages are aligned in promoting cross-border proprietary interests of innovators and manufacturers of knowledge-intensive tangible and intangible goods.

5.2 Globalizing Intellectual Property: From Paris and Berne to TRIPS and Beyond

While the trajectory of cross-border norms and institutions regarding intellectual property has been complex and does not follow a single course, the mid-1990s can be viewed as a point of significant change, with the establishment of the World Trade Organization (WTO) and the adoption of the Trade-Related Aspects of Intellectual Property Rights (TRIPS) Agreement as a binding annex to the Marrakesh Agreement Establishing the World Trade Organization in 1994.[28] Prior to discussing this point of legal transition, a few words are in order about the pre-WTO, pre-TRIPS cross-border legal setting for intellectual property rights.

As noted briefly in Section 5.1, the Paris and Berne Conventions were premised on respect for sovereignty, and not on a switch to universalism. Subject to narrow exceptions, nations were free to determine their own innovation policies as long as they did not discriminate against foreigners.[29] Even when countries followed the general framework of the Paris and Berne Conventions and adopted substantive standards for the protection of intellectual property rights, local enforcement of such norms

[26] J. Barnett, "Patent Tigers: The New Geography of Global Innovation" (September 22, 2016), USC Law Legal Studies Paper No. 16–31, available at https://ssrn.com/abstract=2842350 (accessed on March 1, 2018).

[27] Ibid., pp. 3–4.

[28] Agreement on Trade-Related Aspects of Intellectual Property Rights, April 15, 1994, 1869 UNTS 299, 33 ILM 1197. The TRIPS Agreement is Annex 1C of the Marrakesh Agreement Establishing the World Trade Organization, signed in Marrakesh, Morocco, on 15 April 1994, 1867 UNTS 154, 33 ILM 1144.

[29] Dinwoodie and Dreyfuss, "An International *Acquis*," p. 150.

was often lacking and asymmetrical among countries, leading in particular to claims by Western companies that their rights were denied in developing countries.[30]

Moreover, the ability to engage in cross-border norm-setting or dispute-resolution procedures was largely missing from these conventions. The Berne and Paris Conventions do not include detailed jurisdiction and choice of law rules, and many intellectual property experts often resorted to the national treatment principle as making problems of conflict of laws simply irrelevant – an assumption that proved to be erroneous in many actual conflicts.[31] Although under Article 33 of the Berne Convention the settlement of interstate disputes should have been resolved by the International Court of Justice (ICJ), this provision was subject to state reservations and has never effectively resulted in even a single ICJ dispute-settlement process over copyrights.[32]

5.2.1 Sequential/Simultaneous Applications and Regional IP Offices

The interstate coordination mechanisms that did develop over the course of the twentieth century are those that facilitate sequential (or simultaneous) applications for the protection of intellectual property in multiple jurisdictions, based on the principle that allows a certain window of time for such sequential applications, in which the filing date is attributed to the first application. This means that the time-based priority embedded in sequential applications results in principle in legal priority. These mechanisms, administered by WIPO, also aim at standardizing the formalities of submitting such applications. At the same time, the national authority maintains substantive discretion in considering the application, including defining the core standards for eligibility.[33]

30 R. J. T. Corbett, "Protecting and Enforcing Intellectual Property Rights in Developing Countries," *The International Lawyer*, 35 (2000–2001), pp. 1083–1103 at 1084–1086.

31 P. Torremans, "Intellectual Property and Private International Law" (Elgar Research Reviews in Law, 2015), Sect. 1, available at www.elgaronline.com/view/Research_Reviews/9781783471423/intro.xml (accessed on March 1, 2018).

32 J. C. Ginsburg, "International Copyright: From a 'Bundle' of National Copyright Laws to a Supranational Code?" *Journal of Copyright Society USA*, 47 (2000), pp. 265–289.

33 P. Baechtold, T. Miyamoto and T. Henninger, "International Patent Law: Principles, Major Instruments and Institutional Aspects," in D. J. Gervais (ed.), *International Intellectual Property: A Handbook of Contemporary Research* (Cheltenham, UK: Edward Elgar Publishing, 2015), pp. 37–82 at 45–47 (discussing the context of patents).

In the case of patents, such a mechanism is facilitated by the 1970 Patent Cooperation Treaty (PCT),[34] discussed in Section 5.2.3.1. For trademarks, the mechanism for sequential or parallel multiple-jurisdiction applications is governed by the Madrid Agreement concluded in 1891,[35] the Protocol relating to that Agreement concluded in 1989,[36] and the 2017 Common Regulations.[37] This system is analyzed in Section 5.2.3.4. For industrial designs, the coordination system for sequential or simultaneous applications is covered by the Hague System, comprised of a series of instruments from the 1925 Hague Agreement, 1960 Hague Act, 1999 Geneva Act, and up to the 2017 Common Regulations.[38] The Hague system is discussed in Section 5.2.3.3.

In some parts of the world, the system of multiple applications is governed by a regional office. Some regional offices go further beyond simultaneous applications, and offer a single regionwide registration, although disputes over enforcement and validity of the registered right are generally adjudicated at the state level. There are currently seven regional intellectual property offices:[39]

(a) The African Intellectual Property Organization (OAPI) brings together sixteen French-speaking African countries.[40] The filing of a regional application for registration of the various types of intellectual property rights covered (including also patents, trademarks, and

[34] Patent Cooperation Treaty, June 19, 1970, 1160 UNTS 231, as amended on October 3, 2001, available at www.wipo.int/pct/en/texts/pdf/pct.pdf (accessed on March 1, 2018).

[35] Madrid Agreement Concerning the International Registration of Marks, April 14, 1891, 82 UNTS 389, as amended on September 28, 1979, available at www.wipo.int/wipolex/en/treaties/text.jsp?file_id=283529 (accessed on March 1, 2018) (hereinafter: "Madrid Agreement").

[36] Protocol Relating to the Madrid Agreement Concerning the International Registration of Marks, adopted at Madrid on June 27, 1989, as amended on November 12, 2007, available www.wipo.int/wipolex/en/treaties/text.jsp?file_id=283483 (hereinafter: "Madrid Protocol").

[37] Common Regulations under the Madrid Agreement Concerning the International Registration of Marks and the Protocol Relating to that Agreement (as in force on November 1, 2017), available at www.wipo.int/wipolex/en/treaties/text.jsp?file_id=456131 (accessed on March 1, 2018).

[38] For specific references and full-text versions of the instruments, see WIPO, "Hague Agreement Concerning the International Registration of Industrial Designs," available at www.wipo.int/treaties/en/registration/hague/ (accessed on March 1, 2018).

[39] WIPO, "World Intellectual Property Indicators 2017," p. 217.

[40] *Organisation Africaine de la Propriete Intellectuelle* (OAPI), available at www.oapi.int (in French) (accessed on March 1, 2018).

industrial designs) has the same effect as filing an application in each Member State, and a patent granted by the OAPI office located in Cameroon is effective in all Member States. However, infringements of intellectual property rights are dealt with by the courts of each Member State. A final judicial decision of a court of a Member State about the validity of an intellectual property right has authority over all other states, expect for questions of validity based on *ordre public* (public order) or morality considerations, in which local discretion is maintained.[41]

(b) The African Regional Intellectual Property Organization (ARIPO) has seventeen English-speaking African Member States.[42] Covering the different types of intellectual property rights, ARIPO is based on submitting a regional application that is then sent to the different national offices. Each Member State has the possibility to deny the effect of the regional intellectual property based on the respective protocol that relates to the specific type of intellectual property. Disputes regarding the validity and enforcement of regional intellectual property rights are handled by national courts. Moreover, the regional intellectual property right is subject to certain provisions of the applicable national laws, such as those relating to the issuance of compulsory licenses in the case of patents.[43]

(c) The Benelux Office for Intellectual Property (BOIP) is part of the Benelux Organization for Intellectual Property, bringing together Belgium, the Netherlands, and Luxemburg.[44] BOIP handles applications for registration of trademarks and designs. Appeals about BOIP decisions on the eligibility of an application are submitted to the *Cour d'appel* in Brussels, *Gerechtshof* in The Hague, or *Cour d'appel* in Luxembourg, based on territorial connecting factors laid out in the Benelux Convention on Trademarks and Designs.[45]

[41] Baechtold, Miyamoto, and Henninger, "International Patent Law," pp. 62–63.

[42] African Regional Intellectual Property Office, "About," available at www.aripo.org/index.php/about-aripo (accessed on March 1, 2018).

[43] Baechtold, Miyamoto, and Henninger, "International Patent Law," p. 63.

[44] Benelux Office for Intellectual Property, "About BOIP," available at www.boip.int/en/entrepreneurs/about-boip/organisation-and-policy (accessed on March 1, 2018).

[45] Benelux Office for Intellectual Property, Benelux Convention on Intellectual Property (Trademarks and Designs), text as lastly amended by the Protocol of July 22, 2010, entry into force on October 2, 2013, Arts. 2.12, 2.17. The English version is available at www.wipo.int/wipolex/en/other_treaties/text.jsp?file_id=473041 (accessed on March 1, 2018).

(d) The Eurasian Patent Organization (EAPO) brings together nine countries, which were part of the former Soviet Union.[46] Following the entry into force of the Eurasian Patent Convention in 1995, EAPO facilitates patent applications by conducting a prior art search and enabling applicants to submit a request for substantive examination within six months from the publication of a search report. Once a regional patent is granted, the applicant chooses the Member States in which the patent shall be maintained. Jurisdiction in disputes over the validity or infringement of a patent in a given Member State is granted to the respective national court, with such a judicial decision having effect only within that territory. Each country also maintains the right to grant compulsory licenses.[47] In November 2017, EAPO marked the overall submission of 50,000 applications.[48]

(e) The European Patent Office (EPO) brings together thirty-eight European countries (including all EU members),[49] which are signatories to the European Patent Convention (EPC).[50] A European patent is a bundle of individual national patents having effect in the EPO Member States chosen by the applicant. 2016 has seen a record number of granted EPO patents: 95,940 (40% up from 2015).[51] The EPC also provides a centralized post-grant opposition procedure and an administrative appeal procedure to the Boards of Appeal of the EPO.[52] At the same time, each EPO Member State may require a translation of the European patent within a certain time period, such that failure to comply with such a requirement makes the patent void in that state (therefore, making the process of applying for patents across Member States very costly). In addition, the fact that national courts are authorized to decide on the infringement and validity of European patents gives rise to problems of legal uncertainty, forum

46 Eurasian Patent Organization (EAPO), "EAPO: A History of Establishment and Development," available at www.eapo.org/en/history.html (accessed on March 1, 2018).

47 Baechtold, Miyamoto, and Henninger, "International Patent Law," pp. 63–64.

48 EAPO, "EAPO Congregates on the Occasion of the 50,000th Eurasian Application," November 30, 2017, available at www.eapo.org/en/news.php?pressview=view&d=697 (accessed on March 1, 2018).

49 EPO, "Member States of the European Patent Organization," available at www.epo.org/about-us/foundation/member-states.html (accessed on March 1, 2018).

50 EPO, The European Patent Convention, 16th edition (June 2016), available at www.epo.org/law-practice/legal-texts/epc.html (accessed on March 1, 2018).

51 EPO, "Annual Report 2016," available at www.epo.org/about-us/annual-reports-statistics/annual-report/2016.html (accessed on March 1, 2018).

52 EPO, "Boards of Appeal," available at www.epo.org/law-practice/case-law-appeals.html (accessed on March 1, 2018).

shopping, and high costs.[53] Given these deficiencies, as Section 5.2.3.1 will show, the EU is on the verge of establishing a unitary EU patent and a Unified Patent Court.

(f) The European Union Intellectual Property Office (EUIPO), as it is known since 2016,[54] deals with the registration of EU trademarks and community designs. Such trademarks and designs, once registered, are valid across all EU Member States. Appeals on a refusal to register a trademark or design, or a decision regarding an opposition to such a registration, are discussed before the Boards of Appeal,[55] with the General Court of the Court of Justice of the European Union (CJEU) having jurisdiction "to annul or to alter the contested decision" under the 2017 EU Regulation on the European Trade Mark,[56] and the 2002 Council Regulation on Community Designs, as amended.[57] While enforcement of EU trademarks and designs is left for national courts, the EUIPO system is presently the best illustration of a distinctive regional intellectual property.

(g) The Patent Office of Cooperation of the Council for the Arab States of the Gulf (GCC Patent Office),[58] which started operating in 1998, receives applications for regional patents in the Gulf Region. Such patents secure legal protection across all Member States upon validation of the regional patent in the Member States as of the date of grant. The Board of Directors of the GCC Patent Office may issue compulsory licenses in appropriate cases. Disputes pertaining to the infringement of a regional patent are examined by the competent authorities of Member States.[59]

[53] Baechtold, Miyamoto, and Henninger, "International Patent Law," pp. 64–65.

[54] European Union Intellectual Property Office, "About EUIPO," then "Who We Are," available at https://euipo.europa.eu/ohimportal/en/who-we-are (accessed on March 1, 2018). Prior to March 23, 2016, the organization was known as OHIM (Office for Harmonization in the Internal Market (Trademarks and Designs)).

[55] EUIPO, "Presidium of the Boards of Appeal," available at https://euipo.europa.eu/ohimportal/en/presidium-of-the-boards-of-appeal (accessed on March 1, 2018).

[56] Regulation (EU) 2017/1001 of the European Parliament and of the Council of 14 June 2017 (Codification), Art. 72, OJ (L 154/1), June 16, 2017.

[57] Council Regulation (EC) No 6/2002 of 12 December 2001 on Community designs (OJ EC (L 3/1), January 5, 2002), amended by Council Regulation No 1891/2006 of 18 December 2006 Amending Regulations (EC) No 6/2002 and (EC) No 40/94 to Give Effect to the Accession of the European Community to the Geneva Act of the Hague Agreement Concerning the International Registration of Industrial Designs, OJ EC (L 386/14), December 29, 2006.

[58] Patent Office of Cooperation of the Council for the Arab States of the Gulf, "About Us," available at www.gccpo.org/AboutUsEn/AboutUs.aspx (accessed on March 1, 2018).

[59] Baechtold, Miyamoto, and Henninger, "International Patent Law," pp. 65–66.

5.2.2 *Minimum Protection and Interstate Dispute Resolution: TRIPS and WTO*

As explained in Chapter 2, the World Trade Organization (WTO), established in 1994, is the successor of the 1948 General Agreement on Tariffs and Trade (GATT) as the chief international institution for trade issues. The Trade-Related Aspects of Intellectual Property Rights (TRIPS) Agreement is a binding part (Annex 1C) of the Marrakesh Agreement Establishing the World Trade Organization, which is actually made up of about sixty agreements, falling into six main parts.[60] It was the binding of intellectual property with trade, in light of the desire of practically every country in the world to be part of the WTO, especially in the context of tariffs and customs, which facilitated a global binding agreement on intellectual property that goes well beyond the Paris and Berne Conventions. An important amendment to the TRIPS Agreement – following the 2001 Doha Declaration[61] about the use of state-level compulsory licenses to provide access to essential medicines that are patent-protected[62] – was approved in 2005 and went into force in early 2017, when the required majority of two-thirds of WTO members ratified the amendment.[63]

TRIPS serves as a milestone in the design and implementation of globalization strategies for intellectual property in at least three aspects: (1) setting minimum substantive standards of protection for the various types of intellectual property rights covered under the agreement; (2) requiring states to provide "fair and equitable" enforcement proceedings, including remedies such as injunctions and damages, and under some circumstances, criminal sanctions against infringers; and (3) employing the WTO dispute-resolution system to settle interstate disputes about TRIPS.

[60] Marrakesh Agreement Establishing the World Trade Organization, signed in Marrakesh, Morocco, on 15 April 1994, 1867 UNTS 154, 33 ILM 1144, available at www.wto.org/english/docs_e/legal_e/04-wto_e.htm (accessed on March 1, 2018). The WTO started operating on January 1, 1995.

[61] World Trade Organization, Ministerial Declaration of 14 November 2001, WT/MIN(01)/DEC/1, 41 ILM 746 (2002).

[62] For the circumstances leading to the Doha Declaration, its content, and its aftermath, see H. B. Pauwelyn, A. T. Guzman, and J. A. Hillman, *International Trade Law*, 3d ed. (New York: Wolters Kluwer, 2016), pp. 729–732.

[63] See World Trade Organization, "WTO IP Rules Amended to Ease Poor Countries' Access to Affordable Medicines," January 23, 2017, available at www.wto.org/english/news_e/news17_e/trip_23jan17_e.htm (accessed on March 1, 2018). For the consolidated version of the TRIPS Agreement, following the entry into force of the amendment, see World Trade Organization, "TRIPS Agreement (as amended on 23 January 2017)," available at www.wto.org/english/docs_e/legal_e/31bis_trips_01_e.htm (accessed on March 1, 2018).

In terms of setting minimum substantive standards of protection, which may be seen as employing a globalization strategy of minimum harmonization (approximation), TRIPS governs an unprecedented scope of types of intellectual property rights covered under a single agreement: patents, copyrights, trademarks, geographical indications, industrial designs, trade secrets, and layout designs of integrated circuits. For each such category, TRIPS identifies the types of knowledge that may be protected within such a right (thus, for example, defining and protecting works such as computer programs as an object of copyright, and identifying rental rights as part of copyright protection),[64] and a minimal scope of protection for each such component (for example, by requiring that the term of protection of a patent would be at least twenty years from the filing date).[65] For each type of intellectual property, TRIPS also enables states to introduce state-level exceptions to the protection of the right. In the case of patents, for example, TRIPS reads:

> Members may provide limited exceptions to the exclusive rights conferred by a patent, provided that such exceptions do not unreasonably conflict with a normal exploitation of the patent and do not unreasonably prejudice the legitimate interests of the patent owner, taking account of the legitimate interests of third parties.[66]

TRIPS sets out *minimum* standards of protection. As such, it allows Member States to implement more extensive protection in their domestic laws, and to negotiate such extended protection as part of bilateral or multilateral agreements (particularly free-trade agreements) outside of TRIPS. The United Stated has been particularly active in negotiating such "TRIPS-plus" provisions vis-à-vis its trade partners.[67]

As for interstate dispute resolution, TRIPS offers a major institutional step toward globalization by requiring all Member States to accept the authority of the WTO's dispute-settlement mechanism, administered by its Dispute Settlement Body (DSB), which is part of the WTO's General Council.[68] The DSB sets up panels to adjudicate specific disputes among

[64] Pauwelyn, Guzman, and Hillman, *International Trade Law*, p. 714.
[65] TRIPS Agreement, Art. 33.
[66] Ibid., Art. 30.
[67] C. Fink and P. Reichenmiller, "Tightening TRIPS: Intellectual Property Provisions of U.S. Free Trade Agreements," in R. Newfarmer (ed.), *Trade, Doha, and Development: A Window into the Issues* (Washington D.C.: The World Bank, 2006), pp. 285–300.
[68] Pauwelyn, Guzman, and Hillman, *International Trade Law*, pp. 128–138.

states. The panel's final report is referred to the DSB for formal adoption, which takes place within sixty days unless there is a consensus among Member States *not* to adopt it or an appeal has been filed to the WTO Appellate Body.[69] An examination of the intellectual property disputes brought so far before the WTO shows that only a few dozen requests for TRIPS-related consultations were filed, and that between 1995 and 2010 only nine disputes reached a WTO panel and only three of those went before the Appellate Body. Most of these decided cases focused on the interpretation of the TRIPS provisions authorizing exceptions to the protection of copyrights (Article 13), trademarks (Article 17), and patents (Article 30), or on the provisions of Part III of TRIPS, relating to the commitments of Member States for effective domestic enforcement of intellectual property rights.[70]

5.2.3 *Current Intellectual Property: Cross-Border Norms and Institutions*

This section briefly portrays the current state of globalization strategies for intellectual property rights covered by the TRIPS Agreement as well as by other recent instruments and mechanisms.[71]

5.2.3.1 Patents

Patents are covered by Part II, Section 5 (Articles 27–34) of the TRIPS Agreement. As noted, the only amendment to the TRIPS Agreement so far (and actually, to the entire WTO Agreement) was made in regard to the use of compulsory licenses for generic production of patent-protected essential medicines, so that TRIPS now allows also for exporting such generic medicines to other states under the conditions set forth in Article 31bis and the Annex to the TRIPS Agreement.

More generally, TRIPS sets the basic standards for patent protection of inventions provided that they are "new, involve an inventive step and are

[69] Ibid., p. 135. The negative consensus rule is a fundamental change from the previous dispute-settlement system under GATT, where a positive consensus was required to adopt a final report, thus permitting a dissatisfied losing party to block any action on the report. Ibid.

[70] Ibid., pp. 715–727.

[71] This section does not cover utility models, microorganisms, and plant varieties, not covered by TRIPS. See generally WIPO, "World Intellectual Property Indicators 2017," pp. 209–211. It also excludes layout designs (topographies) of integrated circuits, covered by Part II, Section 6 (Articles 35–38) of TRIPS.

capable of industrial application,"[72] while allowing Member States to exclude from patentability inventions due to considerations of *ordre pubic* or morality,[73] as well as certain specific inventions, such as diagnostic or surgical methods.[74] TRIPS lists the types of exclusive rights granted to patent owners (Article 28), while enabling Member States to introduce general exceptions to the protection of patents (Article 30) as well as to allow specific uses that do not require the consent of patent owners (Article 31).

As noted in Section 5.2.1, while there is no global registration of patents, the 1970 Patent Cooperation Treaty (PCT),[75] which has 152 contracting states as of early 2018,[76] allows for a sequential or simultaneous mechanism of applications for registration of patents in national registries. The PCT process falls into two main phases: the international phase and the national/regional phase. At the international phase, orchestrated by the International Bureau of WIPO, the filing of an application is followed by an international search report, a supplementary international search, and an international preliminary examination report, all of which are then communicated to the national/regional offices or the jurisdictions for which the applicant wishes to obtain a patent. At the end of the international phase, the applicant must decide whether he or she wishes to pursue the next phase. If so, the applicant pays national/regional fees, provides a translation, and appoints a local agent, where required, within a certain time limit. The national/regional offices then examine the application and decide whether to grant the patent on the basis of the applicable national/regional legislation.[77]

Finally, as presented in Chapter 2,[78] the European Union is currently in advanced stages of introducing a "unitary patent package," which will include an EU-wide registry for patents and a Unified Patent Court.[79]

[72] TRIPS, Art. 27(1).

[73] TRIPS, Art. 27(2).

[74] TRIPS, Art. 27(3).

[75] Patent Cooperation Treaty, *supra*.

[76] For a list of PCT contracting states, see WIPO, "PCT System," then "The PCT Now has 152 Contracting States," available at www.wipo.int/pct/en/pct_contracting_states.html (accessed on March 1, 2018).

[77] C. A. M. Mulder, "The Patent Cooperation Treaty," in D. J. Gervais (ed.), *International Intellectual Property: A Handbook of Contemporary Research* (Cheltenham, UK: Edward Elgar Publishing, 2015), pp. 312–337.

[78] See Chapter 2, Section 2.3.4.6.

[79] European Patent Office, "Unitary Patent & Unified Patent Court," available at www.epo.org/law-practice/unitary.html (accessed on March 1, 2018).

The unitary patent is based on two EU regulations that went into force in 2013. Regulation (EU) No 1257/2012 on Implementing Enhanced Cooperation in the Creation of Unitary Patent Protection"[80] lays the foundations for a unitary patent, which would be granted by the European Patent Office (EPO), presented in Section 5.2.1. The patent will be granted a unitary effect for the territories of the twenty-five participating states (all EU countries except for Spain, Poland, and Croatia).[81] Council Regulation (EU) No 1260/2012 on Applicable Translation Arrangements[82] sets out the translation arrangements required for the unitary protection across participating states.

Both regulations will be applicable once the Agreement on a Unified Patent Court,[83] signed by twenty-five EU Member States on February 2013, will have been properly ratified. One threshold has already been met with more than half of the signatories – fifteen states as of early 2018 – ratifying the agreement.[84] In addition, the agreement has to be specifically ratified by Germany, France, and the United Kingdom, comprising the three EU Member States in which the highest number of European patents had effect in the year preceding the signature of the agreement.[85] As of May 2018, France has done so, as did the United Kingdom,[86] despite the encertainty created by the 2016 Brexit referendum.[87] Germany has not yet ratified the agreement. Once launched, the Unified Patent Court will have exclusive jurisdiction for litigation over

[80] Regulation (EU) No 1257/2012 of the European Parliament and of the Council of 17 December 2012 Implementing Enhanced Cooperation in the Area of the Creation of Unitary Patent Protection, OJ (L 361/1), December 31, 2012.

[81] European Patent Office, "Unitary Patent," available at www.epo.org/law-practice/unitary/unitary-patent.html (accessed on March 1, 2018).

[82] Council Regulation (EU) No 1260/2012 of 17 December 2012 Implementing Enhanced Cooperation in the Area of the Creation of Unitary Patent Protection with Regard to the Applicable Translation Arrangements, OJ (L 361/89), December 31, 2012.

[83] For the full text of the Agreement on a Unified Patent Court, see http://documents.epo.org/projects/babylon/eponet.nsf/0/A1080B83447CB9DDC1257B36005AAAB8/$File/upc_agreement_en.pdf (accessed on March 1, 2018).

[84] For a list of the current state of ratifications, see European Council, "Agreement on a Unified Patent Court (UPC)," available at www.consilium.europa.eu/en/documents-publications/treaties-agreements/agreement/?id=2013001 (accessed on May 31, 2018).

[85] European Patent Office (EPO), "When Will the Unitary Patent System Start?," available at www.epo.org/law-practice/unitary/unitary-patent/start.html (accessed on March 1, 2018).

[86] European Council, "Agreement on a Unified Patent Court (UPC)."

[87] T. Jaeger, "Reset and Go: The Unitary Patent System Post-Brexit," *International Review of Intellectual Property and Competition Law*, 48 (2017), pp. 254–285.

European patents with a unitary effect. It will include a Court of First Instance, a Registry, and a Court of Appeal.[88] As such, it will enable a full-fledged regional/supranational strategy.

5.2.3.2 Copyrights

Copyrights are covered in TRIPS by Part II, Section 1 (Articles 9–14). Article 9 incorporates the provisions of Articles 1 to 21 of the Berne Convention,[89] such that TRIPS Member States undertake to comply by the said provisions of the Berne Convention, while subjecting the commitment of such countries to the TRIPS system, including the WTO dispute-resolution bodies.

As such, the TRIPS/Berne framework ensures a minimum protection of copyrights and related rights in a number of ways, including through a broad definition of the types of "literary and artistic works" that may be the object of copyright protection.[90] TRIPS clarifies some of the ambiguities in the Berne Convention by providing, on the one hand, that copyrights shall not extend to "ideas, procedures, methods of operation or mathematical concepts as such" (Article 9(2)), and explicitly including computer programs and certain compilations of data (Article 10), on the other. TRIPS goes further to clarify some of the minimum requirements set forth in the Berne Convention, such that the basic term of protection – life of the author plus fifty years (Berne Convention, Article 7(1)) – is set at fifty years from the date of authorized publication when calculated on a different basis.[91] TRIPS leaves untouched the provision of Article 5(2) of the Berne Convention, by which copyrights "may not be subject to any formality," such as registration with a government office.[92]

TRIPS also introduces the concept of rental rights for protected works (Article 11) and provides for the protection of performers, producers of sound recordings, and broadcasting organizations (Article 14), while somewhat reformulating the rules on limitations and exceptions, such that

88 European Patent Office, "Unified Patent Court," available at www.epo.org/law-practice/unitary/upc.html#tab1 (accessed on March 1, 2018).

89 TRIPS Article 9 excludes, however, Article 6bis of the Berne Convention from state commitments under TRIPS.

90 Berne Convention, Art. 2(1).

91 TRIPS, Art. 12.

92 J. G. Sprankling, *The International Law of Property* (Oxford: Oxford University Press, 2014), p. 104.

> Members shall confine limitations or exceptions to exclusive rights to certain special cases which do not conflict with a normal exploitation of the work and do not unreasonably prejudice the legitimate interests of the right holder.[93]

The interpretation of the limitations and exceptions provision has been the object of a WTO panel decision in a complaint against the United States brought by the European Union (triggered by the Irish Music Rights Organization).[94] The European Union argued that then-in-force Section 110(5) of the US Copyright Act – which allowed certain types of restaurants, bars, and retail stores to broadcast music to their customers without paying the copyright holder – does not meet the requirements of TRIPS Article 13 for such an exemption.[95] The WTO panel agreed, reasoning that the broad applicability of the exemption to many types of businesses goes beyond the Article 13 concept of "certain special cases," undercuts a major source of royalties for right-holders (thus not falling under "normal exploitation"), and unreasonably prejudices the interests of right-holders by causing them an "unreasonable loss of income."[96] As this decision shows, the supranational dispute-resolution process by the WTO can have a significant role in interpreting the TRIPS Agreement and in creating a dynamic body of harmonized legal norms.

5.2.3.3 Industrial Designs

Industrial designs are governed by Part II, Section 4 (Articles 25–26) of TRIPS. The provisions are concise, and they essentially require Member States to provide "protection of independently created industrial designs that are new and original," while enabling states not to protect designs that are "dictated essentially by technical or functional considerations" (Article 25). Article 26(3) provides that the duration of protection shall amount to at least ten years. Article 26(2) allows Member States to provide limited exceptions to the protection of industrial designs, only if

> [S]uch exceptions do not unreasonably conflict with the normal exploitation of protected industrial designs and do not unreasonably prejudice

[93] TRIPS, Art. 13.

[94] Pauwelyn, Guzman, and Hillman, *International Trade Law*, p. 717.

[95] World Trade Organization, United States – Section 110(5) of the US Copyright Act, WT/DS160/R (June 15, 2000), paras. 3.1–3.4, available at www.wto.org/english/tratop_e/dispu_e/1234da.pdf.

[96] Ibid., paras. 6.190–6.229.

> the legitimate interests of the owner of the protected design, taking account of the legitimate interests of third parties.

As noted in Section 5.2.1, industrial designs have long been governed by a coordination system for submitting multiple applications for registration, known as the Hague System, and composed of a series of instruments, including the 1925 Hague Agreement, 1960 Hague Act, 1999 Geneva Act, and the 2017 Common Regulations.[97] The 1925 Hague Agreement has sixty-seven signatories,[98] with slightly smaller numbers of counterparts joining subsequent instruments in the Hague System.[99]

The Hague System of international registration of industrial designs is administered by the International Bureau of WIPO.[100] A single international application may include several different designs up to a maximum of 100, provided that all designs included in the same application belong to the same class based on the international classification of Locarno.[101] An international application that complies with the prescribed formal requirements is recorded in the International Register and then published in the International Designs Bulletin.[102] Upon such publication, the office of each designated contracting party can proceed with the substantive examination, if any, provided for by its own legislation. A refusal of protection, if any, must be notified to the International Bureau within six months from the date of publication of the international registration. If no notification of refusal has been sent within the applicable refusal period, the industrial design is protected in the territory of the contracting party, having the same effect as a grant of protection for an industrial design under the law of that country. International registrations are valid for an initial period of five years,

97 WIPO, "Hague Agreement Concerning the International Registration of Industrial Designs," available at www.wipo.int/treaties/en/registration/hague/ (accessed on March 1, 2018).

98 One of the members is the African International Property Organization (OAPI). See WIPO, "Administered Treaties," then "Contracting Parties," then "Hague Agreement," available at www.wipo.int/treaties/en/ShowResults.jsp?lang=en&treaty_id=9 (accessed on March 1, 2018).

99 The 1999 Geneva Act has fifty-three parties. WIPO, "Administered Treaties," then "Contracting Parties," then "Hague Agreement," then "Geneva Act (1999)," available at www.wipo.int/treaties/en/ActResults.jsp?act_id=7 (accessed on March 1, 2018).

100 WIPO, "Hague Guide for Users" (October 2017), available at www.wipo.int/export/sites/www/hague/en/guide/pdf/hague_guide.pdf.

101 WIPO, "Locarno Classification" (11th ed. 2017), available at www.wipo.int/classifications/locarno/en/.

102 WIPO, "Hague Guide for Users," p. 12.

and can be renewed for one or more additional periods of five years, up to the expiry of the total term of protection allowed by each contracting party.[103]

In the European context, as shown in Section 5.2.1, the Hague System is joined by the ability to register a single community design by the European Union Intellectual Property Office (EUIPO), thus further streamlining the cross-border coordination system of designs' registration.

5.2.3.4 Trademarks

TRIPS governs trademarks in Part II, Section 2 (Articles 15–21). It marks a significant step toward (minimum) harmonization, compared with the parts addressing trademarks in the Paris Convention (Articles 6–10), which essentially determined that the "conditions for the filing and registration of trademarks shall be determined in each country . . . by its domestic legislation."[104]

According to TRIPS Article 15(1), "any sign, or combination of signs, capable of distinguishing the goods or services," including for that matter "personal names, letters, numerals, figurative elements and combination of colours" shall be eligible for registration as trademarks. At the same time, under Article 15(2), states may establish other grounds for refusing to register trademarks, provided that such grounds "do not derogate from the provisions of the Paris Convention." More generally, the section on trademarks includes an exceptions clause, by which

> Members may provide limited exceptions to the rights conferred by a trademark, such as fair use of descriptive terms, provided that such exceptions take account of the legitimate interests of the owner of the trademark and of third parties.[105]

Article 16 defines the exclusive rights of use in favor of the owner of a registered trademark, and Article 18 provides that the minimum term of protection shall be seven years and that "the registration of the trademark shall be renewable indefinitely," while Article 19 establishes the conditions under which Member States may cancel the registration in case of non-use by the owner.

Somewhat similarly to the Hague System for industrial designs, the trademark system is governed by the Madrid system, based on the 1891

[103] Ibid., pp. 13–14.
[104] Paris Convention, Art. 6(1).
[105] TRIPS, Art. 17.

Madrid Agreement, 1989 Protocol Relating to the Madrid Agreement, and the 2017 Common Regulations concerning the Agreement and the Protocol.[106] As of mid 2018, the Madrid system includes 117 countries.[107]

According to the Madrid system, an application for international registration is presented to WIPO's International Bureau through the office of origin. Where the international application complies with applicable requirements, the trademark is recorded in the International Register and published in the WIPO Gazette of International Marks. The International Bureau notifies each contracting party in which protection has been requested, and each party has the right to refuse protection within a certain time limit (typically one year). If no such refusal is notified, the protection of the mark in each state is the same as if it had been registered locally. The international registration may be maintained in force indefinitely, upon payment of fees, every ten years.[108]

As with industrial designs, trademarks may be registered by the European Union Intellectual Property Office (EUIPO) so as to have force across all EU Member States. As with the Madrid System for international registration, the EU trademark can be renewed indefinitely every ten years.[109]

5.2.3.5 Geographical Indications

Geographical indications are covered in Part II, Section 3 (Articles 22–24) of TRIPS. Although the Paris Convention addressed the issue of "false indications" of the source of goods, its provisions were largely ineffective, this making TRIPS the first international treaty on intellectual

106 For the respective texts constituting the Madrid System, see WIPO, "Administered Treaties," then "Madrid Agreement Concerning the International Registration of Trademarks," available at www.wipo.int/treaties/en/registration/madrid/index.html (accessed on March 1, 2018). The Madrid Protocol has significantly more signatories than the Madrid Agreement: 101 counterparts as of mid 2018. See list of contracting parties at www.wipo.int/treaties/en/ShowResults.jsp?lang=en&treaty_id=8 (accessed on July 1, 2018).

107 World Intellectual Property Organization (WIPO), "Services," available at www.wipo.int/services/en (accessed on July 1, 2018).

108 WIPO, "Guide to the International Registration of Marks under the Madrid Agreement and the Madrid Protocol" (updated 2016), p. A3, available at www.wipo.int/export/sites/www/madrid/en/guide/pdf/guide.pdf (accessed on March 1, 2018).

109 EUIPO, "Trade Marks in the European Union," available at https://euipo.europa.eu/ohimportal/en/trade-marks-in-the-european-union (accessed on March 1, 2018).

property that substantively governs geographical indications through minimum harmonization.[110]

TRIPS identifies geographical indications as those which "identify a good as originating in the territory of a Member, or a region or locality in that territory, where a given quality, reputation, or other characteristic of the good is essentially attributable to its geographical origin."[111] The underlying goal of the geographical indication is to prevent the use of any means in the designation or presentation of a good "which misleads the public as to the geographical origin of the good."[112]

For wines and spirits, the protection offered to geographical indications is even more extensive, such that Member States should prevent use of the geographical indication "even where the true origin of the goods is indicated or the geographical indication is used in translation or accompanied by expressions such as *kind*, *type*, *style*, *imitation*, or the like."[113]

Article 24 includes detailed provisions about further "international negotiations" aimed at "increasing the protection of geographical indications under Article 23," while making room for exceptions based on criteria such a previous lengthy use of the indication,[114] good-faith registration of a trademark,[115] or where the indication is "identical with the term customary in common language as the common name for such goods or services in the territory of that Member."[116]

The need for such international negotiations highlights the unique cross-border clash of interests in the case of geographical indications, where the intellectual property rights do not necessarily belong to a specific manufacturer with exclusive rights, but rather to all producers within the region, thus making potential disputes a matter of national, regional, or local pride often voiced directly by respective public officials. The proprietary protection of particular geographical indications may thus implicate greater public or state direct involvement on different sides of the border than is the case with other types of intellectual property rights.[117] Such proprietary disputes, embedded in matters of

[110] Sprankling, *International Law of Property*, p. 105, fn 154.
[111] TRIPS, Art. 22(1).
[112] TRIPS, Art. 22(2(a).
[113] TRIPS, Art. 23(1).
[114] TRIPS, Art. 24(4).
[115] TRIPS, Art. 24(5).
[116] TRIPS, Art. 24(6).
[117] D. S. Gangjee, "Proving Provenance? Geographical Indications Certification and Its Ambiguities," *World Development*, 98 (2017), pp. 12–24.

cultural identity, are not restricted to the TRIPS Agreement. Thus, for example, as of early 2018, a lingering dispute between Spain and Mexico about two different types of cheese, both of which named *Manchego*, threatens to stall a new trade deal between Mexico and the European Union.[118] This recent controversy resonates with other disputes, often involving the United States and countries in the European Union, about the use of terms such as *Champagne* (sparkling wine, France), *Parmigiano-Reggiano* (cheese, Italy), or *Habana* (cigars, Cuba).[119]

5.2.3.6 Trade Secrets

The inclusion of trade secrets in TRIPS, referred to as "protection of undisclosed information" in Part II, Section 7 (Article 39), is a novelty in the setting of international conventions. While the Paris Convention generally refers to protection against unfair competition (Article 10bis (2)), the vagueness of this provision has done little to protect trade secrets at the international level.[120]

TRIPS refers to undisclosed information as one that is "secret," "has commercial value because it is secret," and "has been subject to reasonable steps to keep it secret,"[121] and provides that

> Natural and legal persons shall have the possibility of preventing information lawfully within their control from being disclosed to, acquired by, or used by others without their consent in a manner contrary to honest commercial practices.[122]

In the aftermath of TRIPS, numerous national and regional institutions have moved forward with protecting trade secrets. In 2016, US Congress passed the Defend Trade Secrets Act,[123] and in the same year, the European Union promulgated the Directive on the Protection of

118 D. Agren and S. Jones, "Cursed are the Cheesemakers: Spain and Mexico Locked in Manchego Dispute," *The Guardian*, January 15, 2018.

119 D. Makris, "Geographical Indicators: A Rising International Trademark Dispute between Europe's Finest and Corporate America," *Arizona Journal of International and Comparative Law*, 34(1), 2017, pp. 159–185.

120 Sprankling, *International Law of Property*, p. 109.

121 TRIPS, Arts. 39(2)(a)–(c).

122 TRIPS, Art. 39(2). A footnote (footnote 10) to this sentence reads: "For the purpose of this provision, 'a manner contrary to honest commercial practices' shall mean at least practices such as breach of contract, breach of confidence and inducement to breach, and includes the acquisition of undisclosed information by third parties who knew, or were grossly negligent in failing to know, that such practices were involved in the acquisition."

123 Defend Trade Secrets Act of 2016 (Public Law No. 114–153).

Undisclosed Know-How and Business Information against their Unlawful Acquisition, Use and Disclosure.[124] These two instruments are generally similar in following the TRIPS framework, although they exhibit some substantive and procedural variances.[125] While governed by TRIPS, trade secret protection can be seen as located beyond intellectual property law, being rather part of a broader, emerging body of cross-border norms on proprietary aspects of data, discussed in Section 5.3.1.

5.2.4 *The Landscape of Globalization Strategies in Intellectual Property*

The above survey of cross-border norms and institutions for the different categories of intellectual property mandates a principled analysis of the current landscape of globalization strategies, and of the ways in which the various strategies could be combined, rather than opting for a one-size-fits-all strategy. In one sense, the employment of a specific strategy is a sign of the evolutionary stage in which a certain intellectual property right is located such that it could move up the ladder of globalization strategies (i.e., toward approximation or supranationalism) when the time is right and the international circumstances so permit (consider the move from the Paris/Berne Conventions to TRIPS in setting-up minimum harmonization). But the simultaneous employment of various strategies could also reflect a normative choice, one which requires closer unity for some types of intellectual property, but allows for diversity in other aspects. While functional considerations may often push toward supranationalism, normative considerations such as those concerning interstate economic disparities and their implications for access to essential medicines may call to distinguish between different aspects of intellectual property in devising the appropriate globalization strategy, such that uniformity should not serve as a panacea.

Consider, first, the role of soft law. While the TRIPS Agreement and the employment of the WTO dispute-resolution mechanism definitely

[124] Directive (EU) 2016/943 of the European Parliament and of the Council of 8 June 2016 on the Protection of Undisclosed Know-How and Business Information (Trade Secrets) against their Unlawful Acquisition, Use and Disclosure, OJ (L 157/1), June 15, 2016.

[125] For a comparative analysis of these two instruments, see A. B. Patel et al., "The Global Harmonization of Trade Secret Law: The Convergence of Protections for Trade Secret Information in the United States and European Union," *Defense Counsel Journal*, 83 (2016), pp. 472–486.

tilt the pendulum of intellectual property toward more binding cross-border commitments and at least partially effective enforcement, the current jurisprudential and institutional structure of intellectual property law is still highly fragmented. Different levels of binding state commitments to cross-border norms apply to the various categories of intellectual property – allowing in turn for respective disparities among national laws that implement these various commitments – and each such category of intellectual property has a different set of institutions operating at the regional and international levels, with no cross-field coordination between them (consider the different sets of international institutions operating under the PCT, Madrid, and Hague systems, and the seven regional offices discussed in Section 5.2.1).

Given this fragmentation, soft law might play a role in identifying shared principles or concepts that could alleviate some of the problems of legal arbitrages and uncertainty. Graeme Dinwoodie and Rochelle Dreyfuss call to adopt an international property law "acquis" – a set of basic principles that form the background norms driving the intellectual property system.[126] Such an *acquis* broadly considers and balances the major pillars of intellectual property law, such as access-regarding principles; rights of authors, traders, and inventors; national autonomy; and interdependence. It can serve, in turn, as a tool for treaty interpretation or lawmaking templates, while putting developed and developing counties on more equal footing in future negotiations.[127]

Moving to hard law strategies, the disparities that exist between national laws even in matters governed by TRIPS – in view of "exceptions" provisions, the possibility to go above minimum standards, etc. – and the fact that enforcement is done mostly at the national level, leave ample room for the conflict of laws strategy. As for jurisdiction, while the paradigm of cross-border intellectual property law has traditionally looked at the specific territory in which the alleged infringement takes place, in the current age of digital dissemination of content, simultaneous infringements make jurisdictional issues much more challenging. This is especially so when the right-holder argues that the infringement was somehow orchestrated by a certain entity, even if it was carried out by different defendants in multiple jurisdictions ("spider in the web" doctrine).[128]

126 Dinwoodie and Dreyfuss, "An International *Acquis*," pp. 121–164.
127 Ibid., pp. 153–158.
128 Torremans, "Intellectual Property and Private International Law," Part 2 (Jurisdiction).

Similar problems arise in regard to the applicable law. Somewhat similarly to the discussion of choice of laws in the context of tangible and intangible goods in Chapter 4, the inherent right to trade in intellectual property (whether by sale, rent, license, or other kind of contractual right to use) raises a potential tension between party autonomy and the *in rem* trait of intellectual property. Thus, for example, while the question of assignability of a certain right may be addressed by the law of the protecting country (*lex loci protectionis*) – such as the one in which a patent is registered – the terms of the assignment, if principally valid, could be governed by the law of the contract (*lex contractus*).[129] Although such issues are complex and of increasing importance in the global digital economy, international and regional intellectual property instruments sparsely deal with such conflict of laws issues. This deficit requires a comprehensive employment of a conflict of laws strategy, one that addresses the era of digital, mass-scale, multijurisdictional infringements.

Approximation is by far the most dominant hard law strategy devised under TRIPS and other international and regional instruments. It takes the form of minimum harmonization, which on the one hand allows for both downgrades in the form of exceptions and other local exemptions, and upgrades in the sense that countries are at liberty to provide increased domestic protection and negotiate such increased standards in bilateral agreements (e.g., by TRIPS-plus provisions).[130] Approximation can also be seen as characterizing the various mechanisms for application and registration of intellectual property across multiple jurisdictions, such as under the PCT, Madrid, and Hague systems. While the final authority of whether to register a patent, trademark, or industrial design lies with the local registrar, these systems approximate the process and administrative aspects, and to some extent frame the substantive discretion of national authorities.

The soft spot of the approximation strategy probably lies in the enforcement of intellectual property rights in national courts. Despite the general commitments undertaken by contracting states under TRIPS, countries still diverge in enforcement procedures and substantive outcomes, including through different interpretations of international agreements and implementing local legislation.

[129] Ibid., Part 3 (Choice of Law).

[130] See Section 5.2.2.

One such prominent example is the Supreme Court of India's 2013 decision in *Novartis* v. *Union of India*.[131] India's 1970 Patents Act originally excluded the possibility of patenting "substances intended for use . . . as food or as medicine or drug."[132] To conform to TRIPS, India amended its Patents Act effective as of 2005 to delete this section. At the same time, the amended Act limited patentability only to drugs created after 1995 and subject to additional constraints, particularly those enumerated in Sections 2(ja) and 3(d) of the Act, which condition the patentability of a "new product" on "technical advance as compared to . . . existing knowledge" and on "enhancement of the known efficacy."[133] Gleevec, Novartis's original drug for leukemia treatment, was developed in the early 1990s and was thus not patentable in India. In 1998, Novartis filed an application for a beta version of the drug, arguing it was a "new" and "superior" version.[134]

The court articulated the rationale of the 1970 Patents Act as an antidote to the English colonial patent laws that did "little good to the people of the country" and served mostly the interests of foreigners, especially in the context of food and medicine that are "vital to the health of the community" and "must be available at reasonable prices."[135] The court expounded the position of India and other developing countries during and following the negotiations on TRIPS, including those leading to the 2001 Doha Declaration. It identified concern that overbroad patent protection might put "life-saving medicines beyond the reach of a very large section of people."[136] It held that the legislature, "while harmonizing the patent law in the country with the provisions of the TRIPS Agreement, strove to balance its obligations under the international treaty and its commitment to protect and promote public health considerations."[137] Finally, the court held that Novartis did not convincingly demonstrate the required "enhanced efficacy."[138] Whether one accepts the normative premises of the Indian Supreme Court as valid or not, the *Novartis* case points to the limits of the approximation strategy in a system that relies essentially on domestic implementation and enforcement of cross-border norms. It is therefore much short of unification.

131 *Novartis AG* v. *Union of India*, (2013) 6 S.C.C. 1 (India).
132 The Patents Act, No. 39 of 1970, § 5, India Code (1970).
133 The Patents (Amendment) Act, No. 15 of 2005, §§ 2(ja), 3(d), India Code (2005).
134 *Novartis*, para. 8.
135 Ibid., paras. 31, 42.
136 Ibid., para. 66.
137 Ibid.
138 Ibid., paras. 173, 184.

The supranationalism strategy comes in certain varieties in the current landscape of intellectual property. The registration of EU trademarks and of community designs can be seen as creating a hybrid system, in which the substantive examination and consequent registration is made by a supranational entity – the European Union Intellectual Property Office (EUIPO) – with cross-border protection across all EU Member States. Disputes over validity and infringement are done by national courts. Thus, for example, according to Chapter X, Section 2 of the 2017 Regulation on the European Union Trade Mark,[139] each Member State designates courts of first and second instances to decide such disputes. In certain cases, each such court has jurisdiction over any act of infringement committed or threatened within the territory of any of the EU Member States, whereas in other cases, jurisdiction is limited to acts committed and threatened in the court's territory.[140] As for applicable law, the nationally designated EU trademark courts apply the Regulation, but in matters not covered by the Regulation, the court applies "the applicable national law."[141]

A full-scale switch to a supranationalism strategy will take place in the European Union when the unitary patent package, depicted in Section 5.2.3.1, will be materialized. The unitary patent will be granted by the European Patent Office (EPO) and all disputes pertaining to the unitary patent, such as its enforcement or validity, will be resolved by the Unified Patent Court. Until that time, the cross-border protection of patents across the EU will continue to rely on other strategies.

5.3 Data and Digital Assets in a Global Context

This section analyzes the emerging landscape of cross-border norms and institutions that deal with data and digital assets, other than in matters already governed by intellectual property aspects (to the extent that the latter considerations apply to a certain piece of data or digital asset). While the practical cross-border implications of data and digital assets are evident because of the borderless-nature of digital technology, the legal aspects are far from settled. This is so because the proprietary aspects of data and digital assets are still not developed within domestic legal systems, such that the phase of cross-border ordering of proprietary

[139] Regulation (EU) 2017/1001 of the European Parliament and of the Council of 14 June 2017 (Codification), Chapter X, Section 2 (Arts. 123–133), OJ (L 154/1), June 16, 2017.

[140] Ibid., Arts. 125–126.

[141] Ibid., Arts. 129(1)–(2).

rights will often have to await locally based legal development. Accordingly, this section starts by identifying the emerging jurisprudence in national systems about whether data and digital assets are considered "property," and it will then move to consider the few cross-border aspects of data and digital assets that have already been addressed, and those issues that are still located in a *terra incognita*. This section concludes by examining the potential of the blockchain technology to serve as a decentralized, cross-border system for documenting, validating, and registering proprietary rights in a variety of data and digital assets.

5.3.1 Data and Digital Assets as Objects of Property Rights

The term *digital assets* may refer to a broad plethora of resources, such as e-mail and social media accounts, electronic media in digital form such as music, videos, and books, or reward points earned by persons participating in a retail program or using a certain credit card.[142] Similarly, the term *data* may cover a vast array of information, or more accurately, compilations of information that are stored or kept on certain data carriers, either human or nonhuman carriers.[143]

The question whether a digital asset or piece of data can be seen as an object of property, and what are the particular types and contents of property rights that apply to such an asset, involves both conceptual and normative dimensions. Such an inquiry calls for a contextual analysis, such that different types of digital assets or data may be subject to distinctive legal frameworks.

Starting with the conceptual dimension, the principles of property law generally require that the object would be clearly described and delineated,[144] and that the asset's outer limits – whether physical or conceptual – would be known publicly so that unauthorized parties would not encroach on it.[145] While the form of publicity may vary, distant parties should have a practical way of identifying the object and right thereto

[142] N. M. Banta, "Property Interests in Digital Assets: The Rise of Digital Feudalism," *Cardozo Law Review*, 38 (2017), pp. 1099–1157 at 1102–1103.

[143] S. van Erp, "Ownership of Data and the Numerus Clausus of Legal Objects," Maastricht European Private Law Institute Working Paper No. 2017/6 (October 2017), available at https://ssrn.com/abstract=3046402 (accessed on March 1, 2018).

[144] Ibid., p. 12.

[145] T. W. Merrill and H. E. Smith, *Property* (New York: Oxford University Press, 2010), pp. 4–11.

so as to "keep off."[146] Data poses particular conceptual challenges, in addition to normative ones, in the attempt to distinguish between general or abstract information about the world and a particular compilation of information that has been generated through a deliberate process and has a distinct value as such. It should be noted that the question of whether a certain compilation of information amounts to an asset does not hinge solely on its potential protection as intellectual property, such as copyrighted material. The protection of data, such as pictures stored on one's computer or a cloud service, might involve protection against misappropriation or conversion that may be wrongful outside the realm of intellectual property.[147] That said, not all information is considered property, either conceptually or normatively, although digital assets or compilations of data that qualify as an asset are composed of protected information.[148]

On the normative level, the question whether a digital asset or data is worthy of property protection, and who should be entitled to enjoy property rights in regard to the asset, should often be broken down into more particular incidents of access, use, and control in regard to the asset. This is especially so because digital assets and data are typically controlled by an underlying standard contract, such as the one between a social network platform (e.g. Facebook) and an account user, or the one between seller and buyer of a digital asset. Such contracts purport to control issues such as potential limits on resale, transfer, or inheritance, or the right of the digital asset/data provider to extract personal information about the user for commercial purposes.[149] In addition to contract law, the legal landscape referring to digital assets and data also raises questions of intellectual property in the knowledge embedded in the asset. This in turn has implications for incidents of control, access, and use, such as the right of an owner/user of a digital asset or of a "smart property" (smartphone, smart home) to modify the asset's software or definitions.[150] Therefore, digital assets or data raise complicated questions,

[146] F. S. Cohen, "Dialogue on Private Property," *Rutgers Law Review*, 9 (1954), pp. 357–387 at 374.

[147] *Jonathan Dixon* v. *The Queen*, SC 82/2014 [2015] NZSC 147 (New Zealand), paras. 24–25.

[148] J. A. T. Fairfield, *Owned: Property, Privacy, and the New Digital Serfdom* (Cambridge: Cambridge University Press, 2017), pp. 157–161.

[149] Banta, "Property Interests in Digital Assets," pp. 1104–1113.

[150] Fairfield, *Owned*, pp. 4–5.

which go beyond merely defining the identity of the property owner at-large, in governing particular features of access, use, and control.

Some commentators depict the current practices and use of sweeping contractual provisions by corporations who provide digital assets or process data as creating a state of "digital feudalism,"[151] one in which users/consumers become "owned" rather than owners of digital assets or data.[152] They accordingly call to validate the status of users as underlying owners, by granting them certain incidents of property, even in the face of sweeping contractual provisions in favor of such corporations, such as a right to modify, right to sell, right to use, or right to exclude others.[153]

A brief survey of case law from several national jurisdictions may illustrate the type of practical challenges that courts deal with in addressing the proprietary nature of digital assets and data. These dilemmas have obvious implications for the cross-border ordering of such proprietary aspects, which is currently largely missing, with very few exceptions, as Section 5.3.2 will show.

In *Your Response Ltd.* v. *Datateam Business Media Ltd.*, a publishing company engaged a database company to hold and maintain its subscribers' record, which were kept on a database in electronic form. Subsequently, the publishing company terminated the contract and demanded release of the database information on it. The database company refused to release the information, claiming a common law lien over it. The English Court of Appeal addressed the historical distinction drawn in common law between tangible and intangible property, such that tangible property, referred to as *chattels* or *choses in possession*, could be the object of physical possession and thereby physical control, whereas intangible property (known as *choses in action*) could not.[154]

Referring to previous case law about the tort of conversion as a wrongful interference with the possession of tangible property, the court reasoned that "information of the kind that makes up a database ... if it constitutes property at all, does not constitute property of a kind that is susceptible of possession or of being the subject of the tort of conversion."[155] Following its observation that "the essential nature of a common law artificer's lien ... is a right to certain possession of goods delivered to him for the

[151] Banta, "Property Interests in Digital Assets," pp. 1147–1156.
[152] Fairfield, *Owned*, p. 3.
[153] Ibid., pp. 8–10.
[154] *Your Response Ltd.* v. *Datateam Business Media Ltd.* [2014] 3 WLR 887, para. 13.
[155] Ibid., para. 17.

purpose of carrying out work on them,"[156] the court concluded that intangible property "is equally not susceptible to the exercise of a possessory lien."[157] While relevant to all types of intangible property, the case reflects a particularly suspicious stance to the depiction of data (as opposed to a tangible carrier on which it is stored) as an object of property.

In *Jonathan Dixon* v. *The Queen*, the Supreme Court of New Zealand ruled that digital files qualify as "property" for purposes of Section 249(1)(a) of the Crimes Act 1961, by which a person commits a crime of accessing a computer system for a dishonest purpose when he "directly or indirectly, accesses any computer system ... and without claim of right ... obtains any property."[158] The court reasoned that "digital files can be identified, have a value and are capable of being transferred by others."[159] It also had a physical presence and altered the physical state of whatever medium it was stored on.[160] Per the court, whether digital files are classified as tangible or intangible assets, the digital files at issue (video footage) are property, and not simply information.

A 2018 decision by the Federal Court of Justice in Germany (*Bundesgerichtshof*) dealt with the right of parents to inherit the Facebook account of their fifteen-year-old daughter, who died after falling in front of an underground train in Berlin. The parents wanted access to her Facebook chats to see whether she had been victim of online bullying that might have led her to commit suicide. Facebook refused to grant such access, citing data protection and the potential exposure of other users who hold conversations with the understanding that their contents remained private.[161] A state court, weighing late nineteenth-century inheritance laws and doctrines on the right of parents toward minors with contemporary statutory provisions on telecommunications secrecy (*Telekommunikationgesetz*, Article 88), interpreted the latter statute as applying also to online chats, and upheld Facebook's decision to freeze the account and deny access to the parents. The Federal Court reversed, holding that the parents are entitled to inherit the daughter's account.[162]

156 Ibid., para. 16.
157 Ibid., para. 26.
158 *Dixon* v. *Queen*, para. 3.
159 Ibid., para. 25.
160 This is illustrated by the fact that electronic storage space (e.g., disk) can become fully utilized. Ibid., para. 39.
161 K. Connolly, "Parents Lose Appeal Over Access to Dead Girl's Facebook Account," *The Guardian*, May 31, 2017.
162 "Eltern dürfen auf Facebook-Konto ihrer toten Tochter zugreifen," *Frankfurter Allgemeine*, July 12, 2018 (in German).

Finally, national governments and courts are increasingly facing questions about the legal status of cryptocurrencies, such as Bitcoin. In 2014, the US Internal Revenue Service (IRS) issued a guidance, by which "virtual currency is treated as property" for US federal tax purposes, in contrast to "real" currency. This means that general rules for property transactions apply to "transactions in, or transactions that use, virtual currency."[163] In the 2016 case of *In re: Hashfast Technologies LLC*,[164] a California bankruptcy court held that the Bitcoin is not the equivalent of US dollars (i.e., not convertible currency) for purposes of the fraudulent transfer provisions under the US Bankruptcy Code. The ruling was made in the context of an attempt by a bankruptcy trustee to set aside a 2013 transfer from the estate of 3,000 Bitcoin, then worth $360,000, which have appreciated to a value of $1.2 million as of the date of the ruling (February 2016). The trustee argued that Bitcoin is property that can be converted by the estate at its (then) present appreciated value, while the defendant transferee argued that Bitcoin are the equivalent of US dollars, and thus the 3,000 Bitcoin that were transferred retained their lower US dollar value.[165]

The court held that it does not have to decide "whether Bitcoin are currency or commodities for purposes of the fraudulent transfer provisions of the bankruptcy code. Rather, it is sufficient to determine that . . . Bitcoin are not United States Dollars."[166] The court went further to state that if the transfer would indeed be invalidated as fraudulent, it will hold whether the trustee "may recover the Bitcoin (property) transferred or their value, and if the latter, valued as of what date."[167]

These court decisions dealt with particular types of digital assets or data in specific legal contexts, and are thus far from establishing a consolidated theory or comprehensive body of jurisprudence about the proprietary features of digital assets or data. It remains to be seen whether national legislatures will devise statutory schemes to address

163 Internal Revenue Services (IRS), "IRS Virtual Currency Guidance" (March 25, 2014), available at www.irs.gov/newsroom/irs-virtual-currency-guidance (accessed on March 1, 2018).

164 Bankruptcy Case No. 14–30725DM (Chapter 11), *In re: Hashfast Technologies LLC* (US Bankruptcy Court, Northern District of California, February 19, 2016), order on motion for partial summary judgement.

165 Manatt Phelps & Phillips LLP, "California Bankruptcy Judge Rules That Bitcoin Is Property, Not Convertible Currency, for Valuation Purposes under Fraudulent Transfer Laws," *Lexology*, March 24, 2016, available at www.lexology.com/library/detail.aspx?g=d80f280b-43e7-4168-bd7e-2d007a5652f5 (accessed on March 1, 2018).

166 *In re: Hashfast Technologies LLC*, *supra*.

167 Ibid.

the various features of digital assets or data as objects of property, and how they will order specific instances of access, use, and control.

5.3.2 Cross-Border Ordering of Data and Digital Assets

While national legal systems are in the early stages of conceptualizing data and digital assets as potential objects of property, there are presently almost no cross-border norms or institutions that address the proprietary aspects of data and digital assets. Other particular aspects relating to the cross-border ordering of data and digital assets are being dealt with, but in no systematic way. Accordingly, one cannot yet identify a specific globalization strategy that takes hold in the matter.

The contractual aspects of cross-border trade in digital assets are currently being addressed as part of the broader ordering of e-commerce, which includes Internet-based trading in both tangible and intangible assets. The digitization of international trade, and trade relating to digital assets in particular, is posing increasing challenges for the body of norms and institutions that traditionally governs the international sale of goods. At the moment, however, the effort to reconsider the fundamentals of contract law to accommodate the digital trade in digital assets is done mostly through decentralized practices rather than by top-down cross-border norms or institutions.[168] One particularly important development in the world of e-commerce concerns the gradual move to "smart contracts," algorithm-based protocols designed to facilitate self-executing contracts between buyers and sellers (using the blockchain technology discussed in Section 5.3.3). Smart contracts are particularly dominant in the trade of digital assets, such as cryptocurrencies.[169]

A more comprehensive cross-border system of norms and institutions is being developed in the context of data protection, in view of the fact that personal data is being transferred across borders and processed by MNCs operating search engines (e.g., Google), social networks (e.g., Facebook), or online retail (e.g., Amazon), in addition to online surveillance by governmental and intergovernmental agencies (e.g., Interpol). Cross-border mechanisms for the control of data, aimed at adequately balancing between privacy and legitimate commercial or public purposes, have been developed in particular between the United States and the

[168] S. Grundmann and P. Hacker, "Digital Technology as a Challenge to European Contract Law," *European Review of Contract Law*, 13 (2017), pp. 255–293.

[169] E. Turban et al., "Intelligent (Smart) E-Commerce," in E. Turban et al. (eds.), *Electronic Commerce* (New York: Springer, 2018), pp. 249–283.

European Union, in view of the fact that US corporations retrieve and process mass data collected by their European affiliates.

Prior to reviewing the current EU regulation on data privacy and the EU-US Privacy Shield Framework, a note is in order about two decisions by the Court of Justice of the European Union (CJEU), which had a key role in crafting legal instruments within and outside the European Union.

In *Google Spain SL* v. *González*,[170] the CJEU dealt with a complaint by Costeja González, a Spanish citizen, lodged with the national Data Protection Agency against Google Spain SL, Google, Inc., and the Spanish daily newspaper *La Vanguardia*. According to the complaint, a google search of González's name led to two notices published in *La Vanguardia* in 1998 about an auction of his home for the recovery of social-security debts. Stating that the proceedings have been since then fully resolved so that the reference was entirely irrelevant, González requested that the newspaper be required to remove the pages containing this personal data, and that Google be ordered to remove or conceal its search results that contain links leading to these web pages.

The CJEU held, first, that the activity of a search engine such as Google should be classified as "processing of personal data" within the meaning of the then-in-force 1995 Data Protection Directive,[171] and that the operator of the search engine is regarded as "controller" of such processing. Second, the processing of such data is seen as carried out within the territory of an EU Member State when the operator of the search engine sets up in the Member State a branch or subsidiary in order to promote the sale of advertising space by that engine. Third, as for "the right to be forgotten" – individuals have a right, under certain conditions, to ask search engines to remove links with personal information, when the information is excessive or no longer relevant, even if the publication itself is lawful. The right to be forgotten should be weighed, however, not only against the economic interest of the operator of the search engine, but also against the public interest in having access to that information, for example, when the person plays a public role.[172]

[170] Case No. C-131/12, *Google Spain SL, Google Inc.* v. *Agencia Española de Protección de Datos and Mario Costeja González* (CJEU, Grand Chamber), May 13, 2014.

[171] European Parliament and Council Directive 95/46/EC of 24 October 1995 on the Protection of Individuals with Regard to the Processing of Personal Data and on the Free Movement of Such Data, OJ (L 281/23), November 23, 1995.

[172] *Google Spain SL*, paras. 21–99.

In *Schrems* v. *Data Protection Commissioner (Ireland)*,[173] the CJEU addressed a complaint by an Austrian citizen, a Facebook user, against the transfer of data from Facebook's Irish subsidiary to servers located in the United States. The Irish supervisory authority rejected the complaint on the ground that the EU Commission has decided in 2000, based on the EU-US "Safe Harbor" scheme, that the United States ensures an adequate level of protection of the personal data transferred. The CJEU held that the existence of the EU Commission's decision, finding that a third country ensures an adequate level of protection of the data transferred, cannot derogate from powers granted to the national supervisory authority under the EU Charter of Fundamental Rights or the Data Protection Directive. The Court held that EU legislation permitting public authorities to have access on a generalized basis to the content of electronic communications compromises the essence of the fundamental right to respect for private life. The same holds true for legislation that does not provide any possibility for an individual to pursue legal remedies in order to have access to personal data. Finally, the Court ruled that the Commission's decision is invalid also because it does not have the authority to restrict the powers of national supervisory authorities.[174]

In the aftermath of these two decisions, the cross-border protection of data processed and transferred both among EU Member States and outside of the European Union is governed by the 2016 EU regulation on the protection of data and its movement ("General Data Protection Regulation"),[175] and more specifically, by the 2016 EU-US Privacy Shield Framework.[176]

The General Data Protection Regulation (GDPR), which went into full force on May 25, 2018, is designed to "harmonize data privacy laws across Europe, to protect and empower all EU citizens and to reshape the way organizations across the region approach data protection."[177]

173 Case No. C-362/14, *Schrems* v. *Data Protection Commissioner* (CJEU, Grand Chamber), October 6, 2015.

174 Ibid., paras. 37–98.

175 Regulation (EU) 2016/679 of the European Parliament and of the Council of 27 April 2016 on the Protection of Natural Persons with Regard to the Processing of Personal Data and on the Free Movement of Such Data, and Repealing Directive 95/46/EC, OJ (L 119/1), May 4, 2016.

176 Privacy Shield Framework, "Privacy Shield Overview," available at www.privacyshield.gov/Program-Overview (accessed on March 1, 2018).

177 European Union General Data Protection Regulation (EUGDPR), "GDPR Portal: Site Overview," available at www.eugdpr.org/ (accessed on March 1, 2018).

Probably the biggest change between the 1995 Directive and the 2016 GDPR is that the new regulation extends to "all companies processing the personal data of data subjects residing in the Union, regardless of the Company's location."[178] This means that national supervisory authorities, working together with the European Data Protection Board (EDPB), are authorized to enforce the duties under the regulation also on data controllers and processors located outside of the European Union, including by imposing administrative fines (Article 83) and other penalties (Article 84).

The rights of EU subjects – and respective duties of data controllers and processors – include, first and foremost, the requirement of consent, by which the processing of data usually requires the consent of the data subject (Article 6(1)(a)), with a request for such consent being "presented in a manner which is clearly distinguishable" from other matters, "in an intelligible and easily accessible form, using clear and plain language" (Article 7(2)). A related right is the right of access, by which the "data subject shall have the right to obtain from the controller confirmation as to whether or not personal data concerning him or her are being processed, and, where that is the case, access to the personal data" alongside other information detailed in Article 15(1). Finally, the GDPR enshrines the *Google Spain* ruling in that it establishes a right to be forgotten, by which under certain circumstances, "the data subject shall have the right to obtain from the controller the erasure of personal data concerning him or her without undue delay" (Article 17(1)).

Therefore, while the GDPR does not explicitly determine whether data amounts to property, and if so, who owns it, it regulates some of the key sticks in the bundle of ownership, by granting the data subject considerable control over the processing of data, access thereto, and its erasure.

The EU-US Privacy Shield Framework, crafted following the *Schrems* decision, governs the conditions under which personal data may be transferred from the EU (regardless of whether the data subject is a citizen of an EU Member State or not) to a company in the United States

[178] EUGDPR, "GDPR Key Changes," available at www.eugdpr.org/key-changes.html (accessed on March 1, 2018). GDPR applies to the processing of personal data by controllers and processors in the EU, regardless of whether the processing takes place in the EU or not. It also applies to the processing of personal data of data subjects in the EU by a controller or processor not established in the EU, where the activities relate to offering goods or services to EU citizens (even if for free) and the monitoring of behavior that takes place within the EU. Ibid.

for the purposes of processing the data. The Privacy Shield Principles,[179] to which US corporations must adhere if they wish to obtain certification from the US Department of Commerce to engage in data processing, include various obligations that align with the underlying principles of the GDPR. These obligations include informing the data subject about the types of personal data processed, the reasons why it is processed, and ensuring the data subject's own right of access to the data.[180]

Importantly, the Privacy Shield Framework establishes an array of domestic and cross-border institutions for resolving complaints of data subjects against US Privacy Shield corporations. In addition to lodging a complaint to the company itself, the data subject may also approach an independent Alternative Dispute Resolution (ADR) body (if such a body has been chosen by the company as its independent recourse mechanism), the data subject's relevant National Data Protection Agency, the US Department of Commerce, or the US Federal Trade Commission. If the complaint is wholly or partially unresolved using these redress mechanisms, or if the data subject is not satisfied with the way the complaint was handled, he or she may seek a binding arbitration before a "Privacy Shield Panel," as elaborated in Annex I of the Privacy Principles.[181] The protection of personal data, whether it is viewed as owned by the data subject or not, is thus one aspect of data that is being increasingly governed by cross-border norms and institutions.

Finally, another context concerning the cross-border legal ordering of digital assets, which articulates at least to some extent the proprietary aspects of such assets, is that of domain names. Essentially, a domain name is the digital address for a particular computer server, which functions as a portal, by allowing all internet users to interact with the content on the respective server.[182]

Prior to examining the cross-border nature of institutions in charge of registration of domain names and dispute resolution in regard thereto, it should be noted that a number of national courts have come to recognize

179 For the full text of the Privacy Shield Principles and the Annex thereto, see Privacy Shield Framework, "Privacy Shield Framework," available at www.privacyshield.gov/EU-US-Framework (accessed on March 1, 2018).

180 European Commission, "Guide to the EU-U.S. Privacy Shield" (2016), available at http://ec.europa.eu/justice/data-protection/document/citizens-guide_en.pdf (accessed on March 1, 2018).

181 Privacy Shield Principles, *supra*, Annex I, available at www.privacyshield.gov/EU-US-Framework.

182 Sprankling, *International Law of Property*, p. 89.

that a person has a property right in a registered domain name, rather than a mere contractual right. In *Kremen* v. *Cohen*,[183] the US federal Court of Appeals (Ninth Circuit) addressed the question whether a claim in conversion can be brought in the case of assignment of a domain name from one registrant to another based on a forged letter. To establish such a tort, "a plaintiff must show ownership or right to possession of property, wrongful disposition of the property right, and damages."[184] The court reasoned that "property is a broad concept that includes every intangible benefit and prerogative susceptible of possession or disposition,"[185] and applied a three-part test to determine whether a property rights exists: "first, there must be an interest capable of precise definition; second, it must be capable of exclusive possession or control; and third, the putative owner must have established a legitimate claim of exclusivity."[186] It held that

> Domain names satisfy each criterion. Like a share of corporate stock or a plot of land, a domain name is a well-defined interest. Someone who registers a domain name decides where on the Internet those who invoke that particular name – whether by typing it into their web browsers, by following a hyperlink, or by other means – are sent. Ownership is exclusive in that the registrant alone makes that decision. Moreover, like other forms of property, domain names are valued, bought and sold, often for millions of dollars ... Finally, registrants have a legitimate claim to exclusivity. Registering a domain name is like staking a claim to a plot of land at the title office. It informs others that the domain name is the registrant's and no one else's.[187]

Because of the inherent global nature of the Internet, the unique mechanism that developed for the registration of domain names is that of a global registry, which is currently run by a domestic US corporation with a quasi-governmental function and some intergovernmental features. To briefly explain, while the network was initially controlled by the US government, the management of the domain name system was contracted to Network Solutions, Inc., and then to the Internet Corporation for Assigned Names and Numbers (ICANN),[188] a nonprofit

[183] *Kremen* v. *Cohen*, 337 F. 3d 1024 (9th Cir. 2003).
[184] Ibid., p. 1029 (internal citations omitted).
[185] Ibid., p. 1030 (internal citations omitted).
[186] Ibid. (internal citations omitted).
[187] Ibid.
[188] ICANN, "Welcome to ICANN!," available at www.icann.org/resources/pages/welcome-2012-02-25-en (accessed on March 1, 2018).

corporation registered under the laws of California.[189] While ICANN's Board of Directors is made up of members who are not officials of a national government or an intergovernmental entity, ICANN's operations are supervised by the Governmental Advisory Committee (GAC), which is made up, as of early 2018, of 171 members and 35 observers who represent states and other international entities.[190] Generally speaking, registration is made on a first-come, first-served basis, if the domain name is not in current use, does not infringe a trademark, and meets other criteria set forth in the bylaws.[191]

Another key cross-border institutional feature of the domain names system concerns dispute resolution. In 1999, ICANN adopted the Uniform Domain Name Dispute Resolution Policy (UDRP).[192] Under Article 4 of UDRP, all parties who register domain names bind themselves to mandatory administrative proceedings, intended to resolve disputes in response to complaints made to ICANN (such as those asserting that the domain name is identical or confusingly similar to a trademark, or that the domain name has been registered and is being used in bad faith).[193] The complainant selects a "provider" tasked with resolving the dispute, out of a list of providers approved by ICANN.[194] The most dominant provider is the WIPO Arbitration and Mediation Center.[195] As of early 2018, the WIPO Center has processed over 37,000 cases through its Domain Name Administrative Panels, with the year 2016 seeing a record number of complaints filed.[196] WIPO thus serves as a binding supranational institution for dispute resolution over domain names.

[189] Sprankling, *International Law of Property*, pp. 89–90.

[190] ICANN – GAC, "General Advisory Committee," available at https://gac.icann.org/ (accessed on March 1, 2018).

[191] Sprankling, *International Law of Property*, p. 89. See ICANN, Bylaws for Internet Corporation for Assigned Names and Numbers, a California Non-Profit Public Benefit Corporation (as amended on July 22, 2017), available at www.icann.org/resources/pages/governance/bylaws-en (accessed on March 1, 2018).

[192] ICANN, Uniform Domain Name Dispute Resolution Policy (Approved on October 24, 1999), available at www.icann.org/resources/pages/policy-2012-02-25-en (accessed on March 1, 2018).

[193] Ibid., Art. 4.

[194] ICANN, "List of Approved Dispute Resolution Service Providers," available at www.icann.org/resources/pages/providers-6d-2012-02-25-en (accessed on March 1, 2018).

[195] WIPO, "Domain Name Dispute Resolution," available at www.wipo.int/amc/en/domains/ (accessed on March 1, 2018).

[196] WIPO, "WIPO Cybersquatting Cases Hit Record in 2016, Driven by New Top-Level Domain Names" (March 16, 2017), available at www.wipo.int/pressroom/en/articles/2017/article_0003.html (accessed on March 1, 2018).

The current fragmentation of the conceptualization of digital assets and data as potential objects of property is thus mirrored in the context-specific nature of cross-border norms and institutions that govern, if at all, various types of digital assets and data. This means that unlike intellectual property rights, which have come under a consolidated framework under TRIPS (at least to a considerable degree), digital assets and data are in very early stages of devising globalization strategies, and are practically typified by decentralization more than any other asset. As the next section shows, however, decentralization may *explicitly* shape the future path of property ordering.

5.3.3 Blockchain as a New Platform for the Globalization of Property?

The blockchain technology, popularized by the digital currency Bitcoin and other cryptocurrencies, is catching enormous attention as potentially revolutionizing the financial world. Its implications, however, already well exceed purely financial transactions,[197] and offer a decentralized alternative for creating, validating, and recording property rights in multiple assets.

The blockchain technology handles blocks – uniquely identified, linked transaction records – in a chain. A blockchain is a continuously growing, distributed, shared ledger of such blocks, which are sealed cryptographically with a digital fingerprint generated by a hashing function, such that each block is "chained" to the previous one by referring to its hash value.[198] This means that blockchains offer a record of consensus with a cryptographic audit trail that can be maintained and validated by multiple nodes. It allows contracting parties to dynamically track assets and agreements by using a common open-source protocol, thus streamlining verification processes.[199]

The decentralized, self-executing, and verified nature of blockchain-based transactions is facilitated by two core components: distributed

[197] B. Marr, "35 Amazing Real Life Examples of How Blockchain Is Changing Our World," *Forbes*, January 22, 2018.

[198] P. Treleaven, R. G. Brown, and D. Yang, "Blockchain Technology in Finance," *Computer*, September 2017, pp. 14–17.

[199] Ibid.

ledger technology (DLT) and smart contracts. A distributed ledger is a "decentralized, shared, replicated, and synchronized record of transactions between contracting parties, secured by cryptographic sealing." Nodes of a distributed ledger cannot trust other nodes, and so must independently verify transactions before applying them.[200]

A smart contract constitutes the rules that participants have collectively agreed upon to govern the evolution of "facts" in the distributed ledger. When paired with a blockchain that records changes of asset ownership, a smart contract can "serve as a wrapper for a transaction that automatically moves value and executes the contract's terms."[201] The blockchain functionality also allows users to operate with a high degree of confidence because transactions are unchangeable – they cannot be reversed or resequenced – ensuring all parties have an accurate and identical record. While not entirely bulletproof against cases of fraud,[202] blockchain is generally considered as alleviating the risks of deliberate actions that violate the *nemo dat* principle of property law.[203]

It is exactly the features of creating an alternative, decentralized, and verified recording system for transactions and asset ownership that illustrate the enormous potential of the blockchain technology to establish a cross-border *in rem* system of rights in assets that would not have to rely on top-down instruments and institutions, which are in short supply in the global setting. Just as blockchain allows for validating and registering transactions in cryptocurrencies by bypassing traditional centralized channels such as banks on the one hand, while eliminating or at least significantly alleviating problems of conflicting transactions or unauthorized transfers on the other,[204] so could this technology be utilized to establish a cross-border system for other assets.

200 Ibid.

201 Ibid.

202 Imperial College Business School, "Blockchain and Fraud Risk: What Does It Look Like?," undated, available at www.imperial.ac.uk/business-school/executive-education/resources/articles/blockchain-and-fraud-risk-what-does-it-look-like/ (accessed on March 1, 2018).

203 P. Bajpai, "How Stock Exchanges Are Experimenting with Blockchain Technology," *NASDAQ* (June 12, 2017), available at www.nasdaq.com/article/how-stock-exchanges-are-experimenting-with-blockchain-technology-cm801802 (accessed on March 1, 2018).

204 C. Koch and G. C. Pieters, "Blockchain Technology Disrupting Traditional Records Systems," *Financial Insights* (Federal Reserve Bank of Dallas), Vol. 6, Issue 2, 2017, pp. 1–3, available at www.dallasfed.org/outreach/insights/fi1702 (accessed on March 1, 2018).

While other types of digital assets are the natural candidates for such a cross-border system, tangible assets can also be the object of a blockchain-based cross-border system of property rights.

In November 2017, fintech startup Wave announced it successfully conducted a pilot, in collaboration with Israeli shipping company ZIM and Hong Kong-based logistics firm Sparx, using a blockchain-powered application for a paperless cross-border trade in goods. The service allows for the digital exchange and management of all shipping and trade-related documents, such as bills of lading, certificates of origin, certificates of inspection, and invoices, through a secure decentralized network. It targets all types of organizations involved in international trade, including banks, carriers, importers, exporters, customs and chambers of commerce.[205] If successful, blockchain technology can dramatically revise the system that had emerged centuries ago in order to facilitate a cross-border transfer of goods through negotiable documents of title.[206]

In 2018, Sweden has been experimenting with the blockchain technology for real-estate transactions. The landtmëterie, Sweden's nearly 400-year-old land mapping and registration authority, announced a pilot transaction to be facilitated through the blockchain technology, citing time-saving as a key motive for the initiative. Other land registries are also examining this technology.[207]

Digital technology can thus obtain what may have been viewed as trying to square the circle of property law: creating a decentralized *in rem* system trusted by everyone but controlled by none. While this mechanism would have to be further developed not only technologically, but also legally – such as by introducing to the blockchain-based transactions other proprietary rights, such as security interests, alongside ownership – its potential in the global setting is truly remarkable.

[205] S. Wass, "Wave Kicks Off Live Blockchain Pilots for Paperless Trade Solution," *Global Trade Review*, November 20, 2017, available at www.gtreview.com/news/fintech/wave-kicks-off-live-blockchain-pilots-for-paperless-trade-solution/ (accessed on March 1, 2018).

[206] For the proprietary role of documents of title, such as bills of lading and warehouse receipts, see J. Dalhuisen, *Dalhuisen on Transnational, Comparative, Commercial, Financial and Trade Law, Vol. II: Contract and Movable Property Law* (Oxford: Hart, 2016), pp. 627–638.

[207] S. Anand, "A Pioneer in Real Estate Blockchain Emerges in Europe," *The Wall Street Journal*, March 6, 2018.

5.4 Policy Analysis

Intellectual property, digital assets, and data seem at first glance to be ideal candidates for a strong-version globalization strategy in establishing and operating property law norms and institutions. Technology, innovation, and digitization know no national boundaries. They are easily disseminated, duplicated, and processed across all corners of the universe. Being new resources, as opposed to land or old-style chattels and other tangible goods, these assets may be allegedly free of centuries-old constraints that hinder the move from domestic legal systems to unified global governance.

In reality, however, the analysis of globalization strategies in the context of intellectual property, digital assets, and data is not so straightforward. This is so not only because there is already significant national path-dependency that cannot be easily done away with, especially in the context of intellectual property that is governed by national norms for two or three centuries. More importantly, national differences reflect core normative choices and ideological bents, such as those applying to resolving the tension between strong monopoly rights to pharmaceutical innovators and affordable access to life-saving medicines, or to the conflict between the commercial advantages of digital cross-border processing of data and the protection of privacy.

Accordingly, the following conclusions and policy implications can be drawn in examining the current status and potential future trajectory of globalization strategies for such types of assets:

(a) The employment of a specific globalization strategy could be a sign of an evolutionary stage in which a certain intellectual property right is located, such that it can move up the ladder of globalization strategies when the technological, geopolitical, or industry-specific circumstances so permit. Thus, for example, the switch to a (minimum) harmonization or approximation strategy for basically all types of intellectual property rights in the 1994 TRIPS Agreement was made possible because of the ability of Western countries to bind the membership at the new World Trade Organization (WTO) with a stronger commitment to protecting intellectual property rights by countries, such as China, with a strong interest in free trade.

(b) That said, intellectual property issues continue to exhibit genuine normative, cultural, and ideological differences between countries, and these may stand in the way of full-fledged harmonization. This is manifested, for example, in the Supreme Court of India's decision in the matter of *Novartis* and the balancing of India's international commitments with its societal values (discussed in Section 5.2.4), or in the interstate quarrels about geographical indications (analyzed in Section 5.2.3.5), which are as much about local pride as they are about property. This also means that although norm-making is governed mostly by TRIPS, the resolution of intellectual property disputes by national courts remains prone to strategic or genuine disparities in interpreting, implement, and enforcing the TRIPS commitments.

(c) Accordingly, soft law mechanisms, such as an international intellectual property law *acquis*, can play an important role in creating an open interstate dialogue in interpreting current international intellectual property instruments and developing them further. The conflict of laws strategy also remains essential for resolving questions of jurisdiction and applicable law, while addressing the complications that digitization entails, such as identifying the *locus* of mass digital duplication and dissemination of infringing content across national borders.

(d) The (minimum) harmonization or approximation strategy, which is the core of the TRIPS Agreement, definitely goes a long way in narrowing down legal disparities, but as already mentioned above, as long as dispute resolution remains mostly at the national level, intellectual property rights maintain a substantial domestic layer. The emergence of the PCT, Madrid, and Hague systems, alongside regional intellectual property registration offices (discussed in Sections 5.2.1 and 5.2.3), offer yet another variety of approximation that balances the standardization of process and substance with the preservation of national discretion.

(e) A full-fledged supranationalism strategy for intellectual property requires not only a single legislative and administrative setup, but also an adjudicative one. Once approved, the EU unitary patent framework will rely heavily on the operation of a Unified Patent Court to ensure that the EU-wide patent will be administered and enforced in a truly regional manner.

(f) Digital assets and data constitute the new front in conceptualizing, establishing, and enforcing cross-border proprietary rights. For such assets (but not only), the blockchain technology may offer an alternative which is outside the (closed) box of property law: an inherently decentralized system with a transparent and verifiable cross-border *in rem* effect.

6

Security Interests and Proprietary Priorities in Insolvency

6.1 The Growing Need for Cross-Border Norms on Security Interests and Insolvency

In the globalizing economy, in which individuals and corporations increasingly engage in cross-border commerce, investment, and other types of economic activity, the role of financial institutions and other entities, which extend credit or otherwise provide financing, is also changing. Banks, institutional investors, holders of investment securities, venture capital funds, sellers in credit-based transactions, and other actors must follow the economic performance of individuals and corporations, to which they extend credit and financing, across national borders. Moreover, in seeking to protect the funds they make available to their debtors, such providers of credit and financing need to understand their relative legal position vis-à-vis other creditors and financiers, alongside other stakeholders, such as national tax authorities, in different jurisdictions.

In particular, it is the question of proprietary priority in the distribution of the debtor's assets upon default, which requires creditors to realize how their legal position is impacted by the transfer of tangible and intangible assets across borders, multiplicity of creditors located in different countries, and other cross-border elements pertaining to the underlying obligations, identity of stakeholders, and assets available for distribution. This task is particularly challenging because the laws on security interests and insolvency have a strong national basis, featuring marked differences not only across legal families but also within them (such as the disparities between English and American law on security interests, surveyed below). Problems of legal arbitrage among different legal systems, and uncertainty about the jurisdiction, applicable law, and enforcement procedures in cases involving priority among various types of creditors or ranking in insolvency proceedings, might deter financiers from extending credit and thus hinder the efficacy of globalizing markets.

The challenge of legal disparities pertaining to security interests and insolvency results not only from the overall growth in cross-border mobility of assets, as surveyed in the opening section of Chapter 4, but also from the qualitative changes to financing schemes in contemporary economy.

Consider, for example, the mortgage (or hypothec, in civil law terminology), which is considered the quintessential security interest, and which used to have as its paradigm the scenario of a bank extending a loan to a homebuyer against a secured interest on a single real-estate asset. As such, the mortgage has been conventionally very local in nature, registered in a single national real-estate registry, and inherently applying the substantive and procedural norms of the *lex rei sitae*. This is not necessarily the case today. As one author notes:

> Loans secured on real estate today are amended, redeemed, subjected to both initial and subsequent syndication, assigned, certified, secured by charges against more than one property, divided up and sold in part. Refinancing measures, equity optimisation, risk control and diversification now make it increasingly necessary to transfer large portfolios of mortgage loans.[1]

What this new reality means is that individuals, business corporations, and financial institutions constantly engage in practices that move away from the single loan/single asset model for a secured transaction in real estate. Thus, loans for real-estate projects are nowadays regularly syndicated by several financial institutions, including through secondary syndication,[2] by which the bank originally granting the loan passes it on in tranches to other financial institutions, which may very well be located in different countries. Further, securitization of real-estate-based credit, which includes both pooling of multiple loans and the reslicing of such agglomerated debts into different tranches of bonds, and their consequent trade in stock-exchange markets, necessarily engages multiple investors/creditors from across the globe.[3] Moreover, modern credit instruments may also involve portfolio financing, by which multiple real-estate properties collectively serve as security for large-scale financing schemes. Portfolio finance thus adds yet another layer of legal

[1] O. Stöcker, "The Eurohypothec," in B. Akkermans, A. F. Salomons, and J. H. M. van Erp (eds.), *The Future of European Property Law* (Munich: Sellier, 2012), pp. 65–77 at 70.

[2] Ibid., p. 67.

[3] Thus, for example, the 2007 US subprime crisis, which became an international crisis due to the fraudulent securitization of bad debts and their sale in exchange markets, implicated creditors/investors from throughout the world. M. Landler, "U.S. Credit Crisis Adds to Gloom in Norway," *The New York Times*, December 2, 2007 (describing the financial distress of Norwegian villages who lost millions in purchasing dubious real-estate-based securities in US markets).

complexity to security interests, because it involves not only creditors and debtors located across borders, but it also implicates multiple assets that are essentially governed each by different national laws.[4]

Portfolio financing, which may be defined as "a funding package that encompasses a number of properties all owned by the same individual or company,"[5] obviously goes beyond real estate. In fact, it is much more prevalent in the context of movable assets, both tangible and intangible ones. The floating lien, developed in English law in the context of credit granted to companies, is conventionally premised on placing a "charge on assets both present and future," with such assets "expected to change in the normal course of business," thus allowing the company to sell such assets (primarily its commercial inventory) to buyers in the ordinary course of business, while subjecting new and future assets to the charge, and so forth.[6] While the English floating lien, and several functionally similar security interests developed in other common law countries and in civil law ones – allowing companies to enjoy financing while constantly replacing the charged assets in the ordinary course of business[7] – focused on inventories and other tangible assets, the focus in today's economy has largely switched to placing security interests on intangible assets.

Accordingly, probably the most prominent feature of financing to businesses is that of "receivables financing," by which the financial institution that extends credit or another form of financing to the corporation acquires a proprietary interest in the monetary claims (receivables) that the corporation has vis-à-vis its own customers or debtors.[8] Receivables financing typically takes one of two forms. The financial institution may receive a security interest over some or all of the receivables to which the corporation is entitled. Alternatively, the corporation may assign (i.e., transfer) its rights in the receivables to the borrower, a practice referred to as *factoring*.[9] This latter technique therefore uses the transfer of ownership in the receivables as a security device.

[4] Stöcker, "The Eurohypothec," pp. 66–68.

[5] Access Commercial Finance, "Portfolio Finance," available at https://accesscommercialfinance.com/commercial-property-finance/portfolio-finance/ (accessed on March 1, 2018) (commercial website).

[6] D. Sheehan, *The Principles of Personal Property Law* (Oxford: Hart Publishing, 2017), p. 346.

[7] S. van Erp and B. Akkermans, *Cases, Materials and Text on Property Law* (Oxford: Hart Publishing, 2012), pp. 454–464.

[8] G. McCormack, *Secured Credit under English and American Law* (Cambridge, UK: Cambridge University Press, 2004), p. 209.

[9] Ibid., pp. 209–210.

As Section 6.2.2 will show, the distinction between creating a security interest versus transferring ownership in receivables for security purposes may be difficult to make across legal systems, and the legal consequences of opting for each of these options may not always be clear.[10] But for present purposes, it suffices to say that the relative flexibility embedded in using present and future receivables and other streams of intangible benefits that the corporation is entitled to in order to support a financing scheme is increasingly appealing to both borrowers and lenders.

Consequently, international portfolio financing has increased in importance over time,[11] meaning that a corporation may pledge/assign receivables to which it is entitled vis-à-vis customers and other debtors located in different countries where the corporation is doing business. This means that the legal norms applying to the receivables, and to the use of these receivables for security purposes – through either the placement of a straightforward security interest on receivables or their assignment for security purposes – might have implications for multiple jurisdictions in which the assets and/or stakeholders are located. Accordingly, divergences in the laws applying to the creation, perfection, and enforcement of such security mechanisms (including the prospective ranking of creditors in regard to such receivables) might undercut the economic advantages that international receivables financing otherwise offers. The need for some type of a globalization strategy thus seems particularly essential for international receivables financing and similar financing schemes.

Probably the most challenging setup, with implications for competing interests of secured and unsecured creditors located in different jurisdictions and/or questions of proprietary priorities to assets located in different countries, concerns insolvency of multinational corporations (MNCs). From banks and other financial institutions such as Lehman Brothers,[12] to airlines (consider the 2017 collapse of the British Monarch Airlines),[13] manufacturers such as General Motors and Chrysler,[14] and up to telecom or Internet companies such as Nortel[15] and WorldCom,[16]

[10] Sheehan, *Principles of Personal Property Law*, pp. 385–386.

[11] A. J. Auerbach, "The Mirrlees Review: A U.S. Perspective," *National Tax Journal*, 65 (2012), pp. 685–708 at 697.

[12] See Section 6.4.2.4.

[13] G. Topham, "Monarch Airlines Collapse: UK's Biggest Peacetime Repatriation Underway," *The Guardian*, October 2, 2017.

[14] W. Duggan, "The 10 Largest Bankruptcies of all Time," *Yahoo Finance*, January 26, 2015.

[15] See Section 6.4.2.4.

[16] S. Romero and R. D. Atlas, "WorldCom's Collapse: The Overview; WorldCom Files for Bankruptcy; Largest U.S. Case," *The New York Times*, July 22, 2002.

cross-border insolvencies affect multiple stakeholders and assets located in different jurisdictions. This state of affairs requires some sort of a cross-border mechanism to facilitate the essential goal of insolvency or bankruptcy proceedings, that is, holding a collective process in which courts and the insolvency/bankruptcy administrators distribute the limited pool of assets of the debtor to its creditors based on the ranking of *in rem* priorities between the creditors. The establishment of respective priorities between different stakeholders is required for both liquidation and reorganization schemes. This task, which could be essentially viewed as a particular type of a property law challenge,[17] increasingly calls for weighing different globalization strategies, in view of the fact that insolvency laws and proceedings are traditionally governed by national legal orders. Harmonization and globalization strategies can potentially alleviate the risks involved with legal uncertainty,[18] and incentivize financial institutions to extend credit and other forms of financing.[19]

Sections 6.3 and 6.4 will survey the employment of various globalization strategies in an attempt to bridge over the current fragmentation of legal norms pertaining, respectively, to security interests and insolvency. At the outset, however, it is worth considering the broad economic agenda that has been driving initiatives for globalization or harmonization of laws on security interests and insolvency. This economic framework, often associated with the principles of the "Washington Consensus," promoted by international agencies such as the World Bank and the International Monetary Fund (IMF),[20] is invested in a "law and development" agenda that has been seeking to promote privatization and marketization in developing and transitional economies.[21]

A prominent example of the way in which this broader agenda has been specifically related to the goal of expanding credit markets while tying this to property rights and to the use of assets as collateral for credit is found in the highly influential work of economist Hernando De Soto.

[17] B. E. Adler, "Bankruptcy as Property Law," in K. Ayotte and H. E. Smith (eds.), *Research Handbook on the Economics of Property Law* (Cheltenham, UK: Edward Elgar, 2012), pp. 206–220.

[18] W. Rank, "Harmonization on National Security Rights," in U. Drobnig, H. J. Snijders, and E. J. Zippro (eds.), *Divergences of Property Law: An Obstacle to the Internal Market?* (Munich: Sellier, 2006), pp. 201–215.

[19] R. Haselmann and K. Pistor, "How the Law Affects Lending," *Review of Financial Studies*, 23 (2009), pp. 549–580.

[20] See, e.g., J. Stiglitz, *Globalization and Its Discontents* (London: Penguin Books, 2002), pp. 53–54.

[21] G. McCormack, "UNCITRAL, Security Rights and the Globalisation of the US Article 9," *Northern Ireland Legal Quarterly*, 62 (2011), pp. 485–504.

In his book, *The Mystery of Capital: Why Capitalism Triumphs in the West and Fails Everywhere Else*, De Soto seeks to explain the lingering differences in economic performance across different countries.[22] De Soto describes the inherent problem of "dead capital" in developing economies, in which property rights are not adequately documented, protected, and enforced, and as a result, individuals and businesses are unable to use assets as collaterals for credit. He then argues:

> In the West, by contrast, every parcel of land, every building, every piece of equipment, or store of inventories is represented in a property document that is a visible sign of a vast hidden process that connects all these assets to the rest of the economy. Thanks to this representational process, assets can lead an invisible, parallel life alongside their material existence. They can be used as collateral for credit. The single most important source of funds for new businesses in the United States is a mortgage on the entrepreneur's house. These assets can also provide a link to the owner's credit history, an accountable address for the collection of taxes and debts . . . By this process the West injects life into assets and makes them generate capital."[23]

De Soto's account may illuminate not only calls for national reforms in developing and transitional economies, but also calls for harmonization/globalization of laws on security interests and insolvency, and the particular choice of models that should inspire such a strategy. In the case of security interests, as shown in Section 6.3, the American model of Article 9 of the Uniform Commercial Code (UCC) has gained prominence, serving as a source of inspiration not only for other national jurisdictions, such as Australia, New Zealand, and provinces in Canada, but also as an anchor for the UCNITRAL Model Law on Secured Transactions. Based, according to commentators, on a neoliberal economic foundation, which endorses widening the availability of credit and the use of almost all types of assets as security,[24] UCC Article 9 has had a major influence on the work of international organizations, such as the World Bank or UNCITRAL, and consequently on policy-driven instruments such as the comparative *Doing Business* indices.[25]

The normative agenda behind the calls for the globalization of laws on security interests and insolvencies, and the particular choice of models

[22] H. De Soto, *The Mystery of Capital: Why Capitalism Triumphs in the West and Fails Everywhere Else* (New York: Basic Books, 2000).
[23] Ibid., p. 6.
[24] Sheehan, *Principles of Personal Property Law*, pp. 386–388.
[25] International Finance Corporation, "Doing Business," available at www.doingbusiness.org (accessed on March 1, 2018).

that should lead this process, might also shed light on potential objections to such an endeavor and to practical reasons why globalization strategies have so far had limited success in undermining the national basis of such laws. Next to inherent problems of path dependence in bridging over longstanding different jurisprudential concepts or formal requirements in creating, perfecting, and enforcing security rights,[26] as well as the costs of coordination among national registries in which secured rights are registered,[27] the laws on security interests and insolvency entail substantive normative choices. Establishing proprietary priorities between different types of stakeholders is essentially a matter of distribution.

Thus, unlike the UCC approach, not all jurisdictions recognize the full priority of secured claims, such that a proportion of secured asset realizations may be set aside in such countries for the benefit of unsecured creditors and other stakeholders.[28] Such a policy could be based on a concept of fairness, by which stakeholders such as employees and small trade creditors are particularly vulnerable to default of the debtor, but are unable to protect themselves in advance against the risk of default, as opposed to more powerful creditors such as financial institutions.[29] Accordingly, priorities set in national bankruptcy laws often respond to local social, economic, and political conditions, including for that matter pressure exerted by powerful groups.[30] Therefore, full scale harmonization or unification of laws on security interests and insolvency seems unlikely due to the political nature of numerous proprietary priorities set forth in such laws.[31]

6.2 National Approaches to Security Interests: Scope, Creation, and *In Rem* Effect

This section does not offer an exhaustive account of the various features of the laws on security interests in various national legal systems. It seeks, rather, to highlight some of the key disparities among national legal

[26] Rank, "Harmonization on National Security Rights," pp. 206–208.

[27] Z. Akhtar, "Land Registry, Electronic Conveyancing and Harmonisation: A Review of Current Practice," *The Conveyancer and Property Lawyer*, 2 (2014), pp. 106–122.

[28] McCormack, "UNCITRAL," p. 488.

[29] Ibid., pp. 497–498.

[30] J. M. Garrido, "No Two Snowflakes the Same: The Distributional Question in International Bankruptcies," *Texas International Law Journal*, 46 (2011), pp. 459–488 at 481–482.

[31] Ibid.

systems that have a functional bearing on how security interests are created, perfected, and enforced. These differences, some of which continue to exist even in the face of current legal reforms in such countries, can pose obstacles for cross-border markets of credit and financing, thus requiring some type of a globalization strategy or another coordination mechanism. The following sections therefore deal concisely with themes such as the types of assets that may be used as a collateral; functional versus formalistic approaches to quasi-security mechanisms such as reservation of title; the ability to collateralize future assets or bulks; the requirement for registration of security interests as a condition for perfection; and setups of proprietary priorities.

6.2.1 Types of Assets Used as Collaterals

6.2.1.1 Land

Land is often considered the paradigmatic asset that serves as security, and at least traditionally, it was the most valuable asset that a person could offer as a collateral for his or her monetary obligations, whether this obligation was created to finance the acquisition of the immovable asset itself, or for another purpose. It is therefore no wonder that much of the reform efforts in developing and transitional economies, influenced by the privatization and marketization agenda presented in Section 6.1, focused on formalizing property rights in land. Land titling was considered necessary not only for security of tenure, but also to facilitate the extension of credit.[32] While some commentators illuminate the potential disadvantages that Western-modelled land titling reforms may bring about,[33] the key role of land in securing debt remains largely uncontested.

Moreover, as already shown in Section 6.1, secured transactions implicating real-estate assets increasingly move away from the single debt/single asset conventional model, so that the use of land as a collateral seeks to enjoy more flexibility so as to facilitate complex financing schemes.

[32] G. Feder and A. Nishio, "The Benefits of Land Registration and Titling: Economic and Social Perspectives," *Land Use Policy*, 15 (1999), pp. 25–43 (providing evidence that land registration reforms lead to better access to credit).

[33] See, e.g., M. Trebilcock and P. E. Veel, "Property Rights and Development: The Contingent Case for Formalization," *University of Pennsylvania Journal of International Law*, 30 (2008), pp. 397–481.

That said, the fixed location of real-estate assets, the practical monopoly of the national land registry in which the respective land is located, and the continued dominance of the *lex rei sitae* rule at least in private law disputes, maintain the importance of differences among national laws. These disparities, and the legal uncertainties they may entail, posit a challenge for global markets.

While essentially all legal systems currently provide for the use of land as a collateral, the formal mechanisms and substantive rules that developed in each country may vary significantly. Thus, for example, in England, the common law traditionally had no legal interest in land which was by its nature a security interest. Consequently, the legal mortgage developed as a sort of a legal fiction, by which the debtor transferred to the creditor his estate in the land, with the creditor (the mortgagee) undertaking to retransfer the mortgaged estate upon payment of all sums due.[34] Accordingly, if the debtor (the mortgagor) defaulted, it appeared that he had no right to recover the mortgaged estate, even though the transferred estate might be worth much more than the debt. Over time, the Court of Chancery intervened to mitigate such distortions, for example by introducing an equitable right to redeem the estate transferred upon the (late) payment of the debt.[35]

It was not until the comprehensive reform of land law in 1926 that English law recognized, by statute, the ability to create a straightforward charge on land to secure a debt. Currently, for registered land, since the coming into force of the Land Registration Act 2002, a legal mortgage is created by way of a charge, which does not require the mortgagor to part with the legal estate.[36] The English legal mortgage is now functionally equivalent to the civil law hypothec as a nonpossessory limited proprietary interest in the land, which requires registration for its perfection.[37]

That said, substantive and procedural disparities among legal systems remain intact in regard to security interests in land. One such aspect deals with the process of realizing or foreclosing a mortgage upon default by the debtor. German law, for example, requires judicial action to facilitate a compulsory auction or a forced administration, with other systems (e.g., England) allowing for some type of self-help measures such

[34] L. Smith, "Security," in A. Burrows (ed.), *English Private Law*, 3d ed. (Oxford: Oxford University Press, 2013), pp. 307–378 at 308–309.

[35] Ibid., p. 309.

[36] Ibid., pp. 309–310.

[37] van Erp and Akkermans, *Cases on Property Law*, pp. 533–535, 545.

as taking possession of the asset as a prelude for an enforced sale.[38] The European Commission has noted that such disparities may hinder cross-border activity and the employment of financing schemes such as pooling of the mortgaged collaterals.[39]

Another substantial difference concerns the accessory nature of the mortgage or hypothec. Traditionally, the secured interest followed the status of the secured claim or debt, such that if the latter was extinguished or invalidated, the mortgage/hypothec would also be invalidated.[40] An early exception to accessoriness was the *Grundschuld* (Section 1191 of the German Civil Code), which grants a proprietary interest in the land and an entitlement to a certain amount of money out of the value of the burdened land, with such a burden potentially created and continuing to exist independently of a debt between the chargee and the owner of the land. The autonomous status of the *Grundschuld* allows it to secure future obligations, obligations due by several debtors, etc.[41]

Over the past few decades, other legal systems have also been developing mechanisms aimed at granting more flexibility to the real-estate lien – so as to allow, for example, for the assignment, syndication, or securitization of rights to secured debt, without losing the priority to which the original creditor was entitled – but to a varying degree. Thus, for example, while English law offers significant flexibility, Italian law preserves a much more rigid approach to accessoriness.[42] These disparities within Europe have stimulated efforts for the introduction of a "Eurohypothec" – a European-wide system of security interests in immovable assets – but so far to no avail.[43]

6.2.1.2 Goods, Monetary Claims, and Investment Securities

Legal systems have long recognized security interests in corporeal movable objects. In the tradition of the Roman law, the pledge – a limited proprietary right which grants to the pledgee a right to be paid from the proceeds of a forced sale of the asset upon default by the debtor – required a

[38] Ibid., pp. 545–555.

[39] Commission of the European Communities, Green Paper, "Mortgage Credit in the EU" (July 19, 2005), p. 12, available at http://eur-lex.europa.eu/legal-content/EN/TXT/PDF/?uri=CELEX:52005DC0327&from=EN (accessed on March 1, 2018).

[40] van Erp and Akkermans, *Cases on Property Law*, pp. 538–539.

[41] Ibid., pp. 541–543.

[42] Stöcker, "The Eurohypothec," pp. 70–71.

[43] Ibid., pp. 72–75.

transfer of possession of the asset to the creditor.[44] With time, however, it became clear that the mandatory requirement for transfer of possession may hinder commercial life, such that "neither the merchant nor the industrialist is able to repay the secured credit without access to, and disposition of, the assets serving as security."[45] Therefore, legal systems now recognize the nonpossessory pledge, typically requiring registration of the pledge as a condition for its priority.[46] In England, the nonpossessory pledge, known as a charge, was developed in equity, distinguishing between a fixed charge and a floating charge (see Section 6.2.3), and gradually requiring registration of the charge to perfect the security interest. In case of a charge on companies' assets, the Companies Act 2006 provides that all charges must be registered, bar a number of exceptions.[47]

The approach to the use of intangible assets, and particularly monetary claims (receivables), for security purposes, diverges significantly between various legal systems. This is particularly so because of the practical difficulty that may exist in distinguishing between placement of a charge on such assets and their outright assignment or sale to another party, and the need to establish priorities in regard to such assets in cases of conflicting charges and/or assignments of receivables.

Contemporary civil law systems typically provide for a pledge on incorporeal assets, and receivables in particular, and lay out the formal requirements for the validity of such pledges between the parties to the contractual pledge and vis-à-vis third parties. In many of these systems, notification to the debtor (and the date in which it was made) matters not only for perfecting the charge versus the debtor, but also for establishing priorities among conflicting charges or assignments.[48]

Moreover, even in countries where there is some type of a system of publicity by registration for collaterals, security interests over monetary claims are not always subject to the same requirements for registration. In many civil law systems in Europe (including France and Germany), the preferred method for achieving third-party effect and for the determination of priority of such proprietary security devices is still the notification to the account debtor. Nevertheless, some legal systems

[44] van Erp and Akkermans, *Cases on Property Law*, pp. 444–448.
[45] U. Drobnig and O. Boger, *Proprietary Security in Movable Assets* (Munich: Sellier, 2015), p. 205.
[46] van Erp and Akkermans, *Cases on Property Law*, pp. 448–449.
[47] Sheehan, *Principles of Personal Property Law*, pp. 269–270.
[48] van Erp and Akkermans, *Cases on Property Law*, pp. 465–471.

(e.g., Italy) now posit that the proprietary security over monetary claims should be subject to the same requirement of registration that is applicable to proprietary security in tangible assets.[49]

In England, collateralizing receivables can be done in principle by either a legal mortgage (i.e., transferring ownership of the receivables to the creditor with an agreement for retransferring them upon payment) or by an equitable charge, but both these options may be difficult to distinguish from an outright assignment/sale of the receivables.[50] In the case of receivables owned by a company, this distinction carries practical implications for purposes of registration, and consequently for setting priorities in instances of conflicting charges or assignments. A mortgage or charge on receivables owned by a company must be registered, while a sale is not registerable. Conversely, a registrable mortgage or charge that was not registered is void against a subsequent chargee or mortgagee, but it is not void against a subsequent purchaser of the mortgaged or charged asset. In determining whether a transaction is a sale/assignment or a secured loan, English courts look to the substance and the form of the transaction, but the dividing lines may not be clear.[51]

A different approach is advanced by UCC Article 9. As shown further in Section 6.2.2, the American model adopts a functionalist, generic concept of a security interest, which seeks to abolish old, formalist distinctions (such as those still applying in English law).[52] UCC Section 9–109 applies the law of security interests to "any transaction, regardless of its form, that creates a security interest in personal property or fixtures by contract" as well as to "a sale of accounts, chattel paper, payment intangibles or promissory notes."[53] Accordingly, all types of security interests – including those in which ownership in the movable asset is transferred essentially for security purposes – require registration for their perfection.[54] A similar approach is now taken in the common law provinces of Canada, New Zealand,[55] and most recently in Australia.[56] Thus, the Australian Personal Property Securities Act 2009 (which went into

49 Drobnig and Boger, *Proprietary Security in Movable Assets*, pp. 447–453.
50 Smith, "Securities," pp. 336–337.
51 Ibid., pp. 347–348.
52 McCormack, *Secured Credit*, p. 71.
53 Uniform Commercial Code (UCC), Article 9 (Secured Transactions), § 9–109 (American Law Institute, 2012).
54 McCormack, *Secured Credit*, p. 71.
55 Ibid., pp. 71–72; Sheehan, *Principles of Personal Property Law*, pp. 386–387.
56 D. Brown, "Personal Property Security Law: Local and Global Perspectives," *Adelaide Law Review*, 35 (2014), pp. 55–57.

force in 2012) broadly defines the term *personal property* as any "property (including a license) other than land."[57] Similar to the UCC, the Act defines a *security interest* as "an interest in personal property provided for by a transaction that, in substance, secures payment or performance of an obligation (without regard to the form of the transaction or the identity of the person who has title to the property),"[58] and including also "the interest of a transferee under a transfer of an account or chattel paper."[59] Thus, the transfer of an account (monetary obligation) essentially made for security purposes also requires registration or "control" of the interest for its perfection and priority over other claims.[60]

The general unified or functional approach taken in the United States and elsewhere to security interests in assets, and in receivables/accounts in particular, does not mean that the difference between a secured interest and an assignment/sale of the receivable no longer matters. While both types of transactions may similarly require registration or control by the chargee for perfection, in the case of an assignment/sale, the creditor would be considered as owner of the receivables for all other purposes (including in insolvency proceedings) and would be generally entitled to enjoy any surplus value that the receivable has, beyond merely covering any underlying debt or credit.[61]

Investment securities (referred to as *investment instruments* in Australia or *investment property* in the UCC) and intermediated securities (see Chapter 4, Section 4.3.3) are also commonly used as collaterals, with different legal systems providing their particular rules for the attachment of security interests and their perfection by registration, possession and/or control – depending also on the type of record for such an investment security, that is, paper certificate or electronic record.[62]

6.2.1.3 Intellectual Property and Digital Assets

The use of intellectual property as a valuable intangible collateral has gained importance in recent years.[63] That said, the rules applicable to the attachment and perfection of security interests in intellectual property

[57] Personal Property Securities Act 2009 (Cth.), No. 130, 2009, Australian Federal Register of Legislation, Sect. 10.
[58] Ibid., Sect. 12(1).
[59] Ibid., Sect. 12(3)(a).
[60] Ibid., Sect. 21.
[61] Sheehan, *Principles of Personal Property Law*, pp. 385–386.
[62] See, for example, the rules set in Australia in Sects. 21, 24–29 of the Personal Property Securities Act 2009.
[63] Drobnig and Boger, *Proprietary Security in Movable Assets*, p. 214.

are far from being settled in many jurisdictions, and they exhibit substantial differences among the various legal systems.[64] Generally speaking, most legal systems view registration as the only feasible method for giving publicity to security interests in intellectual property, with specific references to such registration being made in some legal systems within specific laws on intellectual property rather than in laws that deal generally with security interests. Thus, for example, the French Intellectual Property Code provides in Article L132–34:

> The right of exploitation of an author of software ... may be pledged subject to the following conditions: ... (2) the pledge shall be entered, failing which it shall not be invoked, in a special register kept by the National Institute of Industrial Property.[65]

The potential split between intellectual property laws and other bodies of law dealing with security interests may lead in fact to a double registration regime in some countries. In England, for example, the Companies Act, which currently requires the registration of security interests in assets owned by companies, applies specifically to "a charge on goodwill or any intellectual property."[66] At the same time, Section 30 (2) of the Patents Act 1977 provides that patents may be assigned or mortgaged, and Sections 24–25 of the Trade Marks Act 1994 state that trademarks may be both mortgaged and subject to equitable charges. A parallel registration in the relevant intellectual property registry may entail its own benefits. Thus, for example, under Section 33 of the Patents Act 1977, registration in the register of patents provides a number of distinct benefits, chief among them is that a registered assignment or mortgage takes priority over an unregistered interest, unless the party claiming priority has actual knowledge of the unregistered interest.[67]

The potential overlap or confusion about the registration of security interests in intellectual property within a certain domestic system, which obviously translates into uncertainly in cases of conflicting interests involving parties across borders, is even more manifested in the

[64] Ibid.

[65] *Code de la Propriété Intellectuelle (Version Consolidée au 1er Janvier 2014)*, L 132–34. A formal English translation is available at www.legifrance.gouv.fr/content/download/1959/13723/version/.../.../Code_35.pdf.

[66] Companies Act 2006, c. 46, Sect. 860(7)(i). The term *intellectual property* is further defined in Sect. 861(4) of the Companies Act as: "(i) any patent, trademark, registered design, copyright or design right; (2) any license under or in respect of any such right."

[67] Sheehan, *Principles of Personal Property Law*, pp. 278–279.

United States. Legal uncertainty exists as to whether federal or state law governs the perfection of security interests in intellectual property.[68] On the state level, secured financing involving the perfection of security interests in intellectual property is generally governed by the local version of UCC Article 9.[69] The Article governs security interests in general intangibles, which are considered personal property. Although trademarks, patents, and copyright are not explicitly included in the definition of *general intangible*, the Official Comment refers to intellectual property as an example of it.[70]

At the same time, UCC Article 9 expressly provides that state UCC perfection laws are neither necessary nor effective to perfect a security interest if federal law preempts state perfection laws.[71] However, the jurisprudence as to whether the various intellectual property federal statutes preempt state UCC perfection requirements remains limited and incomplete.[72] Generally, for registered copyrights, current case law considers the provisions of the federal Copyright Act[73] as preempting the state UCC perfection laws, while no such preemption is currently assumed for unregistered copyrights, patents, and trademarks.[74] That said, lenders resort to dual filings to best protect their legal interests and record their security interests with both the federal office designated under the applicable federal statute and with the state office designated by the state UCC.[75] Calls to establish a national filing system for security interests in intellectual property have not come to fruition so far, and this affects both domestic and international lenders and other stakeholders.

Security interests in digital assets outside the scope of intellectual property, as discussed in Chapter 5, remains pretty much a *terra incognita* in current national systems. This is particularly so because of the

[68] W. A. Gibson, "The Intersection between UCC Article 9 and Intellectual Property: The Need for a National, Centralized Filing System for IP," *The John Marshall Review of Intellectual Property*, 15 (2015), pp. 83–90 at 84.

[69] Ibid., p. 85.

[70] UCC § 9–102, comment 5(d). See D. Orzechovsky and A. Bagdasarian, "Perfecting Security Interests in United States Patents, Trademarks, and Copyrights," White & Case Technology Newsflash (December 18, 2013), available at www.whitecase.com/publications/article/perfecting-security-interests-united-states-patents-trademarks-and-copyrights (accessed on March 1, 2018).

[71] UCC § 9–311(a).

[72] Gibson, "Intersection," p. 85.

[73] Copyright Act, 17 U.S.C. § 205.

[74] Gibson, "Intersection," pp. 85–89.

[75] Ibid. See also Orzechovsky and Bagdasarian, "Perfecting Security Interests."

unclear status of various types of digital assets as "property."[76] Thus, for example, in the 2014 English case, *Your Response Ltd.* v. *Datateam Business Media Ltd.*, the Court of Appeals discussed in *obiter dictum* the possibility of placing a lien on an electronic database, noting that allowing to do so "would be coming close to treating information as property."[77]

In the context of domain names, the creation and perfection of security interests in domain names, through the filing of a UCC filing statement, has become routine in the United States, despite the unclear status of a domain name as *property*. To date, no statutes, regulations, or case law suggest that the creation and perfection of security interests in domain names cannot be achieved under the UCC Article 9 rules set forth for general intangibles.[78] This in mind, there is no systematic jurisprudence on the use of digital assets as an object of security interests, and accordingly, the divergence between different legal systems in the matter may be very substantial.

6.2.2 Security and Quasi-Security Interests: Functional versus Formalistic Approaches

One of the underlying differences between legal systems in regard to security interests concerns the approach to the use of retention or transfer of ownership in assets to secure debts.[79] Some legal systems maintain a more formalistic approach, by which mechanisms, such as

[76] S. van Erp, "Ownership of Data and the Numerus Clausus of Legal Objects," Maastricht European Private Law Institute Working Paper No. 2017/6 (2017), available at https://papers.ssrn.com/sol3/papers.cfm?abstract_id=3046402 (accessed on March 1, 2018).

[77] *Your Response Ltd.* v. *Datateam Business Media Ltd.* [2014] EWCA Civil 281 (Floyd, L.J., para. 42).

[78] R. J. Morgan, "Security Interests in Domain Names and Intellectual Property," *Lexology*, August, 28, 2009, available at www.lexology.com/library/detail.aspx?g=502721a2-599a-4f9c-81d6-3b7ba3bf000b (accessed on March 1, 2018).

[79] Historically, the use of retention or transfer of ownership mechanisms grew, at least in some legal systems, out of limits imposed in those systems on nonpossessory pledges. The need to come up with a practical solution arose initially in the case of a sale credit. Whenever a seller of a movable good allowed the buyer to make deferred payments or to pay in installments, while already surrendering possession of the good to the buyer, the seller was facing the risk that in case of insolvency, the good would be taken over by other creditors or by the bankruptcy administrators, with the creditor's contractual claim vis-à-vis the debtor becoming practically meaningless. van Erp and Akkermans, *Cases on Property Law*, pp. 472–477.

reservation of title,[80] hire-purchase agreements,[81] repurchase agreements (repos),[82] finance leases,[83] consignments,[84] or receivable financing,[85] may be treated differently than secured transactions. Other legal systems, most notably the United States, Australia, New Zealand, and the common law provinces in Canada adopt a functional approach. Under the latter method, any financing mechanism intended in effect to secure a

[80] Under a standard reservation of title clause, a seller hands over the asset to the buyer who has not yet paid in full, whilst the seller retains title to the asset. In the buyer's insolvency, the seller may invoke the right of ownership, which provides full protection. The seller/owner may repossess the sold assets from the bankruptcy estate, subject to due accounting for any payments made by the buyer and counter-claims by the seller for use and wear of the sold goods. Drobnig and Boger, *Proprietary Security in Movable Assets*, pp. 243–244. The conditional-sale nature of this transaction, at least in Germany and in the Netherlands, means that the seller retains a conditional title only, subject to the payment right (and duty) of the buyer who can become full owner at any time. In civil law terminology, both the seller and the buyer have a kind of title. J. Dalhuisen, *Dalhuisen on Transnational, Comparative, Commercial, Financial and Trade Law, Vol. II: Contract and Movable Property Law* (Oxford: Hart, 2016), pp. 512–513.

[81] The legal structure of a hire-purchase agreements is fairly similar to a reservation of title one, except for the fact that the buyer pays in periodic installments until the title automatically passes on to him. Ibid., p. 513.

[82] In a repurchase agreement (repo) of investment securities, an investor who wishes to acquire bonds or shares finances the transaction by obtaining funds from a third party, usually a financial institution, through a sale and repurchase of the same security at a certain date for a pre-agreed price. During the interim period, the seller has a right and a duty to retrieve the asset at the appointed date. Upon a timely tender of the repurchase price the asset would automatically revert to the seller, with implications for attribution of the asset in bankruptcy. Ibid., p. 514.

[83] In a finance lease, the lessee orders the goods from a supplier, but title is officially acquired by a finance company that leases the goods to the lessee against regular payments or installments. Depending on the arrangement, the end-result may be for the lessee to acquire full title after the last installment either automatically or at his or her option. Ibid., p. 513. The finance lease is sometimes difficult to distinguish from an operating lease, in which the lessor wants the asset returned, but it is not always obvious which class a case falls into. Therefore, Australian law requires registration for both types of lease. Sheehan, *Principles of Personal Property Law*, p. 374.

[84] Consignments involve an ultimate seller providing a retailer with goods, with the ultimate seller retaining ownership of the goods but permitting sale to customers. Such a scheme may benefit not only the seller to secure payment, but also the retailer, who is able to return unsold items to the seller. Ibid., p. 374

[85] The concept of receivables financing or factoring was explained briefly in Section 6.1. The transfer of receivables may be conditioned on the approval or collectability by the assignee/financier, such that the receivables may be automatically returned when they are not approved or cannot be collected, or alternatively, when the total of the collections reaches the amount that the assignee/financier has provided plus the interest. Dalhuisen, Vol. II, p. 514.

debt is seen as falling under the general framework of secured transactions, regardless of its form.[86]

These different approaches have consequent implications for the attachment, perfection, or enforcement of the legal interest created in the asset. One such practical implication concerns the need to register a secured interest. A functional approach might subject most if not all types of financing mechanisms to the requirement of registration of the legal interest as a condition for granting its holder broad protection vis-à-vis third parties. A formalist approach might waive such a requirement for transactions that employ mechanisms of reservation or transfer of ownership.[87]

Thus, most European legal systems do not require registration of a reservation of title mechanism, and only part of them mandate that the agreement between the parties be done in writing.[88] The practical result is that in the case of default or insolvency, the party that retained formal ownership in the asset may reclaim possession of the good from the bankruptcy estate, despite the fact that other interested parties may have had no feasible way of publicly knowing about this interest due to the lack of registration. Moreover, in some of the jurisdictions that embrace the mechanism of reservation of title, the retained ownership may remain intact – and accordingly provide its holder with increased protection – to cover not only payment for the original asset sold, but also to secure other or future debts that the buyer–debtor may have toward the seller–creditor (an "all money" title-retention clause).[89] In the legal systems that stick to a more formal approach, the distinction between security interests and ownership-based models might also apply to hire–purchase schemes, and even to finance leases in which the party maintaining title to the asset may be a financier rather than the original seller.[90] Such legal systems may diverge, however, on legally recognizing the transfer of ownership for security purposes, such as in the case of assignment of receivables (receivables financing) or repurchase agreements (repos).[91] German law notably recognizes the fiduciary transfer for security purposes of tangible and intangible assets as a valid act, enforceable versus

[86] Sheehan, *Principles of Personal Property Law*, pp. 371–375.
[87] Drobnig and Boger, *Proprietary Security in Movable Assets*, pp. 467–473.
[88] van Erp and Akkermans, *Cases on Property Law*, pp. 472–477.
[89] Sheehan, *Principles of Personal Property Law*, p. 284.
[90] Drobnig and Boger, *Proprietary Security in Movable Assets*, p. 726.
[91] van Erp and Akkermans, *Cases on Property Law*, pp. 505–515.

third parties.[92] The fiduciary assignment for security purposes of monetary claims to the creditor in Germany follows the general rules of assignment, which do not require any special contractual form or the use of mechanisms of publicity such as registration.[93]

In contrast, UCC Section 9–109 applies its provisions to any "transaction, regardless of its form, that creates a security interest in personal property," and further extends its scope to schemes such as a sale of accounts or consignments.[94] This means that the requirement to submit a financing statement or filing notice under the UCC, or alternatively to gain "control" over the asset to perfect the interest, would also apply to ownership-based models, such as a reservation of title clause.

The Australian approach articulates the concept of *in substance* security interests.[95] Under this approach, any interest in personal property that in substance secures payment or performance of an obligation, is equated to security interests for purposes of creation, perfection, and enforcement. Section 12 of the Personal Property Securities Act 2009 lists types of transactions that could amount to in substance secured transactions, such as reservation of title, hire–purchase scheme, consignment, assignment, transfer of title, and so forth.[96] Australian law therefore adopts a clear functional approach for identifying and regulating secured transactions.

These differences among legal systems persist despite the fact that many of the historical reasons leading to the development of multiple forms of sale- or loan-credit schemes are no longer valid (such as past limits in Continental European systems on nonpossessory pledges).[97] This legal arbitrage leads in practical terms to major variances in the setting of proprietary priorities among stakeholders and accordingly to uncertainty and fragmentation in enforcement procedures.

6.2.3 Priorities among Creditors and Other Stakeholders

The chief goal of a security interest is to provide its holder with a streamlined process to enforce his or her rights vis-à-vis the debtor upon

[92] Ibid., pp. 518–519.

[93] E. M. Kieninger, "Introduction: Security Rights in Movable Property within the Common Market and the Approach of the Study," in E. M. Kieininger (ed.), *Security Rights in Movable Property in European Private Law* (Cambridge, UK: Cambridge University Press, 2004), pp. 6-37 at 11–12.

[94] UCC § 9–109.

[95] Personal Property Securities Act 2009 (Cth).

[96] Ibid., s 12(2).

[97] van Erp and Akkermans, *Cases on Property Law*, p. 505.

default through the realization (e.g., a forced sale) of the encumbered asset, while granting priority to the secured party over other creditors. The ranking of various types of secured and unsecured creditors and other stakeholders thus becomes essential for a system of security interests, with each legal system establishing its own system for ranking priorities to the debtor's assets. This is particularly essential in the case of insolvency or bankruptcy, where the ladder of priorities in different legal systems typically consists of a few main ranks or rungs, e.g., super-priority creditors, priority creditors, *pari passu* creditors, and equity shareholders, with internal ladders within each rung constituting further subclassifications.[98] Every legal system may diverge on defining the relevant sets of legal interests, their respective priority in relation to other interests, the relevance of timing in creating or perfecting the security interest for establishing a priority, the particular features of the registration system, and the implications that these features may have for establishing priorities among creditors, or between creditors and other third parties such as buyers of the asset in the ordinary course of business.[99]

Thus, for example, Section 6.2.2 has shown how in legal systems that validate mechanisms of retention or transfer of ownership for security purposes, such as in a reservation of title clause, the party retaining the formal title to the asset may enjoy a categorical priority over creditors and other stakeholders and reclaim possession of the asset from the bankruptcy estate. Other legal systems, which seek to provide an alternative to this sale-credit dilemma while remaining within a unified system of security interests, may provide a super-priority to the seller or to a financier that provides the purchase money to buy a particular asset.[100] The concept of a purchase money security interest (PMSI) as enjoying a super-priority status, while also requiring special perfection mechanisms to establish a super-priority in PMSIs, is thus legislated in various terms in UCC Article 9 and in the commonwealth legislation.[101] Some differences may exist, however, even among these latter jurisdictions. In Canada, for example, a seller/financier must register the PMSI interest and send a notice describing the inventory covered by the PMSI before the debtor

[98] P. R. Wood., "The Bankruptcy Ladder of Priorities," *Business Law International*, 14 (2013), pp. 209–244.
[99] Sheehan, *Principles of Personal Property Law*, pp. 379–383.
[100] Drobnig and Boger, *Proprietary Security in Movable Assets*, p. 243 (giving the example of Sweden).
[101] Sheehan, *Principles of Personal Property Law*, pp. 381–382.

takes possession of the asset. This advance notice allows a previous creditor to know that priorities will be different in regard to the specific inventory, thus allowing the previous creditor to make an informed decision as to whether to extend further credit to the debtor. Australia does not mandate the seller/financier to send an advance notice, but it does require, upon registration of the PMSI, to explicitly state that it is a PMSI, thus enabling the registrar itself to notify previous/other creditors.[102]

Yet another variety, which cuts through the traditional common law/civil law divide, concerns the floating charge, one that aims at securing also future assets acquired by the debtor, while allowing the debtor to constantly sell assets, such as commercial inventory, as part of its business. The floating charge had developed in equity in English law in the context of companies, and it is not defined in statute in England.[103] The English floating charge becomes perfected only upon a crystallization event (normally such crystallization occurs when the company goes into liquidation, a receiver is appointed, the company otherwise becomes insolvent or it stops trading). Upon crystallization, the floating charge has a relatively low rank, just above nonsecured creditors, and below creditors with a fixed security and preferential creditors such as employees.[104] The ranking of the floating charge is not determined therefore from the date of registration in the company registers, and it generally allows for the creation of fixed charges by other creditors over future or after-acquired property, unless the floating charge explicitly includes also a "negative" pledge.

The relative priority of the floating lien is different under UCC Article 9, which allows for the creation of a security interest in *after-acquired property* (while the term *floating lien* is not explicitly used in the text of UCC Section 9–204, it is referred to in the Official Comment to it),[105] with such future replacement assets also being used to protect future debt (future advances). In such cases, the lien dates back to the date of the original filing, and it thus enjoys priority over liens registered at a later date.[106] Therefore, in the United States, the type of security interest that is equivalent to the English floating charge enjoys better protection and priority over others. This is yet another example of substantial disparities among national systems on security interests.

102 Ibid.
103 Ibid., pp. 345–346.
104 Dalhuisen, Vol. II, p. 540.
105 UCC § 9–204, Official Comment 2.
106 McCormack, *Secured Credit under English and American Law*, pp. 73–74.

6.3 Current Strategies for the Global Governance of Security Interests

The lingering differences between domestic laws on security interests may pose significant challenges for the extension of credit and other forms of financing across national borders. When two or more legal systems become involved, differences relating to issues such as the recognition of a particular security or quasi-security interest, formal requirements for the attachment or perfection of a security interest, relative priority of the security interest vis-à-vis other legal interests, or enforcement procedures affect the respective rights and duties of parties. Such uncertainty due to legal arbitrages may initially deter the extension of cross-border credit. Thus, for example, transnational mortgage lending represents only one percent of the entire real-estate mortgage lending in Europe. Although this low rate can be explained by different considerations, the current legal fragmentation among national legal systems in regard to the creation, registration, and enforcement of such security interests in land is definitely a key factor.[107]

Attempts by courts to overcome the difficulty of legal disparities by adopting the doctrine of transposition, by which a national court seeks to transform or adapt a security interest created in another jurisdiction to the local property system, may often prove shorthanded and incapable of effectively solving disputes.[108] This is especially the case if the jurisdiction, in which the foreign security interest should be recognized or adapted, has a stricter formal or substantive approach to the creation or perfection of a security interest, such as when registration is required in the "receiving" jurisdiction, but not in the original jurisdiction in which the charge was created.[109] In the European context, the lack of an EU-wide mechanism for the recognition of security interests created under the laws of other Member States is viewed as practically hindering the work of the internal market. Some scholars go further to argue that the refusal to recognize a security interest validly created in another Member State is a violation of the principle of free movement of goods in Article 34 of the Treaty on the Functioning of the European Union (TFEU).[110]

107 Akhtar, "Land Registry," pp. 110–111.

108 U. Drobnig, "Recognition and Adaptation of Foreign Security Interests," in U. Drobnig, H. J. Snijders, and E. J. Zippro (eds.), *Divergences of Property Law: An Obstacle to the Internal Market?* (Munich: Sellier, 2006), pp. 105–115.

109 Kieninger, "Introduction," p. 18.

110 B. Akkermans and E. Ramaekers, "Free Movement of Goods and Property Law," *European Law Journal*, 19 (2013), pp. 237–266.

In the face of such constraints, the following sections identify the employment of various globalization strategies that seek to address the divergence of national laws on security interests.

6.3.1 *Soft Law*

Multiple international organizations have been working over the past few decades on texts aimed at approximating, or even harmonizing, laws dealing with security interests. In particular, UNCITRAL, UNIDROIT, and the Hague Conference on Private International Law (all introduced in Chapter 2) have been active along this front. A joint document issued by the three organizations in 2012 surveys and compares the provisions of the relatively few binding conventions, alongside soft law mechanisms, adopted by these organizations to date.[111] The most prominent soft law instrument is the 2016 UNCITRAL Model Law on Secured Transactions,[112] accompanied in 2017 by a Draft Guide to Enactment of the UNCITRAL Model Law on Secured Transactions,[113] and two other documents: Supplement on Security Rights in Intellectual Property[114] and Guide on the Implementation of a Security Rights Registry.[115] Together with a previously adopted Legislative Guide on Secured Transactions,[116] the declared purpose of the Model Law and its accompanying

[111] Hague Conference on Private International Law, International Institute for the Unification of Private Law, United Nations Commission on International Trade Law, "UNCITRAL, Hague Conference and UNIDROIT Texts on Security Interests: Comparison and Analysis of International Instruments Relating to Secured Transactions" (2012), available at www.uncitral.org/pdf/english/texts/security/UNCITRAL-HccH-Unidroit-e.pdf (accessed on March 1, 2018).

[112] United Nations Commission on International Trade Law, UNCITRAL Model Law on Secured Transactions (2016), available at www.uncitral.org/uncitral/en/uncitral_texts/security/2016Model_secured.html (accessed on March 1, 2018) (UNCITRAL Model Law).

[113] United Nations Commission on International Trade Law, Working Group VI (Security Interests), Draft Guide to Enactment of the UNCITRAL Model Law on Secured Transactions (2017), available at https://documents-dds-ny.un.org/doc/UNDOC/LTD/V16/106/31/PDF/V1610631.pdf?OpenElement (accessed on March 1, 2018) (UNCITRAL Draft Guide).

[114] UNCITRAL Legislative Guide on Secured Transactions: Supplement on Security Rights in Intellectual Property (2010), available at www.uncitral.org/uncitral/en/uncitral_texts/security/ip-supplement.html (accessed on March 1, 2018).

[115] UNCITRAL Guide on the Implementation of a Security Rights Registry (2013), available atwww.uncitral.org/uncitral/en/uncitral_texts/security/2013Security_rights_registry.html (accessed on March 1, 2018).

[116] UNCITRAL Legislative Guide on Secured Transactions (2007), available at www.uncitral.org/uncitral/en/uncitral_texts/security/Guide_securedtrans.html (accessed on March 1, 2018).

documents is to "increase the availability and decrease the cost of credit by providing an efficient, modern and certain legal framework for the creation of security interests in movable assets."[117]

While leaving room for flexibility in several matters to adapt the Model Law to the national system, the Model Law calls to stick to a number of underlying policies. One of these policies is "the functional, integrated and comprehensive approach to secured transactions, under which any right created by agreement in any type of movable asset to secure the performance of an obligation is treated as a security right for the purposes of triggering the application of the Model Law, regardless of the terms used by the parties to describe their agreement."[118] In other words, the Model Law largely adopts the functional approach of the American UCC Article 9. It also favors the American notion of providing a categorical priority to secured creditors, unlike the English law that carves out a proportion of collateral realizations for the benefit of unsecured creditors.[119]

Further, the Model Law follows the UCC Article 9 notice-filing system under which the security agreement itself is not filed, but instead only a party-specific financing statement that provides limited information is registered, inviting interested parties to inquire further with the financier.[120] Article 18 of the Model Law determines that a security right is effective against third parties if a notice is registered (with security rights in tangible assets also effective upon their possession).[121] The universal requirement for notice registration of nonpossessory security interests in movable assets is complemented by the provision of Article 29 of the Model Law, by which priority between security rights perfected by registration is determined by the order of registration, regardless of the order of creation (attachment) of the security rights.[122]

As already noted in Section 6.1, the influence on the crafting of the UNCITRAL Model Law by the American UCC Article 9, with its underlying agenda of extending the possibilities for creating security interests in a large variety of assets and granting a clear priority to secured, registered interests, has been criticized as promoting a "neoliberal agenda" that seeks to enhance American economic power in a global economy.[123] The call for harmonization of laws on security interests by

117 UNCITRAL Draft Guide, p. 4.
118 Ibid., p. 7.
119 McCormack, "UNCITRAL," pp. 490–491.
120 Ibid.
121 UNCITRAL Model Law, Art. 18.
122 UNCITRAL Model Law, Art. 29(a).
123 McCormack, "UNCITRAL," pp. 497–502.

the UNCITRAL Model Law arguably undermines distributive policies that have shaped national property laws. Whether this criticism holds true or not, it does attest to the practical difficulty in switching from a soft law mechanism to a binding international convention. Local differences are not only a matter of doctrinal path dependency, but also of value-based divergence.

Another international institution that embarked on the mission of developing a model law and supporting documents for reforming laws on security interests across its Member States is the Organization of American States (OAS), presented in Chapter 2. The OAS Secured Financing Project seeks to "promote and facilitate adequate access to and maintain the flow of secured credit to the private sector."[124] It states that wealth in Latin America has remained almost exclusively land-based, such that for assets located in Latin America "lenders are constrained by outdated laws that are largely based on real property regimes." Therefore, a modern legal framework is viewed by OAS as instrumental to foster the necessary transition to enable businesses, especially small- and medium-size enterprises, to gain access to affordable credit.[125]

Similarly to the UNCITRAL Model Law, the Model Inter-American Law on Secured Transaction[126] and accompanying Model Registry Regulations[127] are impacted by the functional approach of the UCC Article 9, with its liberal policy of expanding the scope of assets that could be encumbered, including future assets, and its universal requirement for perfecting nonpossessory security interests through registration. Thus, Article 2 of the OAS Model Law states:

> The security interests to which this Law refers are created contractually over one or several specific items of movable property, on generic categories of movable property, or on all of the secured debtor's movable property, whether present or future, corporeal or incorporeal, susceptible to pecuniary valuation at the time of creation or thereafter, with the objective of

[124] Organization of American States (OAS), Department of International Law, "Secured Transactions Reform in the Americas" (2013), available at www.oas.org/en/sla/dil/docs/secured_transactions_newsletter_aug_2013.pdf (accessed on March 1, 2018).

[125] Ibid.

[126] Organization of American States (OAS), Department of International Law, Model Inter-American Law on Secured Transactions (2002), pp. 9–35, available at www.oas.org/en/sla/dil/docs/secured_transactions_BOOK_Model_Law.pdf (accessed on March 1, 2018) (OAS Model Law).

[127] Organization of American States (OAS), Department of International Law, Model Registry Regulations under the Model Inter-American Law on Secured Transactions, (2009), pp. 37–75, available at www.oas.org/en/sla/dil/docs/secured_transactions_BOOK_Model_Law.pdf (accessed on March 1, 2018).

> securing the fulfillment of one or more present or future obligations regardless of the form of the transaction and regardless of whether ownership of the property is held by the secured creditor or the secured debtor.[128]

The internalization of the American model in countries rooted in European legal traditions via the former colonial powers of Spain and Portugal has not been an easy process.[129] While OAS reports about several "success stories" of enacting modern secured transactions laws in Latin American countries,[130] other reports point to more limited results.[131] A successful example, the 2014 Colombia Secured Transactions Law is based on the OAS Model Law, although it slightly varies from the Model Registry Regulations in that it allows only for electronic registration.[132]

In 2009 Mexico reformed its Commercial Code and introduced a Single Registry of Security Interests (*Registro Único de Garantías Mobiliarias*), which started to operate in 2010.[133] Replacing the multiple paper-based registries, the reform, which switched to a single registry and digital filing, led to an exponential growth in the number of registered security interests serving mostly micro-, small-, and medium-size enterprises.[134] The Mexican law diverges, however, from the OAS Model Law in several aspects, for example, by offering varying rules on creation, priority, registration, and enforcement for different types of security types.[135] Therefore, modernization of laws on security interests in Latin America has not resulted necessarily in harmonization of laws.

Finally, a highly prominent project, which so far remains a scholarly endeavor with a soft law status, is the European Draft Common Frame of Reference (DCFR) and its Book IX on Proprietary Security Rights in Movable Assets.[136] The key role of DCFR Book IX is to develop a model

128 OAS Model Law, Art. 2.
129 Drobnig and Boger, *Proprietary Security in Movable Assets*, pp. 210–211.
130 OAS, "Secured Transactions Reform in the Americas."
131 Drobnig and Boger, *Proprietary Security in Movable Assets*, p. 211.
132 I. N. Isunza, "The Impact of Secured Transactions Reforms in Mexico and Columbia," *Arizona Journal of International and Comparative Law*, 33 (2016), pp. 125–138 at 134–137.
133 *Secretaría De Economía, Registro Único de Garantías Mobiliarias*, available at www.rug.gob.mx./Rug/home/inicio.do (accessed on March 1, 2018) (in Spanish).
134 Isunza, "The Impact of Secured Transactions," pp. 126–134.
135 Ibid., p. 135.
136 Study Group on a European Civil Code and Research Group on EC Private Law (Acquis Group), "Principles, Definitions and Model Rules on European Private Law: Draft Common Frame of Reference (DCFR)," outline edition 2009, available at http://ec.europa.eu/justice/policies/civil/docs/dcfr_outline_edition_en.pdf (accessed on March 1, 2018).

of common principles, which would not only serve to facilitate the free movement of goods within the European Union but would also consider longstanding characteristics of the European legal traditions. Accordingly, while the DCFR may be seen as generally opting for a functional approach, and it accordingly regulates reservation of title as a specific part of the system of proprietary security in movables, it does not go so far so as to fully equate reservation of title with standard, limited proprietary security rights. Article 1:104 of Book IX generally refers to the scope of applicability of rules on security interests to reservation of ownership devices, and to areas of divergence, thus rejecting the UCC Article 9's one-size-fits-all approach.[137]

Beyond the drafting of common principles on the various aspects of security interests and retention of ownership devices, including creation, third-party effects, priorities, and enforcement, the most harmonizing feature of Book IX is probably the call to establish a European register of proprietary security (Article IX – 3:301). The underlying notion of the register is that subject to some exceptions:

> The publicity by registration required by these rules can only be achieved if a security right or retention of ownership device is registered in the European register of security rights. A registration in any register already established under national law for proprietary security in general (such as the English register for company charges) is not sufficient for the purpose of achieving effectiveness of the security right concerned under these rules. Due to the differences between the various national positions as to the details of a registration, its requirements and effects, these rules could not opt for a solution on the basis of the continuing operation of these registers only.[138]

The DCFR – currently a soft law mechanism – therefore calls to adopt a hard law measure that would facilitate the harmonization of laws on security interests through the quintessential mechanism of a supranationalism strategy: the establishment of a single registry that would create a set of European-wide security interests and retention of title mechanisms. This proposal echoes the call to establish a Eurohypothec to establish an EU single system of security interests in land.[139]

137 Drobnig and Boger, *Proprietary Security in Movable Assets*, pp. 211–216.
138 Ibid., p. 437 (Comment E).
139 Stöcker, "The Eurohypothec."

6.3.2 *Conflict of Laws*

The *in rem* feature of proprietary rights, and security interests in particular, curtails in principle the extent of party autonomy in designing transactions that purport to have an impact also on third parties. This trait of property law, which has been discussed in Chapter 1 in the context of domestic legal systems, also affects the scope of party autonomy in choosing the law that would apply to cross-border transactions.[140] This means that while parties to a cross-border contract are free to choose the law that would apply between them, this party autonomy does not apply to third parties and in particular to the *in rem* rights held by such parties.[141]

Thus, for example, the EU Rome I Regulation on the law applicable to contractual obligations provides in Article 3(1) that "a contract shall be governed by the law chosen by the parties."[142] The Regulation remains, however, silent in regard to the *in rem* rights of third parties, such as those external parties who hold a security interest in the asset which is the object of the contract. The Rome I Regulation has thus been interpreted as not extending the parties' choice of law to cover property law aspects, with the Dutch Supreme Court providing a rare exception in a 1997 case concerning the proprietary aspects of an assignment of future claims.[143]

[140] van Erp and Akkermans, *Cases on Property Law*, pp. 1012–1014.

[141] Kieninger, "Introduction," pp. 16–17.

[142] Regulation (EC) No 593/2008 of the European Parliament and of the Council of 17 June 2008 on the Law Applicable to Contractual Obligations (Rome I), Art. 3(1), OJ (L 177/6), July 4, 2008.

[143] *Brandsma qq/Hansa Chemie AG*, HR May 16, 1997, NJ 1998, 585 (Neth.) (in Dutch). The Dutch court interpreted the previous version of the Rome I Convention (dating to 1980) as applying also to the proprietary assignment of claims. In that case, the assignment of a future claim was crafted as part of a reservation of title clause, protecting a German seller of chemical products against a Dutch buyer while assigning to the seller the right to future claims of the buyer vis-à-vis subsequent purchasers. The Dutch buyer went bankrupt prior to paying the German seller, but after receiving payment from a subsequent buyer of the products, creating a conflict between the German seller and the Dutch trustee in the insolvency proceedings. While German law – which governed the original contract of sale including the assignment provision – allows for transfer of claims for security purposes, Dutch law generally restricts it. The court's decision to apply German law to the proprietary aspects of the assignment, in view of the fact that the parties to the original contract agreed to apply it, established the priority in favor of the German seller, although such an interest was not otherwise recognized in Dutch law. See T. H. D. Struycken, "The Proprietary Aspects of International Assignment of Debts and the Rome Convention, Article 12," *Lloyd's Maritime and Commercial Law Quarterly*, 3 (1998), pp. 345–360.

A proposal to amend the regulation so as to expressly determine the choice of law in such cases has not materialized.[144]

A different set of EU instruments adopt a somewhat different approach to the applicability of party autonomy to proprietary aspects of rights and claims to assets, and security interests in particular.

Thus, for example, the EU Council Regulation implementing enhanced cooperation in matters of matrimonial property regimes,[145] presented in Chapter 2, establishes in Article 21 the concept of unity, by which the law applicable to the matrimonial property regime "shall apply to all assets falling under that regime, regardless of where the assets are located."[146] Article 22 enables the spouses to choose the applicable law governing the matrimonial property.[147] While these provisions may be seen as applying the law chosen by the parties also to proprietary aspects and the rights of third parties, other provisions in this regulation offer a more nuanced approach.

Thus, Article 2(g) excludes from the scope of the regulation "the nature of rights *in rem* relating to the property,"[148] and Article 2(h) excludes "any recording in a register of rights in immoveable or moveable property, including the legal requirements for such recording, and the effects of recording or failing to record such rights in a register."[149] The latter provision, which governs also the registration of a mortgage in land or a security interest in movable property, means that

> It should therefore be the law of the Member State in which the register is kept (for immoveable property, the *lex rei sitae*) which determines under what legal conditions, and how, the recording must be carried out and which authorities, such as land registers or notaries, are in charge of checking that all requirements are met and that the documentation presented or established is sufficient or contains the necessary information."[150]

Another provision in the regulation on matrimonial property recognizes the potential differences in the legal status of an *in rem* right, such

[144] T. C. Hartley, "Choice of Law Regarding the Voluntary Assignment of Contractual Obligations under the Rome I Regulation," *International and Comparative Law Quarterly*, 60 (2011), pp. 29–56 (surveying this failed proposal).

[145] Council Regulation (EU) 2016/1103 of June 24 2016 Implementing Enhanced Cooperation in the Area of Jurisdiction, Applicable Law and the Recognition and Enforcement of Decisions in Matters of Matrimonial Property Regimes, OJ (L 183/1), July 8, 2016.

[146] Ibid., Art. 21.

[147] Being either the law of the state of habitual residence or the law of the state of nationality of either spouse. Ibid., Art. 22.

[148] Ibid., Art. 2(g).

[149] Ibid., Art. 2(h).

[150] Ibid., Preamble, paras. 27–28.

as a security interest, between the law governing the matrimonial property regime and the law of state of the court which has jurisdiction over the case. Article 29, titled, "adaptation of rights in rem," provides that

> Where a person invokes a right *in rem* to which he is entitled under the law applicable to the matrimonial property regime and the law of the Member State in which the right is invoked does not know the right *in rem* in question, that right shall, if necessary and to the extent possible, be adapted to the closest equivalent right under the law of that State, taking into account the aims and the interests pursued by the specific right *in rem* and the effects attached to it.

The concept of *adaptation* or the *closest functional equivalence*, without requiring the court with jurisdiction over the matrimonial property case to automatically embrace an *in rem* right it does not know, may therefore affect not only the recognition of the *in rem* right – such as a security interest – created in a different legal system, but also its relative priority vis-à-vis other rights. This means that the party autonomy in selecting the law that would apply to the matrimonial property as a whole would have to adapt *in rem* rights of third parties created or enforced by a different legal system. The same kind of process is embraced, *mutatis mutnadis*, for the EU Council Regulation on registered partners[151] and the EU Council Regulation on succession.[152] While spouses or the testator, respectively, are able to choose the law that would apply to the spousal property or to the succession as a whole, the incorporation of an *in rem* right, and a security interest in particular, created under a different legal system requires a process of functional adaptation. The principle of party autonomy in the choice of law thus remains bounded in its *in rem* applicability.

Outside of the limited domain of party autonomy, questions of jurisdiction and applicable law in cases of cross-border disputes over security interests are governed by private international law. The most dominant rule in respect to tangible assets – immovable and movable ones – remains

[151] Council Regulation (EU) 2016/1104 of 24 June 2016 Implementing Enhanced Cooperation in the Area of Jurisdiction, Applicable Law and the Recognition and Enforcement of Decisions in Matters of the Property Consequences of Registered Partnerships, OJ (L 183/30), July 8, 2016.

[152] Regulation (EU) No 650/2012 of the European Parliament and of the Council of 4 July 2012 on Jurisdiction, Applicable Law, Recognition and Enforcement of Decisions and Acceptance and Enforcement of Authentic Instruments in Matters of Succession and on the Creation of a European Certificate of Succession, OJ (L 201/107), July 4, 2012.

the *lex rei sitae*.[153] As such, it governs also the law that applies to the status of security interests pertaining to the asset. The prevalence of this conflict of laws principle finds expression also in the UNCITRAL Model Law on Secured Transactions, which reads in Article 85, paragraph 1:

> Except as provided in paragraphs 2 to 4 and Article 100, the law applicable to the creation, effectiveness against third parties and priority of a security right in a tangible asset is the law of the State in which the asset is located.[154]

While the *lex rei sitae* principle seems clear and straightforward, it can nevertheless create legal friction and uncertainty, such as in situations in which a chattel moves across borders after a security interest has been created. If the security interest (or the use of retention or transfer of ownership in the chattel for security purposes) was created when the asset was located in one country, but enforcement of the interest is sought after when the asset has moved to another country, then two different and potentially diverging property law systems are applied consecutively. Such a conflict (known as *conflit mobile*) may particularly arise when the security interest created in one country is not recognized in another country, or when the relative priority of the security interest vis-à-vis competing interests diverges between the two different systems.[155]

The solution that national courts have come to adopt over the years, although in a decentralized country-specific manner, is to engage in so-called transposition or transformation, in which the court with jurisdiction examines whether it can recognize, and if necessary adapt, a security interest created in a different jurisdiction than the state within which the asset is currently located.[156]

This process remains, however, entirely at the discretion of the court and is not entrenched in the principle of *lex rei sitae* or is otherwise recognized as an international norm. Accordingly, national courts can adopt different approaches to the scope and content of recognizing or adapting foreign security rights, and formal constructions of functionally equivalent devices are often not recognized as such.[157] As a result,

153 S. van Erp, "Lex Rei Sitae: The Territorial Side of Classical Property Law," in C. Godt (ed.), *Regulatory Property Rights: The Transforming Notion of Property in Transnational Business Regulation* (Leiden and Boston: Brill Nijhoff, 2016), pp. 61–81 at 64.

154 UNCITRAL Model Law, Art. 29(1).

155 Kieninger, "Introduction," p. 17.

156 Drobnig, "Recognition," pp. 106–113.

157 A. Veneziano, "The DCFR Book on Secured Transactions: Some Policy Choices made by the Working Group," in B. Akkermans, A. F. Salomons, and J. H. M. van Erp (eds.), *The Future of European Property Law* (Munich: Sellier, 2012), pp. 123–135 at 125–126.

creditors run the risk of losing their protection when the asset moves across borders and another legal system comes into play – thus potentially deterring creditors from providing sale- or loan-credit when the asset is likely to move across borders.

One case that illustrates the perils of legal arbitrage in the context of security interests and the invocation of the *lex rei sitae* rule is the 1990 decision by the Court of Justice of the European Union (CJEU) in the matter of *Krantz*.[158] The petitioner, a German company, sold and delivered a machine to a Dutch company under a reservation of title clause. The machine was installed on the premises of the Dutch company. When the latter company entered financial hardships, the Dutch Tax Authority seized the machine on the premises using a special right provided for by Dutch statutory law, which grants such a right even if the asset is owned by a third party. What this means is that even if the Dutch legal system is willing to recognize a German reservation of title clause, its relative priority changes when the asset moves across borders and Dutch law takes over because of the special priority given to the tax statutory lien under Dutch law (as opposed to German law). The Dutch court referred the matter to the CJEU for a preliminary ruling because of the argument made by the plaintiff, by which the Dutch rule constitutes in effect a restriction on the principle of free movement of goods within the European Community under the then-in-force Article 30 of the EEC Treaty[159] (currently Article 34 of TFEU). The CJEU dismissed the claim, reasoning that

> The possibility that nationals of other Member States would hesitate to sell goods on instalment terms to purchasers in the Member State concerned because such goods would be liable to seizure by the collector of taxes if the purchasers failed to discharge their Netherlands tax debts is too uncertain and indirect to warrant the conclusion that a national provision authorizing such seizure is liable to hinder trade between Member States.[160]

Therefore, the CJEU indirectly validated the employment of the *lex rei sitae* rule by the Dutch court, even though the effect of applying such a principle resulted in undermining the secured status of the German creditor as owner of the movable asset for security purposes. Despite numerous critiques of this decision and its implications for the internal market, the EU has so far not come up with a coordinated mechanism to reconsider the scope of the *lex rei sitae* rule in case of a cross-border *in rem* right such as a

[158] *H Krantz GmbH & Co* v. *Ontvanger der Directe Belastingen and Staat der Nederlanden*, Case c-69/88 [1990], ECR I-594.

[159] Ibid. at I-596.

[160] Ibid. at I-597.

security interest or reservation of title.[161] Given the lack of an EU-wide coordination mechanism in the matter, it has really been up to individual national courts across the EU to practically alleviate the problem by adopting a pragmatic approach that recognizes and validates foreign security interests.[162] This problem remains, however, much more challenging outside of the EU context, leading UNCITRAL and other bodies to suggest coordination mechanisms such as the UNCITRAL Model Law.[163]

The conflict of laws rule in regard to security interests in intangible assets, and monetary claims in particular, is less clear.[164] Across Europe, different national courts have taken varying approaches in identifying the conflict of laws rule, with no European instrument (including the Rome I Regulation) explicitly covering this question.[165] Across the world, the rule that seems to be gaining ground establishes the debtor's place of residence or business as governing the proprietary status of a security interest.[166] In the United States, the UCC Article 9 establishes in Section 9–301 the general rule, by which the law of the jurisdiction of the debtor's location governs "perfection, the effect of perfection or nonperfection, and the priority of a security interest in collateral."[167] This rule applies to all debtors, foreign and domestic. It thus orders both interstate conflict of laws within the United States and international ones.[168] Intangible assets are thus differentiated under Section 9–301 from "tangible documents, goods, instruments, money, or tangible chattel papers" – that is, tangible assets. With respect to the latter category, when the debtor is located in one jurisdiction, and the tangible asset is located in another jurisdiction, the debtor's location governs questions of perfection whereas the asset's location governs matters of priority (a bifurcated model).[169]

The growing prevalence of the rule by which the debtor's location determines the applicable law on security interests in intangible assets is also manifested in UNCITRAL Model Law of Secured Transactions, which provides in Section 86:

161 Akkermans and Ramaekers, "Free Movement of Goods and Property Law," pp. 238–239.
162 Ibid., pp. 258–259.
163 See Section 6.3.1.
164 Kieninger, "Introduction," p. 17.
165 Ibid., pp. 18–20.
166 Ibid.
167 UCC § 9–301.
168 Ibid., Official Comment 8.
169 Ibid., Official Comment 7. Section 9–307 then establishes the criteria for identifying the debtor's location, whether within the United States or outside of it.

> Except as otherwise provided in articles 87 and 97–100, the law applicable to the creation, effectiveness against third parties and priority of a security right in an intangible asset is the law of the State in which the grantor is located.[170]

Focusing on the location of the debtor, rather than trying to construct the location of an intangible asset for purposes of establishing a conflict of laws rule, seems to offer more security and predictability to the creditors. While the possibility of a *conflit mobile* may nevertheless occur when the debtor itself moves across borders, this scenario is relatively rare, especially in regard to corporations registered in a certain jurisdiction.

Finally, with respect to security interests in intellectual property, the applicable law would usually follow the jurisdiction in which the intellectual property is protected, especially when the intellectual property is registered (such as in patents, trademarks, and industrial designs). UNICTRAL Model Law on Secured Transactions thus provides in Article 99(1) that

> The law applicable to the creation, effectiveness against third parties and priority of a security right in intellectual property is the law of the State in which the intellectual property is protected.

While intuitively appealing, this conflict of laws rule may also run into difficulties or result in legal arbitrages. This would be so, for example, when a patent is registered in multiple jurisdictions, and each of these jurisdictions has different rules on perfection and/or priority of security interests. Obviously, if creditors are prudent enough to register the security interest in both the relevant company's register and in the intellectual property register, then the specific jurisdiction in which the double registration was made will most likely determine the location in which the intellectual property is protected for purposes of identifying the applicable law.

6.3.3 *Approximation*

Section 6.3.2 has already identified what could be viewed as one type of an approximation strategy: recognizing foreign security interests by finding the closest functional equivalent of such a foreign interest in the domestic legal system. This strategy is, however, constrained in the sense that it relies on the willingness of the local courts to do so, without a clear statutory set of rules on how to engage in such approximation, or a supranational norm that requires such approximation.

170 UNCITRAL Model Law, Art. 86.

This section looks at the utilization of an approximation strategy in the context of security interests in two institutional settings: OHADA (Organization for the Harmonization of Business Law in Africa) and the European Union. While in both cases, the choice of the globalization strategy could be even seen as located between approximation and supranationalism, I nevertheless attribute them to the approximation strategy, because the instruments described below rely on legislating harmonized *domestic* provisions, rather than on creating a single supranational order.

Chapter 2 outlined the main institutional features of OHADA, including the Common Court of Justice and Arbitration (CCJA) being the court of cassation for all disputes related to the various Uniform Acts.[171] This section focuses on OHADA's new Uniform Act on Organizing Securities ("Securities Uniform Act"), which went into force in 2011,[172] replacing a previous version from 1997.[173] The Securities Uniform Act determines the types of security interests recognized across OHADA's Member States. It distinguishes, first, between personal securities (surety-bonds and autonomous guarantees) and transferable securities.[174] As for the latter, Title 2 of the Securities Uniform Act defines and elaborates on the various types of security interests in movable property – distinguishing between possessory liens, property retained or transferred as security, pledge on tangible property, pledge on intangible property, and preferential rights[175] – and setting up the institutional framework of registering transferable securities in the national Trade and Personal Property Rights Register.[176] It should be noted that by recognizing distinctive mechanisms for the retention or transfer of ownership for security purposes – while requiring registration of such a mechanism in the Trade and Personal Property Rights Register to be binding on third parties[177] – the Securities Uniform Act opts for a more formal model rather than the American/Commonwealth functional approach. Title 3 of the Securities Uniform Act sets the rules for mortgages in land.[178]

171 See Chapter 2, Section 2.3.4.4.

172 *Acte Uniforme Portant Organisation des Sûretés* (Uniform Act on Organizing Securities), OHADA Official Gazette, February 15, 2011, available at www.droit-afrique.com/uploads/OHADA-Uniform-Act-2010-securities.pdf (accessed on March 1, 2018).

173 The previous version of OHADA'a Uniform Act on Organizing Securities (no longer in force) is available at www.juriscope.org/uploads/pdf/ohada/OHADA_en/surete-gb.pdf (accessed on March 1, 2018).

174 Securities Uniform Law, Title 1 (Arts. 12–49).

175 Ibid., Title 2, Arts. 67–178.

176 Ibid., Title 2, Arts. 51–66.

177 Ibid., Art. 74 (registration of retention of title); Art. 82 (registration of an assignment of a debt as security).

178 Ibid., Title 3 (Arts. 190–223).

Having identified the types of security interests, and the conditions and procedures for their creation and perfection, the Securities Uniform Act proceeds in Title 4 to consolidate the concept of uniformity at the enforcement stage, by setting up the order of distribution of funds among various types of creditors in the case of the sale of real property (Article 225) and personal property (Article 226). In so doing, the Securities Uniform Act covers the various stages concerning security interests, from their creation to their enforcement, by establishing uniform substantive and procedural provisions to be carried out by state institutions. While the implementation of the Securities Uniform Act at the local level leaves open the possibility for divergences among OHADA states that would emerge over time, due to different practices or modes of interpretation by state institutions, the Common Court of Justice and Arbitration maintains in principle its interpretative role in preserving uniformity across the Member States.[179]

Moving to the European Union, one instance in which a binding instrument has been adopted in the context of secured transactions is the 2002 European Union Financial Collateral Directive, amended in 2009 and 2014,[180] and implemented in domestic legislation by the Member States.[181]

The underlying purpose of the Financial Collateral Directive is to create a "harmonised EU legal framework for the receipt and enforcement of financial collateral."[182] Importantly, the Financial Collateral Directive distinguishes between a "title transfer financial collateral arrangement," in which full ownership or entitlement is transferred to the collateral taker, such as in a repurchase agreement (repo),[183] and a "security financial collateral arrangement" in which the collateral taker receives a security interest, but ownership or full entitlement remains with the collateral provider.[184] The Financial Collateral Directive thus

179 See Chapter 2, Section 2.3.4.4, for an analysis of the role of CCJA under Article 14 of the OHADA Treaty.

180 EU Directive 2002/47/EC of the European Parliament and of the Council of 6 June 2002 on Financial Collateral Arrangements, OJ (L 168/43), June 27, 2002, as amended. The consolidated version is available at http://eur-lex.europa.eu/legal-content/EN/TXT/?uri=CELEX:02002L0047–20140702 (accessed on March 1, 2018).

181 For the implementation of the Directive in the UK, see Sheehan, *Principles of Personal Property Law*, p. 271.

182 European Commission, "Financial Collateral Arrangements," available at https://ec.europa.eu/info/business-economy-euro/banking-and-finance/financial-markets/post-trade-services/financial-collateral-arrangements_en (accessed on March 1, 2018).

183 Financial Collateral Directive, Art. 2(1)(b) (definition of "title transfer financial collateral arrangement").

184 Ibid., Art. 2(1)(c) (definition of "security financial collateral arrangement").

follows and consolidates the formal model traditionally embraced in Europe rather than opting for the American functional model. Moreover, the Financial Collateral Directive accepts various methods for "providing" a financial collateral with third-party applicability, including any measure that provides the collateral taker with control over the collateral, thus replacing methods such as registration or possession.[185]

6.3.4 *Supranationalism*

The most prominent manifestation of a supranationalism strategy in the context of security interests is embedded in the UNIDROIT Convention on International Interests in Mobile Equipment ("Cape Town Convention"),[186] and the Protocol to the Convention on International Interests in Mobile Equipment on Matters Specific to Aircraft Equipment.[187] As Chapter 2 (Section 2.3.4.7) briefly showed, the constant movement of aircrafts across borders raises proprietary concerns, especially in regard to security interests in aircrafts and their equipment, and the enormous difficulties that financiers/creditors might face in enforcing their property rights in such footloose tangible assets. Thus, when a security interest over the aircraft is registered in one country, but the vehicle is located in another country when enforcement is required, conflict of laws rules, and the *lex rei sitae* principle in particular, may prove problematic for the creditor or other stakeholders. This problem is even more acute than in the case of conventional commercial goods, in which the financier/creditor may have some advance knowledge about the cross-border destination of the goods. In the case of an aircraft, the asset may be found anywhere in the world at any given time.

To meet this challenge, the Cape Town Convention establishes an international interest in aircrafts or their equipment – airframes or aircraft engines – that is recognized by all ratifying states.[188] The Cape Town Convention sets up an international registry, which provides for the electronic registration of the international interest, with priority in

[185] Ibid., Art. 2(2). See also Sheehan, *Principles of Personal Property Law*, p. 272.
[186] International Institute for the Unification of Private Law (UNIDROIT), Convention on International Interests in Mobile Equipment, November 16, 2001, 2307 UNTS 285.
[187] Protocol to the Convention on International Interests in Mobile Equipment on Matters Specific to Aircraft Equipment, November 16, 2001, 2307 UNTS 517.
[188] International Registry of Mobile Assets, available at www.internationalregistry.aero/ir-web/ (accessed on March 1, 2018).

case of conflicting interests being determined on a first-to-file basis.[189] A registered international interest prevails over an unregistered interest, even if the holder of the registered interest knew of the unregistered interest.[190] International interest holders are provided various remedies in the event of default.[191]

The Cape Town Convention establishes the Registrar, as well as the Supervisory Authority, which create together the administrative institutional framework required to operate the international registry and to register the international interests. At the same time, the Cape Town Convention does not establish a supranational court or another adjudicative body in charge with interpreting and applying the Convention, or with enforcing the international interests.

Moreover, the Cape Town Convention does not establish a self-sufficient legal system that covers all aspects of conflict of laws issues regarding both jurisdiction and applicable law. As for jurisdiction, the Convention does not include a default rule. This means that if a legal proceeding under the Cape Town Convention is not covered by one of the specific scenarios set out below, the question of jurisdiction would be decided by the court of the forum state in which proceedings have been initiated, based on its internal conflict of laws rules.[192]

The specific scenarios that are covered by the Cape Town Convention in regard to jurisdiction include (1) freedom of the parties to choose the court of any of the contracting states, and to award exclusive jurisdiction to such a court;[193] (2) authority of the court chosen by the parties, or of a court in whose territory the equipment is located, to grant some types of temporary relief under Article 13 of the Convention, with other types of temporary relief-granting authority granted to the court in whose territory the debtor is situated;[194] and (3) exclusive authority to award damages or make orders against the Registrar to the courts in which the Registrar has its center of administration.[195] In the case of the registry of aircrafts, this center is

[189] Ibid.

[190] Sprankling, *International Law of Property*, p. 61.

[191] Ibid.

[192] K. F. Kreuzer, "Jurisdiction and Choice of Law under the Cape Town Convention and the Protocols Thereto," *Cape Town Convention Journal* (September 2013), pp. 149-164 at 149–151.

[193] Cape Town Convention, Art. 42.

[194] Ibid., Art. 43.

[195] Ibid., Art. 44.

located in Ireland.[196] Moreover, the Convention explicitly provides that the jurisdictional rules will not apply to insolvency proceedings.[197] The rules on jurisdiction are thus incomplete in a number of ways.

As for the applicable law, although the international interest should be supranational in nature, many substantive and procedural issues may still require further articulation during the legal proceedings. Questions concerning matters within the scope of the Convention, but not settled by its substantive law provisions or by agreement of the parties, would be resolved by domestic substantive laws. Article 5 of the Convention gives the gap-filling mandate mostly to the court of the forum state to determine the complementary substantive law that would apply.[198]

Summing up, the Cape Town Convention is truly innovative in its particular application of the supranationalism strategy for property law. It is the first global (applying to 73 states) registry system for any form of property rights. Moreover, although it focuses on security interests, the ability to register the title of the seller/financier under a reservation of title clause also expands the scope of the system to include an ownership registry.[199] In the sense of defining a genuine international interest, it is the most ambitious manifestation of the supranationalism strategy.

At the same time, the lack of a supranational court or adjudicative body may allow for locally based arbitrage in interpreting the Convention and its application. Moreover, the reliance of the Convention's rules, regarding both jurisdiction and applicable law, on the domestic conflict of laws rules of the forum state allows for some uncertainty among the various stakeholders. This somewhat undermines the ability of the international registry to truly prevail over national rules.

6.4 *In Rem* Rights and Priorities to Assets in Cross-Border Insolvencies

Insolvency law is often analyzed as a distinct legal field, having potential interfaces with the law of obligations (especially in the case of default by individuals), and with corporate law, when corporations become insolvent and face either liquidation or some sort of a reorganization plan. It is

[196] Kreuzer, "Jurisdiction and Choice of Law," p. 154.

[197] Cape Town Convention, Art. 45.

[198] Kreuzer, "Jurisdiction and Choice of Law," pp. 156–157, 163–164.

[199] J. G. Sprankling, *The International Law of Property* (Oxford: Oxford University Press, 2014), p. 61.

also very much associated with procedural law and issues of court jurisdiction, especially in a country such as the United States, where bankruptcy is generally governed by a federal statute.[200]

That said, the substantive core of insolvency or bankruptcy law[201] lies in governing mutually insupportable obligations to creditors, and it thus requires legislatures, courts, and insolvency officers to settle claims through a system of priorities and rules of distribution among otherwise distant parties. This makes the heart of insolvency/bankruptcy law a matter of property law.[202] Accordingly, this section does not deal with the various process-oriented aspects of insolvency or bankruptcy proceedings. It focuses, rather, on proprietary questions of priority and distribution of assets among creditors, and on how various globalization strategies deal with cross-border insolvencies, such as when creditors and/or the debtor's assets are located across national borders.

As already noted in Section 6.1, national rules on priorities and distribution of assets in insolvency are not merely technical. They reflect an economic or social agenda about which interests should be served in the case of insolvency, alongside organizational principles for the optimal collection of debts. Priority for secured creditors is usually premised on granting financiers an *ex ante* incentive to extend credit to individuals and corporations, although it may also embed a tacit distributive agenda whenever powerful creditors, such as financial institutions, have stronger bargaining power to ensure a secured status.[203] This is also the case when certain bodies, such as tax authorities, enjoy priority though a statutory lien in the case of insolvency.[204] On the other hand, granting preferential rights to employees or insurance creditors over unsecured creditors (as is the case in Australia, for example)[205] represents a normative principle of prioritizing the interests of parties considered particularly vulnerable in

200 The Bankruptcy Code of 1978, as amended, is coded in 11 U.S.C. 101 et seq. (Title 11 – Bankruptcy).

201 The use of the terms *insolvency, bankruptcy* or equivalent terms changes between different legal systems. See, e.g., S. A. Davydenko and J. R. Franks, "Do Bankruptcy Codes Matter? A Study of Defaults in France, Germany and the U.K.," *Journal of Finance*, 63 (2008), pp. 565–608 at 602–607 (surveying the details of bankruptcy codes, including terminology, in three countries). For purposes of this chapter, I use these terms interchangeably.

202 Adler, "Bankruptcy as Property Law," p. 206.

203 McCormack, "UNCITRAL," pp. 497–498.

204 Dalhuisen, Vol. II, p. 525, fn. 321.

205 See S. Gopalan and M. Guihot, *Cross-Border Insolvency Law* (Chatswood, Australia: LexisNexis Butterworths, 2016), p. 11 (on preference to employees); Garrido, "Snowflakes," p. 461 (on preference to insurance creditors).

the case of an economic meltdown. National principles may also shape the particular features of the preferred status of claimants such as employees in insolvency, for example, whether specific sectors of employees are preferred over others, or whether the priority for covering employees' wages is capped at a certain amount.[206]

A different normative principle that is dominant to varying degrees in national insolvency laws is the "essential notion of equality of treatment of creditors,"[207] which builds on a general normative principle of equality and requires that distribution among creditors within the same rank would be made on a *pari passu* basis (i.e., proportionate to the respective amount of debt).[208] That said, the *pari passu* principle within each rank is subject to the ranking and prioritizing of distinct categories of claims. This has been the case across both civil law and common law systems.[209]

In addition, normative considerations for liquidation versus reorganization of insolvent firms might also impact the distributive outcomes of national insolvency laws. Thus, for example, reorganization-oriented bankruptcy laws will often limit the ability of secured creditors to repossess assets through self-help or other measures outside of the insolvency proceedings in order to prevent a situation in which a reorganization scheme would become practically impossible.[210]

More generally, the collective nature of insolvency proceedings, orchestrated by courts and appointed officers (such as receivers or trustees), is intended to optimize the process of mapping the different claims, identifying debtor assets, and distributing proceeds in an efficient manner.[211]

Every national system advances its own normative preferences and balancing of interests, and as a result, the scheme of priorities and rules of distribution in insolvency may vary significantly.[212] Accordingly, while most legal systems generally recognize some sort of priority for secured creditors, employees, and taxes, these priorities vary significantly in their scope and internal ranking in the ladder of priorities.[213] Such differences may also manifest themselves in the recognition (or lack thereof) of

206 Garrido, "Snowflakes," p. 486.

207 I. F. Fletcher, *Insolvency in Private International Law*, 2d ed. (Oxford: Clarendon Press, 2005), p. 9.

208 Gopalan and Guihot, *Cross-Border Insolvency Law*, p. 9.

209 Dalhuisen, Vol. II, pp. 359–362.

210 Ibid., p. 524.

211 Gopalan and Guihot, *Cross-Border Insolvency Law*, pp. 9–12.

212 Garrido, "Snowflakes," p. 461.

213 J. L. Westbrook, "Bankruptcy Control of the Recovery Process," *American Bankruptcy Institute Law Review*, 12 (2004), pp. 245–257 at 253.

reservation of title clauses and other mechanisms of retention/transfer of ownership for security purposes. Legal systems that recognize reservation of title clauses would grant such suppliers/creditors the power to reclaim the assets and remove them from the bankruptcy estate.[214] Differences in rules of priority and distribution exist also among legal systems that otherwise share a certain set of values or that are particularly invested in coordinating economic activities, such as across the European Union,[215] or more generally across market economies.[216] The divergence in national rules governing priorities and distribution of assets thus poses a significant legal challenge in ever-increasing cases of cross-border insolvency.

6.4.1 *Insolvency between Territorialism and Universalism*

At the core of the deliberation about globalization strategies to govern cross-border insolvencies is the longstanding debate between two pole positions: territorialism and universalism, and the increasing prevalence of various interim approaches, such as one of *modified universalism.*[217]

Under a strict territorialism approach to cross-border insolvency law, jurisdiction is dispersed among the courts of the various states in which a multinational debtor has assets, such that each local court is authorized to open insolvency proceedings that govern assets located in its territory, and it applies its local law to priorities and distribution of local assets among local creditors.[218] Under the opposite universalism approach, the bankruptcy of a multinational debtor would result in only one proceeding under a single body of substantive or procedural bankruptcy law, such that the single proceeding would distribute all of the debtor's assets

[214] S. M. Franken, "Cross-Border Insolvency Law: A Comparative Institutional Analysis," *Oxford Journal of Legal Studies*, 34 (2014), pp. 97–131 at 109–110.

[215] For a comparative survey of the insolvency ranking of liabilities across nineteen European states that are members of Banking Union (bringing together the EU members that are part of the Euro zone), see Banking Union, Single Resolution Board (SRB), "Insolvency Ranking in the Jurisdictions of the Banking Union," April 2017, available at https://srb.europa.eu/sites/srbsite/files/ldr_-_annex_on_insolvency_ranking_v042017.pdf (accessed on March 1, 2018).

[216] Wood, "Bankruptcy Ladder of Priorities," pp. 225–234 (comparing national rankings of priority creditors). See also J. L. Westbrook et al., *A Global View of Business Insolvency Systems* (Washington D.C.: The World Bank and Leiden: Martinus Nijhoff Publishers, 2010), pp. 37–44.

[217] Garrido, "Snowflakes," pp. 471–474.

[218] Franken, "Cross-Border Insolvency Law," p. 102.

to the creditors worldwide. This jurisdiction would normally be the debtor's "home country" or its "centre of main interests."[219]

Proponents of universalism point to the maximization of the debtor's assets as its key advantage, due to the decrease in transaction costs and administrative costs of the process, alongside improved certainty for creditors, equality among similarly ranked creditors located across borders, and higher possibility of successful reorganization.[220] At the other end, those advocating the territorialism approach voice concern over the imposition of the debtor's home bankruptcy law on remote stakeholders to their disadvantage, alongside the fear that debtors will manipulate the "centre of main interests" for purposes of bankruptcy forum shopping.[221] But probably most manifestly, it is the fear of loss of sovereignty that practically drives many states to object to ceding the jurisdiction of their local courts in favor of universalism.[222] Accordingly, differences among the territorialism and universalism approaches across various states may also point to disparity in power and influence. Powerful economically independent states prefer to apply their local insolvency law to transnational insolvencies, while placing pressure on dependent countries to apply a more universal approach that enables the application of the dominant country's bankruptcy laws and priority rules even for assets located in the dependent country. Countries' approaches to cross-border insolvency are thus not necessarily reciprocal in nature.[223]

Moreover, market-dominant countries such as the United States or the United Kingdom adopt what can be termed *asymmetric universalism*, or *asymmetric overreaching*.[224] Thus, according to the US Bankruptcy Code, proceedings involving either liquidation (Chapter 7) or reorganization (Chapter 11) have a low barrier of entry for essentially non-US corporations. According to Section 109 of the Code, bankruptcy proceedings can be initiated for a debtor that "resides or has a domicile, a place of business, or property in the United States."[225] US courts have ruled that

219 J. Altman, "A Test Case in International Bankruptcy Protocols: The Lehman Brothers Insolvency," *San Diego International Law Journal*, 12 (2010–2011), pp. 463–495 at 471; Franken, "Cross-Border Insolvency Law," p. 102.

220 A. Walters, "United States' Bankruptcy Jurisdiction over Foreign Entities: Exorbitant or Congruent?" *Journal of Corporate Law Studies*, 17 (2017), pp. 367–404 at 375–376.

221 Ibid., pp. 376–377.

222 Garrido, "Snowflakes," pp. 467–468.

223 Franken, "Cross-Border Insolvency Law," pp. 111–115.

224 Walters, "United States' Bankruptcy Jurisdiction," p. 381.

225 11 U.S.C. § 109(a).

the plain meaning of *property* is any amount of property, however small, such that a foreign entity could qualify as a debtor for purposes of Section 109 even if it has only a nominal amount of property, such as cash or shares, in the United States.[226] Importantly, the motive for initiation of a US bankruptcy proceeding for essentially a foreign debtor often comes from the debtor itself, which may seek to enjoy the benefits of swift reorganization under Chapter 11 even prior to bankruptcy, often in the form of turning bondholders (creditors) into equity owners.[227]

The US proceeding creates a worldwide estate comprising all legal and equitable interests of the debtor in property "wherever located."[228] Commencement of a US case also results in an automatic stay of individual enforcement actions, meaning that creditors that are subject to US personal jurisdiction (such as foreign companies having an office or doing business in the United States) face the threat of being held in contempt for taking unauthorized enforcement actions against the debtor outside of the United States.[229] This means that foreign creditors, and in particular foreign financial institutions such as banks that do business in the United States, are practically deterred from initiating enforcement proceedings against the debtor in their home jurisdictions, thus granting the US stay an extraterritorial reach in effect.[230]

That said, US courts have proven pragmatic enough not to open bankruptcy proceedings under Chapter 7 or Chapter 11 of the Bankruptcy Code when the debtor's interests in the United States are remote, or that the ability to hold a single bankruptcy proceedings is otherwise impractical, thus constraining the abuse of "corporate bankruptcy tourism."[231] The failed attempt of Yukon, the Russian oil company that filed for a Chapter 11 proceedings in Houston in 2004 by virtue of having a small deposit in a US bank account – in order to avoid an expropriatory tax auction of Yukon's Russian assets organized by the Russian government – serves as a vivid reminder of the limits of asymmetric overreaching in insolvency even in otherwise-dominant jurisdictions.[232]

226 Walters, "United States' Bankruptcy Jurisdiction," p. 379.

227 O. Couwenberg and S. J. Lubben, "Corporate Bankruptcy Tourists," *Business Lawyer*, 70 (2015), pp. 719–745 at 721.

228 11 U.S.C. § 109(a).

229 Walters, "United States' Bankruptcy Jurisdiction," pp. 380–381.

230 Ibid.

231 Couwenberg and Lubben, "Corporate Bankruptcy Tourists."

232 Walters, "United States' Bankruptcy Jurisdiction," pp. 390–392.

6.4.2 *Globalization Strategies for Cross-Border Insolvencies*

This section analyzes the various *reciprocal* – bilateral or multilateral – globalization strategies for cross-border insolvencies currently in operation. The various strategies can be portrayed as representing various degrees of modified universalism, being a "universalist approach in which some concessions are made to territorial interests for the sake of ensuring the effective functioning of the international bankruptcy system."[233] The complexity of cross-border insolvencies, and the lack of an international convention or international courts/tribunals with jurisdiction over cross-border insolvencies, somewhat challenge the depiction of current legal instruments as falling within one of the globalization strategies analyzed in this book. For example, as Section 6.4.2.4 shows, it is the bottom-up coordination among bankruptcy administrators or national courts that actually comes closest to holding a single process with a single ranking of priorities over assets in case of cross-border insolvencies of multinational corporations.

6.4.2.1 Soft Law

UNCITRAL is playing a particularly dominant role in crafting soft law mechanisms, mostly through model laws dealing with both domestic and cross-border insolvencies. Between 2004 and 2013, UNCITRAL published the four-part Legislative Guide on Insolvency Law,[234] which deals with the various procedural and substantive aspects of insolvency law, including "priorities and distribution of proceeds."[235] While the Legislative Guide does not offer a single blueprint for the ranking of priorities and distribution of assets, it does state in its recommendations that "the insolvency law should minimize the priorities accorded to unsecured claims. The law should set out clearly the classes of claims, if any, that will be entitled to be satisfied in priority in insolvency proceedings."[236] The Legislative Guide therefore adopts what is largely a market-based

233 Garrido, "Snowflakes," p. 471.

234 UNCITRAL Legislative Guide on Insolvency Law, Parts One and Two (2004); UNCITRAL Legislative Guide on Insolvency Law, Part Three: Treatment of Enterprise Groups in Insolvency (2010); UNCITRAL Legislative Guide on Insolvency Law, Part Four: Directors' Obligations in the Period Approaching Insolvency (2013). All parts are available at www.uncitral.org/uncitral/en/uncitral_texts/insolvency.html (accessed on March 1, 2018).

235 UNCITRAL Legislative Guide on Insolvency Law, Part Two (2004), Section VB, pp. 266–275.

236 Ibid., Sect. VB, p. 275 (recommendation 187).

(some would say, a neoliberal) agenda, by which secured claims should be granted priority in insolvency, whereas priority for unsecured claims such as taxes or employee's wages should be narrowed.

The more influential instrument developed by UNCTAD is the Model Law on Cross-Border Insolvency (1997) with Guide to Enactment and Interpretation (2013).[237] The underlying approach taken by the Model Law on Cross-Border Insolvency ("UNCTAD Model Law") is one of a *co-operative territorial approach*,[238] or a relatively modest version of modified universalism.[239]

The UNCTAD Model Law is intended to be incorporated directly into the law of enacting states on a statutory, rather than a treaty basis.[240] The main idea is one of enabling the local court to open an ancillary or secondary proceeding at the request of a foreign representative of an insolvency proceeding that is pending in another country. The foreign proceeding is considered a foreign main proceeding if it takes place "in the State where the debtor has the centre of its main interests,"[241] or a foreign non-main proceeding if it takes place "in the State where the debtor has an establishment."[242] The local court maintains discretion on whether to open such an ancillary proceeding so that it is not inherently bound by an extraterritorial reach of the foreign bankruptcy court. According to the UNCTAD Model Law, once the foreign proceeding is recognized by the local court, it can grant the foreign representative a number of reliefs, including a stay on individual actions or execution proceedings. Most importantly, under Article 21(2) of the Model Law:

> Upon recognition of a foreign proceeding, whether main or non-main, the court may, at the request of the foreign representative, entrust the distribution of all or part of the debtor's assets located in this State to the foreign representative or another person designated by the court, provided that the court is satisfied that the interests of the creditors in this State are adequately protected.[243]

The UNCTAD Model Law therefore relies on the ability to extend the scope of territorial coverage of the debtor's assets beyond the jurisdiction in which the original (main or nonmain) proceeding was opened,

237 The integrated text is available at www.uncitral.org/uncitral/en/uncitral_texts/insolvency/1997Model.html.
238 Franken, "Cross-Border Insolvency Law," p. 116.
239 Garrido, "Snowflakes," pp. 472–473.
240 Franken, "Cross-Border Insolvency Law," pp. 111–115.
241 Model Law on Cross-Border Insolvency, Art. 2(b).
242 Ibid., Art. 2(c).
243 Ibid., Art. 21(2).

but it relies on the discretion of the local court in deciding whether to assist the foreign proceeding. In so doing, the court considers whether the interests of local creditors and other stakeholders are sufficiently protected.[244] This form of cooperative territorialism or modified universalism relies therefore on the willingness of states to embrace the Model Law, recognize foreign proceedings, and assist foreign representatives in materializing assets located in the territory. At the same time, the Model Law does not set a binding system of private international law rules on jurisdiction, choice of law, or enforcement, but relies on the cooperation of states and their national courts in facilitating cross-border insolvency proceedings.

The adoption of the UNCTAD Model Law across states has had a slow start. The United States had a major influence on crafting the law, which was largely inspired by then Section 304 of the 1978 Bankruptcy Code. It resonated well with the preference of the United States for a territorial albeit cooperative approach to insolvency law in the case of foreign corporations, thereby encouraging American citizens to trade with and invest in establishments of foreign firms in the United States.[245] The 2005 Bankruptcy Reform Act[246] repealed Section 304 and replaced it with Chapter 15, which incorporated with virtually no amendments the Model Law into the Bankruptcy Code.[247] Other common law countries were relatively quick to adopt the Model Law: Great Britain and Canada in 2005, New Zealand in 2006, and Australia in 2008.[248] European civil law systems are still slow in following the Model Law, focusing rather on EU law analyzed in Section 6.4.2.2. A significant boost came in 2015 when OHADA countries in Western Africa adopted the Model Law through a Uniform Act. As of the end of 2017, the Model Law has been adopted in 43 states.[249]

6.4.2.2 Conflict of Laws

The most prominent binding instrument on private international law in respect to cross-border insolvency is the EU Regulation on insolvency

244 Franken, "Cross-Border Insolvency Law," p. 127.
245 Ibid., p. 116.
246 Bankruptcy Abuse Prevention and Consumer Protection Act of 2005, Pub. L. 109–08.
247 Franken, "Cross-Border Insolvency Law," p. 127.
248 UNCITRAL, "Status: UNCITRAL Model Law on Cross-Border Insolvency (1997)," available at www.uncitral.org/uncitral/en/uncitral_texts/insolvency/1997Model_status.html (accessed on March 1, 2018).
249 Ibid.

proceedings, promulgated originally in 2000,[250] and recast in 2015.[251] The EU Regulation is not a measure of substantive harmonization of national insolvency laws, but one aimed at advancing a conflict of laws strategy by allocating jurisdiction to open insolvency proceedings and determining applicable law in respect to such proceedings.[252]

The EU Regulation reflects a "philosophy of Euro universalism," by which main insolvency proceedings purport to have universal scope and encompass all of the debtor's assets.[253] Article 3, titled "international jurisdiction," provides that the "courts of the Member State within the territory of which the centre of main interests of the debtor's main interests is situated shall have jurisdiction to open insolvency proceedings ('main insolvency proceedings')."[254] Article 7 states: "Save as otherwise provided in this Regulation, the law applicable to insolvency proceedings and their effects shall be that of the Member State within the territory of which such proceedings are opened (the 'State of the opening proceedings')."[255] These two provisions read together might create the impression of EU universalism, by which a single process and a single law – that of the State of the debtor's centre of main interests (COMI) – control the entire insolvency estate, including the setting of priorities and distribution of assets. But, at the same time, the EU Insolvency Regulation allows for theme-specific carve-outs and for the opening of secondary insolvency proceedings that are governed by the national laws of the respective states in which the secondary proceedings take place.[256] The mechanism of specific carve-outs, alongside the writ-large exception to the COMI insolvency law enabled by the opening of secondary insolvency proceedings, undercut the practical effect of EU universalism,[257] and thus settle essentially for a conflict of laws strategy.

[250] Council Regulation (EC) No 1346/2000 of 29 May 2000 on Insolvency Proceedings, OJ (L 160/1), June 30, 2000.

[251] Regulation (EU) 2015/848 of the European Parliament and of the Council of 20 May 2015 on Insolvency Proceedings (recast), OJ L 141/19), June 5, 2016, p. 19 (EU Regulation).

[252] G. McCormack, "Something Old, Something New: Recasting the European Insolvency Regulation," *Modern Law Review*, 79 (2016), pp. 121–146 at 123.

[253] Ibid.

[254] EU Regulation, Art. 3(1). The Article further states that "[t]he centre of main interests shall be the place where the debtor conducts the administration of its interests on a regular basis and which is ascertainable by third parties").

[255] Ibid., Art. 7(1).

[256] Ibid., Arts. 34–35.

[257] J. A. E. Pottow, "Beyond Carve-Outs and toward Reliance: A Normative Framework for Cross-Border Insolvency Choice of Law," *Brooklyn Journal of Corporate Finance and Commercial Law*, 9 (2014–2015), pp. 197–220 at 200–201.

The theme-specific carve-outs are located in Articles 8 to 18 of the EU Regulation. One prominent provision is set forth in Article 8, titled "third parties' right in rem," which reads:

> The opening of insolvency proceedings shall not affect the rights *in rem* of creditors or third parties in respect of tangible or intangible, movable or immovable assets, both specific assets and collections of indefinite assets as a whole which change from time to time, belonging to the debtor which are situated within the territory of another Member State at the time of the opening of proceedings.[258]

Article 8 goes further to identify such rights *in rem*, which include not only security interests such as a mortgage or lien, but also rights to repossess assets or require restitution for them, as well as "a right in rem for the beneficial use of assets" and rights recorded in a public register.[259] As the preamble to the EU Insolvency Regulation states:

> There is a particular need for a special reference diverging from the law of the opening State in the case of rights *in rem*, since such rights are of considerable importance for the granting of credit. The basis, validity and extent of rights *in rem* should therefore normally be determined according to the *lex situs* and not be affected by the opening of insolvency proceedings. The proprietor of a right *in rem* should therefore be able to continue to assert its right to segregation or separate settlement of the collateral security.[260]

The divergence from the principle of EU universalism, by which a secured debtor is entitled to continue its individual action regardless of the collective bankruptcy proceeding, while applying the *lex situs* rather than the *lex fori concursus* (the law of the Member State within the territory of which the main insolvency proceedings are opened, or the COMI State) can be justified by the particular reliance that a financier has had when extending credit.[261] That said, this particular carve-out for *in rem* rights, followed by other exceptions in the EU Regulation for themes such as set-offs (Article 9), reservation of title (Article 10), or contracts of employment (Article 13) undermine the proclaimed one proceeding/one set of priorities aspiration of the EU Regulation. As suggested above, these multiple carve-outs turn the EU Insolvency Regulation into a mechanism which employs a conflict of laws strategy, splitting the

[258] EU Regulation, Art. 8(1).
[259] Ibid., Art. 8(2).
[260] Ibid., Preamble, para. 68.
[261] Pottow, "Beyond Carve-Outs," pp. 205–207.

debtor's pool of assets located across EU Member States into distinctive sets of priorities and distribution of assets under national property laws.

6.4.2.3 Approximation

Section 6.3.3 analyzed the work of OHADA in adopting the 2011 Uniform Act on Organizing Securities (Securities Uniform Act),[262] and explained how the direct application of this Uniform Act to the domestic laws of all OHADA Member States, alongside the power of the Common Court of Justice and Arbitration (CCJA) to interpret the Securities Uniform Act, work to approximate the national laws on security interests within the OHADA region, and, moreover, contain certain aspects of supranationalism.

Following along the same lines, in 2015 OHADA adopted the Uniform Act on Bankruptcy Proceedings ("Bankruptcy Uniform Act").[263] The Bankruptcy Uniform Act established a ranking of priorities and distribution of proceeds from the sale of the bankruptcy assets. Article 166 sets up such a ranking in the case of a sale of immovable assets, and Article 167 does so for the sale of movable assets.[264] This uniformity should eliminate, or at least significantly alleviate, the disparities that may exist in a cross-border insolvency within the OHADA region. Because the Bankruptcy Uniform Act, applied directly in all Member States and superseding any contradicting statutory law in them, provides for a certain set of procedural and substantive norms on priorities and distribution, this single ranking should apply for all assets, provided, however, that national bankruptcy courts do not practically diverge in interpreting and/or enforcing the Bankruptcy Uniform Act. Moreover, the Bankruptcy Uniform Act specifically orders the recognition of bankruptcy proceedings opened in other OHADA Member States.[265] It provides in Article 247 that authorized decisions made by bankruptcy courts in one Member State shall be considered *res judicata* in the territories of other Member States.[266] Article 251 provides that the effects of main

[262] *Acte Uniforme Portant Organisation des Sûretés* (Uniform Act on Organizing Securities), OHADA Official Gazette, February 15, 2011, available at www.droit-afrique.com/uploads/OHADA-Uniform-Act-2010-securities.pdf (accessed on March 1, 2018).

[263] *Acte Uniforme Portant Organisation des Procedures Collectives D'apurement du Passif* (Uniform Act on Bankruptcy Proceedings), OHADA Official Gazette, September 25, 2015. An unofficial English translation is available at www.ohada.org/index.php/en/aupc-insolvency-law/presentation-and-innovations.

[264] Ibid., Arts. 166–167.

[265] Ibid., Title VII, Ch. I (Arts. 247–255).

[266] Ibid., Art. 247.

bankruptcy proceeding "shall apply to all the assets of the debtor located in the territory of States Parties," whereas the effects of a secondary bankruptcy proceeding shall be limited to the assets of the debtor in the territory of the Member State in which the secondary proceeding was opened.[267] The reciprocal commitment of OHADA Member States to enforce main bankruptcy proceedings opened in another Member State, alongside the harmonization of national laws on insolvency, should therefore come close enough to holding a single process with a single tanking of priorities.

Finally, the Bankruptcy Uniform Act adopts the key provisions of the UNCITRAL Model Law on Cross-Border Insolvency in regard to the recognition of bankruptcy proceedings opened in countries outside the OHADA region,[268] authorizing local courts to grant various types of reliefs to foreign representatives, such as a stay on local enforcement proceedings, or entrusting the "administration or realization of part or all of the assets of the debtor situated in the territory to the foreign representative of the recognized foreign bankruptcy proceeding."[269] Like their counterparts in other countries that have adopted the UNCITRAL Model Law, courts within the OHADA region are granted discretion to refuse such request reliefs, for example, when the "measure is manifestly repugnant to the public policy of the State party concerned."[270] The Bankruptcy Uniform Act thus complements intra-OHADA uniformity with extra-OHADA recognition of foreign proceedings.

6.4.2.4 Supranationalism

Currently, no supranational court or tribunal is authorized to run a bankruptcy proceeding or to otherwise establish a single set of priorities or asset distribution for cross-border insolvencies (with the limited exception of the CCJA in the case of OHADA's Bankruptcy Uniform Act).[271] While the growing adoption of the UNCITRAL Model Law on cross-border insolvency, with its mechanism for recognizing foreign bankruptcy proceedings, may work to improve the coordination between courts and bankruptcy administrators located in different countries,

267 Ibid., Art. 251.
268 Ibid., Title VII, Ch. II (Arts. 256-1 to 256-30).
269 Ibid., Art. 256-20.
270 Ibid., Art. 256-5. Compare Article 6 of the UNCITRAL Model Law ("public policy exception").
271 See Section 6.4.2.3.

cross-border insolvencies may be still prone to legal fragmentation, including in the setting of priorities.

Somewhat counterintuitively, the best proxy for employing a supranationalism strategy in the context of cross-border insolvency nowadays lies in the creation of innovative bottom-up mechanisms for synchronization of insolvency proceedings involving debtors, creditors, and assets across national borders. Rather than relying on top-down supranational instruments or institutions which are currently lacking, bankruptcy officers and national courts are employing avant-garde techniques that come close to governing cross-border insolvencies by a single system of priorities.

This section examines two such instances: The Lehman Brothers insolvency, in which bankruptcy officers in dozens of countries entered into a private agreement on running the process, and the Nortel insolvency, where the US and Canadian courts authorized a landmark cross-border trial to resolve competing claims to the same assets, finally issuing perfectly consistent judgments.

On September 15, 2008, Lehman Brothers Holdings Inc. filed a Chapter 11 petition with the US bankruptcy court. Prior to this, Lehman Brothers was the fourth-largest US investment bank, with over 900 operating entities in more than 40 countries, and over $600 billion in assets.[272]

In the face of this biggest bankruptcy in world history, the filing resulted in over 80 proceedings, under the purview of 16 Official Representatives. Proceedings were adjudicated in nine countries, and the laws in each country varied widely.[273] The fragmentation of the Lehman Brothers Group therefore posed a litany of complicated issues and practical barriers to managing the insolvency proceedings for the hundreds of Lehman Brothers Affiliates, including the dispersion of assets and activities of Affiliates across jurisdictional borders[274] and led to the fear that bankruptcy officers would enter a state of frenzy by which they would seize assets in an inefficient and uncoordinated manner, quickly

272 Official Representatives and Other Participating Affiliates Pursuant to the Cross-Border Insolvency Protocol for the Lehman Brothers Group of Companies, "Report of Activities through January 15, 2010," p. 2, available at http://dm.epiq11.com/#/case/LBH/info under "Key Documents," then "Cross-Border Insolvency Protocol and Reports" (Lehman Brothers 2010 Report).

273 Ibid. See also Altman, "A Test Case in International Bankruptcy Protocols," p. 464.

274 Lehman Brothers 2010 Report, p. 2.

auctioning assets well below their market value.[275] Due to the presence of these issues, Official Representatives of many of the Affiliates-debtors recognized the necessity for cooperation among bankruptcy administrators and creditors across borders. To promote this goal, the Cross-Border Insolvency Protocol for the Lehman Brothers Group of Companies was developed and submitted to the various courts in May 2009.[276] The Protocol was the result of a thick series of meetings and information-exchange between the Official Representatives, which included the preparation of a Global Close Balance Sheet between November 2008 and January 2009.[277] The Global Close was considered a critical source of information because it represented the last consolidated set of books and records of the Lehman Group prior to insolvency.[278] The Protocol states the need for devising this innovative mechanism:

> Given the integrated and global nature of Lehman's businesses, many of the Debtor's assets and activities are spread across different jurisdictions, and require administration in and are subject to the laws of more than one Forum. The efficient administration of each of the Debtors' individual Proceedings would benefit from cooperation among the Official Representatives. In addition, cooperation and communication among Tribunals, where possible, would enable effective case management and consistency of judgments.[279]

Importantly, while the Protocol refers to the need for cooperation and communication among courts, it is really the direct collaboration among Official Representatives of the Affiliates-debtors that allows for a consolidated process. As the Lehman Brothers 2010 Report states

> The Protocol is a nonbinding agreement, the stated aim of which is to minimize costs and maximize fair recoveries for all creditors through information sharing, by coordination of activities and by a commitment to finding consensual, negotiated solutions wherever possible, in order to keep to a minimum the need to involve courts or other dispute resolution forums.[280]

275 Altman, "A Test Case in International Bankruptcy Protocols," p. 467.

276 Cross-Border Insolvency Protocol for the Lehman Brothers Group of Companies, May 26, 2009, available at http://dm.epiq11.com/#/case/LBH/info under "Key Documents," then "Cross-Border Insolvency Protocol and Reports" (Lehman Brothers Protocol or Protocol).

277 Lehman Brothers 2010 Report, p. 3.

278 Ibid.

279 Lehman Brothers Protocol, p. 2.

280 Lehman Brothers 2010 Report, p. 2.

Therefore, the true innovation of the Protocol lies in the functional and geographical division of labor between the Official Representatives and creditors in various countries to minimize the risk of interjurisdictional friction and incongruent decisions made by local courts and tribunals. One such principle is stated in Section 8 of the Protocol, titled "claims," which is intended to govern a situation where there is more than one proceeding related to the same debtor (i.e., specific operating entity or Affiliate), including main proceedings and non-main proceedings, such that

> Without prejudice to secured claims or rights *in rem*, and subject to applicable law, Official Representatives should adjust distributions so that a creditor who has received payment with respect to its claim in one Proceeding may not receive a payment for the same claim in any other Proceeding as to the same Debtor, so long as the payment to the other creditors of the same class is proportionately less than the payment the creditor has already received in respect of that claim.

In this and other ways, the Protocol seeks to create mechanisms that would coordinate the proceedings across numerus jurisdictions so as to mimic to the best possible extent a single process in which priorities are set and assets (or proceeds from their sale) are distributed to creditors. While the principles set out in the Protocol rely on the goodwill of Official Representatives, creditors, and courts to exchange information, coordinate activities and negotiate solutions, the track record of the bankruptcy proceedings across the various jurisdictions points to considerable success.[281]

A different type of groundbreaking cross-border collaboration, leading in effect to a single process for allocating priorities to assets of an insolvent multinational corporation, has taken place between the US and Canadian bankruptcy courts in the case of Nortel Networks Corporation, the giant telecom and data networking equipment manufacturer headquartered in Canada. The insolvency proceedings started actually as an example of interjurisdictional fragmentation and conflict, when three separate "main" insolvency proceedings were opened in three countries. Nortel's US subsidiary and affiliates filed in Delaware under Chapter 11, the Canadian parent corporation and its affiliates filed in Ontario, and the affiliates from

[281] By way of example, for the current state of the bankruptcy proceedings in the US Bankruptcy Court of the Southern District of New York, see *Lehman Brothers Holdings Inc.* (Chapter 11), Case No. 08–13555, available at http://dm.epiq11.com/#/case/LBH/info (accessed on March 1, 2018).

Europe, the Middle East, and Africa (EMEA) were placed under the control of joint administrators in the United Kingdom.[282]

Because the American, Canadian, and EAME companies began the process to sell Nortel's businesses and intellectual property, but each estate claimed a stake in the operations that comprised the global Nortel brand, the various Nortel Group's affiliates agreed that they would sell the assets first, and negotiate in good faith on how to allocate these sale proceeds after. In the meantime, the sale proceeds were placed in escrow ("the lockbox") until such decision would be made. However, while the business and intellectual property sales raised approximately $9 billion (most of which were kept in the lockbox), the parties failed to agree on how to allocate the escrowed funds or on a protocol governing an allocation process.[283]

Following petitions made by Nortel's US and Canadian officers to their respective courts, in April 2013, the Delaware bankruptcy court and the Ontario Superior Court of Justice issued two congruent decisions, by which they would hold a joint evidentiary trial to determine how to divide the sale proceeds.[284] Although Nortel's EMAE officers objected to the process, their appeal was denied and in May 2014 the cross-border insolvency trial commenced, and continued for six weeks. Using an innovative software for the delivery of live video, audio, and text to dozens of end-users who were participating in the joint courtroom proceedings that simultaneously took place in Delaware and Ontario,[285] The two courts heard testimony of dozens of witnesses and admitted into evidence over 2,000 exhibits and designations from numerous depositions. Two full days of closing arguments were made in September 2014.[286]

In May 2015, the Delaware and Ontario courts issued their separate but consistent decisions, allocating the funds in the proverbial lockbox between the various debtors, based on a *pro rata* allocation principle.[287]

282 L. L. Peakok, "A Tale of Two Courts: The Novel Cross-Border Bankruptcy Trial," *American Bankruptcy Institute Law Review*, 23 (2015), pp. 543–570 at 544.

283 Ibid., pp. 544–545.

284 See, respectively, *In re Nortel Networks, Inc.*, No. 09–10138 (Bank. D. Del., April 3, 2013), aff'd F.3d 265 (3d Cir. 2013) and *Nortel Networks Corp. (Re)*, 09-CL-7950, 2013, ONSC 1757 (Can. Ont. Sup. Ct. J., April 3, 2013).

285 PRWeb, "LiveDeposition Releases Case Study of Nortel Networks, Inc. Bankruptcy Trial," November 24, 2014, available at www.prweb.com/releases/2014/11/prweb12344852.htm.

286 Peakok, "A Tale of Two Courts," pp. 545–546.

287 See, respectively, *In re Nortel Networks, Inc.*, No. 09–10138 (Bank. D. Del., May 12, 2015); *Nortel Networks Corp. (Re)*, 09-CL-7950, 2013, ONSC 2987 (Can. Ont. Sup. Ct. J., April 3, 2013). The two courts justified the use of the pro rata allocation principle in that:

To be clear, The two courts establish an allocation principle among the multiple *debtors* (i.e., Nortel's operating entities located across borders), such that the proportionate share of each such debtor was based on the overall amount of all allowed claims brought against the debtor by its respective creditors, such that at a later stage "all claims against each Nortel Debtor, including intercompany claims and court approved settlements, will receive distributions from the separate Debtor Estates."[288] This in mind, the proceeds were thus brought into a single pool for purposes of allocation among the numerous entities making up the Nortel global group, based on a single priority principle. It is probably the closest that a cross-border bankruptcy case came to the long-sought ideal of establishing a supranational bankruptcy court.[289]

6.5 Policy Analysis

Security rights and proprietary priorities in insolvency probably manifest most clearly the tension between property law as a closed system of *in rem* rights and cross-border economic activities. The extension of credit and other forms of financing is essential for individuals and corporations to take up business opportunities in markets that increasingly defy national borders. This is definitely the case with intangible goods and services in the digital markets, but also with tangible commodities, and even with immovable assets in the current landscape of real-estate investment. Both borrowers and lenders have an interest in opening up market opportunities across borders, but at the same time, parties extending sale- or loan-credit

"In this unprecedented, complex and massive dispute involving highly integrated MNE's, the U.S. Court has the authority to adopt a pro rata allocation ... In an international case such as this, there is the principle 'that assets should be collected and distributed on a worldwide basis' ... The Court's adoption of pro rata allocation is the only outcome that reflects uncontroverted evidence and leads to a just result. The master facts are that Nortel functioned as a unified global enterprise and there was no agreement which governed how the individual entities would or could allocate their assets in the event of an insolvency." *In re Nortel Networks, Inc.*, No. 09–10138 (Bank. D. Del., May 12, 2015), pp. 98–100.

288 Ibid., pp. 99–100. As an aside, on January 24, 2017, the Delaware Bankruptcy Court confirmed a Chapter 11 Plan for all of the debtors (except Nortel Networks India International Inc.). See EPIQ, *Nortel Networks Inc.*, Case No. 09–10138, available at http://dm.epiq11.com/#/case/nortel/info (accessed on March 1, 2018) under "Overview," then "Plan Confirmation."

289 Gopalan and Guihot, *Cross-Border Insolvency Law*, pp. 178–179 (suggesting to set up a supranational insolvency court in The Hague with power to resolve multinational corporate insolvencies).

may be anxious that when the underlying collateral moves or when the debtor incurs liabilities in another jurisdiction, the creditor's priority to the debtor's assets would either be unrecognized or move down the ladder of priorities. The analysis in the chapter mandates the following conclusions about the prospects and limits of various globalization strategies to mitigate the problems of such cross-border divergences.

(a) With relatively few exceptions, such as the Cape Town Convention and its Protocol, or the Uniform Acts of OHADA, the problems of legal arbitrage and consequent creditor uncertainty are currently not resolved by binding instruments, global registries of security interests, or adjudicative institutions that create a top-down supranational body of law of security interests and proprietary interests in bankruptcy. Moreover, the universalism agenda of governing a global process of bankruptcy by grating jurisdiction to a single national court located in the debtor's COMI territory, and applying its national law to govern priorities to worldwide assets through a single process of priority-setting and distribution, comes across a variety of normative, political, and practical obstacles.

(b) With such first-best options being generally unavailable in the global setting, various forms of modified universalism or cooperative territorialism take over globalization strategies that are currently at play. Such second-best options may include the employment of a conflict of laws strategy, such as in the case of the EU Regulation on matrimonial property analyzed in Section 6.3.2, or the EU Regulation on insolvency discussed in Section 6.4.2.2. To address the problem of *conflit mobile*, in which security interests or sets of proprietary priorities in insolvency created under one legal system may become fragile when considered under a different legal system, such instruments either allow for carve-outs in applying the relevant law or rely on national courts to transform or adapt foreign property rights. Such mechanisms still leave room for uncertainty and potential conflict among creditors.

(c) Model laws and other soft law mechanisms, such as the UNCITRAL Model Law on Secured Transactions presented in Section 6.3.1, or the UNCTAD Model Law on Cross-Border Insolvency discussed in Section 6.4.2.1, are playing a relatively significant role in trying to mitigate the disparities among national laws and to facilitate the recognition of proceedings taking place in other jurisdictions. Thus, the adoption by forty-three states up to 2017 of the Model Law on

Cross-Border Insolvency, with its mechanism for recognition of foreign bankruptcy proceedings and the granting of various reliefs to foreign representatives of such proceedings, creates a platform for cross-border exchange of information and coordination.

(d) Accordingly, the real promise for coming close to a supranational ordering of security interests or proprietary priorities in insolvencies lies not in a top-down universal mechanism, but in innovative bottom-up schemes that take information-exchange and interjurisdictional coordination to the next level. The Lehman Brothers Protocol exemplifies how a nonbinding agreement among debtors and creditors in the context of a specific cross-border setting can provide practical solutions that alleviate creditor anxiety, optimize asset realization, and increase the likelihood of coordinating the proprietary ranking of creditors. The Nortel cross-border bankruptcy trial shows how national courts can work together to create a single process with a cross-border reach and a fresh approach to global lawmaking. Property law can and should be innovative in meeting the challenges of a globalizing world.

INDEX

This is the first comprehensive analysis of J. A. Hobson's writings on international relations. Hobson is most famous for developing the neo-Marxist theory of imperialism, but in this book David Long argues that Hobson was also a key figure in the history of liberalism. He shifted liberal international theory away from its *laissez-faire* origins towards a focus on international organisation, making him a forerunner of the functional approach in international relations. The book outlines the philosophical outlook and political economy which informed Hobson's theory, and challenges the narrow interpretation of imperialism which has dominated international relations. Setting out the sources of and contradictions within Hobson's proposals for international government, this book is a contribution not only to the study of international relations, but also to the history of political thought and British liberalism.